Bloom's Modern Critical Views

Bloom's Modern Critical Views

Bloom's Modern Critical Views

Miguel de Cervantes

Edited and with an introduction by
Harold Bloom
Sterling Professor of the Humanities
Yale University

CHELSEA HOUSE
PUBLISHERS
A Haights Cross Communications Company®

Philadelphia

Library of Congress Cataloging-in-Publication Data

Bloom, Harold.
  Miguel de Cervantes / Harold Bloom.
     p. cm. — (Bloom's modern critical views)
  Includes bibliographical references and index.
  ISBN 0-7910-8138-9 (alk. paper)
  1. Cervantes Saavedra, Miguel de, 1547-1616—Criticism and interpretation. I. Title. II. Series.
PQ6351.B56 2004b
  863'.3—dc22

                                            2004026640

Contributing Editor: Pamela Loos

Cover designed by Keith Trego

Cover photo: © Bettmann/CORBIS

Layout by EJB Publishing Services

All links and web addresses were checked and verified to be correct at the time of
publication. Because of the dynamic nature of the web, some addresses and links may
have changed since publication and may no longer be valid.

Every effort has been made to trace the owners of copyrighted material and secure
copyright permission. Articles appearing in this volume generally appear much as they did
in their original publication with little to no editorial changes. Those interested in
locating the original source will find bibliographic information on the first page of each
article as well as in the bibliography and acknowledgments sections of this volume.

Contents

Editor's Note

My Introduction contrasts Shakespeare's Falstaff both to Don Quixote and to Sancho as advocates of the play of the world.

Howard Mancing emphasizes Sancho as the reality principle, while Alban K. Forcione centers upon the *Exemplary Novels* of Cervantes.

The admirable ideals of Quixote are stressed by E.C. Riley, after which Terrence Doody brings together Sancho and Poldy of Joyce's *Ulysses*.

Cory A. Reed sees Cervantes's theatrical *Interludes* as instances of "novelistic indeterminacy," while Diana de Armas Wilson analyzes the late romance, *Persiles and Sigismunda*.

Cervantes's poetry, hardly his strong achievement, is read for autobiographical intimations by Nicholas Spadaccini and Jenaro Talens, after which Dominick Finello describes the pastoral romance, *Galatea*.

Ian Watt dwells upon interpretive puzzles in *Quixote*, while Henry W. Sullivan expounds the purgatorial grotesque of the great book's Part II.

Manuel Durán gives a lively account of picaresque writing in Cervantes, after which Roberto González Echevarría superbly introduces the mastery evidenced by Cervantes in his great work.

In this volume's concluding essay, David Quint finds Part I of *Don Quixote* to be unhappy both with the way things are in Cervantes's age, and with the way they were earlier. Quint rightly intimates that, a decade later in Part II, Cervantes and Don Quixote make something like a separate peace with their era.

HAROLD BLOOM

Introduction

"The text of Cervantes and that of Menard are verbally identical, but the second is almost infinitely richer." That superb irony is the culmination of "Pierre Menard, Author of *Don Quixote*," one of the earliest of the fictions of Jorge Luis Borges. Hidden in it is a deeper irony; Cervantes is one of those few Western writers who cannot be surpassed. The Yahwist (primary author of Genesis, Exodus, Numbers), Homer, Dante, Chaucer, Montaigne, Shakespeare, Milton, Tolstoy, Proust; these are the masters of representation who have fashioned a reality that contains us. In contrast to these, even writers as strong as Virgil, Spenser, Goethe, Blake, Wordsworth, Dickens, Whitman, Flaubert, Joyce, Kafka, Freud, seem partial. The Virgilian and Freudian reality principle is ultimately a taking into account of all the conditions imposed upon us by nature, yet Virgil and Freud do not compel us to see aspects of nature or the given that otherwise we might not come to see. Cervantes and Shakespeare so represent reality as to cause otherwise hidden aspects of reality to appear.

Carlos Fuentes tells us that Don Quixote "illustrates the rupture of a world based on analogy and thrust into differentiation," the world of Cervantes and of Shakespeare. If that is correct, then it pertains also to Homer and Dante, Tolstoy and Proust, which is to say that Fuentes has expressed not a temporal truth but an insight into the highest order of literary representation. Something vital in the individual rhetoric of the strongest masters of representation destroys traditional analogies and creates fresh differences. We can name that vitality in Cervantes by Hazlitt's critical

1

term gusto. Don Quixote and Sancho Panza both incarnate a primal exuberance—at once ethos or character, logos or cognition, pathos or personality—that is utterly memorable through its gusto.

Nietzsche taught us that the memorable always is partly reliant upon pain. We forget easier pleasures, but not those so difficult that they also comprehended severe pain. This Nietzschean, pragmatic test for the Sublime is akin to Wittgenstein's test for love, probably because both Nietzsche and Wittgenstein were the sons of Schopenhauer. "Love is not a feeling," Wittgenstein wrote, because, "Love, unlike pain, is put to the test. We do not say: that was not a true pain, because it passed away so quickly."

We remember the Don and Sancho, always, because they give us a difficult pleasure, in which much pain is mixed, and we love them, always, because Cervantes puts our love for them to the test. Their greatness is dialectical in regard to one another; they educate one another in reality, and in all the orders of reality. One of those orders is play, as beautifully outlined in the *Homo Ludens* of J. Huizinga. Like their great contemporary, the Falstaff of Shakespeare's *Henry IV, Part 1*, the Don and Sancho achieve their essential being in the world of play, or freedom. If everything is a metaphor, except when we play, then Falstaff, the Don, and Sancho achieve a reality beyond the metaphoric. And the Don and Sancho are more fortunate than Falstaff, because they have one another, whereas poor Falstaff learns, in *Henry IV, Part 2*, that he has no one.

The play of the world, as Don Quixote conceives it, is a sublimely purified vision of chivalry, a game of knights-errant, damsels beautiful and virtuous, enchanters both wicked and potent, ogres, giants, and island kingdoms where the shrewd Sancho might exercise his pragmatic wisdom. Falstaff, surveying the corpse of the chivalric Sir Walter Blunt, splendidly declares: "I like not such grinning honor as Sir Walter hath. Give me life, which if I can save, so; if not, honor comes unlook'd for, and there's an end." Don Quixote, though committed to precisely the opposite stance, nevertheless shares with Falstaff the kingdom of play, and we do not sense that there would be any spiritual conflicts between these superb figures if they met in that kingdom. We hear the Don in Falstaff, and a reduction of the grand Sancho in the hypocritical Prince Hal, when they prepare to play the scene in which King Henry IV will denounce his heir:

> FALSTAFF. Well, thou wilt be horribly chid tomorrow when thou comest to thy father. If thou love me, practice an answer.
> PRINCE. Do thou stand for my father and examine me upon the particulars of my life.

FALSTAFF. Shall I? Content. This chair shall be my state, this
dagger my scepter, and this cushion my crown.
PRINCE. Thy state is taken for a join'd-stool, thy golden scepter
for a leaden dagger, and thy precious rich crown for a pitiful bald
crown!
FALSTAFF. Well, and the fire of grace be not quite out of you,
now shalt thou be mov'd ...

The fire of play is almost quite out in the Prince, and he is not much moved,
but we are. As in Falstaff (until Hal destroys him by renouncing him), the fire
of play cannot abandon Don Quixote. Cervantes, more even than Rabelais,
more even than the Shakespeare of the great clowns and of Falstaff,
represents reality with a continuous gusto and buoyancy. What counts most
about the Don is neither his obsession nor his courage. It is the greatness or
sublimity of his unflagging playfulness, as when his neighbor protests to him
that "your Grace is neither Baldwin nor Abindarraez but a respectable
gentleman by the name of Senor Quijana," and the Don replies:

I know who I am, and who I may be, if I choose: not only those I
have mentioned but all the Twelve Peers of France and the Nine
Worthies as well; for the exploits of all of them together, or
separately, cannot compare with mine.

"I know who I am, and who I may be, if I choose," is the Don's credo, even
as Falstaff's is: "No, that's certain, I am not a double man; but if I be not Jack
Falstaff, then am I a Jack." As for the difference between these grand
representatives of *homo ludens*, we may start with Don Quixote confronting
the possibility of battling lions and saying, with a slight smile: "lion whelps
against me?" and then rejecting, with contempt, the lion keeper's insistence
that his lions have no thought of attacking the knight:

My dear sir, you had best go mind your tame partridge and that
bold ferret of yours and let each one attend to his own business.
This is my affair, and I know whether these gentlemen, the lions,
have come to attack me or not.

This is only the apparent antithesis to Sir John Falstaff declining to
have been slaughtered by Douglas, "that hot termagant Scot":

Counterfeit? I lie, I am no counterfeit. To die is to be a
counterfeit, for he is but the counterfeit of a man who hath not

the life of a man; but to counterfeit dying, when a man thereby
liveth, is to be no counterfeit, but the true and perfect image of
life indeed. The better part of valor is discretion, in the which
better part I have sav'd my life.

There is only a touch of discretion in the Don's valor, but there is a plethora
in Sancho's, yet like Falstaff, Sancho pragmatically is as playfully valorous as
the Knight of the Mournful Countenance. Don Quixote's dolefulness and
Falstaff's wit, the Don's mad courage and Falstaff's vital discretion, are the
same qualities turned inside out. An essential gaiety informs the sense of
freedom in Cervantes and Shakespeare alike, a freedom that incarnates the
will to play. The world awaits the writer who could bring the Don and
Falstaff onto one stage simultaneously, or into the pages of one book, to hold
converse together. For the Don is no more insane than the superb Falstaff is.
They are the two authentic literary representations that Nietzsche longed
for: true overmen, figures without a superego, humans beyond the necessity
of turning aggression against the self, or most simply, defiers and deniers of
the death drive.

Had Cervantes given us only Don Quixote, it would have been more than
enough. The astonishment of his masterwork is that its title is inadequate,
since the book is not only *The Adventures of Don Quixote de la Mancha*, but just
as much the adventures of Sancho Panza. "The Truth about Sancho Panza"
is the title of perhaps the finest of Kafka's parables, a parable that is certainly
the most illuminating criticism of Cervantes yet written:

> Without making any boast of it Sancho Panza succeeded in the
> course of years, by devouring a great number of romances of
> chivalry and adventure in the evening and night hours, in so
> diverting from him his demon, whom he later called Don
> Quixote, that his demon thereupon set out in perfect freedom on
> the maddest exploits, which, however, for the lack of a
> preordained object, which should have been Sancho Panza
> himself, harmed nobody. A free man, Sancho Panza
> philosophically followed Don Quixote on his crusades, perhaps
> out of a sense of responsibility, and had of them a great and
> edifying entertainment to the end of his days.

What is strongest in Kafka's insight is the primacy given to Sancho Panza,
whose corporeal understanding or bodily ego provides the ground from
which imagination or the Don rises up. Don Quixote cannot harm the world

or disturb the flow of the mundane, because there is no object for his exploits except Sancho, and Sancho has diverted the demonic drive out into the "perfect freedom" of the beyond, as in the magnificent chapter 28 of part 2, where the two inseparables quarrel, the occasion being a rare Falstaffian moment on the Don's part.

We are never more moved by and with Sancho than when he cries out: "'Fore God, your worship has taken me out of a huge uncertainty, and resolved the doubt in delicate terms. Body o'me! Was the cause of my pain so mysterious, that there was a necessity for telling me, I feel pain in those parts that were cudgeled?" Sancho, I think, might have desired to dispute Erich Auerbach's contention that Cervantes does not take his work's play very seriously: "He looks at it; he shapes it; he finds it diverting; it is also intended to afford the reader refined intellectual diversion." That makes Cervantes rather too much like Walt Whitman's "real me" or "me myself," who is both in the game and out of it, and watching and wondering at it. Cervantes is both Sancho and the Don, and all three of them take the game very seriously indeed, but taking play seriously is a mode very much its own, the mode we call freedom.

As a fierce lover of Falstaff, I find that all his moments are my favorite moments, but the best of all comes in the midst of battle, when Prince Hal requests the knight's sword, and is offered the great wit's pistol instead:

PRINCE. Give it me. What? Is it in the case?
FALSTAFF. Ay, Hal, 'tis hot, 'tis hot. There's that will sack a city.
The Prince draws it out, and finds it to be a bottle of sack.
PRINCE. What, is it a time to jest and dally now?
He throws the bottle at him. Exit.

Falstaff, like Cervantes, has both the Don and Sancho in him. It is indeed always the time to play, to jest and dally, even in the very midst of battle. The order of play is the only idea of order that Falstaff acknowledges. The Don and Sancho, in their very different ways, are shadowed by darker intensities than Falstaff is, though his prophetic fear of being rejected by the Prince is dark and intense enough. Don Quixote plays until reality intrudes and destroys the game, and then he dies. Sancho survives, even though he has learned to play as well as his teacher, though in an earthier mode. Perhaps the Don was the writer in Cervantes, and Sancho the reader in Cervantes; perhaps they are the writer and the reader in each of us.

HOWARD MANCING

Knighthood Compromised

Que la oreja me duele más de
lo que yo quisiera (I, 10, 108)

(for my ear pains me more than I could wish, p. 71)

2.1 SANCHO PANZA: REALITY

The most important single event in Cervantes's novel, after the original exposition, is the introduction of Sancho Panza. Once Sancho with his nonchivalric reality rides beside Don Quijote, the latter can never again be the same. Sancho's effect on Don Quijote's rhetoric can be considered in three ways. First and most important is the squire's role as "Reality Instructor."[1] Sancho's nagging voice asking (I, 8, 88) "¿Qué gigantes?" ("What giants?") and adding more specifically, "Mire vuestra merced ... que aquellos que allí se parecen no son gigantes, sino molinos de viento" ("Look, your worship ... What we see there are not giants but windmills"), can never be effectively silenced by Don Quijote's mere will (pp. 88–89)—"Bien parece ... que no estás cursado en esto de las aventuras: ellos son gigantes" ("It's easy to see ... that you are not used to the business of adventures. Those are giants," p. 59). The knight's chivalric fantasy must from now on attempt to withstand repeated assaults of reality from his squire.

A second concern is one of practicality. On his first sally, Don Quijote traveled all day until he and Rocinante were exhausted, his only conversation

From *The Chivalric World of Don Quijote: Style, Structure, and Narrative Technique.* © 1982 by the Curators of the University of Missouri.

7

being with himself as he imagined how his history would be written by a benevolent wizard and as he invoked (with appropriate chivalric archaism) the support of Dulcinea (I, 2, 41–42). In contrast, his second sally begins with a conversation with Sancho Panza that deals partly with the *ínsula* that the squire is to receive and partly with the nature of the latter's wife (I, 7, 86–87). This discussion contains no archaism. Luis Rosales has shown how beginning with this conversation an essential change in Don Quijote's character takes place. Previously he has employed a "borrowed" language, using only his chivalric style and never really communicating with anyone. Now, with the simultaneous introduction of Sancho Panza and practical social dialogue, Don Quijote becomes more humanized.[2] One of the main reasons why Don Quijote's frequency of archaic speech declines is that it is simply not practical to sustain such an artificial style in his conversations with Sancho.

Third, Sancho Panza introduces into the novel an element of humor that even Don Quijote cannot ignore. In the early chapters, there is not recorded a single instance of laughter by Don Quijote: madmen do not sustain their visions of fantasy through humor. But when the knight-errant explains (I, 8, 90) to his squire "si no me quejo del dolor es porque no es dado a los caballeros andantes quejarse de herida alguna, aunque se le salgan las tripas por ella" ("if I make no complaint of the pain it is because knights-errant are not permitted to complain of any wound, even though their bowels be coming out through it"), Sancho responds, "De mí sé decir que me he de quejar del más pequeño dolor que tenga, si ya no se entiende también con los escuderos de los caballeros andantes eso del no quejarse" ("For my part, I confess I must complain however small the ache may be, unless this rule about not complaining applies to the squires of knights-errant also"); and the narration adds: "No se dejó de reír don Quijote de la simplicidad de su escudero" ("Don Quixote could not help laughing at his squire's simplicity," p. 60).[3]

Throughout the novel, Sancho will point out reality, will engage Don Quijote in nonchivalric conversation, and will make his master laugh. The cumulative effect of Sancho's influence will be the gradual undermining of Don Quijote's chivalric fantasy. Ironically, Sancho Panza himself will become increasingly caught up in that fantasy world and will at times seem as quixotic as his master, but his effect on Don Quijote will consistently be contrary to the sustaining of a chivalric role.

Reality is not, however, first introduced into Don Quijote's chivalric world by Sancho Panza; it is present from the very first chapter when, after destroying the week's work that went into the making of a helmet, he prudently decides not to test the strength of his second effort (I, 1, 37): "él quedó satisfecho de su fortaleza, y sin querer hacer nueva experiencia della, la diputó y tuvo por celada finísima de encaje" ("he was satisfied with its strength. Then, not caring to try any more experiments with it, he accepted and commissioned it as a helmet of the most perfect construction," p. 28).[4] It is also possible that the surreptitiousness of his departure on both his first and second sallies (I, 2, 40)—"Y así, sin dar parte a persona alguna de su intención, y sin que nadie le viese, una mañana, antes del día, ... por la puerta falsa de un corral salió al campo" ("So, without informing anyone of his intentions, and without anybody seeing him, one morning before dawn ... by the back door of the yard sallied forth upon the plain," p. 29)—and (I, 7, 86)—"sin despedirse Panza de sus hijos y mujer, ni don Quijote de su ama y sobrina, una noche se salieron del lugar sin que persona los viese" ("without taking leave, Sancho Panza of his wife and children, or Don Quixote of his housekeeper and niece, they sallied forth, unseen by anybody, from the village one night," p. 57)—belies a tacit recognition that his chivalric intention is inappropriate.[5]

The first major incursion of reality that directly contradicts Don Quijote's chivalric vision is the loss of half of his ear in the battle with the Biscayan. Previously, physical pain had been readily accepted by Don Quijote as part of the rigors of knight-errantry. His first serious, painful beating occurs at the time of the adventure of the Toledan merchants. Don Quijote is left lying on the ground unable to rise, but with his chivalric spirit intact (I, 4, 62): "Y aún se tenia por dichoso, pareciéndole que aquélla era propia desgracia de caballeros andantes, y toda la atribula a la falta de su caballo, y no era posible levantarse, según tenia brumado todo el cuerpo" ("Yet he considered himself fortunate, as it seemed to him that this was a real knight-errant's mishap and entirely, he believed, the fault of his horse. However, battered in body as he was, to rise was beyond his power," p. 44). His next adventure is that of the windmills, and though he receives a hard and painful fall, he announces to Sancho, in the words previously cited, that knights-errant were not permitted to complain when they were wounded.

Cervantes describes the wound inflicted by the Biscayan with brilliant comic understatement.

> mas la buena suerte, que para mayores cosas le tenía guardado, torció la espada de su contrario, de modo que, aunque le acertó en el hombro izquierdo, no le hizo otro daño que desarmarle todo aquel lado, llevándole, de camino, gran parte de la celada, con la mitad de la oreja; que todo ello con espantosa ruina vino al suelo, dejándole muy maltrecho. (I, 9, 103)

(But that good fortune which reserved him for greater things turned aside the sword of his adversary so that, though it smote him upon the left shoulder, it did him no more harm than to strip all that side of its armor, carrying away a great part of his helmet with half of his ear. It all fell to the ground with a fearful din, leaving him in sorry plight.) (p. 68)

Don Quijote completes the adventure, an authentic chivalric victory, as previously observed, and goes on his way, inflated with pride, without mentioning his wound. It is, appropriately, his Reality Instructor, Sancho, who advises his master (I, 10, 107) to take steps to cure himself, "que le va mucha sangre de esa oreja" ("because a great deal of blood is flowing from that ear," p. 70). Don Quijote ecstatically raves about the magic universal healing balm of Fierabrás but is forced to admit (p. 108) that "la oreja me duele más de lo que yo quisiera" ("my ear pains me more than I would like," p. 71). An authentic fictional knight-errant from the romances of chivalry does not complain about his wounds, but Don Quijote—who is thus implicitly inauthentic according to his own norms—does, and does again (p. 109)—"porque yo lo voto a Dios que me va doliendo mucho la oreja" ("for I swear to God, this ear is giving me great pain," p. 72)—and again (I, 11, 118)—"sería bien, Sancho, que me vuelvas a curar esta oreja, que me va doliendo más de lo que es menester" ("it would be well if you would dress this ear of mine again, for it is giving me more pain than it should," p. 78).[6]

The reality is that the ear hurts. Sancho's first-aid kit is insufficient and Don Quijote does not have any magic balm of Fierabrás. Finally the ear is cured not by chivalric ideals or chivalric magic but by simple, rustic, practical knowledge. One of the goatherds, on seeing his guest's wound, offers a cure by applying a mixture of a few rosemary leaves, saliva, and salt to the ear and covering it with a bandage. This treatment, he assures, will be sufficient (I, 11, 118): "y así fue la verdad" ("and so it proved," p. 78); Don Quijote never again complains of the pain of his ear. Later, when he is again bleeding and in pain (I, 17, 166)—"porque se me va mucha sangre do la herida que esta fantasma me ha dado" ("I am losing much blood from the wound that the phantom gave me")—Don Quijote, in a tacit admission of the efficacy of this remedy, recalls the identical ingredients when he prepares to manufacture the balm of Fierabrás: "procura que se me dé un poco de aceite, vino, *sal* y *romero* para hacer el salutífero bálsamo" ("have him give me a little oil, wine, *salt*, and *rosemary* to make the salutary balm," p. 113; my italics). The reality of physical pain cannot be dismissed by Don Quijote; his many stonings, beatings, falls, and various battle wounds, like the presence of Sancho Panza, have a cumulative destructive effect on his chivalric career.

2.2 CHAPTERS 11–14: A PASTORAL INTERLUDE

Chapters 11–14 represent a deliberate and effective change in the pace of narration and a disaster for Don Quijote's career. Knight and squire arrive at the camp of some goatherds and are invited to join them for a simple, rustic dinner. In a long, uninvited postdinner speech (I, 11, 113–14), Don Quijote contrasts the "Dichosa edad y siglos dichosos" ("Happy the age, happy the time," p. 74) of a mythical Golden Age with "estos nuestros detestables siglos" ("this hateful age of ours," p. 75) in order to justify, with considerable rhetorical skill and eloquence, the establishment of knight-errantry—"Para cuya seguridad ... se instituyó la orden de los caballeros andantes" ("In defense of these ... the order of knights-errant was instituted")—and his own adherence to this order—"Desta orden soy yo" (p. 115). Unfortunately, this standard set-piece is wasted on the unlettered goatherds (but not on Sancho Panza; see section 2.5), who maintain a respectful, probably slightly embarrassed, silence.

With the arrival of Antonio and his song to Olalla, chivalric matters are thrust into the background. The subsequent news that the feigned shepherd (I, 12, 119), "aquel famoso pastor estudiante" ("the famed student-shepherd"), Grisóstomo, has died of love for the pseudoshepherdess Marcela—"aquella que se anda en hábito de pastora por esos andurriales" ("the girl who wanders about in these lonely places in the dress of a shepherdess," p. 79)—introduces a brilliant series of ironic contrasts, especially literature versus life (the literary pastoral of Grisóstomo and Marcela in contrast with the genuine pastoral of the goatherds) and literature versus literature (the literary pastoral of Grisóstomo as opposed to the literary chivalric of Don Quijote). Grisóstomo has played his role to the ultimate extreme, dying of love—or committing suicide—for the disdainful Marcela. Don Quijote, meanwhile, has found it increasingly difficult to suffer even the loss of part of an ear for the nonexistent Dulcinea.

The next day's journey to the site of Grisóstomo's burial is enlivened by the presence of the cultured and slightly malicious Vivaldo, who is described (I, 13, 128) as a "persona muy discreta y de alegre condición" ("person of great shrewdness and with a merry disposition," p. 85) and is implicitly—and unfavorably—contrasted with the reserved and respectful goatherds. Vivaldo is the first cultured person Don Quijote meets who is very familiar with the romances of chivalry[7] and who amuses himself at Don Quijote's expense, drawing him out in matters of chivalry, concentrating on the vulnerable point of the knight's near sacrilegious devotion to his lady. Don Quijote has obviously met his match in Vivaldo and is forced into an overstatement (p. 130)—"digo que no puede ser que haya caballero andante sin dama ... y a buen seguro que no se haya visto historia donde se halle caballero andante sin amores" ("I say it is impossible there could be a knight-errant without a lady ... Quite assuredly no history has ever been written concerning a knight-errant without a lady," p. 86)—which is exposed by Vivaldo who cites Amadís de Gaula's brother, Don Galaor, who never devoted himself to a single lady.[8] Don Quijote, trapped, reacts in a manner that anticipates the classic Sancho Panza, by citing a proverb (p. 131)—"Señor, una golondrina sola no hace verano" ("Sir, one solitary swallow does not make a summer")—and then by contradicting himself with an outright lie: "Cuanto más, que yo sé que de secreto estaba ese caballero muy bien enamorado ...; averiguado está muy bien que él tenía una sola a quien él había hecho señora de su voluntad, a la cual se encomendaba muy a menudo y muy secretamente" ("Moreover, that knight, as I am aware was in secret very deeply in love.... it is well established that he had one alone whom he made mistress of his will. To her he commended himself very frequently and secretly," p. 87). Vivaldo continues to press on this matter and on the identity of Dulcinea, and Don Quijote is saved only by their arrival at the funeral. Don Quijote's lie is important. Since later in the novel he will state (I, 25, 263) that "las órdenes de caballería ... nos mandan que no digamos mentira alguna" ("the ordinances of chivalry ... forbid us to tell any lie," p. 182), the statement about Galaor is a clear sign that Don Quijote has failed to maintain his own chivalric standards during the conversation with Vivaldo.

Don Quijote is again thrust into the background during the funeral but is able to assert himself dramatically and, perhaps, effectively in his defense of Marcela at the very end of chapter 14. Clearly, Don Quijote finds his chivalric role more difficult to sustain in the face of nonchivalric pastoral reality and well-executed pastoral-inspired literature. Overall, Don Quijote comes off quite badly in these chapters. In the company of the simple but generous and attractive goatherds, he looks foolish in forcing Sancho to sit beside him in order to illustrate the universality of chivalry, absurdly and uselessly rhetorical in his Golden Age speech, and unnecessarily pedantic in his frequent corrections of Pedro's speech. He is on the defensive throughout the conversation with Vivaldo and clearly loses their debate. He is superfluous at the funeral of Grisóstomo, whose ultimate literature-inspired act makes those of Don Quijote pale in contrast. Even his defense of Marcela may have been ineffective (I, 14, 144): "O ya que fuese por las amenazas de don Quijote, o porque Ambrosio les dijo que concluyesen con lo que a su buen amigo debían, ninguno de los pastores se movió ni apartó de allí" ("Whether it was because of the threats of Don Quixote, or because Ambrosio told them to fulfil their duty to their good friend, none of the shepherds moved or stirred from the spot," p. 96).

2.3 ROCINANTE

After attending the burial of Grisóstomo and searching in vain for Marcela, Don Quijote and Sancho pause to rest (I, 15, 146) in "un prado lleno de fresca yerba, junto del cual corría un arroyo apacible y fresco" ("a meadow covered with tender grass. Alongside ran a pleasant cool stream," p. 99). In this lush meadow, typical of the setting for Neoplatonic love laments in the pastoral romances, Sancho unbridles his *rucio* and Don Quijote's Rocinante to graze, confidently assuming that the latter is (p. 147) "tan manso y tan poco rijoso, que todas las yeguas de la dehesa de Córdoba no le hicieran tomar mal siniestro" ("of [such a] staid, continent temperament, that all the mares in the Córdoba pastures would not lead him into error," p. 99). However, Sancho misjudges Rocinante's tastes, for it turns out that the horse's sexual interests are indeed aroused by some nearby mares. Their rejections of his overtures and the beating that ensues for the knight, squire, and erotically inclined horse provide the framework for a highly comic situation.

In this scene, there is another level of comedy involving linguistic subtleties that deserves analysis and comment. The first mention of the mares is in a reference to "una manada de hacas galicianas" ("a drove of Galician ponies"). What is important here is the use of *hacas* rather than the alternate form *jacas*. While it is possible that Cervantes's orthography could be the result of mere coincidence, or even of a deliberate intent to create alliteration in the phrase "una manada de *ha*cas *gal*icianas de unos arrieros *gal*legos," an even more plausible explanation of his preference for the *h*-spelling is his desire to set up a phonetic contrast with the comic archaic *f*- in the beginning of the following paragraph (p. 147): "Sucedió, pues, que a Rocinante le vino en deseo de refocilarse con]as señoras facas" ("It was at this moment that Rocinante took a fancy to disport himself with the ladies," p. 99). Although the comic personification and irony implicit in the phrase "las *señoras* hacas," especially in the light of what follows, might have been sufficient to achieve a considerable comic effect, the substitution of *facas* for *hacas* cannot help but remind the reader of Don Quijote's frequent use of the archaic *f*-. Reinforcing the assumption of a deliberate choice of the *h*– < *f*– archaism is the subsequent presence of the equally archaic, *ál*: "Mas ellas, que ... debían de tener más gana de pacer que de ál" (p. 147) ("They, however, seemed to prefer their pasture to him").[9] It is almost as though Rocinante takes on human and even, like his master, chivalric characteristics (see note 15); the horse seems to be "thinking" in *fabla* about his erotic chivalric adventure.[10]

The significance of this scene, which casts an ironic light on the preceding episode of pure and idealized love in the case of Marcela,[11] is augmented by what occurs in the following chapter in the inn of Juan Palomeque el Zurdo where Don Quijote and Sancho take refuge.[12] The Manchegan knight, unable to sleep, imagines that the daughter of the lord of the castle in which he is lodged is smitten with love for him—in accord with what takes place in many romances of chivalry—and intends to visit him in his bedchamber. In fact, the innkeeper's daughter is sound asleep; up and about, however, is the servant girl Maritornes, who intends to keep an appointment with a mule driver whose bed is located near that of Don Quijote (I, 16, 157): "Había el arriero concertado con ella que aquella noche se refocilarían juntos" ("The mule driver had made an arrangement with her for recreation that night," pp. 106–7). Noteworthy is the use of the same verb, *refocilarse*, that was associated with Rocinante's misadventure (which also involved *arrieros*) in the previous chapter. This word appears only one other time in the novel (II, 22, 742), and then with no sexual connotation.

Don Quijote used some archaic words on his arrival at the inn (p. 157): *fermosa* (twice), *este vuestro*, *habedes fecho*, and *pluguiera*. Now in bed (pp. 159–60), lying "mal *ferido*" ("sorely wounded"), he imagines that the approaching maiden has come looking for him "a *furto* de sus padres" ("without the knowledge of her parents"), and as she passes, he reaches out his arms "para recebir a su *fermosa* doncella" ("to receive his beauteous damsel," p. 108). These archaisms occur in narration, perhaps reflecting Don Quijote's thoughts, as was the case in the scene dramatizing Rocinante's amorous disaster in the previous chapter. Thus, holding the girl tightly, he says (p. 160): "Quisiera hallarme en términos, *fermosa* y alta señora, de poder pagar tamaña merced como la que con la vista de vuestra gran *fermosura* me *habedes fecho*" ("Would that I found myself, lovely and exalted lady, in a position to repay the favor that thou, by the sight of thy great beauty, hast granted me," p. 108). While stating his intention to defend his chastity and remain faithful to Dulcinea, Don Quijote's actions strongly suggest an inclination to do just the opposite.[13] The scene, of course, ends in chaos.

Rocinante's aborted sexual adventure takes place in a perfect setting for an idealized human love scene, but that of Don Quijote takes place in a garret that (p. 155) "daba manifiestos indicios que había servido de pajar muchos años" ("showed signs of having formerly served for many years as a hayloft," p. 105), in fact, a stable, "aquel estrellado [star-lit] establo."[14] The presence of the muleteer, with his bed made of (p. 158) "las enjalmas y ... todo el adorno de los dos mejores mulos que traía" ("the packsaddles and all the trappings of the two best mules he had," p. 107), contributes to the animal imagery that informs the scene. If Celestina's proverbial statement is that donkeys do it better in the field (see note 9), the implicit corollary is that people do it worse in the hayloft.[15]

There is an interesting recollection of this scene later in the novel when Don Quijote, at the same inn, goes outside to guard the "castle." In order to play a trick on him, Maritornes and the innkeeper's daughter, the two "semidoncellas" ("demi-damsels"), have him reach his hand up to (I, 43, 478) "un agujero de un pajar" ("a hole in the wall of a straw-loft," p. 349)—probably the same one where the previous action took place—where they tie his wrist and then leave him to spend the night, arm uplifted, standing on Rocinante's back. In the morning, some travelers arrive at the inn. One of their mounts sniffs at Rocinante who after all, being made of flesh and bone (p. 483), "aunque parecía de leño" ("though he looked as if he were made of wood"), cannot resist responding to "quien le llegaba a hacer caricias" ("the one who had come to offer him attentions," p. 348). Whereupon, he moves and leaves his master dangling by his tied wrist. Don Quijote's pride and belief that the daughter of the lord of the castle is in love with him get him into difficulties; his horse's erotic interests compound his misfortune.

The attempts of both Rocinante and Don Quijote at erotic adventures end in frustration and disaster. In both cases, chivalric archaism, especially the *f-*, provides a key to interpretation. Rocinante, with his own version of his master's style of speech and sexual desires, anticipates and parodies Don Quijote in the Maritornes adventure. Again, as always in the novel, there are multiple images and structural and thematic relationships that make a simple, comic scene much richer and more significant than it seems at first glance. If there is a single cardinal principle to be observed when dealing with *Don Quijote*, it is that nothing is as simple and obvious as it first appears.

2.4 CHAPTERS 15–22: CHIVALRIC ADVENTURES

Chapters 15–22 form what may be artistically the best section of *Don Quijote*. In a series of brilliant—and brilliantly narrated—scenes, knight and squire come alive as have no other characters before them, and few after them, in the history of literature. The comic genius of these pages, properly called "la cumbre del humor" ("the pinnacle of humor") by Carlos Varo,[16] has seldom been rivaled. In this part of the novel, the figure of Sancho Panza receives its fullest development (see the following section) and that of Don Quijote simultaneously declines in knightly perfection and grows in human stature.

After the frustration and humiliation that Don Quijote experiences during the Grisóstomo episode, the knight wisely turns down the offer of Vivaldo and his friends to accompany them to Seville (I, 14, 145), "por ser lugar tan acomodado a hallar aventuras, que en cada calle y tras cada esquina se ofrecen más que en otro alguno" ("this being a convenient place for finding adventures, which rose up in every street and around every corner oftener than anywhere else," p. 96).[17] Don Quijote conceivably realizes that he would continue to be an object of ridicule and mockery among these people, for his reason for turning them down is an outright lie. He says that "por entonces no quería ni debía ir a Sevilla, hasta que hubiese despojado todas aquellas sierras de ladrones malandrines, de quien era fama que todas estaben llenas" ("he could not go to Seville until he had cleared all those mountain's of the highwaymen and robbers who were said to infest them"), but in fact he has made up his mind to "ir a buscar a la pastora Marcela y ofrecerle todo to que él podia en su servicio" ("go in quest of the shepherdess Marcela and offer her all the services he could render," p. 97).

In the episode of Rocinante's unfortunate attempt to satisfy his sexual desires, Don Quijote does not transform reality at all. He realizes from the start that he is dealing with (I, 15, 147) "gente soez y de baja ralea" ("base people of low birth," p. 100). Sancho's realistic observation that they are outnumbered by more than ten to one piques Don Quijote's pride and evokes his famous response (p. 148), "Yo valgo por ciento" ("I count for a hundred," p. 100). After their drubbing, when Sancho calls his master in a voice described as "enferma y lastimada" ("weak and doleful"), Don Quijote—in anger, humiliation, frustration, and pain—answers "con el mesmo tono afeminado y doliente" ("in the same feeble, suffering tone"). Don Quijote is able to rationalize this defeat, blaming himself for having exceeded the laws of chivalry by raising his sword against men who were not knights-errant. He is still able to boast (p. 149) of "el valor de este mi fuerte brazo" ("the might of my strong arm"), which leads the narrator to comment that "tal quedó de arrogante el pobre señor con el vencimiento del valiente vizcaíno" ("Such was the poor gentleman's arrogance, because of his victory over the stout Biscayan," p. 101). Later, he attempts to console his squire by delivering a lecture (p. 151) on how "la vida de los caballeros andantes está sujeta a mil peligros y desventuras" ("the life of knights-errant is subject to a thousand dangers and teverses," p. 102), and by citing examples of how famous knights-errant, Amadís de Gaula and the Caballero del Febo, were able to overcome adversity. Unfortunately, his statement about the lashing given to Amadís by his archrival Arcaláus is either a lie or the result of a confused memory.[18]

The famous night of Maritornes described in the last section comes about (I, 16, 158–59) because "los pensamientos que siempre nuestro caballero traía de los sucesos que a cada paso se cuentan en los libros autores de su desgracia, le trujo a la imaginación una de las estrañas locuras que buenamente imaginarse pueden" ("the thoughts, ever present to our knight's mind, of the incidents described at every turn in the books that were the cause of his misfortune, delivered up his imagination to the most extraordinary delusion that one could possibly conceive," p. 108). In the aftermath of the beating he receives, Don Quijote resorts to his classic excuse (I, 17, 163–64): "sin duda ... o yo sé poco, o este castillo es encantado" ("Assuredly ... for either I know little about it, or this castle is enchanted," p. 111). This ought to obviate any possible intrusion of reality, but there is a subtle, tacit acknowledgment of reality in Don Quijote's request for ingredients (suspiciously reminiscent of those used by the goatherd who cured the knight's ear) for the balm of Fierabrás. There is, shortly after, when Sancho has been incapacitated by the magic healing potion, an even more startling implicit admission of nonchivalric reality on Don Quijote's part. According to the narration, Don Quijote (p. 168), "aliviado y sano" ("relieved and well"), is anxious to depart in order to go "buscar aventuras, pareciéndole que todo el tiempo que allí se tardaba era quitársele al mundo y a los en él menesterosos de su favor y amparo, y más, con la seguridad y confianza que llevaba en su bálsamo" ("in quest of adventures. It seemed to him that all the time he lingered was a deprivation for the world and those in it who stood in need of his help and protection, and all the more since he had the security and confidence his balm afforded him"), and so, "forzado deste deseo, él mismo ensilló a Rocinante y enalbardó al jumento de su escudero, a quien también ayudó a vestir y a subir en el asno" ("urged by this impulse, he saddled Rocinante himself and put the packsaddle on his squire's beast. He also helped Sancho to dress and to mount the ass," p. 114). It would be, to say the least, an extraordinary breach of propriety for an authentic knight-errant to saddle not only his own horse but also his squire's and then, even worse, to help his servant to get dressed and mounted. It is proper and even common for someone who has just inadvertently caused a close friend to suffer innocently to do such things, but these acts are thoroughly out of keeping with the practices of the order of chivalry.

Finally, when Sancho Panza is tossed in a blanket (p. 170) by some "gente alegre, bien intencionada, maleante y juguetona" ("lively fellows all, well-disposed, fond of a joke and playful," p. 116), Don Quijote is unable to come to his assistance (p. 171): "Probó a subir desde el caballo a las bardas; pero estaba tan molido y quebrantado, que aun apearse no pudo" ("He tried to climb from his horse on to the top of the wall, but he was so bruised and battered that he could not even dismount," p. 116). The narration here directly contradicts its own words of just three pages before when it stated that Don Quijote felt "aliviado y sano" and was so anxious to continue his quest that he acted as servant to his squire. "Molido y quebrantado" ("bruised and battered")—and, one might add, humiliated and repentant for the harm he has caused Sancho—rings more true here than the alternative. Furthermore, the blanketing, which Sancho Panza will never forget nor let his master forget, proves a constant source of embarrassment for the ineffective Don Quijote, who will repeatedly change his lies to his squire in no fewer than four attempts to find one that might be acceptable:

1. "no me fue posible subir por ellas, ni menos pude apearme de Rocinante, porque me debían de tener encantado" (I, 18, 173) ("it was beyond my power to climb it [the wall] nor could I even dismount from Rocinante, because they no doubt had me enchanted," p. 117).

2. "Fue porque no pude yo saltar las paredes del corral" (I, 19, 186) ("it was because I was unable to leap the walls of the yard," p. 126).

3. "Que, bien apurada la cosa, burla fue y pasatiempo; que, a no entenderlo yo ansí, ya yo hubiera vuelto allá, y hubiera hecho en tu venganza más daño que el que hicieron los griegos por la robada Elena" (I, 21, 211) ("For jest and sport it was, properly regarded, and had I not seen it in that light I would have returned and done more mischief in revenging you than the Greeks did for the kidnap of Helen," p. 144).

4. "que si así fuera, yo te vengara entonces, y aun agora; pero ni entonces ni agora, pude ni vi en quién tomar venganza de tu agravio" (I, 46, 506) ("for had it been so, I would have avenged you that instant, or even now. But neither then nor now could I do so, not having seen anyone I could punish for it," p. 365).[19]

It is immediately after his humiliating tossing in the blanket that Sancho Panza introduces his return-home motif (I, 18, 174)—"sería mejor ... el volvernos a nuestro lugar" ("The best and wisest thing ... would be for us to return home," p. 118). For a knight-errant to be abandoned by his squire would be an embarrassing experience; for a squire to talk a knight-errant into giving up the quest and returning home would be utterly unacceptable. From now on, Don Quijote will periodically have to face the pressure of coming up with inducements to keep his squire at his side. On this first occasion, he creates one of his greatest spectacles, that of the warring armies of sheep. The narration states that Don Quijote "tenía a todas horas y momentos llena la fantasía de aquellas batallas, encantamentos, sucesos, desatinos, amores, desafíos, que en los libros de caballerías se cuentan, *y todo cuanto hablaba, pensaba o hacía* era encaminado a cosas semejantes" (p. 175; my italics) ("At all times and seasons his fancy was full of the battles, enchantments, adventures, reckless feats, loves, and challenges that are recorded in the books of chivalry, *and everything he said, thought, or did* had reference to such things," p. 119; my italics), but, as we have already seen, this statement has less validity than it would have had earlier in the novel. Still, Don Quijote's fantastic description of the knights-errant who compose the two armies is a chivalric masterpiece. Sancho believes his master for a while but finally sees the reality of the situation. Don Quijote enters the fray convinced that he can, like so many of his fictional heroes, decide the question (p. 179): "que solo basto a dar la victoria a la parte a quien yo there mi ayuda" ("for alone I suffice to bring victory to the side I choose to aid," p. 122).[20] Defeated and wounded again, Don Quijote once more resorts to the excuse of enchantment but is unwilling to have Sancho put the matter to a test:

> porque te desengañes y veas ser verdad lo que te digo: sube en tu asno y síguelos bonitamente, y verás cómo, en alejándose de aquí algún poco, se vuelven en su ser primero, y, dejando de ser carneros, son hombres hechos y derechos, como yo te los pinté primero ... Pero no vayas agora, que he menester tu favor y ayuda. (p. 181)

> ("to undeceive yourself, and grasp that what I say is true. Mount your ass and follow them quietly, and you will see that when they have gone some little distance they will return to their original shape. Ceasing to be sheep, they will become men exactly as I described them to you. But do not go just yet, for I want your help and assistance.") (p. 123)

In order to placate his obviously dejected squire (p. 182), Don Quijote modifies his "sube en tu jumento. Sancho el bueno, y vente tras mí" ("Sancho the Good, mount your beast and come along with us," p. 124) to (pp. 183–84) "y guiá tú por donde quisieres; que esta vez quiero dejar a tu eleción el alojarnos.... Sube, amigo, y guía, que yo te seguiré al paso que quisieres" ("and lead on where you will, for this time I leave our lodging to your choice.... Mount, friend, and lead the way, and I will follow you at whatever pace you wish," pp. 124–25).

The nocturnal encounter with the funeral procession gives Don Quijote a chance to recover some chivalric stature in a classic adventure.[21] Don Quijote's challenge is appropriately archaic.

> Deteneos, caballeros, o quienquiera que seáis, y dadme cuenta de quién sois, de dónde venís, adónde vais, qué es lo que en aquellas

andas lleváis; que, según las muestras, o vosotros habéis *fecho*, o
vos han *fecho*, algún *desaguisado*, y conviene y es menester que yo
lo sepa, o bien para castigaros del mal que *fecistes*, o bien para
vengaros del tuerto que *vos ficieron*. (I, 19, 187)

("Halt, knights, or whoever ye may be, and render me account of
who ye are, whence ye come, where ye go, and what it is ye carry
upon that bier. To judge by appearances, either ye have done
some wrong or some wrong has been done you, and it is fitting
and necessary that I should know, either that I may chastise you
for the evil ye have done, or that I may avenge you for the injury
inflicted upon you.") (p. 127)

The challenge, "Deteneos" ("Halt"), is repeated (p. 188) with the traditional
"si no, conmigo sois todos en batalla" ("Otherwise ye must all do battle with
me," p. 127). Don Quijote is able to rout his adversaries and evoke the
admiration of his doubting squire: "Sin duda este mi amo es tan valiente y
esforzado como él dice" ("Clearly, this master of mine is no less bold and
valiant than he says he is," p. 128). After learning that the man has died a
natural death and that the knight's opportunity for vengeance is thus
obviated, Don Quijote goes on to announce his identity (p. 189): "Y quiero
que sepa vuestra reverencia que yo soy un caballero de la Mancha, llamado
don Quijote, y es mi oficio y ejercicio andar por el mundo enderezando
tuertos y *desfaciendo* agravios" ("I would have your reverence know that I am
a knight of La Mancha, Don Quixote by name, and it is my business and
calling to roam the world straightening out wrongs and redressing injuries,"
p. 129). Incongruously, broken leg and Don Quijote's potential wrath
notwithstanding, Alonso López mocks Don Quijote's chivalric mission
through a series of puns: "No sé cómo pueda ser eso de enderezar tuertos ...,
pues a mí de derecho me habéis vuelto tuerto ...; y el agravio que en mí habéis
deshecho ha sido dejarme agraviado ...; y harta desventura ha sido topar con
vos, que vais buscando aventuras" ("I do not understand the part about
straightening out wrongs ... for from straight you have made me crooked....
The injury you have redressed in my case has left me so injured.... It was the
height of misadventure for me to fall in with you, on your search for
adventures"). Don Quijote's response is the inane "No todas las cosas ...
suceden de un mismo modo" ("Things do not always happen in the same
way"). The knight is brought to nonchivalric laughter by Sancho's
explanation of the new chivalric name he gives his master—El Caballero de
la Triste Figura (The Knight of the Mournful Countenance)—and his
comments about Don Quijote's appearance.

The adventure of the fulling mills will be analyzed in the next section as one of Sancho Panza's finest moments. Don Quijote's pompous self-inflation (I, 20, 194)—"Sancho amigo, has de saber que yo nací, por querer del cielo, en esta nuestra edad de hierro, para resucitar en ella la de oro, o la dorada, como suele llamarse. Yo soy aquel para quien están guardados los peligros, las grandes hazañas, los valerosos hechos" ("Friend Sancho, know that I by Heaven's will have been born in this iron age to revive in it the age of gold, or the golden as it is called. I am he for whom perils, mighty achievements, and valiant deeds are reserved," p. 132)—is neutralized by Sancho's *industria* in "enchanting" Rocinante. The comedy of the next morning's anticlimactic reality is perceived by both knight and squire, who break into rollicking laughter. Sancho, however, goes too far and parodies his master's words, impertinently exaggerating the rhetoric and escalating the chivalric archaism (p. 204): "'Has de saber, ¡oh Sancho amigo!, que yo nací, por querer del cielo, en *esta nuestra* edad de hierro, para resucitar en ella la dorada, o de oro. Yo soy aquel para quien están guardados los peligros, las hazañas grandes, los valerosos *fechos*'" ("Friend Sancho, know that I by Heaven's will have been born in this our iron age to revive in it the age of gold, or the golden as it is called. I am he for whom perils, mighty achievements, and valiant deeds are reserved," p. 140).[22] In spite of his ire, Don Quijote admits (p. 205) that the episode is "cosa digna de risa" ("worth laughing at") but goes on to affirm that "no es digna de contarse; que no son todas las personas tan discretas que sepan poner en su punto las cosas" ("it is not worth making a story about, for not everyone is shrewd enough to put things in the right place," p. 140). What he really means, of course, is that he recognizes that what has happened is incompatible with the maintenance of his chivalric vision—another tacit recognition of reality—and must therefore be suppressed.

In a very revealing speech, Don Quijote attempts to establish a new relationship with Sancho. He begins with praise for his squire (p. 206)—"eres discreto y sabes que los primeros movimientos no son en mano del hombre" ("you are shrewd enough to know that our first impulses are beyond our control")—and then imposes the condition that Sancho talk less and with greater respect, for, he adds—correctly—"en cuantos libros de caballerías he leído, que son infinitos, jamás he hallado que ningún escudero hablase tanto con su señor como tú con el tuyo" ("In all the books of chivalry I have read, and they are innumerable, I never met with a squire who talked so much to his lord as you do to yours," pp. 140–41). As stated in section 2.1, the mere fact that Sancho talks and forces Don Quijote to talk about nonchivalric matters in a nonchivalric style compromises Don Quijote's chivalric world. Don Quijote takes advantage of Sancho's ignorance of the romances of

chivalry in order to describe the comportment of Amadís de Gaula's squire
Gandalín (if Amadís is his own model, he reasons, Gandalín should logically
be Sancho's): "se lee dél que siempre hablaba a su señor con la gorra en la
mano, inclinada la cabez y doblado el cuerpo, *more turquesco*" ("We read of
him that he always addressed his lord with his cap in his hand, his head
bowed down, and his body bent double, *more turqúesco* [in Turkish fashion]").
This is, purely and simply, another lie, unethical, unscrupulous, and very
unbecoming of one who claims to adhere to the rules of chivalry.[23]

The winning of Mambrino's helmet allows Don Quijote to transform
reality (gray ass to dappled gray steed, barber to knight-errant, basin to
helmet) (I, 21, 209): "que todas las cosas que veía con mucha facilidad las
acomodaba a sus desvariadas caballerías y malandantes pensamientos" ("For
he made everything he saw fall in with his crazy chivalry and aberrant
notions"); issue a mildly archaic challenge, "¡Defiéndete, *cautiva* criatura,
o ...!" ("Defend thyself, miserable being, or ..."); and win another outright
victory. Don Quijote seems to waver only on thei matter of the nature of the
animal ridden by the barber (p. 212): "Así que, Sancho, deja ese caballo, o
asno, o to que tú quisieres que sea" ("Therefore, Sancho, leave this horse, or
ass, or whatever you will have it to be," p. 145).

Don Quijote's summary for the benefit of his squire of the life cycle of
a typical knight-errant, another carefully structured and modulated piece of
oratory that has the desired effect—Sancho listens attentively and exclaims
(p. 216), "Eso pido, y barras derechas ...: a eso me atengo" ("That's what I
want, plain and simple! ... That's what I'm waiting for," p. 148)—is the
longest speech in the novel in which Don Quijote employs archaism
(*fenestras, fermosos, fablar, furto, Levantarse han, tablas, fermosas, pro, talante,
fablado, prométerselo ha*), though their effect is diminished by their
comparative infrequence in such a long speech.

The encounter with the galley slaves enables Don Quijote to exercise
his chivalric mission (I, 22, 221)—"aquí encaja la ejecución de mi oficio:
desfacer fuerzas y socorrer y acudir a los miserables" ("here is a case for the
exercise of my office, to put down force and to succor and help the
wretched," p. 151)—although he fulfills the letter rather than the spirit of
that calling. Don Quijote does not transform reality; rather he interprets
reality according to his own, very strictly literal preference. The stoning he
receives (p. 231) leaves the knight "mohinísimo de verse tan malparado por
los mismos a quien tanto bien había hecho" ("[fuming] at finding himself
treated thus by the very persons for whom he had done so much," p. 159).

Overall, Don Quijote seems to vacillate during the events of this
series of chapters. He is still capable of willfully transforming reality to
conform to his chivalric vision, of speaking in archaism and using all the

formulaic clichés of his chivalric rhetoric, of gloating with pride over his victories and rationalizing his nonencounters or defeats. In short, during this period Don Quijote still maintains a reasonable degree of faithfulness to his chivalric vision. But at the same time, it is undeniable that Don Quijote is unable to sustain his chivalric role with the same degree of fidelity as in the earlier chapters. In virtually every adventure, Don Quijote makes minor but very important concessions to physical and psychological reality, and the degree to which he does this is directly proportional to the degree to which he invalidates his original concept of himself and his chivalric world. The most important single cause of these concessions to reality is Sancho Panza.

2.5 SANCHO PANZA: CHIVALRY

Sancho Panza enters the novel, for better or worse, in order to play a major role in Don Quijote's chivalric world. The manner in which he undermines that world from within has been discussed earlier. But Sancho is more than just another element in a consideration of Don Quijote's progression from chivalry to reality. Sancho's own development is a major aspect of Cervantes's novel, and this development too can be more fully understood when considered in terms of the rhetoric of chivalry.

In section 1.4, in a brief comment following Table 1.2, I observed that the distribution of Sancho's speech reflects his comparatively minor role at the beginning and at the end of part I of *Don Quijote*. More specifically, it is between chapters 15 and 31 that Sancho's role is most prominent. To look at Sancho's figures in a different way, 206 of his 277 speeches, that is, 74 percent, fall within the section between chapters 15 and 31, which include the adventures discussed in the last section and the events that take place in the Sierra Morena.

It is significant that the pattern of Sancho Panza's archaic speech also centers on the same part of the novel. Sancho uses no archaism before chapter 15 nor any after chapter 31, as seen in the figure. This figure indicates a gradual adaptation to Don Quijote's rhetoric of chivalry, as well as a growing linguistic self-confidence on Sancho's part. The squire's first archaism comes after the beating by the Yanguesans when he asks his master (I, 15, 148) for "dos tragos de aquella bebida del feo Blas" ("a couple of sips of that potion of Fear-o'-brass," p. 100), reasoning that it might "de provecho para los quebrantamientos de huesos como to es para las *feridas*" ("serve for broken bones as well as for wounds"). This is typical of Sancho's use of archaism, which usually consists of a single *f-*, the most frequent and most easily perceived archaic form used by his master. There is one occasion, however, when Sancho Panza employs a string of archaisms: when he delivers his most sophisticated and rhetorical speech in part I.

Figure 2.1   Sancho Panza's Archaic Speeches (Part I)

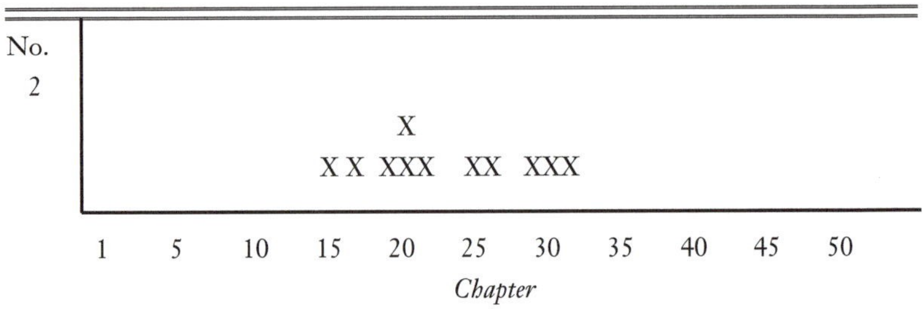

No.	
2	

```
                               X
                       X X XXX   XX  XXX

      1    5    10   15   20   25   30   35   40   45   50
                                Chapter
```

In chapter 20 (p. 193), Don Quijote and Sancho hear the sound of "unos golpes a compás, con un cierto crujir de hierros y cadenas, ... acompañados del furioso estruendo del agua" ("strokes that fell with a measured beat, and a certain rattling of iron and chains. Together with the furious din of the water," pp. 131–32). The mysterious nature of this unknown noise is heightened by the absolute blackness of the night. Sancho is at least as frightened, if not more so, as he was by the spectral lights in the night not so long before. Don Quijote proposes separating from his squire in order to go and discover the source of the noise. Sancho, terrified by the prospect of being left alone in such circumstances (p. 195), begins to "llorar con la mayor ternura del mundo" ("weep in the most pathetic way," p. 132). In this context, motivated by fear, in the midst of tears and trembling, Sancho delivers the following extraordinary speech.

> Señor, yo no sé por qué quiere vuestra merced acometer esta tan temerosa aventura; ahora es de noche, aquí no nos vee nadie, bien podemos torcer el camino y desviarnos del peligro, aunque no bebamos en tres días; y pues no hay quien nos vea, menos habrá quien nos note de cobardes; cuanto más que yo he oído predicar al cura de nuestro lugar, que vuestra merced bien conoce, que quien busca el peligro perece en él; así, que no es bien tentar a Dios acometiendo tan desaforado hecho, donde no se puede escapar sino por milagro, y basta los que ha hecho el cielo con vuestra merced en librarle de ser manteado, como yo lo fui, y en sacarle vencedor, libre y salvo de entre tantos enemigos como acompañaban al difunto. Y cuando todo esto no mueva ni ablande ese duro corazón, muévale el pensar y creer que apenas se habrá vuestra merced apartado de aquí, cuando yo, de miedo, dé miánima

a quien quisiere llevarla. Yo salí de mi tierra y dejé hijos y mujer por venir a servir a vuestra merced, creyendo valer más y no menos; pero como la cudicia rompe el saco, a mí me ha rasgado mis esperanzas, pues cuando más vivas las tenía de alcanzar aquella negra y malhadada ínsula que tantas veces vuestra merced me ha prometido, veo que, en pago y trueco della, me quiere ahora dejaren un lugar tan apartado del trato humano. Por un solo Dios, señor mío, que non se me *faga* tal *desaguisado*; y ya que del todo no quiera vuestra merced desistir de acometer este *fecho*, dilátelo, a lo menos, hasta la mañana; que, a lo que a mí me muestra la ciencia que aprendí cuando era pastor, no debe de haber desde aquí al alba tres horas, porque la boca de la bocina está encima de la cabeza, y hace la media noche en la línea del brazo izquierdo. (pp. 195–96)

(Señor, I do not know why your worship wants to attempt this dreadful adventure. It is night now, no one sees us here, we can easily turn around and take ourselves out of danger, even if we don't drink for three days to come. As there is no one to see us, all the less will there be anyone to call us cowards. Besides, I have heard the priest of our village, whom your worship knows well, preach that "he who seeks danger perishes in it." So it is not right to tempt God by trying so tremendous a feat from which there can be no escape except by a miracle, and Heaven has performed enough of them for your worship in delivering you from being blanketed as I was, and bringing you out victorious and safe and sound from among all those enemies that were with the dead man. If all this does not move or soften that hard heart, let it be moved by this thought and reflection, that you will have hardly left this spot when from pure fear I shall give my soul up to anyone that will take it. I left home and wife and children to come and serve your worship, trusting to do better and not worse. But as "greed bursts the bag" it has torn my hopes open, for just as I had them highest about getting that wretched, unlucky island your worship has so often promised me, I see that instead and in exchange for it you mean to desert me now in a place so far from human contact. For God's sake, master, let not so great an injustice be done to me. And if your worship will not entirely give up attempting this feat, at least put it off till morning. According to what I learned when I was a shepherd, dawn cannot be more than three hours off, because the Little Dipper is overhead and its handle shows that it's midnight.) (pp. 132–33)

The first thing that strikes the reader is the length of the speech, which is over 50 percent longer than anything Sancho has said previously.[24] But more than the length, the careful, logical construction; the rhetorical embellishment; and the shifts in style make it truly remarkable. Sancho begins with a brief introductory statement, or *exordium*, in which he succinctly states his purpose: to dissuade Don Quijote from undertaking the adventure. He launches immediately into his *narratio*, describing the facts— "es de noche, ... no nos vee nadie" '("it is night ... no one sees us")—and the logical consequence of these facts—"pues no hay quien nos vea, menos habrá quien nos note de cobardes" ("As there is no one to see us, all the less will there be anyone to call us cowards"). Next he appeals to recognized authority (as he has often heard Don Quijote appeal to the authority of the romances of chivalry)—in this case, the local priest—citing the truism, both popular and Christian, that "quien busca el peligro perece en él" ("he who seeks danger perishes in it"), and the logical corollary that "no es bien tentar a Dios" ("it is not right to tempt God"), and offering the opinion that God, who intervened to spare Don Quijote in earlier adventures, might exhaust his patience. After the first sentence,[25] which ends with the word *difunto*, we can assume that there is a pause, during which Don Quijote's silence is observed.

With the failure of his logical petition, the *logos* of classical rhetoric, Sancho modifies his technique, employing the other two standard means of rhetorical persuasion, *pathos* and *ethos*; that is, if he cannot evince a response from Don Quijote with an intellectual appeal, he will speak to him in emotional terms and will even allude to his own moral character. The eloquent squire announces this change, saying, "Y cuando todo esto no mueva ..., muévele el pensar y creer que" ("If all this does not move ..., let it be moved by this thought and reflection"). He speaks now of his personal sacrifice—"Yo salí ... y dejé ... creyendo valer más" ("I left ... and I abandoned ... trusting to do better")—which has never been rewarded properly—"mis esperanzas ... aquella ... ínsula que tantas veces vuestra merced me ha prometido" ("my hopes ... that ... island that your worship has so often promised me")—but which has terminated in rejection—"me quiere ahora dejar" ("you mean to desert me").

This progression from fact and universal (that is, theological) truth to personal appeal, the progression from logos to *pathos* and *ethos*, is accompanied by a variety of stylistic devices, the *elocutio* of classical rhetoric:

   1. Preplaced adjectives: "tan temerosa aventura," "tan desaforado hecho," "ese duro corazón," "aquella negra y malhadada ínsula."
   2. Exaggeration with *tan* and *tanto*: "tan temerosa," "tan desaforado," "tantos enemigos," "tantas veces," "tan apartado."

3. Parallel constructions: "ahora es ... aquí no nos vee," "torcer el camino y desviarnos del peligro," "pues no hay quién nos vea, menos habrá quien nos note," "quien busca ... perece," "en librarle ... y en sacarle," "cuando ... no mueva ... muévale," "apenas se habrá vuestra merced apartado ... cuando yo ... dé mi ánima," "Yo salí ... y dejé."

4. Sententious statements: "quien busca el peligro perece en él," "la cudicia rompe el saco."

5. Near synonymous pairs of adjectives, verbs, and nouns: "libre y salvo," "no mueva ni ablande," "pensar y creer," "negra y malhadada," "pago y trueco."

6. Hyperbolic paraphrase: "tan desaforado hecho" ("so tremendous a feat") for "esta aventura" ("this adventure"), "ese duro corazón" ("that hard heart") for "vuestra merced" ("your worship"), "dé mi ánima a quien quisiere llevarla" ("I shall give my soul to anyone that will take it") for "meura" ("I will die"), "un lugar tan apartado del trato humano" ("a place so far from human contact") for "aquí" ("here").

We can suppose another pause after *trato humano* during which Sancho sees that his rhetoric has not, in fact, moved Don Quijote's "duro corazón." Abruptly changing tactics, Sancho replaces rhetorical logic with the heaviest concentration of chivalric archaism that he ever employs—"que non se me *faga* tal *desaguisado* ... este *fecho*" ("let not so great an injustice be done to me ... this feat")—and then switches again, this time to a stylistically more appropriate account of a shepherd's popular astronomy. While the astronomical calculations briefly engage Don Quijote's curiosity—"¿Cómo puedes tú ... ver donde hate esa línea?" ("How can you see ... where the handle is?")—the knight remains determined to continue "hater to que debía a estilo de caballero" ("fulfilling knightly usage") and "acometer ahora esta tan no vista y tan temerosa aventura" ("to undertake now this so unexampled and terrible adventure"). The result is that Sancho must resort to the device he knows best: "Viendo, pues, Sancho la última resolución de su amo, y cuán poco valían con él sus lágrimas, consejos y ruegos, determinó de aprovecharse de su industria, y hacerle esperar hasta al día, si pudiese" ("When Sancho realized that this was his master's final resolve, and saw how little his tears, counsels, and entreaties prevailed, he decided to employ his own ingenuity and compel him, if he could, to wait till daylight"). Sancho ties Rocinante's feet and suggests that it is divine intervention (or perhaps, by implication, an "enchantment") that keeps the knight from leaving his squire.

It is ironic that Sancho's eloquent speech, combined with an appeal in his master's own chivalric archaism, has no effect on Don Quijote. But its ineffectiveness in no way diminishes the fact that this is a remarkable speech to have been articulated by Sancho Panza. It is equally remarkable that, as far as I know, no critic of the novel has ever commented on this extraordinary passage. Perhaps this inattention is due in part to the fact that other, more obviously comic scenes in the same chapter have attracted greater attention: Sancho's amusing folkloric tale; the scatological scene (p. 201) in which the squire must do "lo que otro no pudiera hacer por él" ("what no one could do for him," p. 137); and the absurd discovery of the fulling mills. Another factor in the lack of recognition accorded this passage is its incongruity: how could Sancho have ever learned such a mode of discourse? I suggest that, although he has had no formal training in oratory, Sancho has a good ear for style and a natural ability to mimic speech patterns. For years, he has heard mass and sermons at church—recall his statement that he has "oído predicar al cura de nuestro lugar" ("heard our priest preach")—and is therefore familiar with the rhetoric of the pulpit. Then, of course, he has recently been in the company of a truly outstanding orator, Don Quijote. More specifically, within the last few days, Sancho has witnessed and has undoubtedly heard with admiration Don Quijote's celebrated rhetorical discourse on the Golden Age and Marcela's equally rhetorical harangue at the burial of Grisóstomo.[26] With such recent impressive examples of classical rhetoric still fresh in his mind, it is less difficult than one would have expected to accept the squire's eloquence in this scene.

Furthermore, this speech is not a sudden and incongruous event; rather, it is possible to see it as a logical culmination of an increasing sophistication on the part of the squire. Sancho Panza is introduced (I, 7, 85) as an "hombre de bien ... pero de muy poca sal en la mollera" ("a good man ... but with very little grey matter in his skull," p. 57), and it is generally assumed that Don Quijote recruits him as his squire simply by appealing to his material interests by promising him an *ínsula* to govern and exploit.[27] The scene of this recruitment is merely summarized by the narrator, but there is a suggestion that the appeal is to more than mere greed: "En resolución, *tanto* le dijo, *tanto* le per suadió y prometió ... Decíale, *entre otras cosas*, ... Con estas promesas y *otras tales*" (p. 85; my italics) ("Finally, Don Quixote convinced him with such persuasions and promises ... *among other things*, told him ... On these and *the like* promises," p. 57; my italics). We can never know all that Don Quijote said to Sancho Panza, but it is at least possible that some of the knight's appeal was to Sancho's higher instincts.

From the beginning, Sancho fails to impress as genuinely stupid ("de muy poca sal en la mollera")[28] but is at first comparatively timid and submissive, believing naively that his master's victory over the Biscayan can bring him his governorship (I, 10, 105). He demonstrates an ability to make subtle distinctions when he corrects Don Quijote's oath of vengeance against the Biscayan (p. 108). Sancho stays in the background and merely observes the events leading up to and during the burial of Grisóstomo, but immediately thereafter, following Rocinante's amorous misadventure, he begins to use the chivalric archaisms that he has heard so often in his master's speech.

When they arrive at the inn, Sancho lies for the first time in the novel, saying (I, 16, 154) that Don Quijote "había dado una caída de una peña abajo" ("had fallen down from a cliff," p. 104). The innkeeper's wife almost catches him up by suggesting that "también debistes vos de caer" ("then you must have fallen also"), forcing Sancho to lie again (pp. 155–56): "No caí ...; sino que del sobresalto que tomé de ver caer a mi amo, de tal manera me duele a mí el cuerpo, que me parece que me han dado mil palos" ("I did not fall, but from the shock I got at seeing my Master fall, my body aches so that I feel as if I had had a thousand whacks," p. 105). The innkeeper's daughter rescues Sancho from her mother's suspicions by supporting this last absurdity. Thus reinforced, Sancho proceeds very condescendingly to explain (p. 156) to Maritornes what a "caballero aventurero" ("knight-adventurer") is: "¿Tan nueva sois en el mundo que no lo sabéis vos?" ("Are you so new in the world that you don't know?," p. 106). During all of this, Don Quijote has been silent; Sancho has had to maintain on his own for the first time the chivalric world of his master, and he has responded well to the pressure, finding out in the process how advantageous lying can be.

Fear seems to bring out both the best and the worst in Sancho, for it is after Don Quijote's nocturnal victory over the white-shirted mourners that the enthusiastic squire, without any prompting, invents for his master the genuinely chivalric name of El Caballero de la Triste Figura (I, 19, 190). After this adventure, Sancho, both euphoric and anxious to get Don Quijote to a safe refuge, combines a bit of rhetoric and his first proverb (I, 19, 192): "El jumento está como conviene, la montaña cerca, la hambre carga, no hay que hater sino retirarnos con gentil compás de pies, y, como dicen, váyase el muerto a la sepultura y el vivo a la hogaza" ("This ass is properly loaded; the mountains are near at hand; we are hungry. All we have to do is retreat at a reasonable walk and, as the saying is, 'Let the dead man sleep; a live one has to eat,'" p. 131). Then he continues to assert himself over an uncharacteristically silent and submissive Don Quijote: "Y antecogiendo su asno, rogó a su señor que le siguiese; el cual, pareciéndole que Sancho tenía razón, sin volverle a replicar Ie siguió" ("And leading his ass, he begged his master to follow. Feeling that Sancho was right, Don Quixote did so without saying a word in reply"). A short while later, it is again Sancho who suggests that the abundant grass they see speaks for the presence of a nearby fountain or brook and that they should proceed to find it; the comment is added (p. 193) that "Parecióle biers el consejo a don Quijote" ("The advice seemed good to Don Quixote," p. 131).

Thus, with accelerating frequency, there have been numerous indications of Sancho Panza's growing self-confidence as he settles comfortably into his assigned role. His oratorical masterpiece is then a height in his psychological ascent. Don Quijote's attempt, discussed in the last section, to force Sancho into a more subservient role is a recognition that the squire's stature has increased and rivals his own.

Don Quijote will not be able to reduce the prominence of Sancho, whom he will follow into the Sierra Morena (I, 23, 233), whose explanation he will accept in place of his own theory concerning the dead mule (p. 236), and who will bravely rush to the defense of his master in the fight with Cardenio (I, 24, 252). But if Sancho steadily gains in self-confidence and self-assertion while largely alone with Don Quijote in chapters 15–25, his chance meeting with the priest and the barber reduces him to performing a stereotyped, comic routine for their benefit as he tries to recite the letter to Dulcinea (I, 26, 278). Sancho recovers somewhat during the excitement of the Princess Micomicona adventure, chapters 29–31, but goes into a sharp decline when he is relegated to a very minor role during the long stay in the inn. As we shall see later, he recovers in certain strategic ways on the return to the village.

Sancho Panza, like his master, is commonly supposed to remain a static character in the first part of the novel, but all evidence indicates that this is by no means true. It is no rustic, myopically realistic, comic farmer "de muy poca sal en la mollera" who delivers the rhetorical speech in chapter 20, but rather an extraordinarily intelligent, perceptive, and self-confident man who has already acquired from his equally extraordinary companion a new vision of life and the levels of style with which to express a variety of sophisticated thoughts.

2.6 CHAPTERS 23–28: IN THE SIERRA MORENA

After Don Quijote frees the galley slaves, Sancho, fearing the rural police, advises flight, prudently cautioning (I, 23, 232) that "con la Santa Hermandad no hay usar de caballerías" ("chivalry is of no account with the Holy Brotherhood," p. 160). Don Quijote agrees condescendingly but insists that he does so only for Sancho's benefit and that it should never be so much as hinted that it is done out of fear. It appears that Don Quijote protests too much, and he covers his concession to reality with yet another lie.

As in chapters 11–14, Don Quijote and Sancho meet a goatherd as a prelude to the introduction of an important secondary character, this time Cardenio, whose furious penance has the obvious literary parallels of Amadís de Gaula and Orlando Furioso. After the fight with Cardenio and the goatherd (I, 24, 252–53), Sancho proposes returning home. In order to placate his squire, Don Quijote lifts the ban on speaking (which had not been effective at any rate, since in the four chapters between its imposition and its suspension there is no noticeable change in Sancho's frequency or style of speech) and then announces (I, 25, 256–57) that since "todo cuanto yo he hecho, hago e hiciere, va muy puesto en razón y muy conforme a las reglas de caballería" ("everything I have done, am doing, or shall do, is well founded on reason and in conformity with the rules of chivalry"), he intends now to perform "una hazaña, con que he de ganar perpetuo nombre y fama en todo lo descubierto de la tierra; y será tal, que he de echar con ella el sello a todo aquello que puede hacer perfecto y famoso a un andante caballero" ("something that will win me eternal name and fame throughout the known world. It shall be such that thereby I shall set the seal on all that can make a knight-errant perfect and famous," p. 177). Next Don Quijote delivers his lecture on imitation cited in section 1.2 and reveals that he now intends to imitate Amadís, who responded to Oriana's anger by retiring to the Peña Pobre and calling himself Beltenebros, while simultaneously imitating Orlando in his fury after learning of Angelica's infidelity. The logical Sancho points out (p. 259) that "los caballeros que lo tal *ficieron* fueron provocados" ("the knights who behaved in this way had provocation"), while there is no evidence that Dulcinea "ha hecho alguna niñería con moro o cristiano" ("has been trifling with Moor or Christian," p. 179). That is precisely the point Don Quijote wants to make: "si en seco hago esto ¿qué hiciera en mojado?" ("if I do this without an excuse, what I would do if I had one?").

Don Quijote commits a tactical error[29] in revealing to Sancho the reality behind the myth of Dulcinea and then compounds his mistake by implying a base carnal motivation for his interest in her (pp. 265–67),[30] thus opening a little further the cracks made by reality in his chivalric construct. Don Quijote's letter to Dulcinea is a carefully executed masterpiece of chivalric rhetoric, imitating perfectly the epistolary practices of the fictional knights-errant. But any guise of nobility that the penitential act might have had is eliminated by the bare-bottomed acrobatics (p. 272) designed to illustrate his madness for his lady that he performs before Sancho goes off to deliver the message.

The very gratuity of Don Quijote's penance, which makes it a pinnacle in the knight's efforts to live according to artistic norms,[31] paradoxically reduces in great measure the authenticity of the art-inspired existence that is the hallmark of Don Quijote's chivalric world. The fictional knights-errant who withdrew from the world always believed that they had good reason to do so.[32] Amadís or Orlando would appear silly—as silly as Don Quijote—if they went sulking off to be alone with no cause. Don Quijote's early adventures always had, at least in his own eyes, some degree of substance as well as form: he really did stand vigil over his armor and really was dubbed a knight; Juan Haldudo really was beating poor Andrés; he really did defeat the Biscayan in a sword battle. Now Don Quijote is merely playacting out of frustration with the harsh encounters he has had with reality; he has ceased to be a knight-errant and has become a jester.

Although Don Quijote's stated models for his penance are Amadís and Orlando, his real models are Cardenio, who told the goatherds (I, 23, 241–42) that he had come to these mountains and was acting as he did "porque así le convenía para cumplir cierta penitencia que por sus muchos pecados le había sido impuesta" ("since he was obliged to do so in order to work out a penance which for his many sins had been imposed upon him," p. 166), and Grisóstomo.[33] One reason (besides the fact that it is easier) why Don Quijote finally decides to imitate Amadís rather than Orlando is that Cardenio has already preempted that role in his raving madness that has so disturbed the goatherds. Just as the genuine death of Grisóstomo put Don Quijote in an unfavorable light earlier, Cardenio's authentic penance in the Sierra Morena makes the feigned one of Don Quijote all the more hollow.

During most of chapter 26, all of 27 and 28, and the beginning of 29, Don Quijote is ignored in his solitude as the narrative interest shifts to Cardenio and Dorotea and the decisive reentry of the priest and the barber into the story. Whenever the reader's attention is drawn away from Don Quijote, his chivalric world becomes more remote.

NOTES

1. I borrow this term as being both concise and accurately descriptive from the character of Simkin in Saul Bellow's very Cervantine novel *Herzog* (New York: Viking Press, 1964), p. 30. For a discussion of Sancho's role in pointing out reality to Don Quijote, see Carlos Varo, *Génesis y evolución del "Quijote,"* pp. 153–56.

2. Luis Rosales, "Pequeña historia de un mito," pp. 155–56. Alfred Schutz makes the same point from a psychological and philosophical point of view, citing William James's essay on the relative reality of different individuals' "sub-universes" and concluding that Don Quijote "has to establish a 'sub-universe of discourse' with the fellow-men with whom he shares a face-to-face relationship within the world of common sense. This refers first of all to Sancho Panza, his squire"; "Don Quixote and the Problem of Reality," p. 142. See also Hans Jörg Neuschäfer, "Don Quijote como ser social. Nuevo aspecto de la dialéctica cervantina," 2:406–7.

3. See Varo, *Génesis y evolución*, p. 170.

4. Salvador de Madariaga, *Don Quixote: An Introductory Essay in Psychology*, p. 110.

5. I say that this is possible because a secret departure is a characteristic of the knights-errant whom Don Quijote imitates. See Daniel Eisenberg, "*Don Quijote* and the Romances of Chivalry: The Need for a Reexamination," pp. 520–21.

6. Varo (*Génesis y evolución*, p. 177) notes that Don Quijote's ability to feel pain further humanizes his character. Both Marthe Robert and Arthur Efron must ignore these passages in order to make a similar erroneous point. Robert states that Don Quijote "refuses to believe in the reality of his wounds ... It is impossible to make any contact with him, even by the radical means of cruelty and violence"; *The Old and the New: From Don Quixote to Kafka*, pp. 135–36. Efron discusses the issue at some length before concluding that "like the ideals of the Knight, his pain and his sorrow exist only so that they may be perpetuated further. They become goals in themselves, stock roles blithely masquerading as the height of life's possibilities. The possible emergence of real value from the experience of pain ... is thus truncated"; *Don Quixote and the Dulcineated World*, p. 47.

7. Obviously, Vivaldo anticipates the type of character that Don Quijote will encounter more frequently later in the novel: Dorotea, the duke and duchess, Don Antonio Moreno, and so on.

8. In effect, as Galaor has no need to remain faithful to any particular lady, he is able to sleep with several whom he rescues during the four volumes of *Amadís de Gaula*. Place calls Galaor (*Amadís*, III (1962), 934) "un alegre seductor, realmente más donjuanesco que don Juan" ("a merry seducer, really more Don Juan-like than Don Juan"). See also Clemencín, *Don Quijote*, p. 1134, note 38.

9. The use of *ál* here recalls the well-known line of Celestina to Pármeno: "Este es el deleyte; que to al, mejor to fazen los asnos en el prado" ("That's the real pleasure. As for the other thing, the donkeys in the field can do it better than we can"); Francisco de Rojas, *La Celestina*, 1:108 (*The Spanish Bawd*, trans. J.M. Cohen, p. 51). In fact, it is quite likely that Cervantes had this specific passage (largely responsible, perhaps, for making *ál* less than acceptable in polite language) in mind when writing this scene.

10. This aspect of the personification of Rocinante, together with any consideration of archaism in the passage, is absent in the stylistic analysis and subsequent discussion of this paragraph by Charles W. Steele in his article "Functions of the Grisóstomo–Marcela Episode in *Don Quijote*: Symbolism, Drama, Parody," pp. 14–15.

11. Helena Percas de Ponseti, *Cervantes y su concepto del arte*, 1:132. See also Steele, "Grisóstomo–Marcela Episode," pp. 15–16.

12. Joaquin Casalduero, noting the setting of Rocinante's misadventure, sees it as a burlesque exaggeration of pastoral elements that sets up a parody of chivalric love in the Don Quijote–Maritornes scene in the next chapter; *Sentido y forma del "Quijote*," p. 91. There is a fusion of pastoral and chivalric elements here, but the literary *parody*—which must involve a distortion of "the most striking peculiarities of subject matter *and style*" (my italics) of a work—is specifically chivalric. See the definition of parody cited in Chapter 1, note 20.

13. The contrast between Don Quijote's words and his deeds is also pointed out and commented on by Efron, *Don Quixote and the Dulcineated World*, p. 53.

14. Henry Mendeloff describes it as "more fit for animals than humans," but his subsequent analysis of the farcical aspects of the scene in the inn contains no reference to the related events in the previous chapter; "The Maritornes Episode (*DQ*: I, 16): A Cervantine Bedroom Farce," pp. 753–59.

15. The humanization of Rocinante and the *rucio* is a process that goes on throughout the novel. The friendship between the two animals is described at some length and a

comparison is made with classical heroes (II, 12, 662–63). After Rocinante's unfortunate erotic episode, Sancho refers to him (I, 15, 150) as a "persona casta y tan pacífica como yo" ("a virtuous person and as quiet as myself," p. 102) and (p. 152) as a "caballero andante" ("knight-errant," p. 103). On his first sally, Don Quijote refers to Rocinante (I, 2, 42) as "compañero eterno mío" ("constant companion," p. 30); the tearful Sancho who leaves his governorship calls the *rucio* (II, 53, 987) "compañero mío y amigo mío" ("comrade and friend and partner," p. 720), and when he falls into the pit (II, 55, 1000), he observes that "nunca Sancho Panza se apartó de su asno, ni su asno de Sancho Panza" ("Sancho Panza is never separated from his donkey, nor his donkey from Sancho Panza," p. 729) and again calls his ass "compañero y amigo mío." In general, the relationships between tall, thin Don Quijote and long, lanky Rocinante and between short, fat Sancho Panza and his well-fed *rucio* tend to blur the distinctions between man and beast. Completing the process of animal–human reversal are statements by Sancho (II, 11, 653)—"Señor, las tristezas no se hicieron para las bestias, sino para los hombres; pero si los hombres las sienten demasiado, se vuelven bestias" ("Sadness, señor, was made not for beasts but for men, but if men give in to it they turn beasts," p. 478)—Don Quijote (II, 28, 799)—"Asno eres, y asno has de ser, y en asno has de parar cuando se te acabe el curso de la vida; que para mí tengo que antes llegará ella a su último término que tú caigas y des en la cuenta de que eres bestia" ("Ass you are, ass you will be, and ass you will end when the course of your life is run; for I know it will come to its close before you perceive or discern that you are a beast," p. 585)—and Cide Hamete Benengeli (II, 29, 807)—"Volvieron a sus bestias, y a set bestias, don Quijote y Sancho" ("Don Quixote and Sancho returned to their animals—and to their beastly life," p. 590). In the inn, Sancho is tossed in a blanket like a dog (I, 17, 170–71) and later Don Quijote is incited like a dog (*azuzado*) by the people watching him fight with the goatherd (I, 52, 551; see section 3.4). Maese Pedro owns an ape who can talk to him (II, 25); men bray like donkeys (II, 25, 27, 55); enchanters turn human beings into grotesque statues of animals (II, 39, 876); Dulcinea is compared (quite suggestively) with a rabbit (II, 73, 1127); and so on. The novel's rich underlying animal-human imagery, especially in part II, is a topic worthy of further study.

16. Varo, *Génesis y evolución*, p. 187.

17. Clemencín (*Don Quijote*, p. 1143, note 37) notes that Seville would be the worst possible place for chivalric adventures. He is obviously correct: when Don Quijote visits a comparable big city, Barcelona, in part II, he acts more like a tourist than a knight-errant (see section 4.5). When Sansón Carrasco, whose fun-loving personality is anticipated here by Vivaldo, plays the role of the Caballero de los Espejos, he tells Don Quijote that he has defeated the famous Sevillan giantess Giralda (II, 14, 674), which could be a hint of the type of adventure that Vivaldo and his friends might have prepared for Don Quijote had he accepted their offer.

18. See Clemencín, *Don Quijote*, p. 1149, note 28.

19. See also Don Quijote's comment that he (spiritually) shared fully in Sancho's (physical) pain (II, 2, 593).

20. See Clemencín, *Don Quijote*, pp. 1439–40, note 37. Daniel Eisenberg also discusses such an adventure but perhaps goes too far in rationalizing the relative verisimilitude of his hero's feat; Ortúñez de Calahorra, *Espejo de príncipes y cavalleros*, 4:98–99, note for lines 21 ff.

21. Riquer points out that, while the modern reader might well find this adventure absurd, Cervantes's contemporaries readily perceived it as a conscious parody of a particular episode from *Palmerín de Inglaterra; Don Quijote*, p. 184, note. See also Clemencín, *Don Quijote*, p. 1178, note 11.

22. See John J. Allen, *Don Quixote: Hero or Fool?*, 1:57; see also 1:37.

23. Clemencín (*Don Quijote*, p. 1193, note 64) notes that Don Quijote does not tell the truth here but rationalizes that the knight should be excused on account of his madness. In the following note, Clemencín observes that Don Quijote's statement that the squires of knights-errant were typically silent is in error.

24. The speech occupies thirty-one lines in the Riquer edition. Sancho's longest speech prior to this, when he described his blanketing and suggested returning home, was nineteen lines (I, 18, 173–74). The only time that Sancho speaks at greater length (about thirty-eight lines) is when he learns that Dulcinea del Toboso is really Aldonza Lorenzo (I, 25, 265–66). The longest of his other speeches are: twenty-nine lines, when he narrates the story of Torralba (I, 20, 199–200); twenty-five lines, when he reproaches the priest for "enchanting" Don Quijote (I, 47, 515–16); twenty lines, when he discusses chivalric procedures with his master (I, 21, 213); and twenty lines, when he learns that a princess in distress is searching for Don Quijote (I, 29, 316–17).

25. This sentence is one of the longest and most sophisticated ever uttered by Sancho. However, simply measuring the length of Sancho's sentences is less revealing than might be hoped because of the sometimes arbitrary punctuation in the Spanish passage, as seen in these examples: "tres días; y pues" and "al difunto. Y cuando."

26. See the excellent analyses of the speeches by Don Quijote and Marcela by Mary Mackey, "Rhetoric and Characterization in *Don Quijote*," pp. 51–66; and Thomas R. Hart and Steven Rendall, "Rhetoric and Characterization in Marcela's Address to the Shepherds," pp. 287–98.

27. See, for example, Franklin O. Brantley, "Sancho's Ascent to the Spheres," pp. 37–38.

28. Gonzalo Torrente Ballester makes the same observation; *El "Quijote" como juego*, p. 91. Unfortunately, Sancho's natural stupidity is assumed by the great majority of the novel's readers, including, for example, one of his best biographers, Hipólito R. Romero Flores, who calls Sancho "un porro" ("a dolt"); *Biografía de Sancho Panza, filósofo de la sensatez*, p. 107.

29. Jorge E. Sorensen calls this confession "inexplicable"; "The Importance of Sierra Morena as a Point of Transition in *Don Quijote*," p. 48.

30. Don Quijote cites the folkloric anecdote of the cultured widow who defends her love for a stupid *mozo motilón* ("young lay-brother") by saying (p. 267) "para lo que yo le quiero, tanta filosofía sabe, y más, que Aristóteles" ("Because for all I want with him, he knows as much and more philosophy than Aristotle," p. 184), and then he adds "por lo que yo quiero a Dulcinea del Toboso, tanto vale como la más alta princesa de la tierra" ("for all I want with Dulcinea del Toboso, she is just as good as the most exalted princess on earth"). The switch from *para*, indicating the use to which the man is to be put, to *por*, suggesting the motivation for Don Quijote's love for Dulcinea, is significant (and, sadly, lost in translation), but the fact that such an analogy should even occur to Don Quijote can only put Dulcinea in an unfavorable light. See Mac E. Barrick, "The Form and Function of Folktales in *Don Quijote*," pp. 127–28.

31. The essential critical study on this important subject is Juan Bautista Avalle-Arce's essay on "La vida como obra de arte," included in revised form as chapter 5 of *Don Quijote como forma de vida*, pp. 144–72. See also "Vital and Artistic Structures in the Life of Don Quixote," p. 104–21.

32. See Edward C. Riley, *Cervantes' Theory of the Novel*, p. 67.

33. Luis Rosales has commented on the many details of Cardenio's penance that are copied by Don Quijote; *Cervantes y la libertad*, 2:305–7. For Grisóstomo as a model for Don Quijote, see Harold G. Jones, "Grisóstomo and Don Quixote: Death and Imitation," p. 88.

ALBAN K. FORCIONE

Madness and Mystery:
The Exemplarity of Cervantes's
Novelas ejemplares

In his literary testament, the mock-epic *Viage del Parnaso*, Cervantes describes his frustration when, on entering Apollo's dazzling garden, he finds himself excluded from the ceremonial gathering of the great poets beneath the laurels of Parnassus. Likening the indignity to the mistreatment of Ovid in his exile, he allows his "Juvenalian anger" to vent itself in the composition of some autobiographical verses. Addressing his complaint to the god of poetry, he reminds him of the authenticity of his vocation and proceeds to pass review of his considerable achievements as a writer. Cervantes prefaces his surrender to anger with an acknowledgment that the literary products of the indignation of fools are generally full of perversity. But a more interesting note of self-deprecation. sounds in the middle of his list of accomplishments, in the qualification attached to his defense of his collection of short stories, *Las novelas ejemplares*:

> Yo he abierto en mis Nouelas vn camino,
> por do la lengua castellana puede
> mostrar con propiedad vn desatino.[1]

> (In my novels I have opened a way,
> Whereby the Castilian tongue can display
> An absurdity with propriety.)

From *Cervantes and the Humanist Vision: A Study of Four Exemplary Novels*. © 1982 by Princeton University Press.

In its reference to the "desatino con propiedad," the tercet presents the exemplarity of the tales in an odd perspective, a perspective that is all the more striking when one considers it beside the emphatically doctrinaire pronouncements of Cervantes's prologue to the tales: "I have given them the name of *Exemplary*, and if you look at it well, there is not one of them from which a profitable example could not be extracted ... perhaps I would show you the savory and honest fruit which could be derived from them.... If in any way it comes to pass that the reading of these novels could tempt one who should peruse them to any evil desire or thought, rather should I cut off the hand with which I wrote them than bring them out in public."[2] The paradoxical understatement of the *Viage* is much more elusive than the closed, conventional discourse of the prologue, but its ambiguities might, in fact, tempt us to suspect disingenuousness in the latter and to read both as implying Cervantes's awareness that the exemplarity of his tales is not to be sought where expected.

If we look at the testimony of one of Cervantes's most illustrious contemporary readers, we discover a striking failure to find any notable exemplary content in the tales. Introducing his own collection of novellas, *Novelas a Marcia Leonarda*, Lope de Vega praises the formal excellence of Cervantes's tales, but adds: "I confess that they are books of great entertainment and that they could be exemplary, like some of the *Tragic Histories* of Bandello, but they should be written by men of learning or at least by great courtiers, men who are able to discover in a 'disillusionment' (*desengaño*) remarkable *sententiae* and aphorisms."[3] Apart from what it reveals about Lope's ambivalent personal feelings toward the literary successes of his great rival, the commentary is most interesting in its insistence that the excellences of Cervantes's short stories are to be found exclusively in their pleasant fictions. Quite explicitly, Lope refuses to acknowledge that the *Exemplary Novels* offer any edifying doctrine commensurate with their entertaining effects, and in making his judgment, he invokes a narrow and well-defined conception of exemplarity in short fiction. His emphasis on erudition, wit, courtly philosophy, and a type of discourse in which univocal doctrinal content can be clearly isolated and indeed even dissociated from its fictionalization through reductive *discursus*, aphorism, and *sententia* recalls methods of novella writing which had developed in courtly circles of Italy in the sixteenth century and were to flourish in the academic novellas of seventeenth-century Spain. As Walter Pabst has demonstrated in his comprehensive account of the historical development of the early European novella, the sixteenth century witnessed a striking transformation of the genre in its form, its social function, and its reception by its readers. The change paralleled an increasing interest throughout Europe in the vulgar tongues as the proper instrument of self-expression and communication for the new culture of court and city, and it was undoubtedly a response to the ascendance of the courtly society with its widely orchestrated ideal concerning the individual as a socially perfectible being. Castiglione himself gave the genre a type of canonization which was to be frequently repeated and which we find echoed in Lope de Vega's observations on Cervantes. If the courtier is indeed to achieve the polish required to distinguish himself within his society, he must master the arts of good speech ("bel parlare") and the strategies of competitive conversation. The proper models for wit, verbal resourcefulness, propriety, and grace in the use of Italian lie in the tales of Boccaccio, and the successful courtier would do well to study them in order to cultivate the arts of extemporaneous composition.[4] While such a conception of the art of the short story brought with it the elevation of a genre which had been traditionally consigned to the marginal and even subliterary spheres of man's reading experience, it undoubtedly blinded its adherents to the numerous possibilities which the form had cultivated in its historical development and excluded from serious consideration all narrative procedures and even types of tales that failed to focus on the social graces and urbane wisdom of "courtly philosophy."[5] It is surely such a blindness which Lope, the most worldly of Spain's great writers, reveals in his failure to find any exemplarity worthy of comment in Cervantes's tales. It is even possible that Cervantes's refusal to employ the traditional frame—a courtly society of teller and recipient—with its conveniences for both reader and author as a closed, determining structure which reduces the contained fictions to a univocal exemplarity and thereby fixes the reader's response to them, was for Lope a sign that the *Novelas ejemplares* belonged to a conventional type of writing aiming at the modest goal of entertaining its audience.

If Lope and, presumably, numerous readers who shared his expectations concerning the form and proper subject matter of the novella were inclined to discount the exemplarity of Cervantes's tales, we must consider the possibility that Cervantes's allusion to the "proper *desatinos*" of his fiction was in fact an admission of their modest intention of supplying permissible entertainment for a public which did not always welcome the edifying assaults on its sensibilities of traditional devotional readings or of the more austere genres of "honest entertainment." Apart from the salaciousness of some of the tales in the collection, Cervantes's willingness to use the designation "*desatino*" may be his way of acknowledging and dealing with the disdain which the short story had suffered in official circles from its very beginnings and which persisted through the sixteenth century despite the peculiar sanction it received in the courtly society of Italy. The authors of early novella collections frequently had to recognize the embattled status

of their fiction, its disruptive subject matter, its potential for debasing its
readers, and the contempt that it excited in orthodox quarters. The excesses
of their justifications can, in fact, be read as testimony to the validity of their
opponents' claims. If the genre was generally looked upon as a vulgar form
of entertainment, the designation *novella* and its cognates were themselves
occasionally invoked as terms of derogation. For example, Chrétien de
Troyes, Ramón Lull, and Juan Manuel suggested that one of the worst insults
a knight could endure was to be regarded as a *novelero*, a teller of novellas.[6]
One of Cervantes's predecessors in Spain, Juan de Timoneda, intitled his
volume of tales and anecdotes "the collection of lies"—*El patrañuelo*—,
suggested to his reader that his creations should be taken purely for
"pasatiempo y recreo humano," and added: "my native Valencian tongue
intitles such confusing imbroglios (*marañas*) *Rondalles*, and the Tuscan calls
them *Novelas*."[7] And it is possible that Lope's introduction to his collection
of novellas, which attributed their composition to the persuasiveness of a
"woman reader," his beloved Marta de Nevares, remarking: "I never thought
that it would occur to me to write novellas," is to some extent motivated by
the traditional scorn with which the genre was treated in academic circles.[8]

At the same time, in referring to his absurdities as proper, Cervantes
may well have been adopting a defensive posture, ironically acknowledging
the traditional disrespect for short fiction and carefully reminding his
audience that his own tales should not be judged according to conventional
prejudices. His words may in fact be simply a translation into a more severe
paradox of a contradiction latent in the phrase "*novela ejemplar*" and as such
a characteristically indirect way of pointing simultaneously to the literarily
revolutionary and the morally legitimate character of his literary
undertaking.[9] The same intention could well have motivated the
exaggerations and reiterations concerning their exemplarity in the prologue.
Cervantes, as we have noted, is prepared to cut off his hand before allowing
it to write a word that might provoke an evil thought in his reader. E.C. Riley
is certainly right in suggesting that "the excessive insistence of Cervantes
undoubtedly reflects anxiety," and that he may have been eager to dissociate
himself from the notoriety enjoyed by the classical Italian *novellieri*, whose
names, well known in Spain, had become "bywords for salaciousness."[10]
However, there is something yet more revealing in the paradox which he
voices while complaining of his mistreatment in the garden of Parnassus, and
it explains in part why for Lope de Vega the true exemplarity of the tales may
have passed unnoticed. It is perhaps well to recall Cervantes's self-
deprecatory discussion of the literary merits of *Don Quixote* I on the eve of
Don Quixote's third sally. In the midst of the various denunciations of the
work—the improvisational monstrosity resembling Orbaneja's formless

paintings, the masterpiece for an audience composed of the "stultorum infinitus numerus," the hodgepodge of "baskets and cabbages"—Don Quixote notes that "to say amusing things and to write humorously is the gift of great geniuses" because "the cleverest character in comedy is the clown, for he who would make people take him for a fool, must not be one."[11] In its association of the "discreet madman" and the *Quixote*, the phrase casts a revealing light on the "proper absurdities" which Cervantes offers as the designation of his tales, and in both cases the paradoxes look back to the fundamental paradox animating the thought and writings of the Erasmian reformers, men inspired by their profound sense that ultimate truth lies beyond the canonized forms of culture—the deadening letter—and that it can be reached only if one transcends the logic of the letter. As Erasmus asked repeatedly, was not the most sublime source of truth veiled in the humble form of a carpenter's son in Nazareth? And did not the wisest of the ancient sages pronounce his universal truths from an oafish face and a slovenly figure laughable to all who gazed upon it until they beheld the wonders of the spirit concealed within?[12]

Cervantes's description of his tales as "*desatinos*" is, then, neither the defensive invocation of a *topos* of novella composition nor an admission that his tales are primarily aimed at furnishing pleasing entertainment. In the tradition of Erasmus's meditation on the *Sileni Alcibiadis*, it is rather an invitation to look for the truth beneath the surface, in the remote or concealed areas where Lope de Vega, a man of radically different disposition and a man whose spiritual formation was the product of very different historical circumstances, was temperamentally unprepared to look. As Cervantes insinuates in his prologue, "lofty mysteries" lie concealed within his trifles: "they hold hidden some mystery which elevates them" ("algún misterio tienen escondido que las levanta"). "He who says 'mystery' says 'pregnancy' (*preñez*), an impending truth which is hidden and recondite, and any truth which exacts a price in its communication is more highly esteemed and more pleasureable," Gracián was to say in his poetics of wit a few years later.[13] For the critic, a reader whose business it is to transcend, insofar as it is possible to do so, the historical rootedness that inevitably mediates and conditions our perception of the past, Cervantes's words offer not only an invitation to look within, but a challenge to look backward in history as well, to the humanist writings of nearly one hundred years earlier, the writings of Cervantes's spiritual fathers, men who understood that the loftiest teachings concerning man's religious, ethical, political, social, and domestic life could be conveyed perhaps most effectively in the disjointed discourse of a fool.

Since Américo Castro's declaration in *El pensamiento de Cervantes* (1924) that "without Erasmus, Cervantes would not have been the writer he was,"[14] the attempts to locate the spiritual and intellectual sources of Cervantes's fiction in Erasmus's writings have retreated from the forceful conclusions of Castro's epoch-making study. The reaction was in part attributable to the gradual revision in historical studies of the excessively secularized conception of the European Renaissance, rooted in Burckhardt's classical interpretation, which informs Castro's entire argument, and in part due to the closely related correction of a traditional misconception of the modernity in the critical tendencies of Erasmus's philosophy. If the crucial period in Cervantes's spiritual development was no longer to be viewed as an era of unbounded individualism, audacious free inquiry, subversive ethical naturalism, heroic hypocrisy, and exhilarating liberation from confining religious traditions, the greatest humanist of the late Renaissance could no longer be regarded as simply the iconoclastic precursor of modern rationalism, the "Voltaire of the Sixteenth Century." However, more important among Cervantists was the emphatic change of direction that marked Castro's own thinking in the twenty years that followed the publication of *El pensamiento de Cervantes*. During this period, years of cultural breakdown and exile for Castro, he devoted his inexhaustible intellectual energies to comprehending the structure of a text larger and, in its contradictions, even more complicated than the *Quixote*—that of Spain itself. As he focused his attention on the peculiar dynamics of Spanish history and looked more searchingly and exclusively for inspiration in contemporary existentialist and vitalistic philosophy in his efforts to deal with the intractable complexities of historical process, he found himself compelled to doubt the fundamental premises and methods of the intellectual history (*Geistesgeschichte*) which he had practiced so successfully, and ultimately to deny the validity of its privileged categories of historical understanding—the generalized structures of ideas and values, the *Weltanschauungen*, as well as their specific historical formulations such as Renaissance, Counter-Reformation, and Rationalism—the very categories that he had taken for granted in his previous efforts to account for Spain's position in Occidental history and for its principal cultural creations such as the *Quixote*.[15] One of the results of the profound reorientation in his thought was a thorough disdain for the lifelessness and inauthenticity of abstraction and a heightened sensitivity to its potential—in the form of ideology, unexamined assumptions, cultural commonplaces and axioms—for the suppression of human freedom, the curtailment of individual growth, and the general impoverishment of man's experience. Castro is not the first Spaniard whose intellectual evolution is mirrored perfectly in his rereadings of Cervantes's multifaceted and ultimately elusive masterpiece. Whether as guide or provocation, the *Quixote*, the work that revolutionized literature by calling into question all traditional assumptions concerning literary value, implicitly disclosing the poverty of the ideologies reflected in them, and endowing the nontranscendent particulars of ordinary experience with poetic dignity, now offered Castro something far more profound than the monument to Renaissance ideas and cultural tensions which he had constructed so painstakingly and persuasively in his *El pensamiento de Cervantes*. If the vision and structural dynamics of the work itself seemed to vindicate the value and integrity of the individual human life in all its singularity, the very possibility of its creation in Spain of the early seventeenth century by a man driven by a particular sense of his own marginality and alienation pointed to the very concrete preoccupations and tensions which account for the peculiar historical life of Spain and its uniqueness in the Occidental world.

Castro's insight into the depths of Spanish historical life and into *Don Quixote* as a creation within a particular historical scenario led him to his most profound writings on Cervantes's art. As a result of his effort, we understand the uniqueness, the value, and the place of the *Quixote* in literary history as never before, and his quixotic refusal to permit the republication of *El pensamiento de Cervantes* until shortly before his death in 1972 is a characteristic sign of the intensity and intellectual integrity which marked his own life-long quest for truth. However, as valuable as it is, *El pensamiento de Cervantes* is not the most precious victim that Castro sacrificed on the altar of the vitalism informing his new conception of historical process and value. In his general hostility to the abstracting tendency in thought and literary creation and in his particular disdain for the official set of values that stultified the consciousness of Cervantes's contemporaries and blighted their institutions, Castro came to look upon all of Cervantes's overtly exemplary writings that fail to dignify the sphere of individuality and ordinary experience as somehow lifeless, worthy of historical recuperation only as documents of the tensions alive in Cervantes's consciousness. While brilliantly illuminating the perspective of marginality from which the *Quixote* appears to have been conceived, Castro's influential essay, "The Exemplarity of Cervantes' Novellas," has had the effect of widening the historical gap separating us from the tales, the very gap that his early *El pensamiento de Cervantes*, which considered Cervantes's *oeuvre* as a unified totality and the product of a single consciousness, had undertaken to overcome.[16] With Castro's essay we find the dichotomy of the "two Cervanteses," a conception which, in one form or another (see below), has plagued a good deal of modern Cervantine criticism, resurrected in a particularly disturbing version. Castro would appear to be no longer interested in the content of the tales, reads Cervantes's emphatic assertion in the prologue—"the clamorous pretension to morality"—as a confirmation of the absolutely doctrinaire and trivial nature of the ethical vision exemplified in his fictions, finds in his willingness to create characters according to ideas—that is, the conventional technique of exemplary fiction—a renunciation of his artistic self, and devotes the major arguments of the essay to an analysis of the motives for Cervantes's silencing of his authentic voice. No longer writing from the perspective of the outsider, creating "madmen in collision with society's normal ways of thinking," subjecting all "vulgar experience" to ironic treatment, and affirming the primacy of a "profound and imperishable vital reality" over the lifeless "truth of moralization," Cervantes conceived the *Novelas ejemplares* from a vital situation firmly fixed within the cultural horizons of the official Spain, a Spain that had finally consented to make him its own after he had endured a life of frustrated ambitions, physical exile, poverty, social degradation, and spiritual alienation. Cervantes's affirmations in the prologue to the exemplary stories are the revealing statements of a new man, one "circumspect and tranquil," who "proceeds with a consciousness of being a responsible member of a community in which he is of some importance." The greatest writer of Spain determined to "moralize from above," assuming, as moralists generally do, that society would reward his concerned pronouncements with status and esteem. While acknowledging that this change of perspective, the "swing of the pendulum of Cervantes's art toward exemplarity," must be viewed as the necessary result of the complex personal, social, and historical circumstances of Cervantes's existence, Castro's analysis of the process is frequently marked by a disapproving, even disdainful tone: Cervantes wishes to "pontificate in that society in which he believed himself to be duly established." In his stories he chooses to offer his public "archetypes of social perfection, in order to become respectable," and, as an exemplary writer, he can feel important within the social hierarchy. He writes as an "inoffensive conformist," a "gentle moralist," proposing an ideal "valid and acceptable for the people among whom he lived and desired to live in a respectable way and not as a pariah." A severe judgment of Cervantes's inauthenticity is clearly audible throughout the explanation of his apparent determination to endorse the official convictions of his society, and, when Castro goes on to consider the way in which this development is reflected in *Las novelas ejemplares*, he does not stop short of implying that their composition was in a sense an act of self-betrayal. Two of the novellas, which are most interesting and valuable because their author's authentic voice asserts itself and appears to be in conflict with his exemplary voice, require revision if they are to be allowed in the collection. They must be "pruned and touched up." If the concealed metaphor of grooming might hint at pretentiousness or a desire to please finer company, the harsh figure of excision suggests the spiritual violence that frequently accompanies self-betrayal. The lifelessness of academic art is the ultimate result of the savage self-repression: "The rebel writer becomes, in a certain way, an academic." With the *Persiles* the process is complete: no longer can we discern, as is still the case in "some of the twelve novellas," the coexistence of the "Cervantes who lives his art 'from outside' and the Cervantes who aspires to implant himself 'within' the area of the currently reigning codes of value."[17]

Castro's basic thesis is engaging, and, whether or not his speculations concerning the motivations and tensions troubling Cervantes's consciousness are valid, his analysis of the singular features and effects of the artistic product of the author's "authentic" voice is an incisive and convincing summary of the interpretations advanced in his major essays on the *Quixote*. However, as a study of the exemplarity of Cervantes's fiction, the argument falls victim of its narrow, polemical assumptions concerning the nature of exemplary art—"exemplarity, as a goal which is utilitarian, goes beyond and deforms authentic art"—and fails to offer its reader any insight into the particulars of the rich exemplary vision that informs the short stories. Indeed, Castro's abbreviated description of the tales as conformist, abstract, and devitalized, a description that in reality amounts to defining them by negative contrast with the *Quixote*, would suggest that they belong to a type of conservative fiction which has flourished in every age since the invention of printing and which owes its stability and resiliency to its fulfillment of the primarily social function of confirming established values, supporting vulgar prejudices, cultivating pleasurable sentiments, and trivializing subversive preoccupations. The short stories, which enjoyed an extraordinarily rich and productive historical life and which, as recently as 1795, were celebrated by Europe's most imposing man of letters as providing the classical models, both in form and vision, for modern writers of novellas, are reduced to the status of bland and comforting entertainment, the kind of literature which H.R. Jauss, in a metaphor which no doubt would have been pleasing to Cervantes for reasons very different from those informing it in Jauss's studies of literary reception, has referred to as "culinary reading." Indeed Castro at one point in his argument refers to the "formas de vida apetecible" of Cervantes's exemplary fiction, resurrecting at once one of the age-old *topoi* of derogation that have beset the European novella from the earliest period of its history.[18] The fact is that Castro's reading of the *Novelas ejemplares* in some ways represents the culmination in the development of the central tendencies of the Romantic reading of Cervantes's works, which, while leading to a profound understanding of the *Quixote*, a full appreciation of the essential qualities of novelistic fiction, and the due recognition of the revolutionary role of Cervantes's masterpiece in the evolution of literary forms and the creation of the novel, has resulted in the loss of Cervantes's works in which the potentialities are more restricted by the cultural and literary horizons surrounding their original creation.[19] Castro himself noted in his reconsideration of the blindness in his own early reading of the *Quixote* that Cervantes's masterpiece could be recovered from the drastic reductions of its potentialities which generally characterized its readings in the first two centuries of its historical existence only following the radical modification of consciousness and the revisions in philosophical and literary orientation brought about in the period of European Romanticism.[20] What Castro's writings do not indicate so explicitly is that the reformation of the European literary horizon which enabled the expansion of the *Quixote* to the fullness of historical life which was potential but unrealized in it earlier would lead to the severe attenuation of Cervantes's exemplary fiction, which, to be sure, speaks much more directly and exclusively to its immediate audience.[21]

If the *Novelas ejemplares* are to be recuperated in the extraordinary fullness of *their* original historical existence, an effort must be made to probe their exemplarity and its historical sources more searchingly than Castro's pronouncements on their dubious authenticity would encourage. Castro is, of course, perfectly aware of the direction that such an undertaking must follow, as he, more than any other literary historian, first opened our eyes to the matrix of cultural values, spiritual preoccupations, and literary systems in which they were born. Even in the grudging tones of his late work, Castro implies that the fundamental conclusions concerning the origins of Cervantes's ideas and values in Erasmian thought, presented in his now forbidden *El pensamiento de Cervantes*, are still valid. He argues that, following the death of the austere monarch, Philip II, "there flourished in Spain a Christian neo-humanism," concerned with preparing man for the afterlife but at the same time determined "not to forget the flesh and blood individual of this world." And it was precisely in this neo-humanism that Cervantes found inspiration as he structured the fictional shapes of his exemplary works, with their "forms of a life to be desired."[22] Insofar as my study attempts to illuminate the exemplary vision of Cervantes's short stories and situate them within the spiritual climate known for its most influential spokesman as Erasmism, it can be seen as reasserting and developing the tradition in Cervantine studies initiated by Castro's *El pensamiento de Cervantes*. In a sense it is an effort to recuperate through revision the historical-critical context in which that pioneering work had fruitfully elucidated Cervantes's entire literary production, but which Castro and various disciples have subsequently attempted to dismiss as peripheral to Cervantine criticism.[23]

In my consideration of the Erasmism of Cervantes's tales, I am not primarily concerned with the question of the specific nature of the transmission of the humanist's thought to his greatest literary disciple. Noting the inconclusiveness of the various attempts to find concrete evidence that Cervantes read Erasmus's works, Marcel Bataillon has suggested that it is more fruitful to imagine that for Cervantes, educated in the Spain of Charles V, a Spain "impregnated with Erasmus's thought," and exposed as he undoubtedly was to the humanist's essential doctrines both through the instruction of teachers such as López de Hoyos and his youthful readings, Erasmus was a powerful experience of his formative years which took root in his personality and was nourished by his subsequent experiences as a traveller, a soldier, a captive, a husband, an observer, a writer, and a disillusioned patriot and idealist. When the Erasmian vision informed his writings, Cervantes probably had no need for a specific text to borrow from or to imitate. The vision had grown with him, and it was authentically his own, transfigured by his own experience into the vision of a great spiritual heir, possessed of its own integrity, unique in its own right, and productive in its own distinctive way. As in the case of all genuine spiritual families, the disciple was drawn by natural affinities to the master, and his discovery of the predecessor was in reality the discovery of his own authentic self. Certainly the question of Cervantes's Erasmism can be ultimately answered only if one adopts a more sophisticated method of comparative study than that which has limited traditional studies of sources and influences. Bataillon concludes that what is needed are "many comparative studies which take into account not only ideas, but also their expression, and which would seize as their object typically Erasmian ideas."[24] This is the type of approach that I take at various points in my study, seeking configurations of ideas and methods of exposition linking the two writers rather than concrete verbal correspondences.[25] Cervantes's thematically richest tales in fact point quite directly to several of the central preoccupations of Erasmus's program for spiritual *renovatio*—freedom and individual fulfillment, domestic and social organization, knowledge and education, language and literature, sinfulness and moral action, and the need for a general sanctification of the secular world. A good deal of my study is devoted to the careful analysis of the way in which such preoccupations animate the fictional shapes of Cervantes's tales. It attempts to show that the *Exemplary Novels* represent a complex and effective fusion of literary form and philosophical vision and that their narrative methods were so original in their time that, to recall Lope's blindness to the exemplarity which can not be isolated and extracted from its fictional container and fixed in the conveniently assimilable *sententiae* of a controlling moralist narrator, they could be understood properly only with the development of the profound insights into the symbolic nature of fiction following the breakdown in the eighteenth century of traditional rhetorical modes of criticism and the neo-classical literary theories that formulated them so persuasively.[26] Taken in its entirety, Cervantes's collection of exemplary tales, with its imaginative reach extending from the opening celebration of man's divine potential to its concluding exploration of the darkest abysses of his misery, is perhaps Spain's most imposing tribute to the breadth of vision and generosity of spirit inspiring the Christian Humanist movement and distinguishing its enduring literary products.

If we must make an effort in historical recovery in order to be able to appreciate the exemplary vision informing Cervantes's tales, we must make a similar type of effort if we are to comprehend their formal qualities, their genre, and their place in the history of narrative fiction. The European novella came into existence in Boccaccio's *Decameron* as one of the most flexible and multifarious of literary forms, assimilating a variety of traditional narrative structures and techniques, incorporating a considerable range of aesthetic effects, and, as it was widely regarded as an undignified conveyer of amusement, gossip, and novelties, escaping the confining concepts of decorum and the limitations on compositional procedures which canonization in the official poetics of the period would no doubt have brought to it.[27] If such variety had always been a characteristic of the early novella collections, there was, nevertheless, a uniformity visible in the general tendency of the individual tales toward brevity, swiftly paced movement to a climactic point, and spareness in the use of any detail—whether descriptive, rhetorical, psychological, or thematic—that might delay the reader in his movement toward the point.[28] Based on one of the most primitive elements in man's literary experience, the stability of the genre was to a certain extent dependent on severe limitation, and it proved increasingly precarious as writers of the sixteenth century attempted to exploit the fictional resources of the form for radically new purposes and effects. While courtly circles continued to find its traditional qualities well-suited to their cultivation of wit and conversational charm, such writers as Marguerite de Navarre and the French adaptors of Bandello's sensational tales, Belleforest and Boaistuau, were expanding its narrow confines by introducing elements that were ultimately incompatible with its traditional constitutive features: the consideration of philosophical and social problems, the cultivation of sentiment, the exploration of complex psychological motivation, an increased attention to description, and the elaboration of striking narrative units—e.g., the scene of pathos, the rhetorically striking declamation, the generalizing excursus by character or narrator—as independent and hence discontinuous elements within the traditional tightly ordered design. In short, the form, which had always been open in its assimilation of different socioeconomic milieus, different types of character, and different tones, settings, and historical periods, now opened up in a way which was much more radical and which threatened its foundations and hence its very existence.[29] The century preceding Cervantes's decision to *novelar* for the first time in Castilian would appear to be a period of crisis in the historical evolution of the genre, a period of breakdown and redirection in its response to new expressive needs, themselves the result of the complex historical pressures of this age of transition in European history. More than any other collection of short stories of the period, Cervantes's *Novelas ejemplares* would attest to the profundity of the alteration which the genre experienced in this period. On the one hand, they represent the full realization of the effort, initiated sporadically in Marguerite de Navarre's *Heptaméron*, to turn the novella into a vehicle capable of engaging with the most urgent ideological and social preoccupations of the moment. As a novelistic monument to the humanist vision, analogous perhaps in its "belatedness" within its spiritual tradition to Milton's *Paradise Lost* in Renaissance epic literature, Cervantes's collection of tales is a true descendent of the *Heptaméron*, and one cannot begin to account for the evolution in narrative fiction represented by both collections without giving some attention to the possible impact, on the novella of the most highly influential fictionalizations of profound ideas in Europe of the sixteenth century—the *Colloquies* of Erasmus.[30] On the other hand, Cervantes's tales represent the culmination in the quest for new forms that marked the experimentalism occasionally visible in sixteenth-century short fiction as it turned from the brief, pointed forms that had been dominant during the first centuries of the genre's' historical life. Viewed within the tradition of the early European novella, Cervantes's collection is remarkable not only for the length of the individual tales included, but also for the variety of their forms and the generic models to which they point.

While Cervantes's aspirations to be the first to *novelar* in Spanish were high, his imagination was obviously not inhibited in the slightest by an awareness of a particular model to be imitated or a set of codified rules of composition to be followed. His admirers immediately hailed his collection of novellas for its variety:

> aqueste florido abril,
> cuya variedad admira
> la fama veloz, que mira
> en él variedades mil.[31]

At the same time there are indications that his contemporary audience was somewhat bewildered by his claims to offer a collection of novellas. As we have seen, Lope, who in his willingness to consider *Amadís de Gaula* and

Orlando furioso as distinguished examples of the genre seems not to have had a very precise awareness of what a novella was, nevertheless drew attention to the deviations in Cervantes's tales from a type of story which was familiar to him and could be invoked as representing the norms of the genre, Bandello's *Tragic Histories*. The observations of the conservative Avellaneda similarly indicate the disorienting effect which Cervantes's designation of such narratives may have had on his contemporary readers. The works are not only improperly called exemplary, since they are "más satirical que exemplares," but they are also inaccurately described as novellas since nearly all of them are in reality "comedias en prosa."[32] At the same time, in the enthusiastic reception which greeted Cervantes's tales in France, there are clear indications that their failure to match readers' expectations based on established conventions of the short story was so thorough that they were viewed as representing an entirely reconstituted novella, or, in fact, a new literary form. Le sieur d'Audiguier introduced his French translation of the tales as offering his public a completely new type of fiction, and Tallemant des Réaux expressed the view that the Cervantine novella must be considered as a literary form sui generis.[33]

Modern readers and literary historians have found the variety of Cervantes's tales no less challenging than his contemporary readers, but their attempts to render it intelligible in terms of familiar generic categories have been only slightly more helpful than those of his seventeenth-century readers. If one considers the various attempts at systematic classification of the *Novelas ejemplares*, one quickly discovers that critics and literary historians have been content to account for the differences in the tales by invoking some rather vaguely formulated dualistic typology—such as romantic and realistic, fantastic and *costumbrista*, idealistic and skeptical, Italianate and Spanish, imitative and original, literary and representational, normative and vitalistic, early and late, and so on—a duality that in fact turns out to be a translation into the terms of literary genre of the more basic biographical dichotomy that Cervantists continue to cling to—the "two Cervanteses." One scrutinizing it closely, one then discovers that this dichotomy, as well as the various others which it underlies, is in reality the expression of literary preferences of the modern reader, and that it carries with it a strong value judgment. There is, on the one hand, the authentic, "original," and genuinely creative Cervantes, writing the literature that significantly altered the history of prose fiction and man's literary experience, creating, through the ironic engagement with nearly all traditional forms of fiction, the great representational genre of the modern novel. On the other hand, there is a conservative, conformist, and imitative Cervantes, the man of letters who bowed to the conventional literary tastes and values of his society and its repressive institutions, such as the Inquisition, and wrote such perishable imitations of its escapist, naively idealizing forms as *La Galatea*, *El Persiles*, and the so-called Italianate novellas. Since Menéndez y Pelayo's eloquent description of the romantic and the realistic tendencies in Cervantes's fiction, the notion of the "two Cervanteses," in several variations, has shown remarkable powers of survival, and, as I have pointed out above, we find it emerging most recently in a form which is particularly troubling for the student of the *Novelas ejemplares* in Américo Castro's arguments concerning the motivations behind their exemplarity.

The fact is that Cervantes, one of the great experimenters in the history of fiction, was receptive to a wide variety of literary forms. There was nothing exclusivistic about his reading preferences; as he himself put it, he was a man who could not resist picking up, reading, and rescuing from oblivion, as it were, the scraps of paper he found in the streets, and one need only look at the immense variety of forms and styles which he incorporates into the *Quixote* to get some idea of the catholicity of his literary tastes. Neither the single generic designation *novella*, which Cervantes himself offers us, nor the various dualities which literary historians have thus far invoked can account for the variety of the tales or, for that matter, for the form, structure, and effects of a single one. Indeed, in the failure of such attempts at classification Walter Pabst has found confirmation of his thesis concerning the nonexistence of a "classical" European novella and his general view that little is to be gained in literary study by the invocation of such insubstantial entities as types and genres. On examining the tales, Pabst goes on to remark that perhaps the most apt designation for Cervantes's collection of short fiction would be a "labyrinth" (an *Irrgarten*), a metaphor which resurrects the very *topos* by which authors and commentators, from the *Decameron* to the *Novelas ejemplares*, declared the freedom of the form in its unbounded variety.[34] Certainly one must agree with Pabst that a healthy critical nominalism which leaves the eyes open to the integrity of the individual object of study is far preferable to the facile typologies which mediate the object through a screen of modern prejudices concerning literary value. Fortunately, however, one does not have to resign oneself at this point to the choice of these two counterproductive positions. Over the past thirty years our insight into the generic possibilities of prose fiction has increased enormously, and numerous valuable studies of neglected genres, ranging from the simple minor literary forms of folktale, parable, fable, and aphorism to such inexhaustibly rich creations of man's literary imagination as romance and satire and their various subspecies—for example, chivalric, Byzantine, and hagiographic; Menippean, Lucianesque, and picaresque— have rewarded us with an increasingly sophisticated and precise knowledge of the specific forms that make up that gigantic area of non-novelistic narrative fiction, forms which can be viewed both as stable, definable literary systems and as objects with particular historical existentes, involving origination, evolution, transformation, and, in some cases, death and oblivion. Anybody who reads *Don Quixote* quickly recognizes that Cervantes's consciousness of the literary conventions of traditional literary genres is highly developed, so developed in fact, that the novel itself, and particularly Part I, draws its imaginative vitality from the reiterated process of disclosing the artificiality of literary convention in its opposition to reality. The *Novelas ejemplares*, of course, assume a much less subversive attitude toward traditional generic systems, but they are no less wide-ranging in their incorporation of available forms, and they are just as subtle and, in a different way, just as original in their engagement with generic codes as is the great novel. While one part of my study looks toward the problem of their exemplarity, the other part undertakes, generally as the proper point of departure for each chapter, a careful consideration of their structure, genre, and place in literary history. Here my focus is on Cervantes's craft as a writer of short stories, as an experimenter in literary forms, and as a man who was profoundly aware of the potentialities for creative adaptation in traditional narrative. My study of the literary aspects of the works confirms in every case my arguments concerning their exemplarity and the impact of Erasmian thought on their conception. It is not simply that one finds a variety of forms which parallel the extraordinary range of thought and concern animating the tales and which indicate that it would be just as perverse to regard them as representatives of the most lifeless mechanical literature of moral instruction as to conceive their message as a bland confirmation of the most vulgar prejudices of contemporary Spain. Nor is it simply that some of their most original fictional innovations and most sophisticated accommodations of literary forms to doctrine presupposed Cervantes's intense interest in and thorough understanding of the privileged genres of the humanists—the Menippean satire and the Heliodorean romance.[35] The spiritual heritage of humanism is, in fact, visible at the most profound level of Cervantes's activity as an experimenter in narrative, and, in order to glimpse it, we must be fully aware of the generic codes in which his short fiction is conceived and offered to his reader. At this point the study of exemplarity and literary genre converge. Far from being inhibited by the pressures of his culture and captive to its most reactionary literary, preferences, Cervantes, in his aspiration to be the first to *novelar* in Spanish, proceeds with absolute freedom and sovereign control of his medium. His engagement with all available literary resources is that of a writer who understands thoroughly their potentialities and exploits them independently for his own particular needs.[36] His methods of adaptation are always original, and they range from unprecedented hybridization, in the combination of traditional forms of disorder in *El casamiento engañoso y el coloquio de los perros*, and skillful accommodation, in *La Gitanilla*'s complex fusion of ideas and romance conventions, to unraveling and reconstitution, in the critical engagement with a prestigious hagiographic form in *La fuerza de la sangre*, and violent deconstruction, in the unexpected formal disarticulation of *El celoso extremeño*.[37] As the latter case would indicate, Cervantes's tales can become structurally most intricate and elusive precisely when they appear to be most doctrinaire and conventional. Indeed there is hardly a tale that fails to deviate in some radical way from the expectations that its traditional ingredients would arouse in its audience. The disorienting *desatinos*—the "swerves from the destined mark"—are clearly intended. Cervantes, whose stories so frequently strike one as childlike in their simplicity, is at once the most indulgent and the most exacting of authors, and the numerous efforts, from Avellaneda to Unamuno, to rewrite his fiction so as to eliminate "superfluous" or "absurd" elements, while commemorating certain readers' failures to respond fully to the challenge in its refusal to close in the readily intelligible way according to an insinuated "destination," are, nonetheless, continuing testimony of its power to activate its reader and enlist his energies in its own creation. In the sense that the irregularities of Cervantes's "Sileni" refuse to allow their reader the comforts of a stock response and instead burden him with the obligation to cope with unsettling violations of his vocabulary of genre, the *Novelas ejemplares* stand as one of the fullest literary realizations of the characteristic nonlinear discourse of the great humanist writers of the sixteenth century, who turned to dialectical, ironic, and paradoxical modes of exposition in their efforts to explore the complexities of truth, to provoke their readers' collaboration in that exploration, and to revitalize perceptions blunted by the tyranny of familiarity and appearance.[38] The man who thoroughly understands the "familiar" beliefs which he adopts and on which he acts is in a very fundamental way a truly liberated man. To the extent that the *Novelas ejemplares* are composed in this deceptive, demanding discourse, their ultimate message may well lie in the freedom with which they dignify their reader and in the example of the creative use of freedom set by their author. In this sense they are no less progressive in the history of literature than the much more overtly revolutionary *Don Quixote*, for, while the language of its phrasing is frequently quite remote and calls for translation and mediation by the literary historian, the ultimate message to be recovered is no less valid in 1980 than it was in 1613.

NOTES

1. *Viage del Parnaso*, ed. R. Schevill and A. Bonilla (Madrid, 1922), p. 55.

2. "Heles dado nombre de *Ejemplares*, y si bien lo miras, no hay ninguna de quien no se pueda sacar algún ejemplo provechoso ... quizá te mostrara el sabroso y honesto fruto que se podría sacar ... si por algún modo alcanzara que la lección de estas novelas pudiera inducir a quien las leyera a algún mal deseo o pensamiento, antes me cortara la mano con que las escribí que sacarlas en público" (*Obras completas*, ed. A. Valbuena Prat [Madrid, 1956], pp. 769–70).

3. "Confiesso que son libros de grande entretenimiento y que podrían ser ejemplares como algunas de las Historias trágicas del Bandelo, pero habían de escribirlos hombres científicos o por lo menos grandes cortesanos, gente que halla en los desengaños notables sentencias y aforismos" (ed. F. Rico [Madrid, 1968], p. 28).

4. *Novellentheorie and Novellendichtung: Zur Geschichte ihrer Antinomie in den romanischen Literaturen* (Heidelberg, 1967), chap. 2. Pabst traces the novella's intimate connection with courtly values and philosophy from Masuccio's incorporation in his tales (1476) of the qualities of wit prized by the dominant social class of his time through the academic implementations of Castiglione's formulas for *novella*, *facezie*, and *motti*, such as G. Parabosco's *I Diporti* (1550), to Lope de Vega's conception of the writer of novellas as the "grande cortesano," proclaiming the fashionable worldly wisdom of his own times in "desengaños notables." For the extremes to which the dissociation of fiction and erudite commentary could lead, see Pabst's discussion of G. Giraldi Cinzio's *Hecatommithi ouero Cento Novelle* (pp. 89–90). One can contrast Lope's emphasis on "*ciencia*" with G. Sermini da Siena's description of his collection of tales (*Novelle*, 1424) as a modest "basket of salad" which is not for the learned: "di questa non dia ad uomini di grande scienza, perché non é vivanda da loro" (Pabst, *Novellentheorie*, p. 76). Castiglione's theories on the art of facetiae and novellas appear in the *Libro del Cortegiano*, 2:42–100 (see ed. E. Bonora and P. Zoccola [Milano, 1972], pp. 150–205). An indication of the popularity and topicality of Castiglione's discussion is the fact that his basic distinction between insubstantial tales dependent entirely on the oral performance of their teller for success and tales valuable for their inherent, "fixed" content, a distinction which, as Pabst points out, incorporates a *topos* deriving from Cicero's *De Oratore*, is echoed by Cervantes's Cipión in *El coloquio de los perros*. However, the interesting thing about Cervantes's discussion of the "ingenious tales" which, through the "clothing of words" and their teller's gesticulations, make "something of nothing," is its transformation of the literary doctrine. Far from standing as a statement of the author's artistic program and his fundamental theory of the short story, as Ortega has suggested, the *topos* forms part of a dense system of elements in the tale pointing up the universality of illusion in human experience and specifically the deceptive potential in literature.

5. For the "misreading" and resulting impoverishment of the *Decameron* in sixteenth-century Italy—e.g., its readers' concentration on the two days offering triumphs of verbal ingenuity, their perception of the frame primarily as an exemplification of the general aesthetic doctrine of unity, and their condemnation of its plague description for its apparent disruption of a uniform elegant tonality—see Pabst, *Novellentheorie*, pp. 74–79. Though their profound themes are rooted in sixteenth-century thought, Cervantes's tales, in their conceptual density and complex mixture of tonalities, can be seen as representing a rediscovery by the novella tradition of the broad dimensions that are visible in its founder and in all his authentic descendants.

6. See W. Krauss, "Novela-Novella-Roman," *Gesammelte Aufsätze zur Literatur- und*

Sprachwissenschaft (Frankfurt am Main, 1949), p. 64. W. Pabst points out that the term preserved certain despective connotations of its Latin root *novus*—e.g., "surprising," "odd," "comical," "foolish," "fanciful," and "mendacious." A sixteenth-century editor of the earlier novellas wrote: "Nuova, volea dir Piacevole per semplicità, e stravaganza onde è rimaso a noi Nuovo pesce [joke].... Di qui le favole, e li racconti piacevoli Novelle fur dette" (see Pabst, *Novellentheorie*, pp. 15–16, 21–22).

7. "semejantes marañas las intitula mi lengua natural valenciana *Rondalles*, y la toscana, *Novelas*" (ed. R. Ferreres [Madrid, 1971], p. 41). E.C. Riley points out that the "word *novela*, as well as being unflatteringly interchangeable with words like *patraña*, or 'deceitful fiction,' must have conjured up for the public the names of Boccaccio and Bandello," authors associated with licentiousness (*Cervantes's Theory of the Novel* [Oxford, 1962], p. 102).

8. "nunca pensé que el novelar entrara en mi pensamiento" (*Novelas a Marcia Leonarda*, p. 28).

9. An interesting testimony to the paradoxicality and possible audacity in the combination of terms for Cervantes's audience can be found in G. Argote de Molina's prefatory address to the reader in his edition of the *Libro llamado el Conde Lucanor* (Seville, 1575). He justifies the book as an "exemplario," a "libro de buenos consejos," which adopts the methods of the ancient sages, Socrates and Plato, and Jesus Christ in their utilization of "*cuentos*" and "*parabolas*" in order to convey ancient philosophy and divine wisdom. He distinguishes his "*exemplario*" sharply from the popular forms of "*nouela*" and "*fabula*," "los quales tienen vn solo intento que es entretener con apazible, y algunas vezes dañoso gusto." To appreciate the forcefulness of Cervantes's assertion that he was doing something new and valuable, as well as the freedom and originality with which he created the exemplary novella, one must bear in mind the traditional prestige of the *exemplum* in Spain (see Pabst, *Novellentheorie*, p. 100) and the absence both of an established indigenous tradition of novella literature and of the academic-courtly circumstances which in Italy focused attention on and to some extent schematized the Italian short story. In 1590 the Spanish translator of Giraldi's tales introduced his work with the hope that his audience will see "que se estima esto tanto en los estrangeros, para que los naturales hagan to que nunca han hecho, que es componer Novelas" (Pabst, *Novellentheorie*, p. 104).

10. *Cervantes's Theory of the Novel*, p. 102. Riley points out that Cervantes may have intended the title of his collection to be *Novelas ejemplares de honestísimo entretenimiento*.

11. "Decir gracias y escribir donaires es de grandes ingenios: la más discreta figura de la comedia es la del bobo, porque no lo ha de ser el que quiere dar a entender que es simple" (*Don Quijote de la Mancha*, ed. L.A. Murillo [Madrid, 1978], 2:64; all subsequent volume and page references to the *Quixote* in my text are to this edition).

12. See "Sileni Alcibiadis," *The "Adages" of Erasmus*, ed. and trans. by M. Mann Phillips (Cambridge, 1964), pp. 269–72.

13. "Quien dice misterio, dice preñez, verdad escondida y recóndita, y toda noticia que cuesta, es más estimada y gustosa" (*Agudeza y arte de ingenio*, ed. E. Correa Calderón [Madrid, 1969], 1:88).

14. (Barcelona, 1972), p. 300.

15. In elaborating the central category of his new historical method—the *morada vital*—Castro glances at the lifeless abstractions, the disembodied "essences" of *Geistesgeschichte*: "No existe un Gótico, un Renacimiento, un Barroco o un Neoclásico que, desde un espacio irreal, condicione el fluir de la historia como la luna interviene en las mareas" (*La realidad histórica de españa* [Mexico, 1954], p. 49). In Chapter Two, "Enfoque de la historia," Castro reveals the sources and direction of his developing philosophy of

history. He acknowledges the fundamental place of Dilthey's *Lebensphilosophie* in his conception of the dynamic process of history, and he makes it clear how his thought is conditioned and developed in his engagement with the ideas of such prominent spokesmen for vitalism and existentialism as Bergson, Nietzsche, and Kierkegaard. Another disciple of Dilthey whose central conceptions concerning historical process—e.g., the "la razón vital," "la razón histórica," and "la circunstancia"—are clearly influential in Castro's intellectual development and his reconsideration of Cervantes's work is J. Ortega y Gasset.

16. In presenting Cervantes as an embattled pioneer of enlightenment in the repressive era of the Counter-Reformation, Castro insists on the normative and rationalistic tendencies of his art. There were "determinadas realidades, tanto físicas como morales, que para él son de existencia tan evidente como esta luz que nos alumbra. Entre esas realidades morales hay algunas cuya existencia se establece dogmáticamente, y que son en Cervantes verdaderas tesis de combate" (*El pensamiento de Cervantes*, p. 123). Thirty-five years later he writes that the *Quixote* is impenetrable to the reader who would "enfocarlo como un arsenal de ideas y doctrinas" and, in a judgment that would definitively dispose of his early "classic" of Cervantine scholarship, he proclaims: "Los resultados desprendibles y objetivables de todo aquel proceso quedaban en penumbra; los bienes o los males, los pensamientos o las creencias, la doctrina o la retórica perceptibles en el *Quijote* son cosa secundaria en él, mero combustible para que no cese el martillo de la forja vital" ("Prólogo" to *Don Quijote de la Mancha* [Mexico, 1960], pp. xx–xxi). In another influential exposition of his vitalist reading, he admits his error in having argued that "a Cervantes le interesaba en ocasiones determinar cuál fuera la realidad yacente bajo la fluctuación de las apariencias" and insists that "lo dado, las realidades inmutables y objetivadas frente al correr mismo de las vidas, no juega papel esencial en el libro máximo de España." The work presents human experience, and "el vocablo 'experiencia' no se refiere entonces a nada racional y científico" ("La palabra escrita y el 'Quijote,'" *Hacia Cervantes* [Madrid, 1967], pp. 383–84). The characters of the *Novelas ejemplares* are unfortunately born as such rationally determined essences, "tipos alimentados por un ideal trascendente a ellos y válido y grato para las gentes ... son personajes 'sustanciales' aristotélicamente, sustancia de virtud; no se hacen a sí mismos, no poseen un *sí mismo*, van adonde 'les han dicho' que tienen que ir ..." ("La ejemplaridad de las novelas cervantinas," *Semblanza y estudios españoles: Homenaje ofrecido a Don Américo Castro por sus ex-alumnos de Princeton University* [Princeton, 1956], p. 311). In characteristic metaphors Castro emphasizes the historical perishability of all art conceived in such abstract terms. "Envejece ... lo concluso y definido, lo objetivado sin enlace con un vivir incierto. Se agostan incluso los sistemas de pensamiento y las teorías científicas ..." [Works which maintain] "viva su eficaz y perenne realidad" are those "creados por el genio humano, no como entes, sino como existentes" (p. 297). This judgment rests to some extent on the questionable assumption that the historical vitality of a work of literature is dependent on its projection of the dynamic, unpredictable flow of real experience.

17. See "La ejemplaridad de las novelas cervantinas," pp. 297–315.

18. See Goethe's letter to Schiller, December 17, 1795, *Goethes Briefe*, 4 vols. (Hamburg, 1962–1967), 2:210. For Jauss's discussion of the type of literature that avoids troubling the receiving consciousness with the unfamiliar experience that might provoke a change in its comfortably assumed horizons, see *Literaturgeschichte als Provokation* (Frankfurt am Main, 1970), p. 178. For the conventional unfavorable view of novellas as "food for the senses," see the sixteenth-century judgment of J. de Zurita: "algunos libros han de quedar para ocupar la gente sensual, que no sabiendo ocuparse en cosas más altas, por fuerza han de tener algunos manjares gruessos en que se entretengan" (cited by A.

González de Amezúa y Mayo, *Formación y elementos de la novela cortesana* [Madrid, 1929], pp. 82–83).

19. A very different evaluation of the results of the Romantic "misreading" of *Don Quixote* can be found in A. Close's recent *The Romantic Approach to "Don Quixote"* [Cambridge, 1978], a study which reached me after the completion of this introduction.

20. See "Prólogo" to *Don Quijote de la Mancha*, pp. xiii–xiv, also "La palabra escrita y el 'Quijote,'" p. 389. A glance at the complicated historical life of the *Quixote* would confirm the usefulness of a fundamental distinction in the current aesthetics of reception between the immediate and potential meanings of a literary work and the recognition that the distance between the two can vary a great deal in different types of works and as individual works are subjected to the readings of different periods. In fact, in its "expansion," a phenomenon all too readily dismissed by an influential school of contemporary readers as the growth of a distinguished body of "erroneous interpretation," the *Quixote* is the preeminent case of a literary work that, before it can become fully meaningful, requires a profound alteration in its public, a process which can unfold in decades or centuries and which can in some instances be effected by the powers of its own imaginative energy. "Der Abstand zwischen der aktuellen ersten Wahrnehmung eines Werks und seinen virtuellen Bedeutungen, oder anders gesagt: der Widerstand, den das neue Werk der Erwartung seines ernsten Publikums entgegensetzt, kann so gross sein, dass es eines langen Prozesses der Rezeption bedarf, um das im ersten Horizont Unerwartete und Unverfügbare einzuholen" (Jauss, *Literaturgeschichte als Provokation*, pp. 192–93). Clearly there was much in the *Quixote* that was both "unexpected" and "unusable" for Cervantes's contemporary readers, and the impoverishing "improvements" of Avellaneda's reconstruction of the masterpiece, as well as Sancho Panza's indignation at the gluttony and drunkenness of the "impostor" whose life is chronicled by the Tordesillan historian, are eloquent testimony of its "irrelevancies" for its contemporary readers (see *Don Quijote de la Mancha*, 2:488–89). See also M.M. Bakhtin's observations on the "immortal, polysemic" novelistic images which live different lives in different epochs and his judgment of *Don Quixote* as the classic example of the phenomenon of "re-accentuation" in literary history. "The historical life of classic works is in fact the uninterrupted process of their social and ideological re-accentuation. Thanks to the intentional potential embedded in them, such works have proved capable of uncovering in each era and against ever new dialogizing backgrounds ever newer aspects of meaning; their semantic content literally continues to grow, to further create out of itself." Bakhtin notes that the process can bring contraction as well as expansion, and his words on the dangers of "impoverishment" could stand as a summary of the excesses of both the Romantic interpreters of *Don Quixote* and their adversaries, the so-called "hard" readers. "Especially dangerous is any vulgarizing that oversimplifies re-accentuation (which is cruder in all respects than that of the author and his time) and that turns a two-voiced image into one that is flat, single-voiced—into a stilted heroic image, a Sentimental and pathos-charged one, or (at the other extreme) into a primitively comic one" ("Discourse in the Novel," *The Dialogic Imagination*, trans. C. Emerson and M. Holquist [Austin, 1981], pp. 410, 421–22).

21. Ironically Castro is the twentieth-century reader who has done most both to sustain the life of Cervantes's exemplary fiction and to complete the historical process of its loss, and one should not underestimate the severity of the rift separating the rationalism of his original conception of Cervantes as the most distinguished early spokesman for a minority tradition in Spain espousing enlightenment, rationalism, cosmopolitanism, and Europeanism from the vitalism informing his subsequent attachment as a critic to

novelistic values and qualities, a philosophical vision intimately connected with them, and a belief in the causal relationship between their discovery and cultivation and the peculiar tensions of Spanish history. The recent study of Castro's writings on Cervantes by A. Close (*The Romantic Approach to "Don Quixote*,*"* chaps. 4–6), while correctly pointing out the vitalistic elements of *El pensamiento de Cervantes* and hence the general unity of Castro's whole corpus of Cervantine studies as "romantic," fails to stress sufficiently the radical rift separating the early and late criticism. Castro's envisaged dichotomy in Cervantes's consciousness and writings may be a mirror of the conflicting tendencies marking Castro's own development—from the secure spiritual horizons of his early cosmopolitan scholarship and his unquestioning self-identification within Spain's minority liberal tradition (in 1928 Castro associates himself with "Erasmus's 16th-century Spanish friends" in a letter to M. Bataillon concerning the advisability of softening the tone of some of the anticlerical assertions in the tatter's prologue to Dámaso Alonso's edition of the *Enchiridion* for the purpose of assuring its publication in the Spain of Primo de Rivera's dictatorship [M. Bataillon, "Erasmo, ayer y hoy," *Erasmo y el erasmismo* (Barcelona, 1977), pp. 362–63]), to a *circunstancia* painfully problematized by his historical study, a profound sense of alienation from the "illusions" of his earlier understanding, and, in his search for authentic self-knowledge, a recognition of the degree to which he and all his work were conditioned by the distinctive character of the *morada vital* of Spain. This rift is in some ways as radical as that accompanying the shift from "classic" to "romantic" in the historical reception of *Don Quixote*.

22. "La ejemplaridad de las novelas cervantinas," p, 302. Castro's assertion that the reign of Philip III was a period of Christian Humanism appears to be based more on his desire to attribute the doctrinal content of the *Novelas ejemplares*, which he obviously understood as "Christian Humanist," to a thoroughly conformist impulse in Cervantes than on his accurate observation of the cultural life of the period. See J.B. Avalle-Arce's recent discussion of the deep intellectual alienation which Cervantes suffered in the Spain of the Philips, the prominence of Erasmus's ideas and attitudes in his works, and his yearning for "the world of ideas that circulated quite freely in the Spain of Charles V," "Cervantes and the Renaissance," *Cervantes and the Renaissance*, ed. M.D. McGaha (Easton, Pa., 1980), pp. 5–6. As I shall point out in my analyses of the tales, deviations from the norms, values, and expectations constituting the contemporary horizon for literary reception and from the works creating and confirming that horizon are strikingly apparent in nearly every one of them. One of the most interesting threads linking the tales under consideration and pointing to a unified consciousness informing their highly variegated structures is Cervantes's critical dialogue with and disengagement from the contemporary ascetic writings which I refer to as the literature of *desengaño*. It should be pointed out that Castro omits this revealing passage in a later, revised version of his essay. The expurgation is extremely interesting: is it simply a sign of his awareness of the inaccuracy of his earlier description of the cultural life of Philip III's Spain and his consequent recognition that acknowledgment of the *Exemplary Novels'* humanist doctrines would vitiate his central argument that they should be seen as conformist works, or is it a sign of his increasing determination to dissociate all of Cervantes's achievements in writing about man as a concrete being in this world from European humanism and, in effect, to keep his own early critical voice, that of *El pensamiento de Cervantes*, from reasserting its influence? See *Hacia Cervantes*, pp. 451–74.

23. In his subsequent writings Castro disposes of the question of Cervantes's Erasmism more conclusively, limiting his considerations to what can be recovered from the Erasmian vision that to some extent accounted for the achievements of the "authentic"

Cervantes. In *Cervantes y los casticismos españoles* (Barcelona, 1966), for example, he acknowledges that Cervantes "se interesó vivamente por la espiritualidad cristiana de inspiración erasmista," but finds its significance for the writer primarily in its general emphasis on the individual's interior spiritual life and in the way in which the type of consciousness which it nurtured might lie behind the unprecedented and entirely secular act of "structuring a new type of literary character." He argues that Spanish Erasmian should be defined less in terms of a body of received doctrine than in terms of the vital needs that it, as well as other spiritualist movements which preceded it historically, satisfied in the alienated sensibility of the group of Spaniards to whom its appeal was most immediate. "El interés de Erasmo por la espiritualidad de San Pablo fue aprovechado en España para finalidades no exclusivamente teológicas o doctrinales. El erasmismo—como bien se sabe—no tuvo importancia en España como 'idea,' sino como medio protector y defensivo para quienes vivían como Luis de León nos ha dicho sin ninguna reserva, y hoy sabemos por otras vías. Los conversos se aferraban a cuanto sirviera para bastarse cristianamente a sí mismos" (see pp. ix, 109). For a balanced critical exposition of Castro's final view of Cervantes's Erasmism, see M. Bataillon, "El erasmismo de Cervantes en el pensamiento de Américo Castro," *Erasmo y el erasmismo*, pp. 347–59. An intelligent attempt to reconcile Castro's early and late approaches to the question can be found in F. Márquez Villanueva's recent *Personajes y temas del Quijote* (Madrid, 1975), which maintains that Cervantes's relation to Christian Humanist thought is that of an informed and articulate antagonist. The central doctrines of Erasmus's edifying program do inform crucial scenes of the *Quixote*, but the critical scrutiny which they receive from Cervantes discloses in every case their incompatibility with the novelist's vitalism and his existentialist vision of life's manifold complexities. By attesting to the impact of Erasmian thought on Cervantes's intellectual development and creative procedures, the argument resurrects the context of El pensamiento de Cervantes, but in its unsympathetic interpretations of Erasmist doctrines and its failure to consider numerous scenes, particularly in Don Quixote II, in which the humanist vision is forcefully associated with the chivalric enterprise, it ultimately supports the late Castro's continuing disengagement of Cervantes's specific creative achievements from Erasmian inspiration.

24. See *Erasmo y España: estudios sobre la historia espiritual del siglo xvi*, trans. A. Alatorre (México, 1966), pp. 777–801; esp. p. 799. J.L. Abellán's recent *El erasmismo español* (Madrid, 1976) is content to answer the question of Cervantes's Erasmism by restating the conclusions of the studies of Castro and Bataillon (see pp. 265–81). In view of Amezúa's uncompromising rejection of the possibility of any influence of Erasmus's writings and thought on Cervantes's work (*Cervantes, creador de la novela corta española*, 2 vols. [Madrid, 1956–1958], 1:139–99) and the recent endorsement of his conclusion in C. Morón Arroyo's *Nuevas meditaciones del "Quijote"* ([Madrid, 1976], pp. 124ff.), it would appear to be all the more urgent that such studies as Bataillon calls for be made.

25. Bataillon himself and subsequently F. Márquez Villanueva have fruitfully considered the important episode of Don Quixote's encounter with the "Caballero del Verde Gabán" in connection with Erasmus's colloquies, *The Old Men's Chat* and *The Godly Feast*, employing a method of comparison which is not encumbered by the methodological requirements of traditional influence study. Though their analyses yield very different judgments of the episode, they strongly support the conclusion that Cervantes's knew the *Colloquies* and drew on them in a most independent and creative way (see *Erasmo y España*, pp. 792–94; Márquez Villanueva, *Personajes y temas del Quijote*, pp. 159ff.). Similarly A. Vilanova has analyzed successfully the play of ideas marking Cervantes's prologue to *Don Quixote* I in connection with the *Praise of Folly*, supporting his argument for influence with

some interesting correspondences of detail (see "La Moria de Erasmo y el Prólogo del Quixote," *Collected Studies in Honour of Américo Castro's 80th Year*, ed. M. P. Hornik [Oxford, 1965], pp. 423–33, and *Erasmo y Cervantes* [Barcelona, 1949]). See also Bataillon's recent reconsideration of the possible influence of the *Praise of Folly* on such ironists as Cervantes and the author of *Lazarillo de Tormes* ("Un problème d'influence d'Érasme en Espagne: *L'Éloge de la Folie*," *Actes du Congrés Érasme* [Rotterdam, 1969], pp. 136–47).

26. E.C. Riley points out that the traditional interpretation of exemplariness in literature is far too narrow to enable a full comprehension of Cervantes's tales and adds: "Over and above edifying examples and warnings there was a region where the poetically true and the exemplary were at one, and this must have been the generous sense of exemplariness that Cervantes understood" (*Cervantes's Theory of the Novel*, p. 105). A striking alteration in the readers capacity to understand correctly the nature and workings of Cervantes's exemplary art is registered in the description of the *Novelas ejemplares* by the celebrated grammarian, G. Mayans y Siscar, in 1737—"jocosidad milesia," commendable for their style, disposition, and "la agudeza de su invención y honestidad de costumbres" (cited by W. Krauss, *Miguel de Cervantes: Leben und Werk* [Neuwied, 1966], p. 215)—and in Goethe's recognition of the affinities of his own art with that of the master: "Dagegen habe ich an den Novellen des Cervantes einen wahren Schatz gefunden, sowohl der Unterhaltung als der Belehrung. Wie sehr freut man sich, wenn man das anerkannte Gute auch anerkennen kann und wie sehr wird man auf seinem Wege gefordert, wenn man Arbeiten sieht, die nach eben den Grundsitzen gebildet sind, nach denen wit nach unserem Masse and in unserem Kreise selbst verfahren" (letter to Schiller, December 17, 1795, *Goethes Briefe*, 2:210).

27. From Boccaccio's concluding comment on the *Decameron*, "Conviene nella moltitudine delle cose, diverse qualità di cose trovarsi," to Bandello's acknowledgment of the "disorderliness" of his collection, "E non avendo potuto servar ordine ne l'altre, meno m'é stato lecito servarlo in queste; il che certamente nulla importa, non essendo le mie novelle soggetto d'istoria continovata, ma una mistura d'accidenti diversi, diversamente e in diversi luoghi e tempi a diverse persone avvenuti e senza ordine veruno recitati," the major writers of short stories continued to recognize that the appeal of their art rested to a great extent on its variety (see Pabst, *Novellentheorie*, pp. 39, 74). See also R. J. Clements and J. Gibaldi, *Anatomy of the Novella: The European Tale Collection from Boccaccio and Chaucer to Cervantes* (New York, 1977), pp. 12–16. Pabst notes that the most striking feature of the short story in its historical development from the thirteenth to the eighteenth century is the freedom of expression which it allowed its cultivators and its resistance to the confinements of theme or form which prescriptive literary theory generally imposes on the objects of its attention. He emphasizes that Boccaccio "hat ... selbst nie daran gedacht, das Vielfältige und Unterschiedliche als Gattung oder Norm aufzufassen" and that sixteenth-century efforts, under the impact of the increasingly prestigious neo-classical doctrines, to attribute a unified conception to the *Decameron* offer one of the most striking examples of the incompatibility which the genre has shown through history with the sporadic and ineffectual attempts at codification by its commentators. While critics and defenders of short stories invoked principles of traditional rhetoric, they never attempted to derive a theory of the novella that would accurately take into account its fundamental constitutive features and the positive differences separating it from the officially sanctioned genres (see pp. 22–27, 40, 73–79). For the variety of traditional narrative forms which Boccaccio incorporated in his masterpiece, see Pabst, *Novellentheorie*, pp. 28–29, and H.-J. Neuschäfer, *Boccaccio und der Beginn der Novelle: Strukturen der Kurzerzahlung auf der Schwelle zwischen Mittelalter and Neuzeit* (Munich, 1969).

28. See E. Auerbach, *Zur Technik der Frührenaissancenovelle in Italien und Frankreich* (Heidelberg, 1921), and W. Krömer, "Gattung und Wort *Novela* im Spanischen 17. Jahrhundert," *Romanische Forschungen* 81 (1969): 381–434.

29. See Krömer, "Gattung and Wort *Novela* im Spanischen 17. Jahrhundert," pp. 390–96; Clements and Gibaldi, *Anatomy of the Novella*, pp. 216–28; Auerbach, *Zur Technik der Frührenaissancenovelle in Italien und Frankreich*, pp. 63–64.

30. Considering L.B. Alberti i "De amicitia" in connection with the humanists' general search for flexible, "antisystematic;" forms of exposition, F. Schalk notes that "eine persönliche erfinderische, der Novelle verwandte Kunst fliesst in seinen Büchern zusammen mit der mächtigen Einwirkung des Humanismus" and goes on to assert that there is a relationship of reciprocal influence between the novella and the privileged didactic genres of the humanists: "Symposion, Traktat, Dialog—und es gab seit dem Humanismus viele Traktate und Dialoge—... Panegyrikus, Disputatio, Novelle treten in einen inneren Zusammenhang miteinander" ("L.B. Albertis Buch 'De Amicitia' [Della Famiglia IV]," in *Symbola Coloniensia Iosepho Kroll sexagenario ... oblata* [Cologne, 1949], pp. 163–71). E. Auerbach suggests that with Marguerite de Navarre's *Heptaméron* a new and rich phase in the historical development of the novella begins, as the genre situates itself more firmly within the context of the humanist philosophical vision (*Zur Technik der Frührenaissancenovelle in Italien und Frankreich*, p. 64). As I shall point out in my analyses, the *Colloquies* of Erasmus appear to have had an influence on Cervantes's composition of novellas, both in their philosophical content and in their manner of fusing ideas and fictions. W. Pabst's generally unfavorable treatment of the encounter of the European novella with humanism is severely limited by his far too exclusive association of the latter with academic theorizing, rationalistic systematization, inauthentic imitation, and logical attitudes which would inhibit creative freedom (see *Novellentheorie*, pp. 58–59, 78–79).

31. "This flowery April, / Whose variety is admired by / Flying fame, who looks upon / A thousand varieties in him" (prefatory poem by Fernando Bermúdez Carbajal, *Novelas ejemplares*, *Obras completas*, ed. A. Valbuena Prat, p. 771).

32. See *Don Quijote de la Mancha*, ed. M. de Riquer (Madrid, 1972), 1:7–12.

33. See G. Hainsworth, "Quelques opinions françaises (1614–1664) sur les Nouvelles exemplaires de Cervantes (1613)," *Bulletin Hispanique* 32 (1930): 63–70.

34. *Novellentheorie*, p. 117.

35. M. Bataillon has noted the particular appeal which Heliodorus's *Ethiopian History*, rediscovered in the sixteenth century, had for the Erasmists (*Erasmo y España*, pp. 621–22).

36. For the self-consciousness and general independence with which Cervantes manipulates traditional literary genres, see K. Reichenberger, "Cervantes und die literarischen Gattungen," *Germanisch-Romanische Monatsschrift* 13 (1963): 233–46.

37. My examination of *El casamiento engañoso y el coloquio de los perros*, which I consider ideologically the most complex and formally the most revolutionary work of the collection, will appear as an independent study, titled *Cervantes and the Mystery of Lawlessness*.

38. While their liberating discourse, which engages the reader in a dialogue, separates Cervantes's stories decisively from traditional exemplary literature with its "monologic" formulations of doctrine, it links them not only with the characteristic literature of the Christian Humanists but also with *Don Quixote*, for it is the fundamental idiom of the great novel. At various points in my study I consider the central issues and narrative techniques of the short stories as they appear in the *Quixote*. Through comparative analysis I hope both to enhance our understanding of the distinctive character of each work and, by considering their mutual relationships, to contribute to our understanding of the

complexity and fundamental unity of the vision informing them. Several specific points of comparison—e.g., religious attitudes; adaptations of literary conventions; the themes of nature, knowledge, and marriage—indicate the greater modernity of the *Quixote*, but they also disclose a common body of interests and preoccupations underlying both works. If it is undoubtedly naive to accept the Romantics' exaggerated conception of this unity—e.g., Friedrich Schlegel: "Wer nicht einmal sie [die Novellen] göttlich finden kann, muss den *Don Quixote* durchaus falsch verstehen" (*Seine prosaischen Jugendschriften*, 2 vols. [Vienna, 1906], 2:315)—it is perhaps no less so to conceive of an irreconcilable opposition of spirit separating the exemplary and novelistic works. A full clarification of their reciprocal relationships would, of course, require a separate study, but I hope to suggest some directions such a study might take, one of which would be to shift the focus of critical attention from the search for germs of the *Quixote* in the novellas to a careful examination and evaluation of the presence of the novellas in the *Quixote*. Given the renewed interest in the *Persiles* and the theater in recent years, such a shift would appear to be perfectly compatible with contemporary trends in Cervantine criticism, which is clearly no longer dominated by the interest in novelistic values which, because of the inexhaustible richness of *Don Quixote* as the first novel, persisted long after their decanonization by many twentieth-century writers and critics. The prominence of the humanist vision in Part II of the *Quixote* and its elevation through the ascent of Sancho Panza, the increasing conceptual complexity and ambivalence in Don Quixote's madness, and the elegiac tone surrounding his rejection by the world would suggest that the affinities of the *Novelas ejemplares* and the *Quixote* are much deeper than is commonly supposed. In general my study tends to confirm M. Bataillon's view that "La obra de Cervantes es la de un hombre que permanece, hasta to último, fiel a ideas de su juventud, a hábitos de pensamiento que la época de Felipe II había recibido de la del Emperador" (*Erasmo y España*, p. 778).

E.C. RILEY

Ideals and Illusions

It is not possible to sum up *Don Quixote* in the terms of a single general theme. The huge multiplicity of motifs, themes and topics which the work has been held to contain may be seen in the titles listed in any critical bibliography. The range and depth of Cervantes's novelistic invention partly account for this, but his basic choice of subject is also in part responsible—the consequences of a man going mad through reading too much chivalresque literature. Out of this it is in fact easy to abstract a whole range of related conceptual polarities: madness–sanity, illusion–reality, appearances–truth, fiction–fact, art–life, poetry–history, romance–novel, idealism–realism, theory–practice, mind–matter, spirit–flesh. They are open to such infinite speculation, however, that any temptation to ponder them here is easily resisted.

One of these concepts above all others has been especially associated with Don Quixote. Idealism—ineffectual idealism, to be exact. In the major European languages to be 'quixotic' means to pursue impracticable ideals. More or less like Cervantes's hero, the quixotic idealist takes little or no account of practical realities in seeking to implement his aims. He does not see when pursuit of an ideal becomes surrender to an illusion.

Now, although this incapacity is a distinguishing characteristic of Don Quixote, Cervantes offers no direct and explicit commentary on it, as he

---

From *Don Quixote*. © 1986 by E.C. Riley.

does, for example, on the comportment of some of the central figures in his *Exemplary Novels* and other works. His own precise attitude to his hero's deficiency has remained in part elusive. 'In part', because he obviously presents him as a figure of fun, while still leaving ample room for speculation over whether in addition he tacitly condemns, reproves, mocks, pities, sympathizes or admires. Rightly or wrongly, answers have perennially been inferred from the way Cervantes handles the story or from sources outside it. This general area of interpretation has been over the years the most contestable of the whole novel. Most people have taken Cervantes to be defending idealism; a few have thought he was attacking it. Probably he was doing neither. Unamuno canonized Quixote for his idealism ('my Saint Quixote', he calls him: 1967D, e.g. p. 212). Ruskin was inclined to rate Cervantes first 'of all powerful and popular writers [who] in the cause of error have wrought most harm to their race ... for he cast scorn upon the holiest principles of humanity' (1855E, pp. 66–7).

While it is misguided to treat the novel as a moral or philosophical tract, many such questions of a more particular kind do insistently present themselves. Does Cervantes really tend to suggest that ideals are illusions, idealism folly? Is Don Quixote foolish or heroic to persist in his? How is it that we laugh at a man so wholly dedicated to relieving distress and fighting injustice? Has he simply got his ends right and his means wrong? There are many such questions as these and even more answers to them.[1] It is a measure of Cervantes's success in reflecting life through this least dogmatic of books that people have been so disposed to find in it the answers they would like to find there. No one is immune. Centring attention too exclusively on the ideals leads to Romantic distortions of the work; focusing too narrowly on Don Quixote's crazy behaviour eventually reduces the novel to the vacuousness of a comic strip.

The simple connection between Don Quixote's ideals and his illusions is central. The fact that he regains his sanity at the very end means that to all intents and purposes he eventually sheds his illusions, although until he is on his deathbed the separation of ideals and illusions is slow and incomplete. The process is under way at least from the beginning of the third expedition, maybe earlier, when his most obvious physical illusions—ocular delusions— almost disappear. We have also noted signs of the growth of another kind of disillusionment: namely his incipient recognition of the impracticality of literally and completely realizing the ideals of story-book chivalry in the world he fives in, and of doing so on his own. What happens to his idealism in these circumstances is naturally important. There can be little doubt of his intensified melancholy in the later chapters, or of the surge of disappointment after his defeat. But I do not see incontrovertible signs of loss of faith in his ideals *per se*—close though he may come to this—either before or after he regains his wits. Nothing in his deathbed conduct suggests the cynicism, bitterness or broken spirit one might expect of the frustrated idealist. He abjures the books of chivalry and their heroes and looks back on his obsession as ignorance (II, 74; ii, 587); his predominant concern now is to die a good Christian death. The emphasis is on balance of mind restored.

In this general context I shall look at one major motif of the novel and two important episodes in Part II: respectively, Dulcinea, the Cave of Montesinos and the encounter with Don Diego de Miranda. All three are rich in a variety of ways and throw light on Don Quixote's state of mind. The first two do so from within, as it were. In some degree the third does the same from a source outside it, and by means of a complementary figure provides a kind of equilibrating control for the assessment of the hero. Of course one cannot anatomize Don Quixote's entire madness by means of a simple bisection of idealism and illusion, but a careful look at the text with these central concepts in mind may help.

(i) DULCINEA

Dulcinea enters the book almost as an afterthought to Don Quixote's other preparations for his career as knight errant (I, 1), but she plays a major part in his story. She is one of the most extraordinary character conceptions in literature. She exists as pure idea in the mind of the Knight, is the professed motivation or justification for many of his actions, and the occasion for some bravura displays of eloquence. As it turns out, she is not his exclusive property, however, and moves others to action, too. She has no physical presence, but an incarnate original form as Aldonza Lorenzo, who is spoken of, but never 'appears oft the scene' in Cervantes's novel (unlike various modern stage and screen versions of it). Two figures alleged by others to be Dulcinea enchanted do appear. In the circumstances perhaps it is forgivable not to attempt an exact definition of her existential or ontological status!

The contrast between the perfections she represents in spiritual form and the earthiness of her material one is a dominant feature of her persona. The earthiness is captured to some extent in the very name 'Aldonza', which has strong peasant connotations to the Spanish ear.[2] As an idealization of an individual, Dulcinea is to Aldonza rather as Don Quixote is to Alonso Quijano or Princess Micomicona is to Dorotea—only more so. The paired figures have some analogy to the twin terms of a metaphor, and it is no accident that Dulcinea is intimately connected with the metaphorical procedures of enhancement characteristic of the cultivated poetry of the age (see Rodríguez-Luis, 1965-6D, p. 387). Don Quixote envisages her as possessing

> all the impossible and chimerical attributes of beauty conferred
> by poets on their ladies ... such as that her hair is gold, her brow
> the Elysian fields, her eyebrows rainbows, her eyes suns, her
> cheeks roses, her lips corals, pearls her teeth, alabaster her neck,
> marble her breast, ivory her hands, her whiteness snow.

> (todos los imposibles y quiméricos atributos de belleza que los
> poetas dan a sus damas: que sus cabellos son oro, su frente campos
> eliseos, sus cejas arcos del cielo, sus ojos soles, sus mejillas rosas,
> sus labios corales, perlas sus dientes, alabastro su cuello, mármol
> su pecho, marfil sus manos, su blancura nieve: I, 13; i, 176.)

Similarly, when Quixote revises Sancho's prosaic (and plausible) account of his supposed visit to Dulcinea, he transforms grains of wheat into pearls, as a sophisticated poet of the day might have done (I, 31). As an idealization of womanhood, Dulcinea inevitably has some connections with the damsel Poetry who recurs in various of Cervantes's works in forms ranging from outright allegory in the *Viaje del Parnaso* to symbolic association in the gypsy girl Preciosa. Naturally, idealization on the scale of Dulcinea's invites comic deflation. Being another of Don Quixote's imitations from chivalric romance, she is a parody from the start, but she is not *in herself* a comic one. The comedy comes from the material contrast and when the metaphor is stood on its head.

There may be some doubt about Dulcinea's royal lineage (I, 13; II, 32), but there is none about her literary pedigree. A younger sister, as it were, of Oriana and other peerless princesses of chivalric romance, she is the ultimate descendant of those perfectly idealized ladies whom courtly love poets had sung and swooned over, sighed and died for, for centuries, beauties who like her had been loved *de lonh*, and *de oídas*. She is the parody version of the *donna gentile*, and the chaste adored of poets in the Renaissance neoplatonic vain. She is close kin to the Amaryllises and Dianas, Galateas and Phyllises of pastoral, whose flesh-and-blood content is negligible—as Don Quixote actually explains to Sancho in I, 25. More perfect than Petrarch's Laura, Garcilaso's Elisa or Herrera's Luz, she is the beloved whose virtues have etherialized her right out of physical existence. She is the disembodied mistress.

In Part I, Don Quixote establishes her as the conventional absent mistress, for whose sake ... (etc.), and who alone imparts strength to his right arm (I, 30; i, 178). He admits to Sancho that he depicts her in his imagination exactly as he pleases (I, 25; i, 314), but he domiciles her in the real village of El Toboso where, in the novel, Aldonza Lorenzo lived. This gesture towards the actualization of his ideal woman, though consistent with finding giants in wineskins and so forth, is the source of all the trouble later on, when Sancho is required to make contact with her. By attaching a place-label to his ideal, Don Quixote turns it into an illusion which is vulnerable.

This is borne out in Part II, where he suffers the nightmarish experience of having a cherished dream go out of orbit, get taken over by other people and return to haunt him. The moment Sancho talks him into believing that the uncouth peasant girl is Dulcinea under a spell, he loses his freedom to depict her in his imagination as he pleases. His own beautiful parody becomes a crude travesty fashioned by Sancho. The juxtaposition of Don Quixote's beautiful courtly prose with the 'rustically boorish' language of the peasant girl has been described by Erich Auerbach as something which 'had certainly never happened before' in literature (1969D, p. 114). Sancho proceeds to dislocate totally the metaphorical picture of Dulcinea, railing at enchanters for changing 'the pearls of my lady's eyes'—as though she were a codfish, Don Quixote objects later—'into corktree galls, and her hair of purest gold into red ox tail bristles', and so on (II, 10; ii, 112).[3] Dulcinea's recovery of her pristine state is henceforth a major preoccupation for the Knight. Small wonder that he dreams about her in the Cave of Montesinos. Then the Duke and Duchess and their attendants get involved, and the travesty becomes literal at the next appearance of 'Dulcinea', when a page, heavily veiled, burlesques the part of the enchanted damsel (II, 55). The figure of Dulcinea has been debased and transformed, first by Sancho out of self-interest, then by others for their own amusement, and Don Quixote is helpless by himself to break the spell (short of regaining his wits). Worse is to come. Her image is contaminated with money.

The Knight's attitude to money and to any kind of commercial transaction at the outset of his career had been one of superb disregard. However, the first innkeeper amiably persuaded him of the need to be basically provided (I, 3), and so on his second sortie he goes out modestly equipped for his and Sancho's needs. He continues to regard lucre as a drab requirement at times but not the sort of thing a gentle knight worries his head about. He refuses to pay the second innkeeper (I, 17) and is evasive about paying Sancho a salary. Not a few sixteenth-century gentlemen would have behaved in exactly the same way. In Part II, where he is less alienated socially, he accepts the need for money transactions almost as a matter of course, agrees on paying Sancho a salary, tips the lionkeeper and carter two escudos (II, 17), and almost meekly pays for the damage he has caused to Maese Pedro's puppets (II, 26) and to the boat on the River Ebro.

The first intimation of Dulcinea's involvement with money is an incident in the Cave of Montesinos, an incident in Quixote's dream, with symbolic prophetic force.[4] Dulcinea sends a message to Don Quixote asking for a loan of six *reales* and offering a cotton skirt as security. More humiliatingly still, the Knight has only enough change on him to oblige with four (II, 23). Not long after, the whole business of disenchanting Dulcinea, devised at the Duke's castle, takes on the sordid colours of a commercial deal, as depressing for Don Quixote as it is ridiculous to everyone else. Sancho has to 'pay' by receiving 3,300 lashes on his ample posterior (II, 13). Naturally he does not accept this without haggling. Eventually (II, 72) he gets his master to pay him so many *reales* per stroke, raises the price some more, and finally cheats Don Quixote by faking the entire punishment. Could Dulcinea be more debased?

It is hard to say what she 'stands for' precisely in Don Quixote's eyes, apart from being his professed inspiration and object of devotion. As a concept she has been likened to Aristotle's concept of God (Atlee, 1976D) and St Anselm's argument for His existence (Durán, 1960D, p. 160). I do not think she is the *symbol* of anything in particular. All the same, it is clear that her image resides close to the heart of all that chivalry means to Don Quixote. Dulcinea is obviously associated very closely with chivalry for him. In the light of this it is significant that nobody (except perhaps Sancho in moments of confusion) believes in her existence, yet quite a few people (notably the members of a ducal court) pretend to do so and pay lip-service to her. The charade of restoring her to what she once was ends in a fraudulent cash deal. Her image has become a travesty of her original self and tainted with commercialism. It is easy to draw the analogy between Dulcinea and what was left of chivalry in Spain in the early capitalist era, when the buying of patents of nobility was widespread. It was the new age of that powerful *caballero*, Don Dinero, 'the great solvent of the solid fabric of the old society, the great generator of illusion' (Trilling, 1961E, p. 209). It was the age when, as Olivares reminded Philip IV, 'Kings cannot achieve heroic actions without money' (Elliott, 1963E, p. 320).

Dulcinea's appearance as impecunious bumpkin in Don Quixote's dream implies that at the unconscious level of his mind he accepts that something has happened to his ideal mistress. She does not *look* the same to him now. This suggests that a cherished belief of his has been undermined; it points to a deep-level disillusionment, representing a painful step towards sanity. However, at the conscious level, he considers the metamorphosis to be neither fundamental nor irreversible, but a temporary aberration induced by magic. As he reminds Sancho:

> enchantments switch all things around and change their natural
> shapes. I do not mean that they really change them from one thing

into another, but that it looks that way, as we learnt from experience in the transformation of Dulcinea, sole refuge of my hopes.

(todas las cosas trastruecan y mudan de su ser natural los encantos. No quiero decir que las mudan de uno en otro ser realmente, sino que lo parece, como lo mostró la experiencia en la transformación de Dulcinea, único refugio de mis esperanzas: II, 29; ii, 265.)

The distinction between her appearance and her real self is all-important. When Don Quixote now asserts his steadfast belief in Dulcinea's perfections, as he resolutely does at least from the time of the discussion with the Duke and Duchess onwards (II, 32; ii, 289–93),[5] it is of course to her unchanged essential self that he refers. His resolution is strengthened by the news that the false Quixote of Avellaneda was disenamoured of Dulcinea, and he loudly proclaims his undying devotion to her again (ch. 59, p. 486).[6] But the great, the most authentically heroic moment in his whole career is when he lies prostrate beneath the lance-point of the Knight of the White Moon and

battered and dazed, without raising his visor, as if speaking from within a tomb, he said in a low and faltering voice:
'Dulcinea del Toboso is the most beautiful woman in the world, and I am the most unlucky knight on earth, and it is not right that my weakness should discredit this truth.'

(molido y sturdido, sin alzarse la visera, como si hablara dentro de una tumba, con voz debilitada y enferma, dijo:
—Dulcinea del Toboso es la más hermosa mujer del mundo, y yo el más desdichado caballero de la tierra, y no es bien que mi flaqueza defraude esta verdad: II, 64; ii, 534.)

Don Quixote knew nothing of Sansón Carrasco's imposture: for all he did know, he risked being run through by a lance when he said this.

But nothing happens to lift the spell from Dulcinea and Quixote's spirits with it. The pleasure and hope he shows when Sancho completes his whipping (ch. 72, p. 580) are short-lived. He reads the incidents with the running hare and the boys with the cricket's cage as bad omens—'*Malum signum! Malum signum!* Hare runs, hounds give chase: Dulcinea won't appear!' (ch. 73, p. 581). In a brave effort to undo the maleficence of these omens, Sancho buys the cricket-cage, symbolically associated with Dulcinea, for four *cuartos*. Her connection with money is maintained to the end.

However, Don Quixote's pessimistic words are not quite the last he has to say on the subject. All he has just said is that he does not expect to *see* her. When he mentions her next, for the last time, he restores her to all her poetical glory. Fantasizing with his friends about their going pastoral together, he calls her 'the peerless Dulcinea del Toboso, glory of these river banks, ornament of these meadows, pillar of beauty, cream of wit, and, in short, fitting object of all praise however hyperbolical it may be' (p. 584). This final affirmation of faith in her does not so much revive her illusory status as relegate her to the printed page of pastoral romance, where, as he had once told Sancho, her sister Amaryllises and Galateas were all to be found (I, 25).

The only serious doubt Don Quixote betrays over Dulcinea concerns her visible physical presence. In El Toboso he gets cold feet and avoids taking the obvious action required for them to meet face to face. Then he lets his private visualization of her be supplanted by Sancho's, which is diametrically opposed to it. Finally he decides that she will not make the appearance he wants her to. The one thing that he has become unsure about is her palpable existence as a living human being. And this is the strictly illusory side of Dulcinea, since a Dulcinea incarnate is unbelievable. Her status as a mental image, however, as a compendium of womanly perfections is secure. When Don Quixote proclaims that her real beauty is intact, despite the worst that enchanters—and the most sordid materialism of the age, one feels inclined to add—can do, he is symbolically affirming his belief in the ideal qualities she epitomizes. His faith in these does not waver.

(ii) THE CAVE OF MONTESINOS

The adventure of the Cave is the richest and most suggestive in the whole novel, thanks partly to Cervantes's fertile imagination and partly to the fact that caves have always been marvellous repositories of symbol. A modern study of the *Quixote* devotes 177 well-filled pages to the episode.[7]

The very nature of the experience Don Quixote relates is intended to be mysterious. He soon becomes unsure about it himself. Benengeli refuses responsibility and leaves it to the prudent reader to judge (II, 24; ii, 223). The really prudent reader knows that he can never know, but if he cares to put himself on the same level as the characters in the book and join in the discussion he can opt for the most plausible of four possibilities: that the events really physically happened just as they appeared to; that somebody staged them; that Don Quixote deliberately made up the whole story;[8] that it was a dream or some kind of visionary experience. The only evidence is circumstantial and it points to the last of these. Aside from which the episode reads as one of the best dreams in literature before Galdós.

Montesinos, Durandarte and Belerma are figures from a group of Spanish ballads of Carolingian chivalric derivation, closely associated with this region in La Mancha, where, close to the Cave of Montesinos, the Lakes of Ruidera are to be found and the partly subterranean River Guadiana runs. In these circumstances it is natural that the ballad figures mentioned should comprise the principal dramatis personae of the dream. But its mainspring is Dulcinea, even though she plays a smaller role in it. The dark shadow of her enchantment has clouded the otherwise auspicious beginnings of the third expedition. Lifting the spell on her is now the Knight's major preoccupation. It is little wonder that he dreams about redeeming all the inhabitants of the Cave (which include her) from the enchantment imposed on them by the arch-wizard Merlin. His account of the dream offers a unique insight directly into his mind at this point in his career.

Freud said that 'every dream deals with the dreamer himself' (1953E, p. 332). Although they originate in balladry, the main figures have affinities with the dreamer and the lady mainly responsible; they are projections of Don Quixote and Dulcinea (as we have previously remarked). Quixote's role in this wish-fulfilling yet anxious dream is that of messianic deliverer foredestined to release from bondage all the inhabitants of the Cave (some figures from Arthurian lore are mentioned, too). He is frustrated by premature awakening when his friends haul him up to the surface but, quite apart from that, the signs were not encouraging. He had fallen short of Dulcinea's financial needs, for one thing. For another, Durandarte, stretched out on his marble slab, had been disappointingly sceptical about Don Quixote's mission. 'And if it should not be so,' he says in the immortal words, 'if it should not be so, oh, cousin, patience I say, and shuffle the pack' (ch. 22, p. 217). It is not surprising that Quixote's pleasure in recalling his dream is at the same time pervaded by a tone of deep melancholy (ch. 22, p. 210).

The dream is notable for its fine touches of absurdity—the rosary beads the size of ostrich eggs, the scholar's cap and hood worn by Montesinos, the two-pound human heart pickled in brine, the outsize turbans, Belerma's looks, the caper cut by Dulcinea's maid, and so on. While quite appropriate to a dream, the inclusion of such ridiculous details, of a kind which were almost totally absent from Don Quixote's two major, consciously invented, chivalresque fantasies (I, 21 and 50), is significant for another reason.[9]

These ridiculous details puncture the fabric of his chivalric vision. They damage the imagery in which it is couched. They do not *fit*. Their oddity, empirically based (as we shall see later) is at variance with the perfectionism which idealized literary chivalry demands. It is as if his unconscious mind which engendered them were mocking him with their incongruity. And, as usual, the unconscious is well ahead of the conscious

mind here. It seems right therefore to read the Cave experience in the way
most critics have done, as a significant pointer towards Don Quixote's
eventual rejection of chivalric fiction and his recovery of sanity. Indeed,
considered in this light, his attack on Maese Pedro's puppets shortly
afterwards (II, 26) might be seen as a further stage in his psychic
development. They, too, are pseudo-Carolingian ballad figures, and Don
Quixote wreaks destruction on them indiscriminately, 'friend' and 'foe'
alike.

The dream in the Cave has some marked characteristics of myth to
which also we will return later. However, one principal mythic motif is
relevant here. It is metamorphosis. This affects not only the duenna Ruidera
with her brood of children and Guadiana the squire, but the major
characters, too. Montesinos is not the knight of the ballads now, but a wise
old man. Durandarte subsists in a curious condition, intermittently dead and
alive. Belerma has lost her beauty. Each one has changed a lot since the
heyday of his or her existence as recounted in the ballads. Drastic change is
also Dulcinea's problem. Lastly, there is the dreamer himself. Perhaps the
most important change of all is taking place in Don Quixote. Something
certainly seems to have happened in his innermost mind to his chivalric
vision, as it happened to the figure of Dulcinea with whom that vision is
intimately associated. The process of disenchantment, which, in another
sense of the word, was the object of his dream mission to the other world,
appears to have begun to operate upon himself.

The ludicrous details of the physical appearance and manner of existence
of the figures in the Cave signal the fact that their physical embodiment as
witnessed by Don Quixote is unreal, and therefore some kind of illusion. Later
on, the physical reality of the experience in the Cave is precisely what Don
Quixote wonders about.[10] So, just as he does with Dulcinea, he shows doubts
about the physical manifestation, which is the illusory side.

Montesinos, Durandarte and Belerma nevertheless preserve a gravity
consonant with their chivalric status. As Menéndez Pidal observed, although
Cervantes treats them in jest this does not affect their inner nobility (1948D,
p. 22). The absurdity of their manifestation in the flesh, now apparent even
to Don Quixote, does not for him impair the chivalric values they embodied
and exemplified in their conduct (such as valour, fidelity in love,
steadfastness, friendship). As with Dulcinea again, the underlying idealism is
unquestioned. In his dream he does not succeed in liberating either his lady
or the other prisoners of the Cave. Similarly, his self-imposed mission to
restore chivalry to the world is not destined to succeed. Unconsciously at
least, he is beginning to realize this. But he says nothing to suggest that the
impracticality of the task undermines the status of chivalry as an ideal in his

eyes. In the Cave of Montesinos adventure he begins to separate illusion and ideal, which is the beginning of sanity.

(iii) DON DIEGO AND DON QUIXOTE

'J'ai découvert que tout le malheur des hommes vient d'une seule chose, qui est de ne savoir pas demurer en repos dans une chambre,' said Pascal (*Pensées*, no. 205). This rather dismal maxim would have been applauded by a number of figures in the novel—if not by Don Antonio Moreno, who argues quite the contrary (II, 65; ii, 536–7). But staying quietly at home is prescribed for Don Quixote's cure, and on a number of occasions expressly identified with right living by a variety of persons. The Niece gives expression to it at the beginning of the second sortie (I, 7) and the Housekeeper at the end of the third (II, 73). In between, so do Sancho (I, 18, and II, 28), the Housekeeper again (II, 2), Tomé Cecial (II, 13), the odious ducal Chaplain (II, 31), the unpleasant Castilian (II, 62) and the Bachelor Carrasco (II, 64). The Housekeeper's words are representative:

> Stay at home, look after your property, go to confession frequently, be good to the poor, and on my soul be it if any harm come to you.
>
> (estése en su casa, atienda a su hacienda, confiese a menudo, favorezca a los pobres y sobre mi ánima si mal le fuere: II, 73; ii, 585.)

Essentially the sentiment is the same as that of another phrase from a less pious source than the Housekeeper, Voltaire's 'Il faut cultiver notre jardin' in *Candide*.

Since it represents a way of life diametrically opposed to Don Quixote's and is clearly equated with sanity, it would seem natural to take this stay-at-home philosophy as the 'moral' of the book, the panacea for Quixotism and Cervantes's last word on the matter, although the proponents of the view do not look very likely candidates for authorial spokesmanship. In any case, nothing in *Don Quixote* is that simple; Cervantes is too disposed to see both sides of things. It so happens that the Housekeeper's simple message is embodied in Don Diego de Miranda, a figure of many virtues but—since the well-bred gentlemen-farmer type ceased to be universally admired—a not uncontroversial one. However, it is as exaggerated to regard him with contempt as 'a commonplace man of no importance, complacently living in social and cultural stagnation' (Castro, 1971D, p. 93) as it is to set him up as 'the ethical focus for the entire novel' (Mandel, 1957-8D, p. 160).[11] He is a complex figure who must be seen, above all, within his novelistic context and not just in the light of twentieth-century social likes and dislikes.

Sancho's response to Don Diego's brief account of himself is an exaggerated but not incongruous: response to the squirearchical qualities displayed (II, 16; ii, 153–4). The courtesy, generosity and other good points of Don Diego are no less evident to the reader. However, in at least two situations, his behaviour, though entirely sensible, commands something less than admiration and probably induces in most modern readers a certain sympathy for Don Quixote, despite his crazy behavior. The first is Don Diego's disapproval of his son's passion for poetry. Don Lorenzo's enthusiasm is creative, scholarly and a little ingenuous (chs. 16 and 18), but he is not at all one of those ridiculous amateurs of poetry who crop up in Cervantes's writings from time to time. The father's wish that instead he should study for a successful law career anticipates a million unromantic modern fathers. The second is Don Diego's prudence when Don Quixote insists on having the door of the lion's cage opened. Unable to dissuade the Knight from his folly, he puts himself at a safe distance, like the others (ch. 17, pp. 161–2). Nothing could be more reasonable, but there is inescapable irony in the fact that Don Diego claims hunting as his habitual exercise (ch. 16, p. 153). And it is hard not to feel a sneaking regard for Don Quixote when he tells Don Diego to attend to his docile falcon and his plucky ferret and leave this business with lions to him (ch. 17, p. 161). The Gentleman in Green really does look like an early example of the *bon bourgeois*, prudent, a bit of a philistine and, as his self-introductory speech contrives to suggest, a trifle self-satisfied in his Erasmian moderation and his complacent epicureanism.

The intense speculation engendered by the detailed description of Don Diego's mostly green clothing (ch. 16, pp. 149–50) now hardly seems warranted. It is festive enough to earn him the sobriquet of the Gentleman in the Green Coat from Don Quixote, but the outfit seems distinctive rather than exclusive. The vagaries of colour symbolism are merely confusing (see Joly, 1977D). The last word on the subject has probably not yet been said, but it is unlikely that Cervantes meant him to be such a hermeneutic target as he has become centuries later.

Don Diego de Miranda is in fact perfectly well accounted for in terms established by Don Quixote. He sees Don Diego as a 'knight about court', as distinct from himself, the knight errant out in the field and abroad in the world. His first words to him are 'Señor galán', referring to his dress, which has just been described.[12] Don Diego is not literally a courtier; on the contrary, he lives a retired life in the depth of the provinces. But it is natural enough for Don Quixote to see him this way: a knight like himself, but the inactive sort. He had pointed out the differences to his Housekeeper earlier:

and although we are all of us knights, there is a great difference between us; for courtiers, without leaving their rooms or crossing the threshold of the court, can rove round the world by studying a map, and without it costing a penny, and suffering neither heat nor cold, hunger nor thirst.

(y aunque todos seamos caballeros, va mucha diferencia de los unos a los otros; porque los cortesanos, sin salir de sus aposentos, ni de los umbrales de la corte, se pasean por todo el mundo, mirando un mapa, sin costarles blanca, ni padecer calor ni frío, hambre ni sed: II, 6; ii, 80.)

The encounter with the cartload of lions is a heaven-sent opportunity to demonstrate the difference between their roles, and our Knight seizes it eagerly. He follows up this somewhat abortive triumph with another disquisition, delivered meaningfully to Don Diego, on the difference between courtly knights and knights errant (ch. 17, pp. 166–8).[13] It is quite apparent that he is keenly conscious of these two kinds of knight, the former being a lot more abundant in this post-chivalric age. He brings up the topic on other occasions (II, 1; ii, 48, and II, 35; ii, 325). He is also echoed by the seguidilla-singing youth off to join the army, whom they meet on the road a while later. 'I'd rather have the king for lord and master and serve him in war than some hard-up fellow in the capital [*corte*]' (II, 24; ii, 227), says this 'venturesome page', whom Don Quixote also addresses as 'Señor galán', presumably on account of his courtly dress again (pp. 226–7). The parallel and contrast with Don Diego may well be intentional.

No 'story', much less any adventure, attaches directly to Don Diego de Miranda or his son. Although Don Quixote tries to romanticize him a little by calling him the Knight of the Green Coat, and the narrator follows this lead by suggesting that his home is a castle, which it is not, he is as remote from chivalric romances as the books of chivalry are from his portals (ch. 16, p. 153). His sanity and his excellent qualities are marked by an unpoetic, unheroic strain. And it is precisely this unromantic complication which makes him so interesting novelistically. With Don Diego, Cervantes opens a path leading directly to the nineteenth-century novel.

Don Quixote mad has great ideals and great illusions; Don Diego sane has ideals, we infer, but no illusions. Don Quixote ends up sane, as Alonso Quijano, with ideals intact and no illusions (and no time left to cultivate his garden). The equation between the two men is very finely balanced, and perhaps only the reader's personal predilection gives one the advantage over the other. It is hard not to take sides, though, whether it is with the equable

Don Diego, who finds in Don Quixote an object of polite curiosity, or with the visionary Don Quixote who, though overanxious to establish a superior position, succeeds in transmitting to so many readers a degree of the scorn he feels for his counterpart.

The whole episode bristles with subtleties and diverse nuances. Don Quixote argues that true valour is a virtue poised between the extremes of temerity and cowardice, but that it is better to err on the side of excess than of insufficiency, it being easier to turn prodigality into generosity than to do the same with meanness (ch. 17, p. 167). But his recent behaviour with the lion is absurd as a demonstration of this. Analogously, the way of life embodied in Don Diego, which is undoubtedly presented as a counterweight to Quixotism, is shown as having built-in limitations.[14] Don Quixote's conduct is inexcusably excessive; Don Diego's falls short of the mark. Men can have ideals without illusions, but can men without illusions be men of vision?

Cervantes never lets us forget the foolish side of the medal which has *Heroism* inscribed on the other side. Facing the lion is one of the Knight's greatest acts of physical courage. However, it is not only superfluous and anticlimactic, but significantly prefaced by an act of pure clowning, when he unwittingly empties a helmetful of curds over his head (ch. 17, p. 158). Authentic heroic impulse constantly struggles to be realized in the face of misapplied effort, intractable material circumstance and physical inadequacy. *Don Quixote* is a comedy of good intentions confounded, of ideals misdirected, lack of *discreción*, infantile regression and other things besides. But because he overdoes the noble and heroic (and they are not less so because he overdoes the imitation of heroes of chivalry), and also because he learns bit by bit from experience there is, through the zaniness of his antics something in his character to admire.

He is admirable, too, in that he never quite gives up, despite his melancholy and even if at times despair is not far off. For a time he lives with doubts about ultimate success, even before he is forced to retire. To live thus, without throwing over his ideals, takes another kind of heroism—unexciting, humdrum and perhaps more exacting than the traditional sort. It is probably what lies behind Sancho's remark when, at their homecoming, he describes him as 'defeated by another in battle, but victor over himself' (II, 72; ii, 580)— a remark his master impatiently dismisses. Don Quixote, failing hilariously to be the kind of hero he aims to be, somehow succeeds in being the ancestor of the unheroic modern hero. As Lionel Trilling saw, Joyce's Leopold Bloom, the modern Ulysses, stands in direct line of descent from him:

In the existence of both men the ordinary and actual are prepotent; both are in bondage to daily necessity and to the manifest absurdity of their bodies, and they thus stand at a polar distance from the Aristotelian hero in the superbness of his aristocratic autonomy and dignity. Yet both Bloom and Don Quixote transcend the imposed actuality to become what we, by some new definition of the word, are willing to call heroes. (1972E, p. 90)

NOTES

1. In recent years the whole problem has been confronted afresh by Anthony Close, who finds in Cervantes little or no room for approval of Don Quixote's brand of idealism, because his aims as well as his acts are presented as a 'madly literal mimicry of the stereotype behaviour of the heroes of chivalric romance' (1972D, p. 37; see also 1978[2]D, pp. 16 ff.). It is hard to see, however, why this should eliminate our, or Cervantes's, perception of the valid ideals transparently visible through Don Quixote's crazy behaviour.

2. As found in popular saws and phrases like 'moza por moza, buena es Aldonza' and 'Aldonza con perdón'.

3. J. Herrero (1981[1]D) pursues the debasement of the Dulcinea metaphor through to ultimately diabolical associations.

4. See Hughes (1977D), pp. 110 ff. By a not insignificant juxtaposition, Don Quixote's letter to Dulcinea in high chivalresque style and his promissory note for three donkeys, written in commercial jargon, occur together within the space of little more than a dozen lines in I, 25.

5. It now seems perfectly clear that the sentence beginning 'God knows if there is a Dulcinea in the world or not ...' (p. 290) has been much misinterpreted in the past, as Close (1973[1]D, p. 250) and others have pointed out.

6. See also ch. 48, p. 396, and ch. 70, p. 567.

7. Percas de Ponseti (1975D), Vol. 2, pp. 407–583. See also Barto (1923D); Forcione (1970D), pp. 137 ff.; Dunn (1972D, 1973D); Avalle-Arce (1976D), pp. 173 ff.; Hughes (1977D); Redondo (1981D); Riley (1982D).

8. Cide Hamete himself spreads the rumour that Don Quixote on his deathbed confessed to having invented the whole thing. This much misread passage contains a double qualification reducing it to mere hearsay: 'it is *held to be* true that at the end, at the time of his death, *they say* that he retracted it and said that he had invented it' ('*se tiene por* cierto que al tiempo de su fin y muerte *dicen que* se retrató della, y dijo que él la había inventado': p. 223). English translators have regularly mangled the passage, removing the uncertainty. Thus Shelton, Motteux, Cohen, Starkie. Putnam is closer. Ormsby gets it half right (see Allen, 1979D[2], p. 6).

9. Cervantes insisted on the importance of the literary absurdity being deliberate. 'How can an absurdity please, unless it is committed deliberately, guided by a seemly humour?' (*Viaje del Parnaso*, VI, 138). At the same time he was well aware that a work could in fact give pleasure and amusement for the wrong reasons—unintentionally, that is.

10. II, 26; ii, 238, and II, 29; ii, 261, and II, 62; ii, 516. On this last occasion he sees the alternatives as 'truth' and 'dream'.

11. On Don Diego, see also Bataillon (1950D), Vol. 2, pp. 417–19; Sánchez (1961-2D);

Percas de Ponseti (1975D), Vol. 2, pp. 323 ff.; Márquez Villanueva (1975D), pp. 150 ff., and (1980D), pp. 97–8; Joly (1977D); Pope (1979D).

12. 'Galán. El que anda vestido de gala y se precia de gentil hombre' (Covarrubias [1611], 1943C, s.v.).

13. His statement 'Better a knight errant aiding a widow in some deserted spot than a courtly knight wooing a damsel in the cities' (p. 167) obliquely recalls the courting of Cervantes's neighbour, the widow Doña Mariana Ramírez, by a certain Don Diego de Miranda, both of whom were implicated together with Cervantes and members of his family in the Ezpeleta incident of 27 June 1605. See McKendrick (1980B), pp. 235 ff. The possibility of some personal allusion in the figure of Don Diego in the novel cannot be discounted.

14. Though overingeniously elaborate, it seems to me, the arguments of Márquez Villanueva are basically right on this score (1975D), pp. 150 ff.

TERRENCE DOODY

Don Quixote, Ulysses,
and the Idea of Realism

Eat from my plate and drink from the vessel I drink from; for it can be said of knight errantry as of love: that it puts all things on the same level.

—*Don Quixote*, I: xi

Extremes meet.

—*Ulysses*, Circe

I

—*M*aybe, *but in realism you are down to facts on which the world is based: that sudden reality which smashes romanticism into a pulp. What makes most people's lives unhappy is some disappointed romanticism, some unrealizable or misconceived ideal. In fact you may say that idealism is the ruin of man, and if we lived down to fact, as primitive man had to do, we would be better off. That is what we are made for. Nature is quite unromantic. It is we who put romance into her, which is a false attitude, an egotism, absurd like all egotisms. In* Ulysses *I tried to keep close to fact.*

But a writer must maintain a continual struggle against the objective: that is his function. The eternal qualities are the imagination and the

---

From *Why the Novel Matters: A Postmodern Perplex.* © 1990 by Indiana University Press.

> *sexual instinct, and the formal life tries to suppress both. Out of this*
> *present conflict rise the phenomena of modern life.—In my Mabbot*
> *Street scene I approached reality closer in my opinion than anywhere else*
> *in the book except perhaps for moments in the last chapter.*

These remarks, which are quoted from Arthur Power's *Conversations with*
James Joyce, illustrate how difficult it is for anyone, even himself, to define
realism both precisely and comprehensively.[1] In the first passage, Joyce is the
Catholic, classically-tempered writer who developed the theory of
impersonality that Stephen Dedalus pronounces in *A Portrait of the Artist*; in
the second passage, he is the intensely private, openly defiant writer of a
book that managed to be both obscure and obscene. And in this passage, he
confuses the issue further by apparently contradicting himself, for nothing in
Circe seems to be like anything in Penelope. The Bunyan-like voice of Oxen
of the Sun calls Circe "the land of Phenomenon."[2] There everything is
reduced to a single level of being: the self and the world interpenetrate with
no distinction between the inner and the outer, the past and the future, the
living and the dead; clothing is costume; fantasies are immediately realized
and embodied; buttons, among other things, talk; and Joyce's style eschews
characterization and narrative in order to imitate the cinema's speed and
montage.[3] Circe doesn't seem "down to fact" in any way. Penelope, by
contrast, in its artless, unmediated representation of character has the
primitive realism of *Moll Flanders*; and by the time we get to it, after chapters
like Oxen of the Sun, Circe, and Ithaca, Penelope seems conventional.

Joyce's contradictions could be resolved, perhaps, if we knew exactly
what "moments" in Circe he refers to, but the ambivalence of his remarks is
valuable because it expresses unself-consciously the polarity that has always
been intrinsic to the idea of realism, the conflict between the world and self
that he expresses in his desire to stay "down to fact" *and* to resist the
"objective." This polarity, I think, is a fairly direct, traditional expression of
the dualism in human nature. And in English, Raymond Williams explains,
this polarity has meant that the word "real" itself, which is derived from *res*,
has always signified both the physical entity of a thing and the immaterial
principle which lies beneath or beyond mere appearances—what the thing
really is.[4] So, the history of realism has been the history of those ideas of
what *the thing* really is, those essential principles which are the norms of
being and meaning and which have changed throughout time. The course of
their change is recorded in Erich Auerbach's *Mimesis*,[5] and Auerbach's own
great sympathy for so many of these ideas allows us to accept as
uncontradictory Nietzsche's scorn for the ideal of realism—"Realism in art is

an illusion, all the writers of all the ages were convinced they were realistic"—and Harry Levin's praise for its practice and moral purpose—"for all great writers, in so far as they are committed to a searching and scrupulous critique of life as they know it, may be reckoned among the realists."[6]

The novel has flourished in this ambivalence, at least since *Don Quixote,* because it is the fox, not the hedgehog, who wants to write a novel.[7] In *Don Quixote,* at the end of Part I, the Canon makes two long statements which pose in Renaissance terms a parallel to the remarks about realism Joyce made to Power. The first passage is the Canon's own injunction against the egotism of the writer which produces distortions and romance. Like Joyce, the Canon invokes the norm of nature; unlike Joyce, however, he can still invoke a community of taste which makes the reader's own experience a standard of realism as well.

> *"If you reply that the men who compose such books write them as fiction, and so are not obliged to look into fine points or truths, I should reply that the more it resembles the truth the better the fiction, and the more probable and possible it is, the better it pleases. Fictions have to match the minds of their readers, and to be written in such a way that, by tempering the impossibilities, moderating excesses, and keeping judgement in the balance, they may so astonish, hold, excite, and entertain, that wonder and pleasure go hand in hand. None of this can be achieved by anyone departing from verisimilitude or from that imitation of nature in which lies the perfection of all that is written. I have never seen a book of chivalry with a whole body for a plot, with all its limbs complete...."*[8]

This corporeal metaphor for a book's integrity is important because it affirms the physical norm of reality that Sancho uses to oppose the Don's romantic ascesis; and it looks toward one of Joyce's designs for keeping *Ulysses* "down to fact" by organizing the themes of each chapter according to a part of the body. The Canon also anticipates Joyce by apparently contradicting himself and defending the epic for the expressive latitude it gives the writer.

> *Yet he continued that, for all that he had said against such books, he found one good thing in them: the fact that they offered a good intellect a chance to display itself. For they presented a broad and spacious field through which the pen could run without let or hindrance, describing shipwrecks, tempests, encounters and battles; painting a brave captain with all the features necessary for the part; ... now depicting a tragic and*

lamentable incident, now a joyful and unexpected event; here a most
beautiful lady, chaste, intelligent, and modest; there a Christian knight,
valiant and gentle; in one place a monstrous, barbarous braggart; ...
Sometimes the writer might show his knowledge of astrology, or his
excellence at cosmography or as a musician, ... and he might even have
an opportunity of showing his skill in necromancy. He could portray the
subtlety of Ulysses, the piety of Aeneas, the valour of Achilles, ... and, in
fact, all those attributes which constitute the perfect hero, sometimes
placing them in one single man, at other times dividing them amongst
many.... the loose plan of these books gives the author an opportunity of
showing his talent for the epic, the lyric, the tragic and the comic, and
all the qualities contained in the most sweet and pleasing sciences of
poetry and rhetoric; for the epic may be written in prose as well as in
verse. (426)

This is a more generic, more modern theory, and even a description of
many aspects of *Ulysses*. But this is only an accidental connection between
two novels which are connected in so many other, more essential ways that
they can stand as a beginning and an end of the realistic tradition of the
novel. They share what all novels have: a definitive interest in the experience
of the individual in a particular time and place; but they also share an unusual
self-consciousness of their own relation to literature, a variety of styles that
establishes a complicated satire, and a concern for the semantic distance
between the word and the thing it names.[9] Moreover, they suggest a general
definition of realism, a generic idea, that is pertinent to explore because it
contains three propositions about the novel which we must continue to
acknowledge in our effort to establish the novel's poetics.[10] These
propositions are that the novel is a thing—not the author's self expression so
much as it is an object in its own right; that this kind of objective artifact
entails the notion of an impersonal artist; and, most important, that the
novelist who wants to create a thing and remain impersonal will necessarily
be willing to undermine, distribute, or share his own authority in order to
define his meaning by the proposal of a consensus rather than by an appeal
to some superior or antecedent norm. This last proposition also implies that
the author will not even try to rely on the authority of the genre he uses, that
he will try to say this thing is not merely a novel.

Not every realistic novel will embody all of these propositions as clearly
as *Don Quixote* and *Ulysses* do; and, in fact, not even *Don Quixote* and *Ulysses*
embody all of them in the same way. In making the case I want to make about
the idea of realism, it is not necessary to argue that *Ulysses* was intended as a
thing because this is an idea about it we have acknowledged for some time.

It is interesting and necessary, however, to show the reason *Don Quixote* is intended as a thing, just as it is to define the kind of realism in Joyce that can be taken for granted in Cervantes. The incongruity of even these two novels, moreover, is perfectly fitting, for the idea of realism that I want to define has to do with a novel's internal relationships and does not point to any particular consensus that all novels seek—not to the pastoral idea of harmony that John Loofbourow sees as the ground of the Anglo-American novel, and not merely to the rhetorical consensus that Wayne C. Booth recognizes in the meeting of every implied author and his reader.[11] The consensus the realistic novel looks to is broader because it is one that tries to acknowledge the world's plurality and to give everything its due.

Another way of saying this, which does apply to every novel, is that realism achieves its objectivity by recognizing the inviolable subjectivity of all its human characters, the potentially equal value and authority of every individual, the possibility of another point of view. Cervantes himself establishes a model of this attitude by giving his protagonist a partner who is quite different but ambiguously equal and not a mate.[12] The fact that the Don and Sancho (like Stephen and Bloom) cannot resolve their differences sexually is important. For sexual couples like Elizabeth Bennet and Darcy, or Mr. and Mrs. Ramsay, can embody the problem of knowledge at the heart of realism, but pairs of partners can keep these epistemological issues open and unaccommodated by emotional and institutional resolutions like marriage. So, the general narrator of *Bleak House* is a more equal and interesting partner to Esther Summerson than Allan Woodcourt or even Inspector Bucket is; and the tragedy of Anna Karenina seems harsher or more significant than Emma Bovary's because Anna is paired with Levin and set against his reasonably successful, open quest for life's meaning. Pairs of partners keep a balance, an open equilibrium, that resists both identification and an absolute.

This equilibrium is at the center of the generic idea of realism that *Don Quixote* and *Ulysses* together suggest: realism is the idea that man and the world exist in a relationship of intelligibility. Under this idea, things are meaningful in themselves; they do not refer for their significance to some higher or ulterior principle; they are, rather, immediately accessible to man's intelligence and amenable to the meaning he discovers and creates. The idea of realism does not depend upon a particular ontological program, and it does not assume any particular theory of human character or knowledge. What this idea of realism does demand, though, is that the concept of character be commensurate with the theory of things. An imbalance in this relationship means that it is no longer realistic, that the literary situation is something else. For things which are not meaningful in themselves, or are not fully intelligible to man, but which embody some superior force or principle, such things are part of a relationship that is deterministic. There are deterministic principles that are religious and there are those that are secular, and the difference between them can be illustrated by Kafka's "The Metamorphosis." This story maintains all of the surface decorum we expect of realistic narrative, but the principle of Gregor Samsa's transformation is never defined. If the reader decides the principle is religious in any way, then "The Metamorphosis" can be read as an allegory; if, however, the principle is secular, then things have the opacity or hostility we call naturalistic or absurd. Perhaps the most terrifying way of taking the story is in insisting that it is realistic and that there is no ulterior principle which explains it at all.

On the other hand, things which are not meaningful in themselves because they are empty of intrinsic significance, or which have meaning only in man's presence and by his agency, and which offer no limits to his freedom, these things are the props of romance: like the moon in most lyric poems or the paper money is printed on. These things often figure in mythic narratives and in allegories of another kind, and they usually have a different relationship to time than the constituents of realism do. For the fact that things and men exist through time is also definitive of realism. Because things grow, change, decay, they can never be completely known because they can never be known at once; nor can man's intelligence claim any absolute authority when it is changing as the world is. So time itself, under this idea of realism, is the only absolute in so far as it is the ultimate limit of both knowledge and freedom: within time are the "imprevidibilities" of change,[13] beyond it the mystery of death.

The advantage of this idea of realism is that it is not limited to any particular metaphysics, nor to the *style* of realism of any particular nation or era; and it does not posit any single organizing idea of its own except that of the world's intelligibility to man's cognate intelligence, so it tries not to harbor any hierarchies. (And it is not perfect.) Harry Levin's elegant formulations clearly apply to the French novel more aptly than to the English; and Ian Watt's ideas of the eighteenth-century British novel work for much of the nineteenth-century British novel too, but the empiricism and rational psychology he uses to define Defoe and Richardson do not apply to Fielding exactly, much less to Dickens, and not at all to their modern heirs like Joyce and Lawrence who must include in their conception of character the unconscious. Yet Joyce and Lawrence, like Woolf and Faulkner, all now seem to us to be realistic, in at least the honorific sense in which we use that word, and it is important to realize that what once seemed strange, now seems true. And it does seem true because our sense of the world has changed with the changes in our sense of human nature. So, Lawrence's famous letter to Edward Garnett is an important example of the way in which character, the "old stable ego," can be redefined in a realistic way according to principles the author sees in the natural world, in things; as part of the world, the ego can have its deeper, allotropic states just as carbon can.[14] It has become a truism to remark that a scientific theory of the unconscious was developed in the same generation that physicists developed theories of relativity and quantum mechanics. But it is important to remark as well that as man has displaced more and more of the external world into himself, as he has seen more deeply into his own mind and nature, he has also discovered a greater depth and complexity in matter; and in both places, the center of the atom and the center of the unconscious, the laws of time are the same. Neither one is subject to the traditional, "realistic" sense that time is linear and mechanical, and in neither place is the *field* of time eternal.

The literary history of this appropriation of the world by the mind Erich Kahler has called "the inward turn of narrative," but this inward turn can also be figured as a fall. In Northrop Frye's scheme, it is the descent from the mythic and romantic through the high and low mimetic to the ironic; for John Loofbourow, the shift is described in our belief that now the natural man is more authentic than the god or king.[15] Yet whatever nostalgia we may feel for what we have supposedly lost, the idea of realism tried to compensate in the sense that we are also growing less estranged from the world we really occupy. In Stevens' words, we may be descending "downward to darkness, on extended wings," but

> *The sky will be much friendlier then than now,*
> *A part of labor and a part of pain,*
> *And next in glory to enduring love,*
> *Not this dividing and indifferent blue.*

II

Ulysses is at first hard to read because it is so thoroughly realistic; we are not prepared for an ordinary mind like Bloom's to be so spacious, nor for a world as small as DEAR DIRTY DUBLIN to be so rich in significant detail. Telemachus is a relatively easy, naturalistic beginning; the difficulties in Nestor are the ironic result of the characters' self-involvement; in Proteus, however, we begin to see the essence of the equilibrium that Joyce wants to maintain, his position that a human character is most himself not in any social relationship, but alone with his thoughts of the world. Stephen is the most alert and articulate exponent of this position because he is himself in the process of figuring it out, and his most dramatic attention to the world's readiness comes in the opening paragraphs of Proteus, when he is fully alone for the first time.

> *Ineluctable modality of the visible: at least that if no more, thought through my eyes. Signatures of all things I am here to read, seaspawn and seawrack, the nearing tide, that rusty boot....*
>
> *Open your eyes now. I will. One moment. Has all vanished since? If I open and art forever in tire black adiaphane. Basta! I will see if I can see.*
>
> *See now. There all the time without you: and ever shall be, world without end.* (37)

The facts that must be "lived down to" here are both elemental and trivial, "the nearing tide, that rusty boot"; but the incomplete, unaffirmed allusion to the liturgy, "and ever shall be, world without end," suggests that a world endless in time is not finally determined in meaning, that the signatures he is here to read are not a holy code.

In fact, the only other determinant of meaning, balanced against a world meaningful in itself, is what we might call the ineluctable modality of the individual which Stephen formulates later in Scylla and Charybdis. This is the subjective complement of knowledge, the way in which the self imposes the meaning it may otherwise think it discovers, and also a principle which explains the individual self's variety, its own complement to the world's endless detail.

> *He found in the world without as actual what was in his world within as possible. Maeterlinck says*: If Socrates leave his house today he will find the sage seated on his doorstep. If Judas go forth tonight it is to Judas his steps will tend. *Every life is many days, day after day. We walk through ourselves, meeting robbers, ghosts, giants, old men, young men, wives, widows, brothers-in-love. But always meeting ourselves.* (213)

Scylla and Charybdis, in its examination of theories of art, contains a number of ideas about the nature of *Ulysses*—explicitly in Stephen's theory of Shakespeare, implicitly in his theory of the incertitude of paternity and its relation to artistic creation (207), and offhandedly in such remarks as: "They remind one of don Quixote and Sancho Panza. Our national epic has yet to be written, Dr. Sigerson says" (192). Moreover, it contains even more explicitly than Proteus does Stephen's realization that the equilibrium he must maintain between the self and world is a relationship that exists in time.

His opponents, like AE, insist that we are eternal essences and that the truth is too; against such an idealism, Stephen has to assert that his personal identity is temporal, that it is continuous despite its changes, and that it is not totally subject to mere circumstance. He says:

> *Wait. Five months. Molecules all change. I am other I now. Other I got pound.*
>
> *Buzz. Buzz.*
>
> *But I, entelechy, form of forms, am I by memory because under everchanging forms.* (189)

And later he adds: "As we, or mother Dana, weave or unweave our bodies, ... so does the artist weave or unweave his image.... that which I was is that which I am and that which in possibility I may come to be" (194). As part of this intuition Stephen also realizes he is both the agent and the patient of his own life, and he says: "Act. Be acted on" (211), which on this day in particular is an important and complicated pair of imperatives. As W.J. Harvey says: "Novels which portray roughly the same equipoise between Self and World, which achieve the effect of conditional freedom that I have described, we may call realistic."[16]

Bloom states his own version of these fundamental principles of the idea of realism more laconically. He is less abstract than Stephen and more accommodated to the conditions of life, and much of what Stephen comes to formulate in a debate in the library Bloom arrives at on his way to lunch in Lestrygonians. The realistic relationship of intelligibility, which is subject to the changes of both man and the world in time, Bloom almost sums up in the word "Parallax" (154). His sense of his own identity he debates with: "I was happier then. Or was that I? Or am I now I? ... Am I like that? See ourselves as others see us" (168, 169). This kind of distance on himself is a maturity or discipline that Stephen is not quite capable of, for he feels himself this day in too much pain, and he thinks, later in Wandering Rocks: "Stop! Throb always without you and the throb always within. Your heart you sing of. I between them. Where? Between two roaring worlds where they swirl, I. Shatter them, one and both. But stun myself too in the blow. Shatter me you who can. Bawd and butcher, were the words. I say! Not yet awhile" (242). Stephen's reversion to religious belief for an Apocalyptic solution to his problem is not in keeping with the realism of *Ulysses'* first half, but it is appropriate to Wandering Rocks' overture to the second half and a clear foreshadowing of the moment in Circe when he smashes the chandelier with his ashplant and screams "*Nothung!*" (583). Bloom keeps a better balance between the human and the divine when he brackets his very poignant realization, "Me. And me now" (176), between his memory of the moment on Howth when he and Molly passed the seedcake to each other, a moment she will remember in Penelope, and his resolution to investigate later at the library whether or not goddesses have anuses.[17]

The first half of *Ulysses* ends with the meeting of Bloom and Stephen on the library steps. Bloom has seen Stephen from the carriage in the Hades chapter, which is appropriate to the epic convention by which the hero foresees his future in his trip to the underworld.[18] But their actual meeting here is more important because it establishes them consciously in each other's world and predicts their common future. The scene begins in Stephen's mind as he is trying once again to get away from Mulligan:

> *Part. The moment is now. Where then? If Socrates leave his house today, if Judas go forth tonight. Why? That lies in space which I in time must come to, ineluctably.*
>
> *My will: his will that fronts me. Seas between.*
>
> *A man passed out between them, bowing, greeting,*
>
> —*Good day again*, Buck Mulligan said.
>
> *The portico.*
>
> *Here I have watched the birds for augury. Aengus of the birds. They go, they come. Last night I flew. Easily flew. Men wondered. Street of harlots after. A cream-fruit melon he held to me. In. You will see.*
>
> —*The wandering jew*, Buck Mulligan whispered.... (217)

Stephen's ironic prophecy that in meeting himself that night he will meet Bloom, "ineluctably," anticipates the narrative that will join them in Oxen of the Sun and keep them together until Stephen leaves from 7 Eccles Street in Ithaca. It also anticipates the elaborate rapprochement in Ithaca, where they become Stoom and Blephen (682), which parodies in the style of the catechism all of the realistic balances the novel sets up, all the symmetries between the mind and the world that the second half of the novel questions by its variety of styles. But most important here is the manifestation that Bloom and Stephen have had the same dream about an encounter in the street of harlots (see also 57 and 381). Molly will participate in this dream herself, both in the fantasia of Circe (439) and also in her monologue in Penelope (780). Now, the fact they have all had this dream seems to be more significant than the coincidence of Throwaway's victory that makes Bloom seem a prophet, and it also seems to be of another order of being than the interpenetrations of Circe. In fact, their common dream suggests that the isolation each one of them feels in Proteus, Lestrygonians, and Penelope is not inescapable. While this isolation is fostered and reinforced by the stream-of-consciousness style that works best in a character's solitude, it is a style that also recognizes the independence of the world. And since the world itself contains other minds, its complete meaning has to come from a consensus in which others are acknowledged as equals and then joined. In *Ulysses,* not even in dreams can the individual alone claim authority, even for himself.

In *Don Quixote,* dreams are equally important, but in a different way. *Don Quixote* is a book about books, so Cervantes assumes a stability about the world in order to measure certain questions of perception, which Joyce treats as resolved so that he, in turn, can use them to look back at the world. There is nothing in *Don Quixote* like the opening of Proteus because there does not have to be, and there is no book in *Ulysses* like Amadís de Gaul's or the texts of chivalry. When Don Quixote reads the windmills as giants, there is no question about his mistake; when Bloom walks through the meticulously recorded Dublin of 1904, there is no question he is also *lisant au livre de lui-meme* (187). Bloom, therefore, would never have the kind of problem the Don has with the dream he has had in the Cave of Montesinos.

This experience is a singular adventure for the Don because it is not an illusion or "enchantment," but the one experience he has by himself which no one else witnesses and he cannot rationalize. Yet he is bothered by it so much that he seeks a confirmation for it later, a kind of consensus, when he tries to get Sancho to equate his experience in the cave with Sancho's own experience on the wooden horse Clavileno: "Sancho, if you want me to believe what you saw in the sky, I wish you to accept my account of what I saw in the Cave of Montesinos. I say no more" (735). The modesty of the favor the Don requests makes Sancho's refusal even more painful; for Sancho's story of what he saw in the sky, which plays the height of vision off the depth of dream here, is an elaborate, obsequious fabrication, designed to appeal to the Duke and Duchess who are toying with Don Quixote. Sancho could only have learned to make up a story like this from the Don himself, and telling it makes him a fool in the eyes of the Court. The Don, however, is as simple and abashed as Sancho usually is, with no realization that his real dream is very different from Sancho's fake apology. And the dream remains so important to him that it is the only experience of his life that he repudiates on his deathbed (624), where it still seems to him a perversion because it was so authentically private and so unaccommodated by the conventions of chivalry under which he had organized the meaning of his life. His dream is a real experience, but Don Quixote has no idea by which he can "naturalize" it. It is his great irony that he always prefers the apparently realistic, as the convention of chivalry would define it, to the actually real.

Don Quixote makes its essential propositions about the idea of realism by making a continual inquiry into the differences between the real and the realistic, the thing itself and the ideas by which any thing is given meaning, value, or representation. The barber's basin which becomes the helmet of Mambrino is an obvious counterpoint to the adventure in the Cave of Montesinos, for it is an example of a consensus too easily arrived at, a convention too obviously discrepant with individual perception.[19] In order to gull the Don and have some fun with the barber whose basin it is, the priest and the barber from La Mancha, Don Cardenio, Don Ferdinand, and his companions all agree that the basin is Mambrino's helmet. The incredulous barber says:

> 'Well, if this basin is a helmet, then, this pack-saddle must be a horse's harness, as this gentleman said.'
> 'It looks like a pack-saddle to me,' said Don Quixote, 'but, as I have already said, I am not interfering in that.'
> 'Whether it is a pack-saddle or a harness,' said the priest, 'Don Quixote has only to say; for in these matters of chivalry, all these gentlemen and myself defer to him.' (404)

This scene shows the way in which a false consensus or a merely social consensus can become tyranny. It shows too what the Don loses when he does not have his usual passionate belief in what he is doing. When he has discussed the helmet of Mambrino earlier, on his own initiative and according to his own principles, he offers an explanation of its mysterious variety that does not denigrate the potential good faith of anyone involved.

> "Is it possible that all this while you have been with me you have not discovered that everything to do with knights errant appears to be chimaera, folly and nonsense, and to all go contrariwise? This is not really the case, but there is a crew of enchanters always amongst us who change and alter all our deeds, and transform them according to their pleasure and their desire either to favour us or to injure us. So what seems to you to be a barber's basin appears to me to be Mambrino's helmet, and to another as something else. It shows a rare foresight in the sage who is on my side to make what is really and truly Mambrino's helmet seem to everyone a basin." (204)

The Don's explanation of the sage's foresight is not only one of the ways in which viewpoints other than his own are acknowledged, it is also one of those moments when the characters inside the book talk about the book itself, as though they actually are antecedent to it and independent: historical persons before they have become realistic characters.

This trespass across ontological frontiers first occurs when Sancho calls Don Quixote the Knight of the Sad Countenance. He explains that "your worship has lately got the most dismal face I have ever seen. It must be either from weariness after the battle or from your worship's losing his teeth."

> *'It is from neither,' replied Don Quixote, 'but because the sage whose task it is to write the history of my deeds must have thought it right for me to take some title, as all knights did in the olden days.... That is why I say that the sage I mentioned has put it into your thoughts and into your mouth to call me now* The Knight of the Sad Countenance.'
> (147)

What is wonderful about this preposterous explanation is that it is true.[20] It does not obviate Sancho's explanation, which is also true in another way. And these complementary truths promote, even comically, the claim that the full truth of *Don Quixote* resides in its proposal of a consensus that does not violate anyone's individual perception or refer to only one source of authority. Not even to Cervantes himself, who is and is not the sage, for he treats the book as Don Quixote treats the book—as a thing apart from himself, an object.

For the Don, the history the sage writes is an objectification of his most fantastic ideas of himself, his most subjective longings; and this reification that confirms the meaning of his life as a knight errant is the necessary premise on which Part II becomes possible. Part I is picaresque and centrifugal: Don Quixote wanders out to encounter the world. Part II is centripetal and more realistic: it criticizes the false history written as a sequel to Part I, and it presents the Don as a celebrity whom others now seek out. Although he has an itinerary, which includes the Cave of Montesinos, in Part II the world comes to Don Quixote to enter the circle of enchantment that he has created by the intensity of his own idea of himself. And however ironic or condescending they are about their motives to be included in the next installment of the history, figures like the Duke and Duchess confirm the Don's idea of himself by playing his game on his field. Their court is not the Cave.

By the same token, the *thingness* of *Don Quixote* itself, its existence as a text or object, guarantees Cervantes that his fiction is not like the Don's self-delusions and uncertifiable dreams, and Cervantes goes to some lengths to reify his book in order to distance himself from creatures he does not claim. Cide Hamete Benengeli is always presented as the author of this history; and between Cide Hamete and Cervantes, who says he is its "step-father" (and who acts like its "stylist"), there are at least two translators, one of whom is hired on the spot when Cervantes finds a part of the manuscript in the Alacana at Toledo (76). This fragment contains pictures of Don Quixote and Rocinante (77), and Cervantes gives the manuscript even greater historicity by including himself within it as the author of *Galatea* (62) and as the almost unidentified heroic rebel of "The Captive's Tale" (355). In this way, Don Quixote is given the same ontological status Cervantes has as an historical figure, and the various narrators of the interpolated tales, the translators and commentators Cervantes is always referring to as his sources, are treated as his equals too, for they have become his collaborators. They are to Cervantes what the Duke and Duchess are to the Don: confirmation that *Don Quixote* is more like a windmill than a giant, a thing rather than a romance.

In *Cervantes's Theory of the Novel*, E.C. Riley says: "Cervantes handles his work in such a way as to show his complete control over the creation he tries so hard to make seem independent."[21] But Cervantes' control is not what is most interesting here: it is exactly what we expect from art. What is interesting is his effort to make it seem not *his*, to resolve his artistry away and make his book seem life's. This is the effect, I think, of reading Penelope after the self-conscious *literature* of the preceding chapters: in Molly's artless words, Joyce gives his book back to life. And the attitude he shares with Cervantes, that a univocal authority is less valuable and true than the experience of multiplicity, is at the heart of their common idea of realism.

III

In *The Situation of Poetry*, Robert Pinsky claims that the tradition of the "persona," "a borrowed voice or alter-identity, as speaker or central character partly distinct from the poet, constitutes one of the most widely-noted, perhaps overemphasized, critically chewed, and fundamental aspects of modernism.... And 'the speaker' as a method stands in clear logical relation to the modernist goal of moving the poem away from the abstraction of statement, toward the being of an object."[22] It seems, however, that this idea of impersonality is, generally, a *modern* idea, which is not limited merely to modernism and which has been a natural resource and goal of realistic novelists since the time of Cervantes. Yet I don't think it is over-emphasized because it is an idea that has had so many different intentions. Joyce, for instance, seems to have wanted the pervasive, invisible, God-like presence of the dramatist, whereas Eliot wanted both an escape from emotion and a discipline before he got religion. But Yeats wanted to complete or fulfill his identity in the "double" or "anti-self" he defines in "Ego Dominus Tuus," and Wallace Stevens, in poems like "The Snow Man," wanted to keep himself from solipsism and anthropomorphic distortions by maintaining a perfect metonymic balance with the landscape.[23] One of the most interesting versions of the idea was Brecht's, who had the impersonality of the ideologue to add to that of the dramatist, but who also wanted to impose it as a condition on the audience. Still, Wayne C. Booth's objections to the idea of impersonality are given an unintended ratification in the claim Hugh Kenner makes that Pound practiced translation to purge "the contingencies of a personality partly private (Hailey, Idaho; Hamilton College), partly public (the legacy of Rossetti, the emotional climate of 1900–12) but in any case irrelevant to the fullness of poetic achievement."[24] This is a fairly ruthless formulation that suggests a personality purged of its contingencies and therefore reduced to its *necessary* reality may be capable of authenticity and objectivity only at the physiological level.[25] A much more humane defense of the ideal comes from Marx, in the "Economic and Philosophical Manuscripts," when he explains how the objectification of the self in a piece of work not only confirms the self, but affirms as well its essentially communal nature.

> *Supposing that we had produced in a human manner; each of us would in his production have doubly affirmed himself and his fellow men. I would have: (1) objectified in my production my individuality and its peculiarity and thus both in my activity enjoyed an individual expression of my life and also in looking at the object have had the individual pleasure of realizing that my personality was objective, visible to the senses and thus a power raised beyond all doubt. (2) In your enjoyment of use of my product I would have had the direct enjoyment of realizing that I had both satisfied a human need by my work and also objectified the human essence and therefore fashioned for another human being the object that met his need. (3) I would have been for you the mediator between you and the species and thus been acknowledged and felt by you as a completion of your own essence and a necessary part of yourself and have thus realized that I am confirmed both in your thought and in your love. (4) In my expression of my life I would have fashioned your expression of your life, and thus in my own activity have realized my own essence, my human, my communal essence.*[26]

We do not have to claim for this passage that it contains a theory of reading in order to say that it implies a condition of the novel that we often ignore: whereas poems are often songs, and plays are performances, novels are things we must hold in our hands to read. And in such a thing, Marx argues, is objectified not only the individual being of the writer and reader, but also what Marx calls the "species-being" of each: not only the singularity of an

individual identity, but its intrinsic multiplicity as well. This notion of the
self's variety is important to the idea of realism and its proposal of a
consensus because it means that the writer who does not want to speak *in
propria persona* is not confined to a single other voice and that the voices he
does use are not merely prosthetic devices, but real extensions of himself,
part of his human nature. When Don Quixote says:

> '*I know who I am, ... and I know, too, that I am capable of being not
> only the characters I have named, but all the Twelve Peers of France
> and all the Nine Worthies as well, for my exploits are far greater than
> all the deeds they have done, all together and each by himself,*' (54)

he gives a comic correlative to Cervantes' use of so many different
translators, commentators, and narrators; and he emphasizes that both he
and his author are distributing themselves throughout their various roles
quite deliberately and responsibly. Not all the role-playing in *Don Quixote* is
so responsible; in fact, the moral lesson of one of the longest and best of the
interpolated tales, "The Tale of Foolish Curiosity," is that the actor must
guard against being overtaken by his act, that he must not lose himself.

This moral aspect of role-playing is not a problem for Joyce. The
variety of his obvious presence throughout the second half of *Ulysses*, after his
magisterial invisibility throughout all the first half but Aeolus, is an easy
demonstration of one of the principles of modernism Stevens epitomizes in
the "Adagio": "A change of style is a change of subject."[27] The pun on
subject is important, of course, but it should not distract us from the fact that
Joyce's virtuosity expresses quite directly his sense of what it means to be
human. When he discussed the Ulysses theme with Frank Budgen and
George Borach, he emphasized both Ulysses' *humanity* and his *fullness*, the
variety of his roles, until the two seemed to mean the same thing. This long
passage, which Richard Ellmann quotes from Borach's journal, should recall
to us both the Canon's remarks in *Don Quixote* about the expressive latitude
the epic offers a writer and Stephen's remarks in Scylla and Charybdis that
"We walk through ourselves, meeting robbers, ghosts, giants, old men,
young men, wives, widows, brothers-in-love. But always meeting ourselves."

J. J. thinks:
'*The most beautiful, all-embracing theme is that of the Odyssey. It is
greater, more human, than that of* Hamlet, Don Quixote, *Dante,*
Faust. *The rejuvenation of old Faust has an unpleasant effect upon me.
Dante tires one quickly, it is like looking at the suit. The most beautiful,
most human traits are contained in the* Odyssey. *I was twelve years old*

when we took up the Trojan War at school; only the Odyssey *stuck in my memory. I want to be frank; at twelve I liked the supernaturalism in* Ulysses. *When I was writing* Dubliners *I intended at first to choose the title* Ulysses *in Dublin, but gave up the idea. In Rome, when I had finished about half the* Portrait, *I realized that the Odyssey had to be the sequel, and I began to write* Ulysses.

'*Why was I always returning to this theme? Now* in mezzo del cammin *I find the subject of* Ulysses *the most human in world literature. Ulysses didn't want to go off to Troy; he knew that the official reason for the war, the dissemination of the culture of Hellas, was only a pretext for the Greek merchants, who were seeking new markets. When the recruiting officers arrived, he happened to be plowing. He pretended to be mad. Thereupon they placed his little two-year-old son in the furrow. Observe the beauty of the motifs: the only man in Hellas who is against the war, and the father. Before Troy the heroes shed their life-blood in vain. They want to raise the siege. Ulysses opposes the idea. [He thinks up] the strategem of the wooden horse. After Troy there is no further talk of Achilles, Menelaus, Agamemnon. Only one man is not done with; his heroic career has hardly begun: Ulysses.*

'*Then the motif of wandering. Scylla and Charybdis—what a splendid parable. Ulysses is also a great musician; he wishes to and must listen; he has himself tied to the mast. The motif of the artist, who will lay down his life rather than renounce his interest. Then the delicious humor of Polyphemus. "Outis is my name." On Naxos, the oldster of fifty, perhaps baldheaded, with Nausicaa, a girl who is barely seventeen. What a fine theme! And the return, how profoundly human! Don't forget the trait of generosity at the interview with Ajax in the nether world, and many other beautiful touches. I am almost afraid to treat such a theme; it's overwhelming.*'

"It is not surprising," Ellmann comments, "that Joyce's description of Ulysses as pacifist, father, wanderer, musician, and artist, ties the hero's life closely to his own."[28] I think it is no coincidence, either, that a writer so noted for his impersonality would appreciate in a character so favored for his multiplicity the statement, "Outis is my name." For the tie between Joyce and Ulysses that is most important is the one between Ulysses as a model and Joyce as the creator of Bloom. It is obvious we are supposed to see Bloom as a father and a son, husband and lover, pacifist, wanderer, inventor, companion, figure of the artist, and good gentle man. It is also important we see him eating and sleeping, going in Calypso and coming in Nausicaa, at work and at large, through his own eyes and through the eyes of other

Dubliners. For in seeing him through Joyce's eyes, we often see him as he cannot see himself, in Sirens and Oxen of the Sun, for instance, as well as in Circe and Ithaca. These seem not to be realistic chapters in the way Nausicaa and Penelope are because there is in them no more equilibrium between Bloom's intelligence and the intelligibility of the world he is in. He "contains" Lestrygonians beautifully; it is, in fact, one of the novel's great chapters because so much is said so artlessly. But there is no way he can be said to contain even his own identity in Oxen of the Sun, nor that even his unconscious can hold all the phenomena of Circe. And were he allowed somehow to read *Ulysses*, there are parts he would not be able to recognize as his own experience as well as even more parts, probably, that he simply wouldn't get.[29]

This same lack of comprehension can be attributed to many other characters central to the modern novel, yet these characters, like Lawrence's Brangwens or Faulkner's Bundren family, do not now seem unrealistic to us. We have grown to accept them, and other characters like them, as we have grown to accept ideas about human nature that exclude parts of our being from our own self-consciousness or aspects of our most basic experience from the reach of language. In doing so, we have also come to accept the necessity of omniscient authors who make no final claims for their omniscience, who in fact try to disguise or deny it by dealing it away. No one has done this more adamantly than Faulkner has, except Joyce, perhaps, throughout the chapters of *Ulysses'* second half. Whether we want to say that the different styles of Sirens and Circe amount to different "characters" of the narrative (as the narrator of Cyclops in particular seems to be), or that they are rather different aspects of Joyce himself, which I think is simpler and makes more sense, the fact remains that no one of them is given a superior claim. The style of Sirens is not truer than the style of Cyclops; the prose of Nausicaa is not less "Joycean" than that of his favorite chapter, Ithaca. Joyce does not distribute himself throughout Moorish historians and interpolated raconteurs, but he achieves the same value by adopting for himself a series of identities in *Ulysses* as easily, as fluently, as Stephen adopts new identities for himself in Proteus, with little more but with nothing less than the change of style that amounts to a change of subject.[30] Not every one of these last nine chapters of Ulysses is realistic by any definition, but all the chapters together are faithful to realism's commitment to the truth based upon a consensus of equal individual principles. And while it would be hard to draw a simple consensus from what these last nine chapters say about the self and the world, it is easier now to grant that when Joyce said, "In my Mabbot Street scene, I approached reality closer in my opinion than anywhere else in the book except perhaps for moments in the last chapter," he was defining his idea of realism quite exactly:

posing his opinion at the moment against the objectified body of his work and one of his styles against another, claiming nothing absolute for any of them, and leaving an exact definition of "reality" just out of reach.

IV

The polarity intrinsic to the idea of realism, the equilibrium that realistic novels try to maintain, is a recognition of the essentially equal but contending claims that issue from, and yet also bind together, the self and the world, the author and his work, one character and another, the narrator and the reader, readers and their experience. In order to acknowledge all of these relationships and to give them a form, Cervantes and Joyce, who represent a beginning and an end of the novel's most self-conscious tradition, each tried to present his novel as a thing; and then from this thing, each also tried to efface himself in order not to impose a single standard of authoritative meaning. In doing so, each has distributed himself among many different points of view, which is the literary strategy by which they recognize both the great variety of human experience and the possible multiplicity within each individual self. Meaning, they propose, arises from a consensus; identity, they imply, is actually legion. In doing this, they demonstrate how important the anti-authoritarian nature of realism has been to the modern world, and they explain why the correlative of narrative impersonality has been the idea of selflessness that moved Lionel Trilling to call the novel "the literary form to which the emotions of understanding and forgiveness were indigenous, as if by definition of the form."[31] Realism evokes selflessness as an ideal because it is so essentially committed to the value of individuality, to the fullness and freedom of every individual, that it can also comprehend its own limit. For this reason, if for no other, the idea of realism is still necessary to maintain and defend in a world where things and other ideas proliferate so rapidly that a single governing idea, a univocal system of any kind, is seductively restful, reductive, annihilating. There is about the idea of realism a modesty that characterizes Bloom's deference to Stephen and Sancho's to the Don, but this same modesty promotes their survival and suggests that these two shall inherit the world where, as William Carlos Williams says,

> *so much depends*
> *upon*
>
> *a red wheel*
> *barrow*

glazed with rain
water

beside the white
chickens.

NOTES

1. *Conversations with James Joyce*, ed. Clive Hart (London: Millington, Ltd., 1974), pp. 98 and 74–75.

2. *Ulysses* (New York: Random House-Vintage Books, 1961), p. 395. All further citations in the text.

3. A thorough discussion of Circe's anti-realism is contained in Marilyn French, *The Book as World: James Joyce's Ulysses* (Cambridge, Massachusetts, and London, England: Harvard University Press, 1976), pp. 185–206. See also Hugh Kenner, "Circe," *James Joyce's Ulysses*, ed. Clive Hart and David Hayman (Berkeley, Los Angeles, London: University of California Press, 1974), pp. 341–362, for a very discriminating study of the chapter's styles and what actually happens. Also interesting are Alain Robbe-Grillet's remarks about the cinema's influence on prose fiction, in "Time and Description in Fiction Today," *For a New Novel: Essays on Fiction*, trans. Richard Howard (New York: Grove Press, Inc., 1965), pp. 149 and 151.

4. *Keywords: A Vocabulary of Culture and Society* (New York: Oxford University Press, 1976), pp. 216–220.

5. *Mimesis*, trans. Willard Trask (Garden City, N.Y.: Doubleday-Anchor, Inc., 1957). See pp. 484 and 490–491 for Auerbach's explanation of his exemplary method.

6. Nietzsche is quoted in Erich Heller, "The Realistic Fallacy," *Documents of Modern Literary Realism*, ed. George J. Becker (Princeton, N.J.: Princeton University Press, 1963), p. 595. And Harry Levin, *The Gates of Horn: A Study of Five French Realists* (New York: Oxford University Press–Galaxy Books, 1966), p. 83.

7. See Isaiah Berlin, *The Hedgehog and the Fox: An Essay on Tolstoy's View of History* (London: Weidenfeld and Nicolson, 1953). This essay can be construed as a definition of Tolstoy's idea of realism, which is not incongruent with the argument I make here. In a longer essay, Tolstoy could be placed between Cervantes and Joyce to make the case more complete.

8. *Don Quixote*, trans. M. Cohen (Harmondsworth, Middlesex, England: Penguin Books, Ltd., 1976), p. 425. All further citations in the text.

9. These are the general criteria proposed by Ian Watt in *The Rise of the Novel* (Berkeley and Los Angeles: University of California Press, 1969) and by Levin in *The Gates of Horn*. I am also indebted to Robert Scholes' and Robert Kellogg's *The Nature of Narrative* (London, Oxford, New York: Oxford University Press, 1966), especially for the way in which they see *Ulysses* as an end; and to David Goldknopf's *The Life of the Novel* (Chicago and London: The University of Chicago Press, 1972), especially for his fine first chapter.

10. It is interesting that no essay specifically on realism appears in the collection from *Novel*, which is entitled *Towards a Poetics of Fiction* (ed. Mark Spilka, Bloomington and London: Indiana University Press, 1977). Realism is not an issue in Jonathan Culler's *Structuralist Poetics* (Ithaca, N.Y.: Cornell University Press, 1975).

11. John W. Loofbourow, "Realism in the Anglo-American Novel: The Pastoral Myth," in *The Theory of the Novel: New Essays,* ed. John Halperin (New York: Oxford University Press, 1974), pp. 257–270. Wayne C. Booth, *The Rhetoric of Fiction* (Chicago and London: The University of Chicago Press, 1961). Booth, of course, is a great opponent of "objectivity," but his notion of fiction's rhetoric is basically an idea of realism that encourages a consensus. And *The Rhetoric of Fiction* contains a great deal of thinking on the nature and origin of objectivity. See also the section on "The Objective Artifact," in *The Modern Tradition,* ed. Richard Ellmann and Charles Feidelson, Jr. (New York: Oxford University Press, 1965), for additional statements.

12. See Lowry Nelson, Jr., "Introduction," *Cervantes: A Collection of Critical Essays,* ed. Lowry Nelson, Jr. (Englewood Cliffs, N.J.: Prentice-Hall, Inc., 1969), p. 4. See also Edward Mendelson, "Gravity's Encyclopedia," in *Mindful Pleasures: Essays on Thomas Pynchon,* ed. George Levine and David Leverenz (Boston, Toronto: Little, Brown and Company, 1976). He compares *Don Quixote* to *Ulysses,* as well as to other encyclopedic novels, in a number of very interesting ways; for his remarks about partners, see pp. 165–166.

13. See *Ulysses,* p. 696. "Imprevidibility" was coined by Joyce.

14. A fine discussion of this letter is Garrett Stewart, "Lawrence, 'Being,' and the Allotropic Style," in *Towards a Poetics of Fiction.*

15. Kahler, *The Inward Turn of Narrative,* trans. Richard and Clara Winston (Princeton, N.J.: Princeton University press, 1973). Frye, *Anatomy of Criticism* (Princeton, N.J.: Princeton University Press, Bollingen Series LXXXVIII, 1957), pp. 33–35. Loofbourow, "Literary Realism Redefined," *Thought,* 45, 178 (Autumn, 1970); this is a fine brief survey of many ideas of realism—see especially p. 437.

16. *Character and the Novel* (Ithaca, N.Y.: Cornell University Press, 1965), p. 133.

17. On this point, as on many others, I am most indebted for my understanding of *Ulysses* to Richard Ellmann's *Ulysses on the Liffey* (New York: Oxford University Press, 1972).

18. R.M. Adams, "Hades," in *James Joyce's Ulysses,* p. 92, for a different opinion.

19. See Leo Spitzer, *Linguistics and Literary History: Essays in Stylistics* (Princeton, N.J.: Princeton University Press, 1948), pp. 41–86, for a different approach to Don Quixote's realism and a different evaluation of Cervantes' impersonality.

20. See also Cardenio's remark on p. 267: "It is so strange and rare that I do not know whether anyone trying to invent such a character in fiction would have the genius to succeed.

21. *Cervantes's Theory of the Novel* (Oxford: Oxford University Press, 1962), p. 41.

22. *The Situation of Poetry* (Princeton, N.J.: Princeton University Press, 1976), p. 19.

23. Metonymy as a principle of realism is the insight of Roman Jakobson's "The Metaphoric and Metonymic Poles," in *Critical Theory Since Plato,* ed. Hazard Adams (New York, Chicago, San Francisco, Atlanta: Harcourt Brace Jovanovich, Inc., 1971), pp. 1113–1116. The complete essay is contained in Jakobson, *Selected Writings,* II: *Word and Language* (The Hague, Paris: Mouton, 1971), under the title "Two Aspects of language and Two Types of Aphasic Disturbances," pp. 219–259. It is also widely discussed in places like Robert Scholes' *Structuralism in Literature* (New Haven and London: Yale University Press, 1974), pp. 19–22.

24. *The Poetry of Ezra Pound* (Norfolk, Connecticut: New Directions, 1951), p. 134.

25. See Stanley Burnshaw, *The Seamless Web* (New York: George Braziller, 1970), for a physiological theory of art.

26. Quoted in David McLellan, *Karl Marx* (New York: The Viking Press, 1975), pp. 31–32.

27. *Opus Posthumous*, ed. Samuel French Morse (New York: Alfred A. Knopf, 1966), p. 171. In "The Noble Rider and the Sound or Words," Stevens also briefly adumbrates a theory of realism like the one I have proposed here; in the remarks he makes about the pressure of reality and the resistance offered by the imagination, he also sounds like Stephen Dedalus, in *Wandering Rocks*, between two roaring worlds. See *The Necessary Angel* (New York: Random House-Vintage Books, 1965), pp. 22–23, especially.

28. *James Joyce* (New York, London, Toronto: Oxford University Press, 1959), p. 430. See *Ulysses on the Liffey* for similar remarks made to Frank Budgen, pp. 29–30.

29. See Richard Poirier, "The Importance of Thomas Pynchon," in *Mindful Pleasures*, p. 21, for more on who is fit in modern literature to read the books they appear in. There are no more Don Quixotes, who may be the father of the novel because he was so great a reader.

30. See J. Mitchell Morse, "Proteus," in *James Joyce's Ulysses*, pp. 29–50, who has many important things to say about the ideas of identity and time and about the connections between Proteus and the last nine chapters. I also want to remark on behalf of my conclusions about *Ulysses* that the very existence of a book like this, with one critic for each chapter of the novel, also argues for the principle of consensus.

31 "Manners, Morals, and the Novel," *The Liberal Imagination* (Garden City, N.Y.: Doubleday-Anchor Inc., 1953), p. 215.

CORY A. REED

Cervantes and the Novelization of Drama: Tradition and Innovation in the Entremeses

> In an era when the novel reigns supreme, almost all the remaining genres are to a greater or lesser extent "novelized."
>
> —Mikhail Bakhtin[1]

Were Cervantes' *entremeses* bad theatre? If not, why were they perceived by both the writer and his contemporaries to be more suitable for reading than theatrical representation? Such questions have surrounded the interludes since their initial rejection (alongside eight full-length plays) by unnamed *autores de comedias* in the early 1600's. While it is certain that Cervantes' theatre was judged inadequate for the seventeenth-century stage, it remains to be seen exactly how his *entremeses* departed from the theatrical standards of the time or what it was precisely in these plays that made them unacceptable. Critical evaluations of these elusive texts have shown them to be much more complex than performed *entremeses*, but have not examined in detail the internal mechanisms responsible for their intricacy.[2] Nevertheless, the reconsideration of the interludes in light of recent theoretical approaches, including Bakhtin's theory of the novel and novelized genres, reveals that Cervantes' extensive use of novelistic elements in his drama may have rendered his entremeses unperformable within the context of contemporaneous theatrical production. Moreover, the "novelization" characteristic of Cervantes' theatrical work may also provide an important key to understanding his plays' release as texts for reading.

From *Cervantes* vol. 11, no. 1 (Spring 1991). © 1991 by the Cervantes Society of America.

When Cervantes published his *Ocho comedias y ocho entremeses nuevos, nunca representados* in 1615, he essentially readdressed his unperformed drama to a reading public. The appearance of dramatic work in print was not an entirely unusual practice in the time; plays were frequently published (more often than not without the direct intervention of the dramatist) after their success had been proven on the stage. These collections, often plagued with inaccuracies and revisions, provided the means to extend the commercial windfalls of the seventeenth-century Spanish theatre beyond the lucrative business of public performance to include the reading market as well.[3] Cervantes' collection, however, stands as a unique example in that his plays had not been influenced by the process of interpretation and revision by actors and directors which accompanies any theatrical production. Only after his *comedias* and *entremeses* had been deemed inappropriate for the stage did he sell his scripts to a bookseller with the intention of releasing them for the reading public. Apparently Cervantes retained control over the content of his collection until its publication, presumably submitting his authoritative version to the printer as if it had been a collection of short stories. In addition, he was able to draft a prologue as an explanation of his plays' appearance in print and to direct the reader's understanding of the dramatic texts that followed. The printed volume of his *comedias* and *entremeses*, therefore, cannot be classified along with the published collections of commercially successful plays (like those of Lope de Vega, for example), but rather pertains to a new practice of publishing drama based on its value as readable literature, as a dramatic form which has been redefined for initial consumption by a reading audience.

In his prologue, Cervantes relates the roundabout manner in which his plays reached the press, thus beginning the debate over their allegedly problematic theatricality:

> Algunos años ha que volví yo a mi antigua ociosidad, y pensando que aún duraban los siglos donde corrían mis alabanzas, volví a componer algunas comedias; pero no hallé pájaros en los nidos de antaño; quiero decir que no hallé autor que me las pidiese, puesto que sabían que las tenía, y así las arrinconé en un cofre y las consagré al perpetuo silencio. En esta sazón me dijo un librero que él me las comprara si un autor de título no le hubiera dicho que de mi prosa se podía esperar mucho, pero del verso nada.... Torné a pasar los ojos por mis comedias y por algunos entremeses míos que con ellas estaban arrinconados, y vi no ser tan malas ni tan malos que no mereciesen salir de las tinieblas del ingenio de aquel autor a la luz de otros autores menos escrupulosos y más

entendidos. Aburríme y vendíselas a tal librero, que las ha puesto
en la estampa como aquí las ofrece.[4]

Clearly, Cervantes had originally intended his plays to be performed on the
stage and, therefore, conceived each work initially with this end in mind.
Only after being rejected by the *autores de comedias* of whom he speaks did he
consider presenting them to the public through a different medium—in
printed form. The prologue conveys the frustration Cervantes must have felt
as a dramatist, but it is tempered with the understanding that he was
respected for his non-dramatic work, which may have inspired him
consequently to consider the release of his drama exclusively in print.

In the "Adjunta al Parnaso," a fictionalized Cervantes (interestingly in
the neo-dramatic form of dialogue) provides additional reasons for the
redirection of the unperformed works to a reading public. Citing the
necessity of an educated reader's undivided attention, the fictionalized
dramatist ("Miguel") offers the following explanation:

> MIGUEL.   Seis [comedias] tengo, con otros seis entremeses.
> PANCRACIO.   Pues, por qué no se representan?
> MIGUEL.   Porque ni los autores me buscan ni yo les voy a
> buscar a ellos.
> PANCRACIO.   No deben de saber que vuesa merced las tiene.
> MIGUEL.   Sí saben; pero como tienen sus poetas paniaguados y
> les va bien con ellos, no buscan pan de trastrigo. Pero yo pienso
> darlas a la estampa, para que se vea de espacio lo que pasa apriesa,
> y se disimula, o no se entiende, cuando las representan. Y las
> comedias tienen sus sazones y tiempos, como los cantares.[5]

This passage anticipates the same sentiments Cervantes would express one
year later in his prologue. In contrast with the latter, however, the
disillusioned dramatist here justifies the redirection of his drama by referring
to and, in effect, acknowledging the internal complexity of his plays. For
Cervantes, releasing his plays in print would afford the attentive reader the
opportunity to understand "lo que pasa apriesa, y se disimula, o no se
entiende, cuando las representan." Certainly, Cervantes himself believed
there to be more to his *comedias* and interludes than their entertainment value
to a theatrical audience. He must have thought his dramatic work, if not in
demand for theatrical representation, would be suitable as a form of
privatized, even didactic, entertainment for a discriminating reader. Yet this
must not prevent us from reading these works as pieces of theatre composed
originally for the stage. The reader must bear in mind that Cervantes admits

he had his *comedias* and *entremeses* (or at least six of each) already written before he decided to publish them, and that his decision to *print* them (not to *write* them) is based on his desire to direct his plays to a more attentive and discerning audience.[6] Any discussion of Cervantes' interludes must therefore begin with the fact that they are in essence works of theatre, conceived in accordance with certain dramatic principles and conventions, and they must be analyzed as such.

This rather curious occurrence, the publishing of plays before they had fulfilled their artistic potential in performance, has led generations of scholars to underestimate the rich theatricality of Cervantes' interludes. The failure of Cervantes' *entremeses* in their theatrical context leads to an obvious, but puzzling, question: why were his interludes not performed during his lifetime? Cervantes was recognized for his literary talent even in his own day, and today's reader certainly understands his genius. Nonetheless, Cervantes' mastery of literary prose and its conventions may, in fact, be partially responsible for the alleged theatrical inadequacy of his dramatic work. The writing of what we now call literature (writing for a reading public) is by definition substantially different from composition for the stage, where a number of complex semiotic systems are simultaneously at work. While the writer of prose fiction can (and, indeed, must) create a fictional world with verbal imagery and narrative style, the dramatist will also consider the languages of physical gesture and movement, voice quality, spatial relationships, and music, to name but a few. The dramatic text must be conceived with all of these elements in mind, since each one is an essential component which contributes as much to the overall understanding of the work as does the written text. Keir Elam reminds us:

> Literary critics have usually implicitly or explicitly assumed the priority of the written play over the performance, the latter being more often than not described as a "realization" (actual or potential) of the former. The written text constrains the performance in obvious ways.... Since, chronologically, the writing of the play precedes any given performance, it might appear quite legitimate to suppose the simple priority of the one over the other.... But it is equally legitimate to claim that it is the performance, or at least a possible "model" performance, that constrains the dramatic text in its very articulation ... [and that] the dramatic text is radically conditioned by its performability. The written text, in other words, is determined by its very need for stage contextualization, and indicates throughout its allegiance to the physical conditions of performance, above all to

the actor's body and its ability to materialize discourse within the space of the stage.[7]

As an aspiring dramatist, Cervantes most certainly understood the demands and practical restrictions placed on the written text by the intended performance, but his instincts as a novelist also affected the character of his drama. This is not to suggest that he in some way ignored the extra-literary dramatic codes while writing his drama, but rather that his highly developed sense of novelistic discourse may have overwhelmed the theatrical concerns of the interlude, at least in the eyes of the potential producers who rejected his plays. There undoubtedly was something about Cervantes' interludes which set them apart from the performed *entremeses* of the time, something which at first brought about their rejection for theatrical purposes, and simultaneously made them suitable for release in printed form. The differentiating factor, as we shall see, was their overt reliance upon novelistic elements.

Clear, simple distinctions between the "novelistic" and the "theatrical" are not easily made, especially today, when the aims and thematic concerns of each frequently overlap. Theatricality, as Elam suggests, can be defined by the need for stage contextualization, while the novel relies entirely on the written word for imaginative interpretation by a reader. Contrasts between the novelistic discourse and dramatic composition thus usually emphasize the fact that drama is a plastic, representational art, while prose narrative is a written art form. Each genre is also defined by its relationship to its audience; theatre-goers expect temporal, audio-visual entertainment while readers enjoy the more detailed private contemplation of the intricacies of the story or novel. Aside from such broadly-based generic differences, however, there evidently existed in the seventeenth century practical distinctions between theatre and novelistic prose which, perhaps, were more noticeable than those commonly observed today. The commercial success of Lope de Vega in effect defined a specific set of guidelines for Spanish theatre, requiring relatively simple actions, and presenting characters as the subordinated agents of plot.[8] Any definition of character in the *comedia* is limited to those qualities that are necessary and relevant to the exposition of plot events. Thus *Fuenteovejuna*'s Comendador is narrowly-defined as a patently vile and dishonorable personage in order to make possible and justifiable his violent demise later in the work. Still, such subordination of character to plot does not require that each character be completely two-dimensional and devoid of internal conflict. Rather, the implication is that characterization in Golden Age drama typically serves to advance the plot. Conversely, novelistic prose examines the character as an individual and endows plot action with psychological and socio-historical relevance, the plot often serving to elucidate the complexities of character and its position in society.

In addition, the *comedia's* plot consists of a carefully-constructed sequence of events, linked together by dramatic causality, which, once discovered, reveals the thematic meaning of the work as a whole. The full-length play thus ends with the restoration of a previously-disrupted order, often employing poetic justice to punish those responsible for the initial disturbance. In the *entremés*, we see a further reduction of this neatly-composed formulaic style, necessitated by its situation between the acts of the *comedia*. As will be discussed later, characters are drawn almost exclusively according to stereotypical stock-figures, plots consist of one singular action, and the elucidation of thematic meaning is almost non-existent. In contrast, novelistic prose is not regularly constrained by formulaic structure. It is a freer, more flexible form that often explores the internal conflicts of its characters and favors the discussion of complex themes and issues. Novelistic prose is often characterized by thematic indeterminacy and openness, which requires the thoughtful collaboration of the reader for closure. These, precisely, are the elements that Cervantes developed not only in his prose works, but also in his drama, allowing his dramatic texts to execute some of the more profound aims of the novel, while still remaining, essentially, works of theatre.

Cervantes is best known (and justifiably so) as the father of the modern novel, who refashioned prose writing to such an extent that future generations of novelists would continue to follow his leads. *Don Quijote* and the *Novelas ejemplares* show his interest in experimentation and the exploration of the unlimited possibilities of narrative fiction. Nevertheless, Cervantes' drama sometimes has been called excessively traditional, especially when compared to Lope de Vega, whose *comedia nueva* virtually redefined both the production and reception of the dramatic arts in sixteenth- and seventeenth-century Spain.[9] While Lope, in his *Arte nuevo de hacer comedias*, openly admits a disregard for Aristotle's precepts (and, indeed, for many classical artistic concerns) seemingly in order to cater to the tastes of an undiscriminating mass public, Cervantes continues defending the artistic integrity of more traditional drama, and explicitly defies Lope's position in a number of his own writings, including the *Quijote*.[10] The resulting literary polemic has fostered a prevalent and perhaps too convenient impression that Cervantes and Lope were in complete disagreement concerning the value of contemporary dramatic conventions, and that Cervantes the "classicist" refused to accept Lope's innovations, continuing to reject them in his own theatrical works.[11] Contrary to such reductionist critical opinion, however, Cervantes' dramatic creations are not entirely neo-Aristotelian works whose traditional conservatism made them necessarily obsolete before they could reach the stage. Much in the same way he redefines the novella and creates the modern novel, Cervantes also attempts a change in the seventeenth-century conception of drama in Spain, but in a manner far different from Lope de Vega. Cervantes, in short, brings many of the thematic and structural characteristics of prose narrative to the composition of his "novelized" drama.

In his theatrical works as in his novels, Cervantes turns his critical eye inward in order to reconsider the mechanisms of plot, character, and theme: the *mythos*, *ethos*, and *dianoia* of Aristotelian tradition. As a result of changes in these internal components, Cervantes' interludes resemble works of prose fiction in certain ways and depart radically from the accepted drama of the time. William S. Jack asserts:

> ... they belong in some measure to the dialogued story of which Cervantes showed himself to be so complete a master in the *Coloquio de los perros*. It will be recalled that in speaking of one of his comedies, Cervantes says that it was found "larga en los razonamientos." The same thing can be said of his *entremeses*. In this, he stands at the opposite pole from [Lope de] Rueda, but also it may be to some extent because of this that he could be the master who first really brought the form into literature of the highest class.[12]

Pointing to the relationship between Cervantes' interludes and the "dialogued story," Jack confirms the innovative manner in which Cervantes composed his plays, adding a novelistic depth of plot, theme, and character. The elevation of the lowly *entremés*, deeply rooted in the traditions of popular culture and theatrical representation, to the level of "literature"[13] is precisely the effect created by the publication of Cervantes' dramatic works. What was once primarily intended for a mass public is given an additional life as privatized entertainment for the educated reader. This is not to say that the interludes are more similar to novels in dialogue than to theatre, but rather that their novelistic elements include a greater development of the sketchy plots and character-types normally found in conventional interludes. Patricia Kenworthy has observed: "Just as Cervantes extends the boundaries of the form of the genre by including 'novelistic' passages, he extends the limits of subject matter available for dramatic treatment."[14] Thus, the presence of novelistic elements in Cervantes' interludes not only allows the plays to function as reading material, but also effects changes in their theatricality.

As could be expected, Cervantes builds upon the popular foundation of the *entremés* by expanding its range of dramatic possibilities. To the traditional cast of rustic farmers, ruffians, sacristans, and barbers, he adds middle-class mayors, judges, doctors, merchants, and cleverly ingenious women to transform the stage into what Eugenio Asensio has called a "procesión de deformidades sociales"[15] constituted by characters from nearly all social positions. He then places these figures in original situations which extend far beyond the boundaries of the conventional *entremés*. The "malmaridada" of traditional lore is now asking for a divorce, an impossibility in Cervantes' Spain (*El juez de los divorcios*). The beautiful women of the courtly love tradition are transformed into prostitutes, their male counterparts into pimps (*El rufián viudo*). The exploration of the activity of the urban marketplace suggests a burgeoning middle class which reflects Spain's belated but imminent acceptance of the capitalist system (*La guarda cuidadosa* and *El vizcaíno fingido*). In short, Cervantes fuses the popular, theatrical form of the traditional *entremés* and the more thematically profound composition of character and plot found in prose narrative. His characters are more complex and individualized,[16] his situations suggest possible psychological interpretations, and his thematic content invites socio-historical analysis. Such intricacies, common in twentieth-century short drama, but typically characteristic of prose literature in Cervantes' time, were entirely absent from the conventional *entremés* performed between the acts of the *comedia*.

In his insightful chapter titled "El entremés, fecundado por la novela," Asensio plainly states, "Cervantes remoza el entremés importando en su campo temas y técnicas de la novela."[17] That Cervantes redefined the *entremés* by bringing to the theatre his masterful hand as a novelist is a sentiment shared by nearly all who have commented on his interludes. Jill Syverson-Stork sees Cervantes' dual life as dramatist and novelist affecting both his dramatic and non-dramatic work, observing of the former, "Cervantes' primary attention to characterization and the desire to expose his nation's problematical present may well have been the most important causes of his failure as a dramatist ... his plays do tend towards the novelistic."[18] Such novelistic elements may be particularly visible in the brief *entremés*, where temporal restrictions which demand a short, simple action may be incompatible with any depth of character or theme. It seems Cervantes the dramatist was never far removed from Cervantes the novelist, and his proficiency in the creation of prose fiction helped to enrich his dramatic production as well, in effect making a critical literary form out of a previously rough dramatic diversion.

Mikhail Bakhtin (cited above) argues that it is not at all uncommon for a work of drama to display certain characteristics of the novel. Indeed, he asserts that such "novelization" is almost unavoidable in any period in which the novel becomes a primary focus of literature. Consequently, aspects of novelization can begin to manifest themselves in other genres anytime after the appearance of the modern novel, but they do not reach a significant level of importance—or canonical recognition—until much later. This novelization is not due to any superiority of one genre over the other, but rather to the measure of plasticity inherent in the conception and execution of the novel. For Bakhtin, the novel defies canonization; instead it functions as a working literary influence which affects all forms of literature and the manner in which their verbal imagery is composed. Novelization, therefore, can be seen as a liberating process which gives new life to an old form. It is an enrichment of a different genre, in this case drama, which opens up new possibilities, and not an elimination or replacement of its systems and codes. In his essay "Epic and Novel" Bakhtin states:

> The novelization of literature does not imply attaching to already completed genres a generic canon that is alien to them, not theirs. The novel, after all, has no canon of its own. It is, by its very nature, not canonic. It is plasticity itself. It is a genre that is ever questing, ever examining itself and subjecting its established forms to review. Such, indeed, is the only possibility open to a genre that structures itself in a zone of direct contact with developing reality. Therefore, the novelization of other genres does not imply their subjection to an alien generic canon; on the contrary, novelization implies their liberation from all that serves as a brake on their unique development, from all that would change them along with the novel into some sort of stylization of forms that have outlived themselves.[19]

This idea of the novel representing an essence which seems unavoidably to permeate all types of literature is fundamental to the examination of the process of novelization in the time of Cervantes. Following Bakhtin's line of reasoning, one can conclude that the same historical, social, and psychological conditions which constituted and affected Cervantes' environment during the writing of the *Quijote* were also present during the composition of his drama. The same attitudes and thought processes that formed Cervantes' creative genius should logically influence both his prose and theatrical texts. It follows that since Cervantes was one of the first to master novelistic discourse in his prose writing, and, indeed, introduced the western world to the modern novel, his drama would also display a certain novelistic quality. Cervantes' interludes are not weakened, but rather strengthened by this occurrence; as some of the earliest examples of novelized drama, his interludes can be seen as being "ahead of their time."

If the novelization of Cervantes' drama, therefore, is not entirely unexpected or surprising, what effect, precisely, does this process have on his plays? Bakhtin lists a series of modifications which we can expect to encounter in any novelized genre:

> [Novelized genres] become more free and flexible, their language renews itself by incorporating extraliterary heteroglossia and the "novelistic" layers of literary language, they become dialogized, permeated with laughter, irony, humor, elements of self-parody and finally—this is the most important thing—the novel inserts into these other genres an indeterminacy, a certain semantic openendedness, a living contact with unfinished, still-evolving contemporary reality (the open-ended present).[20]

At first glance, these attributes of novelized literature may not seem entirely unusual; in fact, they may appear quite ordinary regarding their application to drama. Most modern drama displays all of these characteristics in some way. But although novelized drama is the norm in the twentieth century, it was only beginning to take root in Cervantes' time. A permanent shift toward novelization in the mainstream short drama would not come at all in the seventeenth century. In Cervantes' interludes, however, we can easily see a number of concrete examples of these qualities.

Heteroglossia is visible in Cervantes' *entremeses*, just as it is present in the *Quijote*. Furthermore, the concepts of heteroglossia and dialogism presented by Bakhtin are absolutely related to the famous "perspectivism" which Américo Castro and Leo Spitzer, among others, have seen as a fundamental characteristic of Cervantes' works.[21] All problems are "dialogized" and given perspective from which no single view of reality can be accepted as the entire truth, often by the simultaneous presentation of conflicting philosophies and language styles. The problematic ambivalence of language manifests itself most overtly in *La elección de los alcaldes de Daganzo* through the comments of the rustic councilmen who argue about correct and appropriate speech and how it affects our perception of truth. Additionally, language is used to deceive in *El vizcaíno fingido* (whose trickster-protagonist employs a stylized Basque dialect), *La cueva de Salamanca* (through the character of the wife who must convince her husband of her devotion, although she has none), and *El viejo celoso* (in which a woman's verbal expression of truth fools the jealous old man). In *El retablo de las maravillas* the power of the artistic word is shown not only to be capable of manipulating the characters on the stage, but also of deceiving the theatre-going (or reading) public, much in the same way the Maese Pedro episode in *Don Quijote* breaks through the borders of fiction to incorporate the reader as well.[22] The increasingly illusory world of *El retablo*'s play-within-a-play allows us to confuse the more verisimilar fiction of its framework play with reality itself, mirroring the characters' own relationship with the drama they are watching. As in Cervantes' prose creations, truth is rendered subjective in the interludes by the dramatist's novelistic and dialogic stance. Multiplicity of language styles is, of course, common in the interlude as a genre, but the fact that Cervantes problematizes language is an important feature related to the process of novelization. Cervantes is not content with the mere presentation of polyglot language in the *entremés* as empirical reality; he explores the limits and philosophical ramifications of language in his drama in a manner not unlike the presentation of language in the *Quijote*.

In pursuing Bakhtin's claim that humor and irony permeate the novelized text, one must proceed with caution, bearing in mind that the *entremés* as a genre itself capitalizes on the maximization of laughter and the comic. In the interludes of Cervantes, however, humor is indeed made ironic, and the above-mentioned "elements of self-parody" do enter the scene. Such irony in Cervantes' *entremeses* seems to be a characteristic quality which distinguishes his drama from more mainstream plays.[23] The most overt examples are *El retablo de las maravillas*, *La cueva de Salamanca*, and *El vizcaíno fingido*, three plays of deception in which the audience maintains a full awareness of the dramatic trickery taking place on stage, while the characters themselves remain in ignorance. Such irony generates much of the humor in these works; the audience or reader can laugh at the foolishness of the characters as they walk readily into their respective traps, seeming at once to be both gullible and deserving of their impending fate. Furthermore, this broad-based ironic humor allows Cervantes to engage in satirical self-deprecation. In *El retablo de las maravillas*, the charlatan Chirinos gives the Governor a lengthy speech on the vices of poets, and particularly dramatists, and *La guarda cuidadosa* has as its protagonist a foolish soldier-poet frequently identified as a semi-autobiographical figure of Cervantes himself.[24] Juan Luis Alborg sees the presence of such satirical wit as the principal factor differentiating Cervantes' *entremeses* from their prototypes, the *pasos* of Rueda:

> [La] agudeza satírica ... bajo la aparente intranscendencia del juguete cómico, apunta también a muchos aspectos de la vida social, a prejuicios y rutinas, a veces a espinosos problemas, a

conflictos de clases, y a todo género de hipocresías; intereses y
egoismos humanos. A diferencia de los pasos de Rueda, la gracia
no es en las piezas de Cervantes de mera situación cómica, sino
de sátira intencionada, lanzada contra ridículas debilidades o
costumbres y corruptelas de las gentes de su tiempo.[25]

The satirical criticism of seventeenth-century Spanish institutions,
prejudices, and hypocrisy is precisely the innovative brand of analytical
profundity which sets Cervantes' interludes apart from the traditional
entremés, and which is certainly more characteristic of prose fiction (as
exemplified in the time by Cervantes' own *Don Quijote*) than of the *teatro
menor*.

Most important, as Bakhtin has suggested, is the openendedness of
novelized literature. Cervantes' interludes, much more so than mainstream
interludes, take place in the "open ended present" of which Bakhtin speaks.
The results of the election in *La elección de los alcaldes de Daganzo* are
postponed until the following day. The resolution of the student's deception
of the nearly-cuckolded Pancracio in *La cueva de Salamanca* is never shown.
The consequences of Lorenza's adultery in *El viejo celoso* are left unexplored.
In contrast, looking at some performed *entremeses* of the time somewhat
similar in theme to those of Cervantes, we see a tendency to conclude on a
note of thematic closure. *La sacristía de Mocejón* (anonymous) resolves an
election, ending the interlude in the celebration of the chosen sacristan, and
in the *Entremés de un viejo ques casado con una mujer moza* (anonymous),
adultery is concealed, the deception of the old man reaches a well-defined
and climactic conclusion, and the play concludes on a self-congratulatory
note by those who have successfully fooled the jealous old man.[26]
Furthermore, the openness of the Cervantine interlude was not to be
incorporated in the subsequent development of the *género chico*. Later in the
seventeenth century, the stylized works of Quiñones de Benavente would
come to define the conventional *entremés* by their strict adherence to
contemporary theatrical demands requiring single actions, one setting, and
complete closure which ensured—and perhaps, reinforced—their
subordinate relationship to the *comedia*. His version of *El retablo de las
maravillas* not only significantly reduces the scope of the Cervantine work
(five characters and two secular "apparitions," as opposed to Cervantes'
eleven personages and six visions of socially and religiously symbolic
importance), but also avoids entirely Cervantes' chaotic ending of beatings
and thrashings, opting instead for a traditionally closed conclusion which
includes a celebratory song and dance. In addition, Quiñones de Benavente's
work does not address the problematic themes of blood purity and racial

intolerance which Cervantes leaves unresolved in the audience's mind and demanding attention.[27]

The structural and thematic openendedness of Cervantes' interludes is thus entirely unique within the short drama of his time and is consistent with the novelistic indeterminacy frequently expressed in his prose works. It is due in part to this irresolution that the interludes invite the intellectually contemplative analysis to which Cervantes referred when he suggested reasons for redirecting his drama toward the discerning reader. The openendedness of Cervantes' interludes requires the collaboration of the reader/audience in order to make sense out of the plays' thematic indeterminacy. These plays often leave the reader or spectator in a state of suspense, which can only be resolved by a thoughtful analysis of the works after they have concluded. In short, the thematic concerns of Cervantes' *entremeses* frequently extend beyond the structural framework of the plays themselves, and require the active participation of the reader to provide closure. This openendedness contrasts directly with the traditional *entremés*, whose location between the acts of a *comedia* required a closed conclusion that rendered its simple plot readily comprehensible to a passive audience— and easily forgettable by the beginning of the play's second act.

Since the interlude is generically a drama of action and the novel is frequently devoted to the presentation of character, the function of character in Cervantes' interludes also provides a glimpse into his process of novelization. Asensio notes the importance of the two-dimensionality of character in the traditional *entremés*, calling it a comedy of "figuras," not of true characters, but of stock types more closely resembling the mechanical puppets displayed in the traveling *retablos* of the time.[28] Of Cervantes, however, Asensio claims, "Pinta no entes de una pieza—lo que llamo *figuras*—sino seres con una sombra de complejidad, con una alternancia de sentimientos que con intención moderna tendríamos la tentación de llamar *caracteres*."[29] These characters are not the faceless stereotypes of the traditional interlude, but are based on realistic, probable situations which could happen in everyday life. They have individual names (Leonarda, Lorenza, Pancracio, Cristina, Ortigosa, etc.), instead of being denoted by the generic terms "bobo," "rufián," or "sacristán" and, although directly descended from the traditional stock-types of the *entremés*, they are put into individual circumstances which require often unique and original solutions. Amelia Agostini Bonelli de Del Rio claims:

> Lo que es en Lope de Rueda simplemente un rufián fanfarrón y pretencioso, adquiere en Cervantes mayor desarrollo y cualidades que le diferencian de los demás rufianes.... En Lope de Rueda nos

reímos de una burla o de un tipo cómico, pero raros son los personajes que se quedan en la memoria, porque el que es pillo es pillo y nada más; se les mira desde un solo punto de vista. De ahí su falta de flexibilidad. Con los de Cervantes pasa lo contrario.[30]

Cervantes' *entremeses*, consequently, make frequent use of the individualized character and not the "type" of the traditional interlude, or, perhaps more accurately, Cervantes individualizes the types themselves, transforming them into characters. For example, Cañizares in *El viejo celoso* is a character drawn from the novella tradition (and particularly reminiscent of Cervantes' own Carrizales in *El celoso extremeño*), and the "vizcaíno" in *El vizcaíno fingido* is not the stereotyped Basque of unintelligible speech, but rather an impostor—a Castilian who imitates the stereotypical Basque (an *entremés* stock-type) and uses stylized speech as a deception. As in Cervantes' other works, the simple base of the *entremés* tradition is problematized, encrusted with layers of artifice which establish each character's individuality on the stage. Another example is *El juez de los divorcios*, in which Cervantes presents the male characters as types ("vejete," "soldado," "cirujano," and "ganapán") and the females as individualized characters (Mariana, Guiomar, Aldonza de Minjaca) who literally attempt to break out of the confines of their dramatic situation by asking for divorce. In *La elección de los alcaldes de Daganzo*, characters are individualized to the extent that their names reflect personal qualities (Estornudo, Panduro, Humillos, Pedro Rana), each of which is a slightly differentiated version of the stock-type of the fool. Even when Cervantes chooses to include traditional, stereotyped characters in his works, he modifies them slightly, often using the type as an agent of the novelistic theme. In *El retablo de las maravillas*, for example, he links the names and personalities of the characters (Juan Castrado, Teresa Repolla, Juana Macha, etc.) to the play's thematic concerns of illegitimacy and *limpieza de sangre*, thus providing a continual, comic reiteration of the characters' anxieties.[31]

In brief, Cervantes bases his characters on the two-dimensional types of the interlude tradition, but he "novelizes" them along with the other elements of his drama. He enlarges his cast (up to fourteen characters in one play, in comparison with Lope de Rueda's maximum of six)[32] and he places them into a series of plots, subplots, and frequent scene changes, which seems far removed from the simple plot and single scene of the traditional *entremés*. His characters, situations, and themes are just as vivid and fascinating in his drama as they are in his novels and short stories, and perhaps this is why his interludes were not seen as performable in 1615. While novelistic profundity is commonplace in today's drama (particularly in the one-act play), Cervantes' novelized *entremeses*, with their many layers of textual complexities, may have been too intricate to function in a position subordinate to the then still "un-novelized" *comedia* without overwhelming it.

The appearance of novelistic elements in the composition of the interludes of Cervantes inevitably leads to a comparison between the short, one-act *entremés* and its equally brief prose counterpart: the novella. Indeed, a case can be made for regarding the two as "sister genres" in light of the unique manner in which Cervantes redefines them both, and considering how these two short literary forms are each related to a larger form, the *comedia* or the novel. Cervantes' novelization of the interlude thus creates an analogous relationship not applicable to the traditional *entremés*: the novella is to the novel as the *entremés* is to the *comedia*. If the novella and the interlude as understood by Cervantes are so closely related, then it logically follows that the master of the Spanish novella would also have much to contribute to the realm of short drama. Novelization and the subsequent redefinition of drama as a purely readable literary work implies a change in both the literary and the theatrical horizon of expectations which must have been met with a certain element of curiosity. Yet the examination of Cervantes' perceived relationship between the novella and the interlude reveals not only the alteration of the role of the dramatic work, but corresponding changes in the novella as well.

The most obvious similarity between the interlude and the novella is their structural brevity. Both forms are, by definition, short. The practical necessity of brevity in the interlude is, of course, a temporal concern. Since the interlude was a form of entertainment presented during the intermission of the *comedia*, concentration of the dramatic action into ten minutes or less was an understood prerequisite for the composition of an *entremés*. This alone may be one of the primary reasons the *autores de comedias* rejected Cervantes' interludes, as his interludes tend to be, on the average, three times the length of contemporary *entremeses*. Brevity in the novella, by contrast, seems to be a stylistic concern of the genre, not a practical problem defined by its position within another form of representation.

Length alone, however, does not justify drawing parallels between the two genres; the analogous relationship depends on each form's interaction with another, longer form. Certainly the *entremés* exists as a counterpoint to the *comedia* in performance, and this relationship has inspired some to view the interlude as a dominated genre, subordinated by the *comedia*, but also sustained by it.[33] Any examination of the traditional interlude must therefore bear in mind its relationship to the *comedia* and to the theatrical spectacle as a whole of which it is part. The novella, however, does not normally interact with the novel in any fundamental way. Yet in Cervantes, we find examples of a complete reversal of the dependence of the *entremés* and the independence of the novella. The publication of his collected interludes at the end of the volume, separated from the text of his *comedias* and removed from the theatrical performance, extracts the interlude from its essential context, treating it more like a short story. Similarly, Cervantes inserts a completed novella, "El curioso impertinente," in the middle of the text of his novel, *Don Quijote*, much in the same way the *entremés* is embedded between the acts of the *comedia*.[34] In a sense, Cervantes at times requires his interludes to act like novellas and his novellas to act like interludes. For Cervantes, the *entremés* seems to be the "novella" of drama—a brief dramatic form in which a single thematic issue can be explored in depth.

If Cervantes was able to recognize structural and functional similarities in the interlude and the prose short story, then the publication of his *entremeses* must have helped this perception to be seen by others as well. Furthermore, the very act of printing his interludes creates an entirely new possibility for their reception which otherwise would have been impossible: the differentiation between a first and second (or subsequent) reading of the text. As Hans Robert Jauss points out, the second reading of a text allows for a more detailed analysis of meaning:

> From now on, the reader will seek and establish the still unfulfilled significance retrospectively, through a new reading, from the perspective of the fulfilled form, in a return from the end to the beginning, from the whole to the particular. Whatever initially resisted understanding manifests itself in the questions that the first going-through has left open. In answering them, one may expect that from the particular elements of significance—in various respects still indeterminate—a fulfilled whole may be established on the level of meaning.[35]

The idea of a meaningful, "fulfilled whole" is precisely one of the goals Cervantes intended to achieve by the publication of his dramatic works, as is evidenced by his above-mentioned comment "pienso darlas a la estampa, para que se vea de espacio lo que pasa apriesa, y se disimula, o no se entiende, cuando las representan." While the dramatic representation only allows a superficial analysis of the interlude by the one-time spectator (and this is further complicated by the interlude being physically surrounded by the *comedia*), the reading public Cervantes hoped for would be able to join the whole and the particular in a more comprehensive second reading. Such constraints of performance do not normally present a problem for the conventional *entremés* in that it is superficial by nature and should not require a "second reading." In addition, the theatre utilizes a variety of communicative systems which assist the spectator in making his "first-reading" analysis of the play as comprehensive as possible. The "reading" of the spectator is therefore different by definition than the analysis of a reader. The information contained within the theatrical piece must be understandable to the one-time theatre-goer, and a series of redundant theatrical codes helps the audience to process the information correctly. The sheer simplicity of the traditional *entremés* assured this proper reception would occur.

Cervantes' interludes, in contrast, are more complex and indeterminate. The author's very mention of wanting (in fact, demanding) a second reading, or at least a contemplative first reading, signals that he felt their content was capable of withstanding more intense scrutiny than a purely theatrical reception could afford, and that such a reading may be necessary to provide closure. This seems to imply that Cervantes was aware of the novelistic qualities of his interludes, and that they might be well received as reading texts. Cervantes' publication expands the reception of his *entremeses*, shifting his audience to the reader, and away from theatre-going *oyentes*, for whom a second or third reading for retrospective analysis of the works is not possible. Moreover, publication allows the interludes to be examined separately, free from the restraints of their position within the *comedia*, so they can be seen for what they are individually. This is a critical difference regarding Cervantes' plays in comparison with novelized drama in general. Whereas most of the novelized drama written after Cervantes (particularly in the nineteenth and twentieth centuries) has remained in the theatre as texts for performance, Cervantes' drama made its first appearance in print, as a text for reading.

The redirection of his drama to the reading public may also explain, at least in part, why Cervantes' novelistic innovations did not influence the subsequent development of the *teatro menor* in Spain. The extent of Cervantes' influence on the dramatic form itself is limited to the borrowing of only his most basic of plot elements, and sometimes characters, by those who later worked the genre into its definitive form. Just as Quiñones de Benavente (mentioned above) eliminated the thought-provoking theme of blood purity and greatly reduced the metatheatrical scope of the internal drama in his version of *El retablo de las maravillas*, "less is more" seemed to be the prevalent rule of thumb for the commercially successful composition of *entremeses* in the seventeenth century. Imitations of *El viejo celoso* and *La cueva de Salamanca* were composed by other dramatists as well, but without the novelistic "baggage" which was probably viewed as superfluous in the context of theatrical performance. Cervantes' novelistic art was apparently not well understood or appreciated in the numerous imitations and appropriations of his drama. Ironically, despite these minor contributions to future *entremesistas*, it was Cervantes' non-dramatic work which provided the most sources for theatrical imitations by other dramatists in the seventeenth century.[36] Perhaps Cervantes' *Comedias y entremeses* continued to be received as reading texts, just like his prose work, throughout the remainder of the seventeenth century and therefore did not influence dramatic composition any more than his other works of non-dramatic nature.

By incorporating in his interludes the serious treatment of theme and interiorization of character generally associated with novelistic prose, Cervantes anticipated a movement which would not affect the performed drama of the canon for more than one hundred years after the appearance of his *Ocho comedias y ocho entremeses*. The resulting works display a level of thematic profundity and structural complexity radically innovative in their time, and fully modern even when judged by the standards of the twentieth century. Certainly, the characteristic elements of novelization in the *entremeses* do not approach the intricacy afforded the novel itself by its length and narrative style. In comparison with their counterparts in the novel, Cervantes' dramatic characters may seem more two-dimensional, his themes less fully developed, and his plots less involved. Yet, when compared with the traditional *entremés*, Cervantes' personages display additional dimensions, and his themes and plots seem highly developed. This is the effect of novelization; the conventional components of drama begin to take on qualities usually associated with the novelistic discourse without sacrificing their theatricality.

Cervantes may have succeeded in creating a new drama, departing from the constraints of conventional dramatic theory and practice, but while the modern reader or theatre-goer recognizes his ingenious innovations, they were evidently not appreciated in the seventeenth century. Here the question which opened this study must again be addressed. Why was his drama not considered appropriate for performance and rejected by the producers and directors of his time? Certainly his *entremeses* may have been too complex to function as mere intermission entertainment between the acts of the *comedia*. The individualized characters, the overt satire of contemporary society, the double-entendre of heteroglot language, and the labyrinthian games of structure may have been excessively intricate for successful juxtaposition alongside (or, more precisely, within) the traditionally dominant *comedia*. The novelized interludes of Cervantes, in short, may have become too autonomous to succeed as a form subordinate to the conventional full-length drama.

Yet the most complicated aspect of Cervantes' interludes is their novelistic openendedness, a quality which in itself may have been responsible for their poor reception as performance oriented scripts. As Alban Forcione points out, Cervantes was obsessed with "the indeterminacy that characterizes all his greatest fiction," often refusing "to endow his works with the rigid structure of definitive pronouncement."[37] Indeterminacy seems to be a characteristic of his writing in general, not exclusively of his dramatic works. What, then, is so disturbing about the indeterminacy of Cervantes' interludes? The key distinction seems to be one of location, not some inherent problem with openendedness in the genre of drama. Whereas openendedness could conceivably conclude a theatrical performance (and, in effect, frequently does in modern drama), the irresolution of the *entremés* and its thought-provoking demands on the audience occur between two acts, in the middle of the performance. Since indeterminacy requires the collaboration of the audience to provide closure, this would be acceptable at the conclusion of a play, but would be problematic in the middle. Many *comedias* open their second acts with lengthy monologues which not only provide actors with the necessary time to change costumes, but also serve to reintegrate the audience into the plot of the play, after having been momentarily entertained by the *entremés*. It seems logical to assume that these monologues reflect the reality of an audience which needed to be reminded of the *comedia*'s action, even after having watched the closed, traditional interlude. An open-ended *entremés* which left the audience to contemplate its themes after its conclusion would be disastrously distracting as intermission entertainment. In order for an *entremés* to be effective in its context within the *comedia*, therefore, its thematic scope would have to be limited and closed so that the audience could make the rapid shift in attention to the *comedia* without leaving any loose ends from the interlude untied.

The novelistic indeterminacy of the Cervantine interlude is thus perhaps too complex to allow the audience to redirect its attention to another work (already in progress) immediately following its conclusion. The single plots, stereotyped characters, lack of intricate themes, and closure in the traditional *entremés* ensured that it would entertain, but distract as little as possible when the moment came to focus on the full-length play's second act. Cervantes' interludes violate this essential simplicity, breaking the conventions which ensure their successful consumption by the mass audience. The novelization and resulting indeterminacy of the Cervantine interlude disrupt the "spell" of mass entertainment, causing unrest and anxiety instead of holding the audience together while they wait for the main play to resume. This openendedness may also help explain why Cervantes' drama has enjoyed relative success in the twentieth century, when one-act plays are either performed as independent, autonomous works or nearly always followed by an intermission if a series of one-acts is presented as part of one program. What may have been perceived as "bad theatre" in the 1600's due to its unconventional openendedness is quite acceptable by today's standards, which encourage indeterminacy as a method of inspiring critical reflection in the audience.

As some of the earliest examples of novelized drama, Cervantes' interludes could not function within the definitive constraints imposed on theatrical production by seventeenth-century dramatic conventions. Yet while the novelization of Cervantes' drama appears to have been at least partially responsible for their rejection as theatrical scripts, the adoption of a more novelistic stance allowed them to be viewed as potentially successful (and lucrative) texts for reading. The very fact that his once-marginal interludes are today considered part of the literary canon, while the traditional, once-successful *entremés* has been marginalized, suggests that the dramatist brought complexities to the genre of short drama which are only now being understood and appreciated.

NOTES

1. M.M. Bakhtin, *The Dialogic Imagination*, ed. M. Holquist (Austin: U of Texas P, 1981) 5.

2. In 1915, Armando Cotarelo y Valledor mentioned novelistic influences in the drama of Cervantes (*El teatro de Cervantes* [Madrid: Revista de Archivos, Bibliotecas y Museos, 1915] 47–49), but did not define them precisely. Américo Castro described, Cervantes' drama as "inferior" and excessively ironic (*El pensamiento de Cervantes* [Madrid: Hernando, 1925] 50–55), but likewise failed to be more specific. While recent scholarly studies of individual entremeses (by Patricia Kenworthy, Bruce Wardropper, Stanislav Zimic, and others) have focused on thematic constructs, exemplarity, and characterization, the approach of Nicholas Spadaccini comes closest to defining the plays' novelistic complexities. Spadaccini, however, writes of their reception as reading texts, and does not analyze the plays in terms of their theatricality. See his "Writing for Reading: Cervantes's Aesthetics of Reception in the Entremeses," *Critical Essays on Cervantes*, ed. R. El Saffar (Boston: Hall, 1986) 162–175.

3. Don W. Cruickshank attributes some inaccuracies in printed Golden Age dramatic texts to the lack of financial incentive. See "The Editing of Spanish Golden-Age Plays From Early Printed Versions," *Editing the Comedia*, ed. F. P. Casa and M. D. McGaha (Ann Arbor: Michigan Romance Studies, 1985) 54.

4. Cervantes, *Entremeses*, ed. N. Spadaccini (Madrid: Cátedra, 1985) 93–94.

5. Cervantes, *Poesías Completas, I: Viaje al Parnaso y Adjunta al Parnaso*, ed. V. Gaos (Madrid: Castalia, 1973) 183.

6. Cervantes does not say "*las escribí ...*" but rather "yo pienso *darlas a la estampa* para que se vea de espacio lo que pasa apriesa...." The frequently-cited passage from the "Adjunta al Parnaso" thus explains why Cervantes sought to print his unperformed plays, but not why he originally wrote them. Indeed, nowhere in his extant writings does

Cervantes suggest that his plays were conceived and composed for any purpose other than theatrical production.

7. Keir Elam, *The Semiotics of Theatre and Drama* (London: Methuen, 1980) 208–09.

8. Alexander Parker defined the formulaic structure of the *comedia nueva* in terms of the relationship between character, plot, and theme. See *The Approach to the Spanish Drama of the Golden Age*, Diamante, 6 (London: Hispanic Council, 1957).

9. Some scholars (among them Castro [49–55]) and editors of anthologies (Linton Lomas Barrett, *Five Centuries of Spanish Literature* [New York: Harper and Row, 1962] 199) have repeatedly dismissed Cervantes' drama as "classical" and therefore subject to failure in a market dominated by Lope's innovative *comedia*. Cervantes did indeed write plays which were relatively classical in nature (i.e. *La Numancia*) during his early period of dramatic composition, prior to Lope's success as a dramatist. Cervantes later abandoned his neo-Aristotelian style and actually adopted that of the *comedia nueva*. His *comedias* and *entremeses* pertain to this second period of dramaturgy.

10. See Chapters 47–48 (Canon of Toledo episodes) in part one of the *Quijote*.

11. Such attitudes (see note #9) have persisted. As recently as 1969, for example, Edwin Honig described Cervantes as "always on the outside of literary society and lagging behind its fashions" in his "On the Interludes of Cervantes," *Cervantes: A Collection of Critical Essays*, ed. Lowry Nelson Jr. (Englewood Cliffs, NJ: Prentice Hall, 1969) 153. Current scholarship in the field is breaking away from this mold. See Patricia Kenworthy, "La ilusión dramática en los entremeses de Cervantes," *Cervantes: su obra y su mundo*, ed. M. Criado de Val (Madrid: 1981) 235–38; Bruce Wardropper, Cervantes' Theory of the Drama," *Modern Philology* 52.4 (1955): 217–251; Jean Canavaggio, *Cervantes Dramaturge: un théâtre à naître* (Paris: Presses Universitaires de France, 1977), and Spadaccini.

12. William S. Jack, *The Early Entremés in Spain: The Rise of a Dramatic Form* (Philadelphia: U of Pennsylvania P, 1923) 125.

13. While Jack's phrase "literature of the highest class" is clearly prejudiced toward the elite canon, it does signal the initial marginalization of the *entremés* and that Cervantes' works are understood as having some canonic, literary value beyond their theatricality.

14. Patricia Kenworthy, "The Entremeses of Cervantes: The Dramaturgy of Illusion," Diss., U. of Arizona, 1976, 12.

15. Eugenio Asensio, *Itinerario del entremés: desde Lope de Rueda a Quiñones de Benavente* (Madrid: Gredos, 1971) 80.

16. Cervantes himself acknowledges the interiorization of character in his plays, writing in his prologue "fui el primero que representase las imaginaciones y los pensamientos escondidos del alma" (*Entremeses* 92).

17. Asensio 99.

18. Jill Syverson-Stork, *Theatrical Aspects of the Novel: A Study of Don Quixote* (Valencia: Albatros, 1986) 9.

19. Bakhtin 39.

20. Bakhtin 7.

21. Bakhtin defines "dialogism" as a crossing of two languages, attitudes, or styles which results in a dialogue between points of view (see Bakhtin 76). "Heteroglossia" describes the potential coexistence of many meanings or nuances within one word, phrase, or language, depending on its social or linguistic context (Bakhtin 272). For a detailed discussion of perspectivism, see Castro 68–109 and Leo Spitzer, "Linguistic Perspectivism in the 'Don Quijote,'" reprinted in *Leo Spitzer: Representative Essays*, ed. A.K. Forcione, H. Lindenberger, and M. Sutherland (Stanford: Stanford UP, 1988) 225–271.

22. See George Haley, "The Narrator in *Don Quijote*: Maese Pedro's Puppet Show," *Critical Essays on Cervantes*, ed. R. El Saffar (Boston: Hall, 1986) 94–110.

23. For Castro (53), Cervantes "no podía competir con el 'Monstruo de la Naturaleza' no por deficiencia de fantasía, sino por carencia de lirismo y exceso de ironía y de crítica."

24. See Stanislav Zimic, "La biografía satírica en *La guarda cuidadosa* de Cervantes," *Segismundo* XV (1981): 95–149 and Luciano García Lorenzo, Experiencia vital y testimonio literario," *Anales Cervantinos* 1 (1951): 73–109.

25. Juan Luis Alborg, "La producción dramática de Cervantes" *Historia de la literatura española*, 4 vols. (Madrid: Gredos, 1967) 2: 71.

26. Both interludes may be found in Emilio Cotarelo y Mori's *Colección de entremeses, loas, bailes, jácaras y mojigangas desde fines del siglo XVI a mediados del XVII*, 2 vols. *NBAE* 17–18 (Madrid: 1911), the former on pp. 60–62, and the latter, pp. 62–65.

27. Benavente's *retablo* is only invisible to cuckolds, and simply in order to make them the butt of a funny joke, not to present cuckoldry as a social problem or to expose hypocrisy, as in Cervantes' version. It should be noted that Quiñones de Benavente (1593–1651) was not exactly a contemporary of Cervantes, having begun his writing career in his early 20's around the time of Cervantes' death. He is frequently credited with being a prolific writer of *entremeses* in a stylized verse form which often appeared to reduce the interlude to a sort of "*comedia* in embryo." See Hannah E. Bergman, *Luis Quiñones de Benavente* (New York: Twayne, 1972) 14.

28. Asensio 84–85.

29. Asensio 101.

30. Amelia Agostini Bonelli de Del Río, "El teatro cómico de Cervantes" *Boletín de la Real Academia Española* 44 (1964): 277–78.

31. See Mauricio Molho's chapter "El retablo de las maravillas" in *Cervantes: raíces folklóricas* (Madrid: Gredos, 1976).

32. Del Rio 275. Theatrical companies of the time employed between eight and sixteen actors, according to N.D. Shergold, *A History of the Spanish Stage* (Oxford: Clarendon, 1967) 505, 510. The large number of roles in Cervantes' interludes may have been impractical for smaller companies, contributing to their perceived theatrical inadequacy.

33. Maria Grazia Profeti, "Condensación y desplazamiento: la comicidad y los géneros menores en el teatro español del Siglo de Oro," *Los géneros menores en el teatro español del siglo de oro (Jornadas de Almagro 1987)*, ed. L. García Lorenzo (Madrid: Ministerio de Cultura, 1988) 33–46.

34. The intercalated novel, of course, is not a creation of Cervantes, but was employed in *Guzmán de Alfarache* and other works published prior to 1605.

35. Jauss, "The Poetic Text within the Change of Horizons of Reading," *Toward an Aesthetic of Reception*, trans. T Bahti (Minneapolis: U of Minnesota P, 1982) 145.

36. See Henri Recoules, "Cervantes y Timoneda y los entremeses del siglo XVII," *Boletín de la Biblioteca Menéndez y Pelayo* 48 (1972): 231–91.

37. Alban K. Forcione, *Cervantes and the Humanist Vision* (Princeton: Princeton UP, 1982) 90–91.

DIANA DE ARMAS WILSON

Plot and Agency

And they are gone: aye, ages long ago
These lovers fled away into the storm.
                            —Keats, *The Eve of St. Agnes*

On some fictive date in or around the 1560s, two young people, a man and a woman, embark on a two-year, thousand-mile journey from "Tile" (Thule, Iceland) to Rome, arriving in the Eternal City in its jubilee year.[1] Only in chapter 12 of the fourth and last book of the *Persiles*—"donde se dice quién eran Periandro y Auristela [where it is revealed who Periandro and Auristela were]" (464)—do we learn that their rightful names are Persiles and Sigismunda. At that point we also learn the real motives for the trip. Ostensibly, Auristela is fulfilling a vow to travel to Rome for Catholic instruction; in fact, she is fleeing Iceland in order to avoid an arranged marriage with Prince Magsimino, a young man whose "barbaric" habits have repulsed his own mother. At the close of the pilgrimage, in other words, readers discover that it was actually founded on a stratagem devised by this widowed queen mother, Eustoquia, to save Auristela for Magsimino's younger brother, her beloved son Periandro. Erotic escape, then, the perennial stuff of romance, fuels the beginnings of Cervantes's main plot.

Quoting from the *Georgics* during the belated revelations in book 4, the

From *Allegories of Love: Cervantes's* Persiles and Sigismunda. © 1991 by Princeton University Press.

hero's old tutor discloses that Thule—"que agora vulgarmente se llama
Islanda [which nowadays people call Iceland]" (469)—was once Virgil's
"última Thule" (465). As the plot of the *Persiles* internalizes the move from
pagan to Christian worlds, it represents a curious blend of geographical
precision and dreamlike *fantasia*. For the first half of the work, Cervantes
deploys the icy cold wastes of the northern European seas, with their
enshrouding mists and—as novels like *Frankenstein* and *Jane Eyre* would later
attest—enduring Arctic romance. But the pilgrims of the *Persiles* are not
always at sea: they sometimes drop anchor in what Spenser's *Faerie Queene*
had earlier called "the six Islands"—Iceland, Norway, the Orkneys, Ireland,
Gotland, and Dacia (Denmark) (3.3.32). Many scholars have concluded that
Cervantes was thoroughly familiar with contemporary northern geography,
and that even his most bizarre-sounding sites (the Isle of the Hermits, for
instance) may be found in maps of the era.[2] The mid-nineteenth-century
English translator of the *Persiles* lamented, however, that Cervantes "should
know so little of England, considering how much his own country had been
connected with her." Louisa Dorothea Stanley then went on to question his
representation of "a perfect land of Romance" whose northern European
inhabitants affect "utterly unknown and barbarous" customs and manners:
"Yet Elizabeth or James the 1st was reigning in England; the queen of James
the 1st was a Danish princess, and Denmark and Sweden were assuredly not
unknown to fame." Stanley's carping, which may appear nationalistic in its
defense of northern European interests, actually echoes the sentiments of an
early nineteenth-century Italian scholar. Simonde de Sismondi spoke of the
Persiles as "the offspring of a rich, but at the same time of a wandering
imagination," chiding Cervantes for "his complete ignorance of the North,
in which his scene is laid, and which he imagines to be a land of Barbarians,
Anthropophagi, Pagans, and Enchanters."[3]

The above critiques of Cervantes's errant imagination reveal a sturdy
ignorance of the genre of allegorical romance. Cervantes's "northern
story"—announced as an "historia septentrional" in the subtitle of the
Persiles—is not staged in the England of Elizabeth I but on a *paysage moralisé*,
a scenic landscape against which the characters act or react, either kindling
or burying their erotic fires in its icy realms. While the elderly Rosamunda
"burns" for the young Antonio on the Isla Nevada (Snowy Island)—"aquí
entre estos yelos y nieves, el amoroso fuego me esta haciendo ceniza el
corazón [here amidst this ice and snow, an amorous fire is turning my heart
to ashes]" (142)—the hermits Renato and Eusehia willfully bury their passion
in the snows: "Enterramos el fuego en la nieve [We buried our fire in the
snow]" (264). Cervantes's so-called wandering imagination is strategically
errant: "Jamás se hace mención de la brújula [There is never any mention of

a compass]," as Schevill and Bonilla remind us, noting the logic of Cervantes's dismissiveness toward history or cartography.[4] The errancy of the ships themselves across the northern seas shows that, for the first half of the journey of the *Persiles*, Cervantes's "wandering imagination" was encompassed by romance.

THE MAIN PLOT

The first installment of the journey across these cold climates is not mentioned until book 2, when Periandro's ten-chapter narration furnishes it as a deferred prologue (2.10–20). Glossing over their royal lineage and falsifying their kinship, Periandro begins by recounting how he and his "sister" Auristela, having escaped from a band of pirates and taken refuge with a community of fisherfolk, expedite a double wedding by rearranging the couples. During the wedding festivities, a band of brigands, shades of Heliodorus, swoops down to steal both Auristela and the new brides (2.12). Periandro and the fishermen become pirates themselves, for a season, during which they comb the North Seas for their lost women. During this watery quest, Periandro has encounters at sea with the aged Danish king Leopoldio, a suffering cuckold, and, soon after, with the Lithuanian widow Sulpicia, an avenging pirate woman (2.13–14), both of whom insert their stories into that of the hero. Periandro also narrates the dream-vision discussed in chapter 3 of the present book, with its parade of personifications (2.15); his vessel's slow drift toward, and ultimate congealment in, the icy Arctic seas, where his party is marvelously rescued by a squadron of Lithuanian skiers (2.16–18); his taming of King Cratilo's barbaric horse (2.20); his springtime sea voyage back to Denmark and, finally, via the Irish coast, to the Barbaric Isle, whose inhabitants imprison him (2.20).

At this juncture we are back to the in medias res beginnings of the *Persiles*, with the hero being hoisted up from an underground dungeon in preparation for the barbarians' ritual sacrifice, which requires, as noted in the preceding chapter, that his heart be charred and pulverized in accordance with the Barbaric Law (1.1). Periandro escapes both executioners and a watery death, this last thanks to Arnaldo, a princely rival who will also pursue Auristela to the very ends of the *Persiles*. Both men sail back to the Barbaric Isle, Periandro disguised as a female this time, in order to rescue the captive Auristela (1.2–3). When the hero's cross-dressed beauty attracts the desire of a barbarian, an erotic explosion foments a civil war and an insular holocaust (1.4). The protagonists are offered refuge from the flames in the sea-cave of Antonio, a Spaniard who interrupts the main narrative with his life story, the first of the *Persiles*'s many interpolations (1.5–6). Antonio and his family will accompany the protagonists on most of the journey to Rome, sharing a series of Northern adventures with them that includes an encounter with the Italian dancing-teacher Rutilio, whose inset story discloses his torpid sexual biography to the pilgrims (1.8–9); a meeting at sea with the dying Portuguese lover Manuel de Sosa Coitiño, whose fatal erotic rejection is related at bemused length (1.10–11); and a reunion of the Irish family of the Mauricios (Fitzmaurices), who narrate their own calamities in tandem (1.12–14).

Book 2 narrates the protagonists' tediously overlong visit, reminiscent of Don Quixote's visit to the Duke and Duchess, with the Irish king Policarpo, an old man who runs about his palace distractedly muttering the Pauline dictum that "es mejor casarse que abrasarse [it is better to marry than to burn]" (1 Cor. 7:9). During their regal captivity, the main personages become involved in a mesh of palace intrigue, largely the result of the old king's grand passion for Auristela, and his daughter's similar desires for Periandro (2.3–17). A narrow escape from Policarpo's burning palace moves the party to the snowy Isla de los Ermitas (Isle of the Hermits), whose resident ascetics Renato and Eusebia recount their former amorous travails within French chivalric court circles (2.18–21). At the close of book 2, the pilgrims bid farewell to the northern latitudes and sail southward to Portugal (2.21).

Their joyous arrival in Lisbon, where the party is feted by the governor and enjoys a pleasant holiday of tourism, marks the beginnings of the Southern adventures and of the second half of the *Persiles* (3.1), which takes place in Portugal, Spain, Provence, and Italy. Wearing pilgrims' habits purchased in Lisbon and taking only one beast of burden for their necessities, the party sets off across Spain on foot, aiming to cover two or three leagues per day. At an inn in Badajoz, they lodge with a cry of players, whose resident poet tries to talk Auristela into becoming a farsanta (comedienne), even though his discourse betrays all the cruelty, hypocrisy, and greed that distinguished the politics of the Golden Age theater.[5] As the pilgrims enter an oak forest in Extremadura, en route to the shrine of Guadalupe, an encounter with an infant suddenly involves them in the misfortunes of Feliciana de la Voz, an unwed mother who recounts her *caso*, and in their felicitous resolution several days later (3.2–5). From Guadalupe, the pilgrims walk through Trujillo and Talavera, on whose outskirts they witness a horseman being thrown by his horse: the shaken victim, a Pole called Ortel Banedre, shares with them the two great crises of his sexual and violent life (3.6–7). Near Toledo, the pilgrims witness a squadron of dancing *villanas*, one of whom is Tozuelo, the male stand-in for his pregnant girlfriend, whose "in-drag" representation we discussed in chapter 4, and whose impromptu wedding the pilgrims help celebrate (3.8). From Aranjuez, the pilgrims walk on to Ocaña, where the long-exiled Antonio reveals his identity in considerate stages to his aged parents (3.8–9). Having dropped off Antonio and his wife Ricla in Ocaña, the remaining pilgrims now head toward "un lugar ... de cuyo nombre no me acuerdo [a place ... whose name I have forgotten]" (3.10), a place forever fixed by the opening sentence of *Don Quixote*. In the plaza of this nameless town, the travelers witness a typical Golden Age scam when two fast-talking students from Salamanca, disguised as recently ransomed Algerian captives, pressure the crowd for alms by narrating the false history of their captivity (3.10). On the road again to Valencia, the pilgrims experience a hairbreadth escape from the hands of some *moriscos* who, as a community, are about to flee Spain aboard Turkish vessels (3.11). When the pilgrims finally arrive in Barcelona, they encounter an Aragonese lady whom they had earlier succoured on the road, Ambrosia Agustina, who narrates the tale of her own cross-dressed quest for her husband (3.12). Although she offers the pilgrims the use of her brother's galleys, the travelers, deferring to Auristela's fear of the sea, continue their journey overland, entering into France through Perpignan (3.12).

While in Provence, three French beauties, all potential brides for a certain Duke of Nemurs, join their entourage (3.13), and while dining alfresco the party is disturbed by the violent drama of the mad Count Domicio, whose wife recounts the tragic results of his mistress's poisoned shirt (3.14–16). Since Periandro's active involvement in this domestic tragedy costs him a near-fatal fall from a tower, the pilgrims must wait out his month-long convalescence before resuming their journey. When they take to the road again, they find themselves lodging in the same inn as a Scottish countess called Ruperta who, while on the road seeking vengeance for her husband's murder, ends up marrying the murderer's son. In the same inn, the pilgrims also encounter the adulterous wife of the Pole Ortel Banedre, who moves them to pity and assistance by a recital of her picaresque wanderings from one man to another (3.16–17). An octogenarian sage called Soldino, a Spaniard who had once served under Carlos V, comes to the inn to predict a kitchen fire which, before long, consumes the entire dwelling. Afterward he conducts the pilgrims to a hidden meadow where he lives in Prospero-style retirement, having, like the hero of Shakespeare's *Tempest*, also forsworn his books (3.18–19). Cervantes's travelers then cross through the Piedmont into Milan, proceeding from there to Lucca, where they participate in the drama of Isabela Castrucha's feigned demonic possession that closes book 3 (3.20–21).

When the party finally arrives on the outskirts of Rome in book 4, their dinner in a local *mesón* is interrupted by a Spanish man of letters, the pilgrim-editor whose verbal *resumé* identifies him as a surrogate of Cervantes himself

(4.1). The next day in a wooded area near Rome, the party happens upon two of Auristela's admirers, the constant prince Arnaldo and the Duke of Nemurs, both wounded from a duel over her picture (4.2–3). After tending to the victims, the travelers enjoy a climactic vision of Rome (4.3) before descending to the city itself, where they soon learn that their muleteer Bartolomé and Ortel Banedre's wanton wife Luisa have been sentenced to hang for a street brawl that took the Pole's life (4.5). While the pilgrims busy themselves bailing out the prisoners (who eventually marry and fare badly in Naples), Auristela begins taking Catholic instruction in all the mysteries, catechism lessons which daily reinforce her ascetic leanings. Apart from visiting Rome's seven churches, a pious custom of all Renaissance pilgrims, the party hears about a curious museum there, whose empty canvases await the portraits of famous future poets, among whom Torquato Tasso is singled out by a Cervantine *vaticinatio ex eventu*.[6]

During their Roman holiday, Periandro is invited to visit a woman from Ferrara, a courtesan ironically called Hipólita, who wishes to show him a storeroom of treasures that includes paintings by Rafael and Michelangelo. Because Periandro flees from her embrace, Hipólita first falsely accuses him of robbery; then recants and publicly confesses her mad passion for him; and, lastly, hires a sorceress to inflict a disfiguring disease upon Auristela (4.7–10).[7] When she recovers, Auristela asks to be released from her vow to marry Periandro, a request that drives Periandro to leave town in a despondent state, wandering south until, in a wood outside of Naples, he overhears a Norwegian conversation between his old tutor and the reformed dancing-master Rutilio. This crucial exchange provides the reader with all the regal politics of Tile and Friesland that led to the pilgrimage in the first place (4.12). Since this conversation also reveals the news that Prince Magsimino has just anchored his ships at Naples in quest of his betrothed Auristela, Periandro returns to Rome instantly. He meets up with a repentant Auristela before the Basilica of Saint Paul, where the lovers undergo their final series of trabajos: first Periandro is seriously wounded in the shoulder by Hipólita's jealous lover, one of Cervantes's gallery of *rufianes*; then Periandro and Auristela both prepare to confront the dreaded Magsimino. When the latter pulls up in a carriage, he is already dying of a fever endemic to the Mediterranean, and the last gesture of this formerly repugnant person is surprisingly magnanimous: he personally joins the protagonists' hands in marriage and then dies. After Periandro recovers from his wound and Auristela kisses the Pope's feet, the couple returns to Thule for a long and fruitful life that—according to an aftertext projected by the closing line of the *Persiles*—even includes "biznietos [great-grandchildren]" (4.14).

The Biblical Pattern in the Plot

What has not been rehearsed in the foregoing synopsis of the *Persiles*, of the main plot of its two-year journey, is the narrative's prefiguration by the story of Israel: Israel captive, wandering and, finally, restored. Let us thicken the plot by retelling it through the grid of Christian typology. The pilgrimage in the *Persiles*, the anxious and vicissitude-filled progress of its protagonists, is from Iceland to Rome, but it may also be read allegorically as a journey from Egypt to the New Jerusalem. There is manifold internal evidence that the Exodus story subtends—or "pennes," to use George Herbert's verb—the main plot of Cervantes's last romance.[8] Allusions to the Exodus event are obtrusive throughout the *Persiles*, as when Clodio promises to liberate Auristela "deste Egipto [from this Egypt]" and take her to "la tierra de promisión [the Promised Land]" (191); or when Lisbon is itself described as "la tierra de promisión" (277); or when Hipólita is labeled as a "nueva egipcia [new Egyptian]," an allusion to Potiphar's wife in Genesis 39 (446). The text's depiction of itself as a pilgrims' progress toward "the Promised Land" has inspired a number of Christian allegorical readings.[9] The remarks that follow, focused on the *Persiles* as Christian allegory, are meant to supplement these interpretations. My own organizing interest in the *Persiles* as Christian allegory has a psychological rather than doctrinal end: in order to understand the strange affectlessness of Cervantes's protagonists, it is crucial to understand the ritualistic nature of the text they motivate, with its special orderliness and repetition of parts.

Three landmarks across the main plot function as vehicles of a kind of typology, in the looser literary, if not desanctified, sense of the word.[10] These are three poems, two religious sonnets framing a hymn: Rutilio's sonnet on Noah's flood, sung near the beginning of the journey (1.18); Feliciana de la Voz's hymn to the Virgin, sung at the midpoint of the pilgrimage (3.5); and the unknown pilgrim's sonnet to Rome, recited near the end of the journey, at a climactic moment, during the pilgrims' epiphanic vision of the Eternal City (4.3).[11] Sandwiched in between these three poems are two episodes of a markedly typological character, representing both Old and New Testament events: the pilgrims' entrapment in the "belly" of their capsized vessel in part 1 of the *Persiles* (2.2); and their betrayal and near-destruction by a dissembling community of moriscos in part 2 (3.11).

The first religious sonnet, which Rutilio sings in Tuscan aboard ship, during an unusually serene night in the North Sea, links the pilgrims in their perilous wanderings to the "reliquias del linaje humano [remnants of the human race]" who found asylum within Noah's ark. The sonnet evokes the ark itself as an "excelsa máquina [sublime machine]" that breaks the laws of

Fate ("los fueros de la Parca"). This particular Fate, one of the three Moirae, is evidently Atropos, who cuts the thread of human lives with her shears, and whose decrees were held to be inexorable. Cervantes has Rutilio picture this Fate as she must have appeared in Noah's day, as "fiera y licenciosa [ferocious and dissolute]" in her destruction of human life (132). In celebrating the ark that subverts the Parca, Rutilio is reiterating what A.C. Charity calls the long and gradual process by which Israel "must deny the mythical cosmos of her neighbours, with its concomitants of eternal repetition, manipulative magic, manipulative ritual."[12] Rutilio, whose exemplary story will be more fully developed in the following chapter, had himself been manipulated by magic while imprisoned in Rome for the sexual kidnapping of one of his dance students. His story about this *hechicera* (witch) represents her as an angel who promised that she would break his chains if he agreed to marry her. After conveying him on a magic carpet to Norway, she turns into a wolf while embracing him, during which metamorphosis he stabs her dead (1.8). Although Rutilio wants to turn his back on the whole magical cosmos his wolfwoman represents, the language of his sonnet shows that she has been displaced onto another "fiera"—projected onto a Parca—and that only the "ark" he is sailing on, the pilgrims' boat, can break her powers. By the end of his sonnet, the analogues between the occupants of Noah's ark and those of the pilgrims' drifting vessel begin to break down, and the romance conventions quickly eclipse the biblical ones. The sonnet itself, however, stands out obtrusively as the first major sign of a prefigurative pattern that has been programmatically drawn across the main plot of the *Persiles*.

Some three months and several shipwrecks later, a tempest completely overturns the pilgrims' vessel, which washes up to an island off the coast of Ibernia (Ireland) with all the passengers trapped within. When the islanders first see the capsized vessel floating into harbor, "creyeron ser el de alguna ballena o de otro gran pescado [they thought it was that of some whale or other great fish]" washed ashore by the recent storm (162). While workmen are busily trying to right the ship, a spectator remarks that he witnessed a similar accident in Genoa with a Spanish galley, "y aun podría ser viviesen agora las personas que segunda vez nacieron al mundo del vientre desta galera [and the people who were born a second time from the belly of that vessel may still be living]." The king responds that it would be a miracle indeed "si este vientre vomita vivos [if this belly vomits up live people]," and the narrator speaks of the great desire of everyone on the beach "de ver el parto [to see the delivery or birth]" of the pilgrims, later described as "resucitados [returned to life]." All of this, of course, adds up to an extended allusion to the biblical captivity of Jonah in the whale (Jon. 1:17–2:10), linking Cervantes's pilgrims to the Leviathan story. The ship's hull is insistently called a "vientre," corresponding to the "belly of the fish" in Jonah's story, and the notion of being "vomited" out of captivity is common to both the *Persiles* and its biblical subtext.

This pattern across the main plot, however, a passage across biblical linear time, is shown to be in constant tension with verisimilitude (to wit, the deliverance of the pilgrims "need not be taken as a miracle" because a similar rescue occurred in Genoa once). A pilgrims' progress is not an easy story to write in the late Renaissance, and Cervantes feels obliged to tell us so. The chapter begins with a criticism of its own fictionality, when the narrator in one of his increasingly obtrusive eruptions[13] confides to us that it cost "el autor desta historia [the author of this story]" some four or five false starts to get this chapter under way, "casi como dudando que fin en el tomaría [almost as if he doubted his purpose in it]" (162). Cervantes's hyperactive narrator here calls attention to the "author's" resistance to a typological pattern that is at odds with the progress of his own pilgrims toward love and intimacy: writing plausibly about "born-again" Christians who still have miles to go in their pilgrimage would make any author hesitate.

Close to the center of the *Persiles*, and soon after the pilgrims have arrived in the so-called "tierra de promisión [Promised Land]," Cervantes inserts into the main narrative Feliciana de la Voz's long hymn to the Virgin of Guadalupe. It is a discourse that spans the whole of Old Testament history, from Genesis to an imaginative point in time just prior to the Annunciation. In twelve stanzas of *octava real* meter, the hymn establishes Mary as the antitype of the gardens of Jericho, the temple of Solomon, and Esther. Mary is also pictured as the "brazo de Dios [arm of God]" which detained Abraham from his sacrifice, in order to give the world the true sacrificial Lamb ("Cordero"). The closing stanza of this long poem depicts that moment in biblical history when the angel Gabriel first flutters his wings prior to visiting Earth for the "embajada honesta [chaste mission]" of the Annunciation (3.5).[14] Ending as it does in the temporal center of biblical history—in the moment between both testaments—and in the virtual center of the text, the hymn reveals the rigid sequence of events that funds the main narrative of the *Persiles*. Cervantes's choice of an unwed mother to sing this hymn to the Virgin Mother will be the organizing interest of chapter 9 of this book. In the present context, it is sufficient for our purposes to show the high degree of organization, rarely acknowledged by critics, that subtends Cervantes's main narrative.

Typology is at work again when the pilgrims, after crossing through Castilla and La Mancha, arrive in "un lugar de moriscos [a place of moriscos]"[15] in the kingdom of Valencia (3.11). The hospitality of the inhabitants there masks their treacherous intentions, a conspiracy to destroy the pilgrims that is virtually foreseen by Periandro, who prefigures the event with a New Testament abstract: "Con palmas ... recibieron al Señor en Jerusalén los mismos que de allí a pocos dias le pusieron en una Cruz [The same people who received Christ in Jerusalem with palms were to crucify him several days later]" (354). And several days later, in point of fact, Cervantes's pilgrims recapitulate Christ's betrayal when the moriscos turn on them; they are saved by some Christian moriscos from being murdered, and after the town is burned to the ground by visiting Turks in "el nombre de Mahoma [the name of Mohammed]," the pilgrims continue their journey. When, after numerous adventures in France and northern Italy, the pilgrims arrive at a hill from where they can look down at the city of Rome, they kneel in adoration to it, "como a cosa sacra [as if to a sacred thing]" (426). At that moment, an unknown pilgrim breaks out into a spontaneous sonnet to Rome, whose closing line establishes it as the great model "de la ciudad de Dios [of the city of God]."[16] This allusion to Augustine's *De civitate Dei*, a work that itself uses the term *city* as a symbolic mode of designation, reminds us of the traces; in the main narrative of the *Persiles*, of the Augustinian theme of human desires and God as their point of repose.[17] Cervantes's fictive Rome, built on soil mixed with martyr's blood ("con la sangre de mártires mezclada"), is the symbolic goal of all Christian pilgrims and the equivalent of their Promised Land. Rome closes the prefigurative pattern established throughout the *Persiles* by strategically placed spots of typology, of which I have selected five: three religious poems—the central one spanning the whole of Old Testament history—and two incidents recapitulating Old and New Testament events. These analogical relations establish a symbolic spread across the *Persiles* from the Flood up to the Papacy. They also reveal a remarkable degree of literary organization, one must conclude, for a writer accused of having produced in the *Persiles* "a farrago of helterskelter fantasy."[18]

THE PRODUCTION OF CHARACTER

The formal controls in the main narrative extend to the character—or more accurately, the agency—of each of Cervantes's titular protagonists, Persiles/Periandro and Auristela/Sigismunda. Because beauty does as beauty is in allegory, these protagonists are predictably beautiful. Modern readers may be dismayed at the frequency of the narrator's panegyrics to the physical beauty of Cervantes's heroes. The opening chapter of book 3, when the entire party of pilgrims is described as they appear to the admiring eyes of Lisbon, may serve to instance this formulaic homage: "En efeto, todos juntos y cada uno de por sí, causaban espanto y maravilla a quien los miraba; pero sobre todos campeaba la sin par Auristela y el gallardo Periandro [In short, both as a group and as individuals, they all excited amazement and wonder in their onlookers; but the peerless Auristela and the graceful Periandro outdid them all]" (279). Schevill long ago lamented the "repetition *ad nauseam*" of the heroine's beauty: "Words seem to fail to express how beautiful Auristela is. The result is that she is nothing else."[19] Except when she is poisoned by Hipólita's hired witch in book 4, during which disease she is colorfully uglified—"se le parecían ... verde el carmín de sus labios [the rose of her lips seemed green]" (458)—we are never suffered to forget that Auristela's beauty is "sin par." And only when Periandro has fallen from Count Domicio's tower and is spilling quantities of blood "por los ojos, narices y boca [through his eyes, nose, and mouth]" (3.14) does he appear less graceful than normal. The Victorian translator of the English *Persiles* (1854), Louisa Dorothea Stanley, speculates on Cervantes's creation of a fair Periandro: "For assuredly those blue eyes and golden ringlets must have been most unlike the visions of beauty that dwelt around him, in his own land of Spain."[20] Lovers of Cervantine realism may miss Sancho's unbeglamoured description of the peerless Dulcinea with her "olorcito hombruno [slightly mannish odor]," or of Don Quixote's dream of Belerma's "oral mensil [monthly periods]." These endearing biological realities remain occulted in an allegorical hero, however, whose physical appearance is cogently depicted as a declaration of what he or she is so that the depiction itself may suffice for identification without any further amplification. Honig succinctly explains the strategy behind the beautification of the allegorical hero: "Before we know who he is, we know what he is."[21]

Even more than for their beauty, Cervantes's heroes have been critically reviled for their moral perfections. The norm for characterization that crystallized in the eighteenth century has dominated the discursive practices of writers of prose fiction until very recently, although even the characters of a contemporary author like John Updike have been dismissed for lacking "the stubborn selfhood and waywardness of the truly memorable figures in literature."[22] The same kind of critics who exalt "stubborn selfhood"—with all its fictions of consistency and closure—have ritually deplored the characters of Persiles and Sigismunda. Entwistle, for instance, accuses them of embodying what he calls "the exemplary fallacy." "The spectacle of unrelieved virtue in the main persons proves intolerable," he laments, adding with remarkable condescension that, had Cervantes lived longer, "he might have agreed that the novel, like tragedy, needs the saving human touch of imperfection." Because Entwistle sees the protagonists as "figures rendered pallid by their aureoles," he speculates that Cervantes himself "must have tired of their perfection." Trying to explain the grounds

of his argument—which I believe belongs to "the perfection fallacy"—
Entwistle concludes that "the portrait of the perfect prince fails to excite
admiration because it is monotonous."[23] In the same critical vein, E.C. Riley
regards perfection in the *Persiles* as a quality that does not make "for great
character-creation."[24] And Byron, too, having pronounced the *Persiles* as a
splendid failure—"a Magnificat, a great cantata to the joyous complexity of
life"—sees the protagonists "as wooden, rolled out on schedule to strike the
hours," hewn from a material, that is, even denser than the so-called
cardboard characters ritually damned by advocates of neorealism. Not only
are Cervantes's main personages "wooden," but also, in Byron's overloaded
criticism, they are chaste and stupid: "Auristela-Sigismunda drifts erotically
throughout the book exciting desire in the men she meets while remaining
as chaste as a holy image. It is hard to think of Periandro-Persiles without
recalling comedienne Anna Russell's description of Siegfried as 'very big,
very strong, very stupid.'" After confidently predicting extratextual "lives of
unflinching rectitude" for the protagonists, Byron feels obliged to conclude
that Cervantes "did not love the population of the *Persiles*," possibly echoing
the earlier and similar judgment of Matilda Pomes.[25]

A robust complacency emerges from the above descriptions, or rather
judgments, of the character of the protagonists of the *Persiles*. The punchy
conjectures regarding Cervantes's immaturity, or his feelings of tiredness
with his own characters, even border on arrogance. The critical reification of
"unflinching rectitude"—entailing various ideological assumptions that
privilege the individual over the collective—turns out, in fact, to be a myth.
The virtue of Cervantes's protagonists, as all close readers will attest, is by no
means "unrelieved." Auristela, in particular, regularly displays for us that
"saving touch" of imperfection. Not only are her chronic fits of gratuitous
jealousy throughout book 2 worth citing (El Saffar writes that "Auristela's
jealousy of Sinforosa nearly overwhelms her, and literally provokes yet
another storm at sea"),[26] but also the more fraudulent traits she has inherited
from her Greek romance predecessor; the heroine of the *Aethiopica*.
Chariclea's similar dedication to virginity, as Northrop Frye reminds us,
"certainly does not imply that she is also truthful or straightforward; in fact
a more devious little twister would be hard to find among heroines of
romance."[27] Auristela's own deviousness, painfully apparent in her
untruthful dealings with the guileless Policarpa in book 2, is by no means her
only flaw. Her obsession with her chastity, a quality that critics other than
Bandera have noted with disapproval, often has a narcissistic edge to it: "¡Oh
hermano!, mires por mi honra [O my brother, look after my honor!]" (296)
is her egotistical response to the sexual sufferings of Feliciana de la Voz,
which she largely takes as cautionary. Auristela is also something of a worrier,

even a whiner, and in a refrain that gathers negative momentum as the book continues, she frets about how she and Periandro will fare when "un mismo yugo optima nuestros cuellos [one and the same yoke burdens our necks]." Directly upon her arrival in Rome, she peremptorily declares her intentions to go to heaven "sin rodeos, sin sobresaltos, y sin cuidados [with no delays, no unpleasant surprises, and no anxieties]" (4.10). Auristela has always wished to escape the sea, that symbol of mutability, and even to avoid "los caminos torcidos y las dudosas sendas [the twisted roads and the doubtful paths]" (4.11). At times she even sounds pertly egotistical: "Que más me debo yo a mi que no a otro [I owe more to myself than to anyone else]" is the curt reason she gives for wanting to be released from her engagement (461). Otis H. Green is not alone in his vision of Auristela as "a self-centered young woman whose only concern [is] for her *pudor* [modesty]."[28] And as for Periandro, his refreshing fallibility has been noted by more than one critic: "Periandro es un llorón [Periandro is a crybaby]," declares Stanislav Zimic emphatically, adding for good measure that, in the horse-taming episode, the hero is "un sujeto jactancioso de la peor especie [an arrogant boaster of the worst kind]."[29] Criticism has also often pointed out Periandro's representation as an insensitive, even defensive, storyteller. Cervantes strategically surrounds Periandro, during his long, serial narration in book 2, with an alert audience of narratees given to censoring many of his narrative procedures. Noting that a reader's attention will be "naturally caught by any suggestion of imperfection in such a hero," Riley asks the blunt critical question: "What critical devil prompted Cervantes to make Persiles a bit of a bore to his companions?"[30]

The frequent critical complaint about the lack of great character-creation in the *Persiles* shows how difficult it is to dislodge character as the touchstone of narrative criticism. It is a given that Persiles and Sigismunda cannot compete with Don Quixote and Sancho for that "stubborn selfhood" ingredient that Cervantes himself gave to Western fiction, but there are other discursive practices—ones that do not oppose the individual to the collective—that critics conditioned by realism seem to have difficulties envisioning. To invoke a conception of character based on the tenets of nineteenth-century realism, as the above critics do, is to forget that the novel works, as Lennard Davis explains, "by turning personality into controlled character": "Like a desirable commodity that seems to offer the promise of an improved life, or like an objectified fashion model who beckons the user of the targeted product into the frame of an advertisement, character holds out the possibility of personal fulfillment in a world that is increasingly making such fulfillment inconceivable."[31] Whether Cervantes may have conceived "the possibility of personal fulfillment" in the closing years of his life, he chose to experiment with the kind of writing in which character was not, as the great novelistic myth would have it, universal. Persiles/Periandro and Auristela/Sigismunda are not wayward and memorable characters because they are allegorical agents, self-divided figures (as their names show). As incomplete personages, they are acting in consort with other agents, the entire cast created to solve a given set of problems. Had Cervantes worked harder to "humanize his protagonists, they may have eclipsed the generic intent of his allegorical romance. As allegorical agents, Cervantes's protagonists do not have solid and memorable characters because, to borrow a phrase from C.S. Lewis, character is what they have "to produce."[32] What is valid for the cluster of heroes of *The Faerie Queene* is also valid for each of Cervantes's titular protagonists: "The moral obligation of a central character may simply be ... to pull himself together."[33] Allegorical heroes seem to be thinly characterized because they are being serially characterized: their cognitive integration is achieved piecemeal in a quest which is a kind of collective self-creation. This may explain, in part, why Cervantes's protagonists are never called by their real names until the last book of the *Persiles*: the "real" Persiles and Sigismunda are by then a kind of composite picture of all the lovers whose exemplary stories they have internalized during a journey of seventy-nine chapters.

Cervantes's rigid control over the behavior of his titular protagonists is generically motivated by his uses of allegorical romance. If Periandro and Auristela have been denied true individualizing character, it is not because Cervantes disliked them or tired of them, but because he envisioned them as representative types with characteristically limited ways of behaving. Fletcher may help readers to imagine a "real-life" analogue of Periandro: "If we were to meet an allegorical character in real life, we would say of him that he was obsessed with only one idea, or that he had an absolutely one-track mind, or that his life was patterned according to absolutely rigid habits from which he never allowed himself to vary. It would seem that he was driven by some hidden, private force."[34] Cervantes's protagonists are driven agents, with characteristically compulsive behavior patterns: Periandro is obsessed with the idea of getting to Rome and to "la dulce posesión esperada [the sweet, long-awaited possession]" of Auristela (413), and Auristela with the idea of getting there *intacta*. Both lovers seem to be acting under compulsion and, despite long colloquies or soliloquies on the subject of their respective desires, rarely do they manifest any evidence of either inner control or active freedom of choice.

Instead of criticizing the protagonists for not being what they are not— that is, novelistic characters—we might try to see them as allegorical agents, as creatures strategically remote from realism and mimesis. Setting aside the chivalric dimensions, Periandro in many ways resembles an allegorical hero like Spenser's Redcrosse Knight, whose identity is revealed to him only after he has endured the trials that attend his sign. Redcrosse "is not so much a real person as he is a generator of other secondary personalities, which are partial aspects of himself."[35] These other secondary personalities then tend to react, either against or with the hero, in a kind of syllogistic manner. Ruth El Saffar suggests a similar dynamics for the *Persiles* when she writes that "through the new secondary characters, Periandro and Auristela once again meet images of themselves."[36] Secondary or subcharacters have long been considered a standard feature of the allegorical repertoire. An understanding of the fragmented conceptual hero in Spenserian allegory is useful for reading Cervantes's protagonists, who may each be said to generate a great crowd of subcharacters—aspects, essentially, of themselves—who then help the heroes to "produce" character. Unaware of the *Persiles*, Fletcher actually mentions "the servant Sancho Panza" as belonging to the type of "subcharacters who arise to help the hero," not an outrageous but an unfortunate example, I think, since it wrenches *Don Quixote* into the category of allegorical romances like *The Faerie Queene* and the *Persiles*. The steady generation of subcharacters across allegory, the refraction of the allegorical protagonist into composite chips of his personhood, has its modern "real-life" analogue in people who "project," who run about, as Fletcher explains, "ascribing fictitious personalities to those whom they meet and live with." By analyzing the projections of such people—the needs, desires, fears, and hates they generate—we determine what is going on in their minds. Similarly, allegorical agents project their selves into refracted "chips of composite character," into personifications that help us to read them.[37]

Apart from the personifications projected by Periandro in his dream of "SENSUALIDAD," earlier discussed in chapter 3, we might consider Auristela's "projection" of a subcharacter in Leonora, the deified and depriving female protagonist in the episode of the "enamoured Portuguese" (1.10) who, in an elaborately staged Christian ritual, rejects and essentially kills her despairing lover. Cervantes manipulates Leonora into service as an "expression," a negative example, of Auristela's potential sexual powers: the conclusion of Auristela's marriage-versus-the-nunnery dilemma in book 4 is predetermined by Leonora's toxic solution to a comparable psychomachia in book 1. Auristela's final destiny as Periandro's wife has been preordained from the first episode of the *Persiles*, where the subcharacters of Antonio and Ricla jointly relate the beginnings of their conjugal love and its resultant fruitfulness. If Auristela seems wooden and pallid to many critics, it is not because she is too virtuous but because she is not free. Her role is not to represent a memorable and convincing individual, but to internalize, through a kind of shuffling technique, the personhood of the female subcharacters. She is like Spenser's Britomart, who internalizes Amoret, the subcharacter she has rescued from the House of Busyrane in *The Faerie Queene* (3.12). As an allegorical character, Auristela's agency is prefabricated.

Periandro is in a similar modal bind. All his erotic desires, as the text slowly reveals, are either personified in his dreams or enacted by his subcharacters. The sexual feelings repressed by the devoted Periandro are expressed for him by the Tuscan dancing-master Rutilio, a "facet" of Periandro. As one of those "subcharacters who arise to help the hero," the reformed Rutilio strategically materializes in Rome during Periandro's final erotic crisis. Another subcharacter who helps to "express" the hero is Isabela's lover: when she describes him as "ese putativo Ganimedes [that so-called Ganymede]" (409), we know him to be a "facet" of Periandro, the man whom Clodio earlier in the book called "este Ganimedes" (182). By working with facets of the protagonist's composite character, in other words, authors can better control the meanings their heroes are meant to carry: but that control implies, of course, some severe limitations on the hero undergoes a change as a result of a psychomachia in which he battles, or of an agony, a progress, a voyage to the moon, or whatever typical story we choose, should not blind us to the real lack of freedom in all these stories."[38] Cervantes's protagonists, in other words, are governed by a rigid destiny, a kind of authorial control that makes us rethink our conventional notions of allegory as a "pilgrim's *progress*." Although they have perhaps seen, and certainly they have heard, everything, Periandro and Auristela seem scarcely changed at the end of their two-year pilgrimage: their characters, as it were, remain predictable and underdeveloped.

Psychoanalysis has assisted literature, and vice versa, in understanding that allegorical heroes are like certain kinds of neurotics, people with patterns of behavior that are anxious, rigid, authoritarian. These modern insights allow us to recognize the "wooden" portrayals of Periandro and Auristela, their one-track minds, as a kind of "frozen agency."[39] The psychoanalytic analogues for allegory are obsession and compulsion, the first as an *idée fixe*, the second as an act, although the two are often closely related. It was via caricature—a mode not unfamiliar to Cervantes—that Freud himself equated compulsion and religion: "It might be maintained," he writes in *Totem and Taboo*, that "an obsessional neurosis is a caricature of religion."[40] The equation of religion—with or without its caricature in the compulsion neuroses—and literary allegory is of course an ancient one: we need only invoke the *Psychomachia*, the *Commedia*, *Everyman*, and *The Faerie Queene* as examples. Allegory, whose natural theme is temptation, is "the most religious of the modes," Fletcher reminds us, "obeying, as it does, the commands of the Superego, believing in Sin, portraying atonements through ritual."[41] Cervantes's allegorical agents may be seen obeying, believing, and atoning across the text of the main narrative, a "compulsive" fiction of Christian romance—with both agents *driven* to reach Rome, the heavenly city, in a quest whose "progress" is repeatedly halted by "digressions." Throughout this laborious process, the *trabajos* of the title, the protagonists are finally disclosed to us through a multitude of generated subcharacters.

Cervantes's discursive practice of subordinating character to agency throughout the *Persiles* is revealed by his own surrogate storyteller, the protagonist Periandro. In a mysterious remark that strongly militates against novelistic individualism, Periandro defends his storytelling techniques by constituting himself as a "place" open to Otherness: "Yo soy como esto que se llama lugar, que es donde todas las cosas caben, y no hay ninguna fuera del lugar [I am like that which is called *place*, where all things fit and nothing is out of place]" (227). This improbable site of coalescence—a narrating self as a locus of attraction for all perceptions, a kind of "one-size-fits-all" narrator—belongs to a quintessentially rhetorical discourse.[42] The question of what constitutes place, however, is especially pertinent to ontological speculations regarding character. We may be led, for example, to cross-discipline rhetorical notions of *lugar* with the "physics" of place, problematized as early as Aristotle, who queried the accepted notion that extant beings had to be in *some* place, if only because nonbeing was in *no* place: where, he asked, with pointed literary flair, were the Goat-stag and the Sphinx? (208a).[43] In comparing himself to "that which is called place," the hero of the *Persiles* embraces not only Aristotle's sphinxes and goat-stags but also all *other* notions of Otherness. This embrace of Otherness, in its inclusion of the disparate and the incongruent, seems peculiarly postmodern. "I am like that which is called place" would seem to anticipate some of the insights of modern psychoanalysis, which has an interest in the concept of place as well as the logic of place (topology). One pioneering instance might be the Lacanian notion of the "margins" of psychoanalytic discourse— "where the ego seems to speak almost at the cost of disintegrating." This place, reminiscent of the subject's origins, is a place Lacan ambiguously calls the "limit experience of the non-existent," of what is *not* created by language.[44] An even more promising gloss on Cervantes's *lugar* may be found in Julia Kristeva's theoretical description of the semiotic chora, which addresses the pre-Oedipal state marginal to language.[45] Kristeva's theory is grounded on Plato's representation, in the *Timaeus*, of the chora, the "nurse of all Becoming": "a Kind invisible and unshaped, *all-receptive*, and in some most perplexing and most baffling way partaking of the intelligible." And so we are led backward, courtesy of revisionary psychoanalysis, to the "baffling and obscure" model for the *place* to which Periandro compares himself, to Plato's "ever-existing Place, which admits not of destruction, *and provides room for all things that have birth*, itself being apprehensible by a kind of bastard reasoning by the aid of non-sensation, barely an object of belief; for when we regard this we dimly dream and affirm that it is somehow necessary that all that exists should exist in some spot and occupying some *place*."[46] As one of the central texts used to assimilate both Greek and Judeo-Christian traditions, Plato's *Timaeus* represents the unformed chaos or "nurse" of all material things as unambiguously feminine. In our time, then, through the framing discourses of Plato and revisionary psychoanalysis, we may begin to dimly enlighten (and be enlightened by) Cervantes's outrageous simile for the all-receptive storyteller. Out of the "place" that resembles both his hero and himself, Cervantes fashions a large and wayward population of subcharacters for his interpolated tales, and it is time to hear their side of the story.

NOTES

1. In 3.18, the prophet Soldino, who claims to have served under Carlos V, foresees certain feats at Lepanto by Don Juan of Austria (1572), as well as the death of Don Sebastián of Portugal at Alcazarquivir (1578), thereby dating the plot as earlier than 1572. The Spaniard Antonio mentions in 1.5 that he had fought under Carlos V in Germany (in his wars, c. 1547, against the Elector of Saxony and other Protestants); the Irishman Mauricio claims in 2.19 to have seen this king after he retired to his monastery at Yuste (1557–1558); and the Frenchman Sinibaldo communicates in 2.21 the death of Carlos V (1558), which dates the plot as later than 1558. In 3.10, two counterfeit captives feign a story of their sufferings in Algiers under the renegade Turk Dragut, a famously cruel Turkish corsair who died in 1565. But just before and after this episode, there are two surprising references to Philip III: one in 3.6 to his newly established court in Madrid (1606) and another in 3.11, albeit prophetic, to his expulsion of the Moors (1609). Searching for an exact chronology is futile: the *Persiles* is not historically rigorous because Cervantes was not aiming for a historical reconstruction. He was simply doing what Gabriel Garcia Márquez claims "all writers do": using historical elements "poetically" (see Raymond Leslie Williams, "The Visual Arts, the Poetization of Space and Writing: An Interview with Gabriel Garcia Márquez," *PMLA* 104 [March 1989: 136).

2. In his edition of the *Persiles*, between pages 144 and 145, Avalle-Arce includes a facsimile of the title page of Olaf Magnus's *Historia de gentibus septentrionalibus*, newly translated into Italian in 1565 and available to Cervantes. This *Historia* included maps that would have helped Cervantes with his itineraries for the *Persiles*. See also Ricardo Beltrán y Rózpide's "La pericia geográfica de Cervantes demostrada en la *Historia de los trabajos de Persiles y Sigismunda*," *Boletín de la Real Sociedad Geográfica* 64 (1923–1924): 270–93. Several critics have noted that Cervantes may have selected the Arctic landscape for the *Persiles* on the strength of Tasso's recommendation that poets seek their materials in, tellingly, the far-off and exotic lands "di Gotia e di Norveggia e di Suevia e d'Islanda" (*Discorsi del poema eroico*, 109). On Norway as a literary symbol, see Américo Castro, "Noruega, símbolo de la oscuridad," *Revista de filología española* 6 (1919): 184–86.

3. Stanley, "Preface," *Wanderings*, x–xi. Sismondi is cited by Stanley on p. viii.

4. Schevill and Bonilla, "Introduction," *Persiles*, xii.

5. Cervantes's failure to succeed "in the cruel patio" of Golden Age theater is instructive: "At a time when largely pre-proletarian audiences were eager to identify themselves with the powerful, the wealthy, the aristocratic—in short, with the fortunate— Cervantes offered then, themselves, sometimes idealized, as often not. He was turning up a side street while the parade went straight ahead, to where Lope was preparing to lead it" (Byron, *Cervantes: A Biography*, 288–89).

6. Beneath the empty canvas with Tasso's name is printed *Jerusalén libertada*, which Tasso "había de cantar ... con el más heroico y agradable plectro que hasta entonces ningún poeta huviese cantado [was to sing ... with the most heroic and pleasing plectrum used by any poet until then]." Cervantes's "after the fact" prediction of fame here also extends to the Spanish poet Francisco López de Zárate, who wrote a Christian epic on Constantine and the discovery of the True Cross (4.6).

7. See Lapesa's "En torno a *La española inglesa* y el *Persiles*." For a magisterial historicist reading of *La española inglesa*, see Johnson, "*La española inglesa* and the Practice of Literary Production," 377–416.

8. "For as the Jews of old by Gods command / Travell'd, and saw no town; / So now each Christian hath his journeys spann'd: their storie pennes and sets us down" ("The Bunch of Grapes," in *The Poems of George Herbert*, ed. F.E. Hutchinson [London: Oxford University Press, 1961], 118).

9. Inarguably the most sophisticated is Forcione's archetypal study of the *Persiles* in Cervantes' Christian Romance, where he links the cycle of catastrophe and restoration in the quests of the characters with the orthodox Christian myth of the Fall and Redemption.

10. Typology in its strict sense—as argued by theologians who find it inappropriate to literature—means God's historical design in which New Testament persons and events (antitypes) recapitulate and fulfill Old Testament persons and events (types). A.C. Charity, who acknowledges the tense relation between the currently available meanings of typology, sees it, in its least dogmatic sense, as "either the broad study, or any particular presentation, of the quasi-symbolic relations which one event may appear to bear to another—especially, but not exclusively, when these relations are the analogical ones existing between events which are taken to be one another's 'prefiguration' and 'fulfillment'" (*Events and Their Afterlife* [Cambridge: Cambridge University Press, 19661, 1). In its loosest sense, typology may offer "a kind of symbolic thought without any necessary Christian presumptions" (Earl Miner, "Afterword," *The Literary Uses of Typology*, ed. Earl Miner [Princeton: Princeton University Press, 19771, 393).

11. See 1.9 and 2.3 for two other interpolated sonnets in the *Persiles*.

12. Charity, *Events and Their Afterlife*, 118.

13. On the inconsistency of the narrator's role in the *Persiles*, see Forcione, *Cervantes, Aristotle, and the Persiles*, chaps. 6–8.

14. Forcione's description of Feliciana's hymn multiplies the typology: "The celestial palace with its gardens is simultaneously Eden, the imperfect temple of Solomon, and the New Jerusalem. Christ is both the lamb of God, the 'true sacrifice,' prefigured imperfectly in Abraham's sacrifice of Isaac, and the Messiah of the Apocalypse. The serpent is both the corrupter of Adam and the dragon slain by the Messiah" (*Cervantes' Christian Romance*, 88).

15. A morisco, also known as a *musulmán converso*, is a convert from the Muslim religion to Christianity. Philip III expelled them as a nation from Spain in 1609, a shameful historical event recalled in the Ricote episode in *Don Quixote* (2.54).

16. Cervantes was correct in saying that poetry was "la gracia que no quiso darme el

cielo [the grace that heaven did not wish to give me]." This last sonnet is the most mechanical of the poems he included in the *Persiles*. One wishes it could have been of the stature of Petrarch's *In Vita* no. 14 ("Movesi il vecchiere canuto e bianco"), about an ancient, white-haired pilgrim, broken down with age ("rotto de gli anni"), who leaves his anxious family to make this same pilgrimage, obviously his last, to Rome. Also far superior to Cervantes's poem is Dante's sublime simile of a Croatian pilgrim who visits Rome during a Jubilee Year (*Paradiso*, 31).

17. See chap. 15 on "The Two Cities in Early Biblical History," where Augustine distinguishes between the earthly city of Babylon and the heavenly city of Jerusalem.

18. Lewis, *The Shadow of Cervantes*, 188.

19. Rudolph Schevill, "Studies in Cervantes. I. 'Persiles y Sigismunda': The Question of Heliodorus," *Modern Philology* 4 (1907): 700.

20. Stanley, "Preface," *Wanderings*, xii.

21. Honig, *Dark Conceit*, 85, 81.

22. Robert Towers, Review essay of *Problems and Other Stories*, by John Updike, *The New York Review of Books*, 8 November 1979, 19.

23. Entwistle, "Ocean of Story," 166, 163.

24. Riley, *Theory of the Novel*, 54.

25. Byron, *Cervantes: A Biography*, 513–19. Pomes had come to the same conclusion: "Cervantes no les ha cobrado afecto ni a Persiles ni a Sigismunda ni a ninguno de sus compañeros [Cervantes did not love either Persiles or Sigismunda or any of their companions]" ("Interés del *Persiles*," *Cuadernos de Ínsula*, Homenaje a Cervantes [1947]: 136).

26. El Saffar, *Beyond Fiction*, 140.

27. Frye, *Secular Scripture*, 73.

28. Green, *Spain and the Western Tradition* 1:201.

29. Zimic, "Novela bizantina," 60, 62.

30. Riley, *Theory of the Novel*, 121.

31. Lennard J. Davis, *Resisting Novels: Ideology and Fiction* (New York: Methuen, 1987), 128. Davis sees novel reading as "the process of falling in love with characters or making friends with signs" (127).

32. Lewis's context bears quoting: "No man is a 'character' to himself, and least of all while he thinks of good and evil. Character is what he has to produce; within he finds only the raw material, the passions and emotions which contend for mastery (*Allegory of Love*, 61).

33. Barney, *Allegories of History*, 43.

34. Fletcher, *Allegory*, 40. I am indebted to Fletcher's study of "daemonic agents" in allegory for a number of my conclusions about Cervantes's heroes.

35. Ibid., 35.

36. El Saffar, *Beyond Fiction*, 138.

37. Fletcher, *Allegory*, 35–38.

38. Ibid., 64.

39. "The tendency of agents to become images, which allowed agents to represent the 'cosmic' order of allegories," as Fletcher notes (ibid., 289) is also played out in the *Persiles*, where images—canvases and portraits and miniatures—are very much in evidence.

40. Freud, *SE* 13:73.

41. Fletcher, *Allegory*, 283. But see the whole chapter on "Psychoanalytic Analogues: Obsession and Compulsion," Allegory, 279–303.

42. Cervantes's energized predication here is the work of what Juan Luis Vives would

call "ingenium," that passionate faculty of the rational soul which discovers new and apt resemblances. See *De anima et vita*, in *Opera omnia*, 8 vols. (1782; rpt. London, 1964), 3:372, 374.

43. Aristotle, *The Physics*, trans. Rev. Philip H. Wicksteed and Francis M. Cornford, 2 vols. (Loeb Classical Library, 1929–1934), 1:277.

44. For this exposition of part of the seminar *Encore* (1972–1973), which addresses the "inexpressible" realm of feminine sexuality, see Bice Benvenuto and Roger Kennedy, *The Works of Jacques Lacan: An Introduction* (New York: St. Martin's Press, 1986), 185–86.

45. Julia Kristeva, "Revolution in Poetic Language," in *The Kristeva Reader*, 93–95. Kristeva's depiction of the *chora*, which avoids fixing it in terms of any sign or position, is as "a non-expressive totality formed by the drives and their stases in a motility that is as full of movement as it is regulated." She sees these drives predominantly as "oral and anal drives, both of which are oriented and structured around the mother's body" (93–95).

46. Plato, *Timaeus, Critias, Clitopho, Menexenus, Epistulae*, trans. R.G. Bury (Loeb Classical Library, 1929), 7:113–27; emphasis added.

NICHOLAS SPADACCINI AND JENARO TALENS

Poetry as Autobiography

In his autobiography Robbe-Grillet, the chief exponent of the *nouveau roman*, made a surprising and, apparently, provocative declaration: "I have never spoken of anything but myself." The sentence points to a fundamental problem that has traversed contemporary theoretical discussions, namely, who speaks in a text, what a text speaks of, and from where it speaks. On the one hand, we know that the limits of our language are the limits of our world, that is, that we can *think* our relation with the real only in terms of discourse. On the other hand, when one speaks, it is impossible to not say "I." How, then, does one resolve what, in these terms, appears to be such an irreducible contradiction? How do we claim objectivity when we know that it is not possible to transcend our bodies, to feel with a skin that is not our own; to look with eyes that, for a moment, forget the untransferable place that our own history makes them occupy? How, on the contrary, does one narrate his or her own life with words that exist precisely because they cannot belong to anyone? As Lautréamont wrote, "These eyes are not yours. Where have you taken them from?" In one form or another, this vicious circle frames and traverses most contemporary writing. Its problematic, however, is not unique to this writing and, in large part, has guided the historical development of literature.

A paradigmatic case may be the discourse of lyric poetry, in which the

From *Through the Shattering Glass: Cervantes and the Self-Made World.* © 1993 by the Regents of the University of Minnesota.

frequent use of the first person does not necessarily imply the presence of an "I" that speaks of itself. Yet, the frequent absence of anecdotal-argumentative support leaves bare procedures of composition and structure and allows one to analyze the traces that are no less real for being invisible. A life is drawn not only from what one tells of it, but also from what is silenced. A gesture, the choice of a certain perspective for approaching some matter, the predilection for an adjective, all tell more than a thousand anecdotes. In this sense Cervantes's poetic work can be seen as paradigmatic, despite the fact that it has not enjoyed much critical acclaim in literary history.

The work of Miguel de Cervantes is composed of three parts, which are well defined in their limits as well as in their function. He is not only the peerless prose writer and creator of a genre in its modern sense, but also the author who, together with Shakespeare, has managed to produce an entire literary continent. Second, he is a playwright who breaks his own paths, distinct from those of Lope de Vega. Finally, he is the poet who perseveres in a task that brings him nothing more than sorrows and none of the praise commensurate with his estimation of its worth. And if critics have been preoccupied with his novel, and have paid attention, though perhaps not enough, to his theatrical work, his poetry has not enjoyed the same fortune. The attitude toward this portion of Cervantes's work is particularly unjust, above all if, as we will attempt to demonstrate, we can see in it not only its substantive value as poetry (with respect to its original conception of poetic work), but also a small-scale model of his entire literary world. The constancy with which Cervantes applies himself to the unpleasant task of *writing verses* throughout his life would otherwise have little justification.

Cervantes begins his poetic adventures in 1569, at the age of twenty-three. The four compositions included by his teacher, Juan López de Hoyos, in his *History and True Tale of the Sickness, Happy Death and Magnificent Funeral Rites of the Most Serene Queen of Spain, Our Lady, Doña Isabel de Valois,*[1] are, indeed, the oldest of his works to have come down to us. In them, there are, as in all beginners, the marks of the teaching of his elders. At the same time, when read from the perspective of his later works, one observes what will become his fundamental tendency: the adoption of the *cancionero* lyric and the Italian model, a double tradition in which he inserts himself and that he then manages to transform. This function of playful craftsmanship—which will later make of him one of the great and original innovators—is what catches one's attention in his poetic work from the very beginning. Such work may be understood as a method on the one hand, and as *salvation of man by beauty* on the other. Both aspects are joined from the beginning, if we consider the simple comparison of texts that are so far apart in time as the

"Elegy" of 1569 and that which Dorotea and Clara hear sung in *Don Quijote* (I, 43):

> He who always enjoys tranquillity in his state of being
> and whose effect leads him to hope
> and of what he wants, nothing is changed:
> It is said that one may have
> little confidence in he
> who enjoys and sees with
> limpid eyes good fortune. ("Elegy" vv. 133–138)

> Sluggards do not deserve
> the glory of triumphs or of victory;
> good luck will never serve
> those who resist not fortune manfully,
> but fall weakly to ground,
> and in soft sloth their senses all confound.
> ("Don Luis's Song" 388)[2]

Nearly half a century of Cervantes's poetic activity compels us to pay more attention to this work. That activity responds to a vocation that was stated in the prologue to *La Galatea* (*The Galatea*): "by which I can prove the inclination toward poetry that I have always had" ("para lo cual puedo alegar de mi parte la inclinación que a la poesia siempre he tenido"), repeated only two years before his death in the fourth song of *Viaje del Parnaso* (*Journey to Parnassus*):

> Since my tender years I have loved
> the sweet art of agreeable poetry and with it
> I will always try to please you.[3]

Some critics have taken this vocation for granted,[4] while the tendency of others to confuse poetry and verse and not to take into account the same presuppositions with which Cervantes confronted his work as a poet, have led even modern editors such as Vicente Gaos to say that Cervantes "was not a born poet."

Cervantes's high esteem for poetry verges on religion (Schevill and Bonilla 1922), but his relationship with poetry turns out to be somewhat ambivalent, for, with the exception of *Viaje del Parnaso*, he never published a book of poetry. These facts, however, should lead us to reformulate the matter of his poetry in other terms, without judging the results of Cervantes's poetry from presuppositions other than those that he himself established. By so doing, perhaps we could break a long critical tradition, initiated in Cervantes's own time, that undervalues his poetic production.

The passages that follow cannot be taken literally, especially in an author who constantly uses irony and double entendre in his work. First there is the shopworn citation of the third tercet of *Viaje del Parnaso*:

> I who always strive and am vigilant
> to appear that I have the poet's wit
> that heaven didn't choose to grant me.[5]

There is also the sentence uttered by the Licenciado Vidriera in the novella by the same title: "I haven't been so foolish as to begin to be a bad poet, or so fortunate as to have deserved to be a good one" ("No he sido tan necio que diese en poeta malo, ni tan venturoso que haya merecido serlo bueno"). Finally, there are the allusions to poetry scattered throughout his works. Let us recall, for instance, the following statement from *Don Quijote* (I, 6): "That Cervantes has been a great friend of mine for many years and I know that he is more versed in misfortunes than in verse" (62) ("Muchos años ha que es grande amigo mío ese Cervantes, y sé que es más versado en desdichas que en versos"). Yet many other quotations that are not so often glossed would lead us to different conclusions. We cite three fragments from *Viaje del Parnaso*:

> Pass on, inventor rare, further advance
> With thy subtle design, and aid supply
> To Delian Apollo, of vast weight—
> Or ere the vulgar squadron comes to call
> E'en more than twenty thousand seven months old
> Poets, whom so to be are much in doubt. (Chap. 1, vv. 223–228)

> Mercy on us! What poetasters rise. (Chap. 2, v. 396)

> He said, Shall it be possible that in Spain
> There be nine bards with laureated crowns? (Chap. 8, vv. 97–98)[6]

One cannot take Cervantes's ironic statements seriously.[7] Rather, it is necessary to underline their humorous and sly character.[8]

For Cervantes, poetry was grounded in the cult of beauty so that a poem could not lower itself to the status of a commercial object directed toward a pleasure-seeking public. In *Don Quijote* (II, 16) he states that poetry should be kept out of reach of "the ignorant vulgar, who are incapable of recognizing or appreciating her treasures" (569). For this very reason, he considers himself a poet by avocation (*afición*) rather than by vocation (*oficio*). He states as much in *La gitanilla* (*The Gypsy Girl*) and in *Don Quijote* (II, 18). The distinction between avocation and vocation has supported those critics who have interpreted Cervantes's attitude toward poetry as being contrary to the normal work of the artist; as being a mere pastime. There is little substance to this view, however, for while Cervantes does not want to lower art to the daily vulgarity of a remunerable job, he never ceases to consider poetry as constant and tiring work. This exclusive attitude already is manifest in the fourth book of *La Galatea*:

> Despite the low esteem in which [poets] are held by princes and common people alike, they communicate with their intellects their lofty and strange concepts, without daring to make them known to the world, and in my opinion, Heaven should order the world in this fashion, because neither the world nor our maligned century deserves to enjoy such tasty repasts for the soul.[9]

A detailed analysis of Cervantes's poetry shows, as much from the point of view of his theoretical statements as from that of his concrete practice, that if we seek to discover his work, it requires us to speak of its articulation based on two presuppositions: consciousness and a search for balance. From the latter will come the elements of Cervantes's poetic scaffolding: (1) the objectification of lyric sentiment, and (2) the existence of shrewd talents that guide the compositional work. The preceptive zeal is evident throughout his extensive poetic career, but Cervantes possesses a poetics without a code, a theory rather than a normative program. His is a poetics that defends the principle of invention, provided that it does not result in the corruption of art in order to meet public demand, and provided that it does not violate the laws of reason. His rules of composition are flexible and variable. Thus, they are less evident than those of his contemporaries. His theory allows for the modification of what is established by the norms of verse, provided that such modification is submitted to a harmonic scheme fashioned by an intellect controlled by reason and in an analogical relationship with the natural processes of the universe. His theory of poetic expression concerns more a meta-aesthetic system of ideas than a treatise on poetic art. He can make a mockery of the rules, given their particular character, in contrast to the scope of the universals in which the poem operates and shows itself, and he can laugh at sterile erudition because of its apoetical nature. His rules of composition are consequently a habit of thought more than norms and orders. His critical scruples as well as his distrust of academic literary judgments derive from that habit. There is nothing but irony and humorous sarcasm behind the "Privileges, Decrees, and Regulations That Apollo Sends to Spanish Poets" in the Appendix to *Viaje del Parnaso*:

> The first essential is that poets be as well known for the slovenliness of their persons as for the fame of their verses.
>
> Also, should any poet say he is poor, that he instantly be credited on his word, without any other oath or verification whatsoever.
>
> It is required that every poet be of a mild and becoming mental habit, and that one should not look at stitches, albeit they appear in his stocking.
>
> Ditto, should any poet touch at the house of a friend or acquaintance, and should stay there for material sustenance, that although he swear that he has eaten, let it not be believed, save that he be made to eat by force, which in that case will be no great thing.
>
> Ditto, that the poorest bard in the world, though neither Adam nor Methuselah, may say that he is in love, though he be not so, and should give as the name of his lady, now styled Amaryllis, now Anarda, now Cloris, Phyllis, or Fílida, or Juana Téllez, or any other name at will, all may be done without asking reasons why....
>
> Again, notify that he be not held for a thief who would appropriate others' verses, and pass them off for his own, whether in conception or in part, in which case he is as much a thief as Cacus.[10]

Likewise, we can say that humor and sarcasm are hidden behind the serious thoughts of the sick poet in *El coloquio de los perros* (*The Dialogue of the Dogs*), when he complains of the failure of his work even while he takes great care to respect "what Horace orders in his *Poetics*" ("lo que Horacio manda en su *Poética*"). If Cervantes's poetics is a habit of thought, his theory is a method of resolving specific artistic problems at a level that is superior to that of codified precepts. In this sense Cervantes associates poetry with life, which he likewise does not subject to precepts. Indeed, his artistic formula is applicable as much to the composition of a poem as to vital processes in general. That principle even appears to rule the world of military affairs, as he states in the first act of *El cerco de Numancia* (*The Siege of Numancia*) in Scipio's speech:

If an army, however small,
is subjected to military order,
you will see that it shines like the bright sun
and achieves the victories it desires;
but if the army conducts itself with indolence,
although the world sees itself condensed in it,
in a moment it will be routed
by a more forthright hand and stronger heart.[11]

In *Cervantes's Theory of the Novel*, E.C. Riley noted that the origin of Cervantes's idea on the function of imaginative literature was one of "instructing while pleasing" (*instruir deleitando*). Cervantes reconciled this classical concept of the artistic with the antinomy inherent in the accommodation of neo-Platonic aesthetic ideas with a plan of life ruled by reason. León Hebreo, whom Cervantes had read and assimilated, according to Américo Castro and Francisco López-Estrada, had established a way of articulating this antinomic relation in his *Diálogos de amor* (*Dialogues of Love*). In the *Dialogues* Philo describes the method to grant to him, a bit paradoxically, first a poetic fiction, a Cabalistic meaning, and, later, a pedagogical function. This is, in principle, something apparently contradictory, but Hebreo saves the antinomy by assigning both elements to differentiated powers:

1. Hermetic, intellectual knowledge is grasped by "creative faculties suitable for divine and intellectual matters and a mind that preserves and does not corrupt the true sciences of those matters."
2. The matter of beneficial instruction (*provecho*) is assigned to three kinds of minds: (a) "the less intelligent can only take from poetry the story with the ornament and melody of verse"; (b) "the more intelligent can digest the moral sense, in addition to the story"; (c) "the most intelligent can digest, in addition to the story and the moral sense, the allegorical repast, not only of natural philosophy, but of astrology and theology as well."[12]

Cervantes's position does not differ much from that of León Hebreo. He reserves the knowledge of universals to a select few and assigns the "instruction while pleasing" to those not apt for the highest knowledge. In prose, this double purpose of serving everyone can be realized, even if everyone does not benefit in the same fashion by what is offered to them. In poetry, however, this realization is not possible because of its very high position in the scale of the harmonic. Poetry aspires to produce pleasure and a supreme good and, therefore, its use is forbidden to the "ignorant vulgar, who are incapable of recognizing or appreciating her treasures" (569) ("ignorante vulgo, incapaz de conocer ni estimar los tesoros que en ella se encierran") as we hear in Don Quijote's speech (II, 16:155).

For Cervantes, the fundamental objective of the poem is enjoyment in the contemplation of beauty. The poem's beneficial effect consists of enriching itself with the truth of this graciously received gift. That thought is similar to what is expressed in the treatises on Christian piety in the sixteenth century. One thinks, for example, of Fray Diego de Estella, who writes in his *Meditaciones devotísimas del amor de Dios* [*Most Devout Meditations on the Love of God* (1576)]: "He who says that he loves You and keeps the Ten Commandments of Your law only or chiefly because You give glory to him, should consider himself abandoned by that glory" ("El que dice que te ama y guarda los diez mandamientos de tu ley solamente o más principalmente porque le des la gloria, téngase por despedido della"). This thought coincides with that of Don Quijote when he speaks of his consecration to his lady Dulcinea (I, 31). There he speaks, in neo-Platonic fashion, of the transfer of concepts of universal courage from the sacred to the profane and vice versa.

According to these ideas, prose, as well as poetry, occasions responses in accord with a reader's specific sensibility. But the poem, in contrast to prose, also has the function of producing what is impossible for prose, namely, mental and spiritual therapy by means of the cessation of emotive processes. This kind of therapy is possible only for those who know how to interpret poetry. This pseudomystical position, of Plotinist derivation, is also characteristic of León Hebreo. From this perspective, we can understand the definition of poetry that Cervantes gives in *Don Quijote* (II, 16), insisting that it is "made of an alchemy of such virtue that he who knows how to treat her will receive in turn the purest gold of priceless worth" ("es hecha de una alquimia de tal virtud, que quien la sabe tratar la volverá en oro purísimo de inestimable precio"). In Cervantes this vision of poetry as an exclusive artistic labor is joined by the consciousness of having both the creative genius and the technical competence necessary to convert this mental schema into verbal discourse. At the same time, he knows that not all of his poetic peers possess this virtue.

In effect, in the length and breadth of his poetic production, Cervantes shows himself to have mastered a fairly ample formal and metrical repertory, including troubadouresque, Italianized, and popular styles. Moreover, even his own variations within the fixed schemas are intricately woven and superimposed without ever privileging any of these modes of composition. A simple examination of his work shows not only technical and strophic variety, but also the balanced perfection with which it is employed. Examples of this perfection include his sonnets; the *silvas* that appear with the same ease and fluency in *Nueve canciones petrarquistas* (*Nine Petrarchan Songs*), fashioned from the news of the defeat of the Invincible Armada in 1588; the poem "A los éxtasis de Nuestra Beata Madre Teresa de Jesús" ("To the Ecstasies of Our Blessed Mother Theresa of Jesus") of 1615; and the ballads or *romances* that, together with those of Lope de Vega and Luis de Góngora, must have influenced the formation of the *Romancero Nuevo*.[13] If his peers considered his romances well made, the same can be said of his *zéjeles* and *villancicos*.[14] In short, Cervantes's formal range encompasses virtually all known varieties of verses and strophes used in his time.

The lack of predilection for one meter compared to another does not imply an eclecticism or indecision, but rather the clear conscience of an instrument for putting into practice what really matters: form, understood as composition, as configuration of all the elements integrated in the superior unity called a poem. Already in *La Galatea* this particular approach to the matter of meter appears, generically speaking, as a form in which the poetic material is embodied, the material that, in the last instance, determines the form and grants value to it. A clear example of this approach is to be found in the eclogue of the third book of *La Galatea*, when Orfinio reiterates in two successive instances the same theme with different versification.

> The fruit that was sown
> by my constant work,
> having arrived in a sweet season,
> with thriving destiny
> was delivered in my power.
> And no sooner had I succeeded in arriving
> at such incomparable ends,
> when I came to know
> the occasion of such pleasure
> to be of sorrow for me. (I, 219)

> To my sight there appeared
> an opulent lair full of a thousand riches;
> I triumphed in its conquest,
> and at the very time that fate
> showed itself most serene
> I saw it changed to black darkness. (I, 222)[15]

Likewise, this approach to meter can be seen when two octaves of the same eclogue, in the words of Crisio (vv. 223–238), appear reformulated as a sonnet, in the words of Cardenio in the first act of *La entretenida*:

> My slim and weak hope flies
> on feeble wings and although the flight
> rises to the zenith of the beautiful heaven,
> never will it attain the point to which it aspires.
> I come to be the dead ringer
> for that youth who left Crete's soil
> and, rivaling his father's zeal,
> propelled himself into the heavens.
> Melted by the amorous fire,
> my audacious thoughts will fall
> in the turbulent and cold sea of fear;
> but the violent courses
> forewarned by time and death,
> will not carry my name
> into oblivion.[16]

Meter and the combination of meters lose their determinate value so that the strength of the poem resides in the structural-compositional form and in the internal order of distribution of the poetic material. In this way the craftsmanlike artifice of the poet-writer is fundamental. And what counts for Cervantes, at the end of the process of writing, is fulfilling the lyric intention and the conceptual and technical harmony of the parts.

In the same way, the function of the acoustic in the poem is a problem of structure, so that its meter and prosody cannot be judged by the metric and prosodic norms of the Castilian poem, but from Cervantes's particular use of both in his form of conceiving the poem. The greatest attack on Cervantes's poetry has taken place nearly always in the territory of prosody, yet it is something that few critics have tried to explain.[17]

In prosodic terms, Cervantes's verse lacks acoustic value in itself. Its value is relative to the structure and function of the poem. The relation is not established between the voice and the phonic group, but between the architectonically elaborated thought and the phonic group that is rhythmically disposed and subordinated to the harmony of the concepts. This Cervantine characteristic comes from the enormous importance conceded to the voice that sings and is not limited to speaking the verse. Indeed, the phonological schemas of song do not correspond to those of spoken language. We cannot, of course, determine from a written text what its musical cadence would be, but in view of Cervantes's constant preoccupation with the form of rhythmically linking strophes, we could envisage the possibility that it would be (structurally speaking) repetitive and balanced.

Only in this fashion can one understand how a poem that fails prosodically to our ears may be considered pleasant and sweet within the work. The melody would lend the necessary acoustic harmony, so that it would correspond to the structural harmony. However, since neither all poems included in texts are written in prose, nor are the individual poems sung, it would be worth exploring what happens in these cases. Let us recall that in the years in which Cervantes initiates his poetic career, the matter of prosody was not part of metric theory. Herrera, in his *Anotaciones* (*Annotations*) to Garcilaso, complained of the strictures of rhyme in 1580: "As those who write in this genre of poetry know, this difficulty of rhymes, which disturbs many beautiful bits of wisdom; they cannot be recounted with so much ease and clarity" (68).[18] In that same year, Miguel Sánchez de Luna in his *El arte poética en romance castellano* (*The Poetic Art in Castilian Romance Poetry*) confronts the problem of the measured verse that sounds worse than unmeasured verse, and he gives it a practical solution:

> The poet should guide himself by sound more than by any other path; and for this purpose some composers usually sing what they are composing.... It is necessary that each composition have its melody.... When I was studying, my teacher read Virgil to me by chanting, because in that way, he said, one felt better the smoothness of the verse. He said that Virgil sung them also as he was composing them.[19]

Cervantes, who was very much a poet of the sixteenth century, would probably have used a melody to look for the fluency and smoothness of his verse. Cervantes's preoccupation with music has already been pointed out by Miguel Querol and by Adolfo Salazar, so that it is not too daring to think that the melody, in its specific concept of poetic composition, could make smooth and faint what to our ears seems harsh today. This manner of focusing on the problem had ceased to be the dominant one in the baroque period.[20]

Despite what has been said above, the use of a musical leitmotiv to overcome the formal pitfalls of prosody is not an excuse for the deficient acoustic qualities that many of Cervantes's poems may have. But that use explains how someone with so much facility for discovering the errors of others could compose verses that seem imperfect to us. Perhaps, in the long run, Cervantes himself might have come to think that, within these particular rules of composition without a code, the superficial, mechanical, and acoustic structure was something secondary to the global structure of the poem which was, in the final analysis, the fundamental consideration.

Cervantes structures his poetry with the precision of a painter, but the important thing for him is not the painterliness of verbal clusters, as Jorge Guillén perceptively noted with respect to Góngora, or the melody of sounds that thereafter become inlaid in words, as Valle-Inclán said of Valéry's "Le cimetière marin" ("The Marine Graveyard"). Rather, Cervantes is interested in the conceptual scaffolding that sustains the verbal clusters. And if the painterly aspect does not appear at times in a specific text, it is because he has decided truly to lay bare that structure, or scaffolding. Therefore, his procedures are of a global nature and attend to the ordering, cohesion, and intensification of the signified. This means that figures and tropes are nearly always secondary; they are resources of a cellular function and accessories to procedures of greater significance: correlation and reiteration, verbal play, the secularization of sacred themes, and the reformulation of the themes and fragments of others, as well as his own. These procedures allow him to say to the Cervantes of the fourth chapter of *Viaje del Parnaso* that he has always seen his poetry "dressed in spring color" ("vestida de color de primavera").

Cervantes's organizing model for his verse was, as stated earlier, a concept of harmony analogous to that of the natural processes of the universe. More specifically, we can allude now to the human body. Already in *La Galatea* he signals his concept of the rhythm of the art of poetry, the relation between the parts of the poem and between the poem and each part (that which some avant-garde theorists refer to as the great discovery of Baudelaire and that, in fact, dates back to Cervantes). He says in *La Galatea* that the natural correspondence of this relation is the human body:

> But just as physical beauty is thus divided into two parts, living and dead bodies, likewise can there be love of physical beauty that may be good. One part of physical beauty shows itself in the living bodies of males and of females, and this consists in that all the parts of the body are good in themselves and that together they all make a perfect whole and form a body proportioned in members and smoothness of colors. The nonliving beauty of the physical part consists of pictures, statues, buildings, a kind of beauty that can be loved without vilifying the love with which one loves.[21]

It is a concept of the rhythm of beauty that Cervantes will apply not only to his verse production, but to his own novels as well. In *Don Quijote* (I,

47) he critiques the romances of chivalry in large part for lacking proportions:

> And even though the principal aim of such books is to delight, I do not know how they can succeed, seeing the monstrous absurdities they are filled with. For the delight that the mind conceives must arise from the beauty and harmony it sees, or contemplates, in things presented to it by the eyes or the imagination; and nothing ugly or ill proportioned can cause us any pleasure. What beauty can there be, or what harmony between the parts and the whole, or between the whole and its parts, in a book or story in which a sixteen-year-old lad deals a giant as tall as a steeple one blow with his sword, and cuts him in two as if he were made of marzipan? And when they want to describe a battle, first they tell us that there are a million fighting men on the enemy's side. But if the hero of the book is against them, inevitably, whether we like it or not, we have to believe that such and such a knight gained the victory by the valour of his strong arm alone. Then what are we to say of the ease with which a hereditary Queen or Empress throws herself into the arms of an unknown and wandering knight? (424–425)[22]

For this formal scheme to be a poem, it needs to be incarnated in a word that represents it. Poetic representation is, for Cervantes, a matter of configuration that subordinates meter and prosody to a structural balance (or to an imbalance motivated by an ironic or burlesque function that demands it) and the active disposition that demands it. Poetic representation orders and distributes elements at the same time that it binds them, with procedures more discursive than imaginative, in the poetic totality. The rhythm of beauty will be the lexicalized construction that enables the embodiment of what was only embryonic thought.

An emblem of the image that is offered to us by rhythm and representation is given by the "most beautiful damsel" of the poet-page in *La gitanilla*; by the nymph, "the universal lady" of *Viaje del Parnaso*; and by the tender damsel of the second volume of *Don Quijote*. Rhythm produces unity and representation produces clarity, while rhythm and representation combined produce harmony or consonance, the three characteristics of universal beauty, according to Thomas Aquinas (*Ad pulchritudinem tria requiruntur integritas, consonantia, claritas*). These three elements, in turn, motivate the image of a beautiful world condensed in the poem, in the same way that the beauty of the universe condenses it in the physical beauty of

man. In the last instance, it is clear that Cervantes is looking for a beauty
beyond the reach of man, because although the poem searches for perfection,
it cannot be in itself perfect, as he already said in the fourth book of *La
Galatea*: "the beauty of which I speak cannot be enjoyed perfectly and
entirely ... because it isn't in man's capacity to enjoy perfectly something that
is beyond him and is not all his" ("la belleza de quien hablo no se puede gozar
perfecta y enteramente ... porque no está en mano del hombre gozar
cumplidamente cosa que está fuera dél y no sea toda suya").

What the poem may contain is an approximation of the beauty
contemplated by the poet. And that mental design both validates the
"invention" and justifies, within Cervantes's work, the value given to the
force of writing, shown as such in the very poem. When Cervantes is seen as
an uncomfortable poet because he transmits to the reader the sensation of
the painful effort that the writer seems to have experienced in shaping his
verses, one points to another element of Cervantes's originality.[23] It is not a
question of acting before the public eye, without artifice or *trompe l'oeil*, but
one of implicating the reader in his sufferings.

The essence of this mental design would be the configuration
structured in the thought of an image or a concept. It can be the mental
design of a face, such as the one that Andrés requests of the poet-page in *La
gitanilla*:

Look, Clemente, the star-studded veil
with which this cold night
competes with the day
of beautiful lights adorning the sky;
and in this resemblance,
if your divine wit perceives so much,
that face figures
where the utmost beauty is present. (vv. 108–116)[24]

Perhaps this is the reason why *La gitanilla* has been considered
Cervantes's macrometaphor for poetry.[25]

Despite everything that has been said, it is indisputable that many of
Cervantes's poems can be characterized as "bad." The problem of bad poems
underscores the importance of Cervantes's adventure. The higher one aims,
the greater the error if the target is missed. The emphasis on the mental
plane is transformed sometimes into a wall against which the verbal
achievement explodes. While the verses of Garcilaso, Herrera, Lope de
Vega, or Góngora leave a mark on the eyes and ears, Cervantes seeks to
impress our intellective capacity without entering through the senses. More

than an error, this is a trademark. There exists in Cervantes a certain mistrust of sensible perception that shows itself with clarity in the *reductio ad absurdam* of the value assigned to the senses in Don Quijote's tale of what he has seen in Montesinos's cave (II, 23):

> I opened and rubbed my eyes, and saw that I was not asleep but really awake. For all that, I felt my head and my bosom to make certain whether it was my very self who was there, or some empty and counterfeit phantom; but touch, feeling, and the coherent argument I held with myself assured me that I was there then just as I am here now. (615)[26]

An example of the intellective, nonsensorial mechanism of his conception of structure as formal manifestation is in the following verses of the first book of *La Galatea*: "a thousand incomparable, indescribable charms / have made me fog to the amorous wind" ("mil gracias que no tienen par ni cuento / niebla me han hecho al amoroso viento"). These verses, which undoubtedly have a high affective level, perform their function within their context (the nine octaves of dialogue between Elicio and Erastro as a counterpoint to the verses that close the previous octave): "and other things I saw as I was blinded / have made me fuel for the invisible fire" ("y otras cosas que vi quedando ciego / yesca me han hecho al invisible fuego"). The syntactical and compositional parallelism (each verse is at the end of the preceding octave) puts two worlds into contact: that of the poetic shepherd, Elicio, who refers to "fuel," "invisible," and "fire" and that of the historical shepherd, Erastro, who refers to "fog," "amorous," and "wind." The worlds are related, harmonizing the universal (poetic) and the particular (historical) to sing to the woman they both love. It is not the isolated verses that count, but the verbal artifice of counterpoint that permits the figure portioned from the whole.

   In addition to Cervantes's refusal to commercialize his poetry, this notion of poetry in the totality of the works, rather than in singular ones, provides a possible answer as to why he did not publish an independent book of poetry, except for *Viaje del Parnaso*. His entire corpus of poetic work is a kind of frame where he integrates his proposal as a poet. Thus, the intercalated poems are not really isolated "exceptions," but are part of the fabric of the prose in his narrative and of the verse necessary to the dramatic plan of his theater. If we extract the poems from his novels and plays, we decontextualize them and, as a result, they lose most of their meaning. In this manner, the poems integrated in *La Galatea* are not simple excursuses in the traditional fashion, but a form of inscribing his critique of the pastoral genre.

What is at stake in Cervantes's work is what could be defined as a kind of baroque integration, in contrast to the merely accumulative character of mannerism.[27] "The Song of Grisóstomo," for example, in *Don Quijote* (I, 14:181) (where Garcilaso's *Egloga tercera* ("Third Eclogue") is cited: "Let all together cry from my aching soul" (104) ("salgan con la doliente ánima fuera")], explains a suicide, whereas the narrative text in which it is inserted only speaks of the death of love. Even in single poems, his tendency to integrate genres is evident.

There is a truly paradigmatic example of this integration in the sonnet "Al túmulo de Felipe II" ("To the Funeral Casket of Philip II"). That boasting, which at the end of the poem visualizes what seems to be the neutral voice of the lyric poet, making of him a soldier and holding him responsible for as much as he says, has a great deal of theatricality. On the other hand, Cervantes does not seem to have much interest in conserving individual poems as discrete entities. Some of his compositions would end up being integrated, with few variants, in his works, whether narrative or theatrical. Such is the case of the "Epístola a Mateo Vázquez" ("Letter to Mateo Vázquez"), which coincides, with slight changes, with Saavedra's speech in the first act of *Los tratos de Argel*, and the case of some of the verses of Elicio's song in book II of *La Galatea*, which are reproduced in the same play:

ELICIO: It is so easy for my faint fortune
         to see bitter death
         joined with sweet life
         and see grief dwell where joy resides.
         Between opposites I see
         hope wane, and not desire. (*La Galatea*, vv. 43–48)

SAAVEDRA: In the fast track
           I see the hurried hours of fleeting time
           conspire against me with heaven,
           with hope left behind, not desire. (*Los tratos de Argel*, I)[28]

Finally, before speaking of *Viaje del Parnaso*, we would like to consider briefly Cervantes's tendency to quote his own works, as much as those of others, as poetic material. It has been said that as a poet he does not seem to have a "personal voice,"[29] or that he used entire verses of Garcilaso.[30] This is not so much a matter of a lack of originality, however, as of the deliberate search for the dissolution of the personal voice. In his poem "A los éxtasis de la Beata Madre Teresa de Jesús" ("To the Ecstasies of Our Blessed Mother

Theresa of Jesus"), Cervantes includes three lines in which Garcilaso praises the Viceroy of Naples in his *Egloga primera* ("First Eclogue"):

> You who by working earned
> renown the world over
> and a rank second to none.[31]

Here he is not taking refuge in Garcilaso in order to hide his inexperience. The text is from 1615 and by then his apprentice years had passed. Perhaps the hypothesis could be put forth that with this citation, Cervantes achieved a certain impersonal generalization by neutralizing his voice among voices foreign to his, some of them incorporated from his own writings. This procedure would not be unique to his poems. Indeed, the imbrication of narrators in *Don Quijote* would likewise make the personal disappear behind the work, in order to resurface as the universal textual voice from that same work; for example, the character who reads the first part of Don Quijote's life is none other than the transcriber/adapter of a previous text of Cide Hamete Benengeli.

Cervantes neither cites sterile erudition nor does he wink at the reader. Such is also the case with *Viaje del Parnaso* (1614). Its date of composition, as well as its considerable length, seems to indicate the importance that Cervantes attached to this work. In ill health, involved with the production of the second part of *Don Quijote* and engaged in writing *Persiles y Sigismunda*, Cervantes might not have dedicated the time that was slipping away from him to a poem with the characteristics of *Viaje* if it were not because he sought to achieve something important and significant.[32]

While *Viaje* is not an essay in literary criticism per se, Cervantes humorously criticizes himself as a literary figure:

> "Oh you!," he said, who canonized
> the poets from the long list
> by indirect reasons and ways.
>
> Where did you hold, evil one,
> the sharp sight of your talent, so that
> though blind, you were such a lying chronicler?
> (Chap. 4, vv. 490–495)[33]

Cervantes's curious affirmation "by indirect reasons and ways" can be taken as a self-vindication, for, although the direct and fundamental thing to do was to speak of oneself, the primordial purpose of Viaje was to leave to posterity an autobiography vindicating Cervantes's function as a poet. And, in truth, the only sincere praise, without the clichés of the time, are the ones dedicated to his own work:

> He who doesn't value being a poet,
> for what reason does he write and proclaim verses?
> Why does he disdain what he most esteems?
>
> I was never happy or satisfied
> with hypocritical fastidiousness; I simply
> wanted praise for what I did well. (Chap. 4, vv. 337–342)[34]

The plot of the book could not be more Cervantine: (a) by means of memory, he leaves his country on an "ideal voyage," to cite the expression of Croce, and returns to the golden Italy of his youth; (b) the Spanish "prosaic" reality of the time in which writers have to survive is ironically pictured by means of the representation of a mythography—evasion and improbability being constant features of his style; and (c) by simultaneously doubling as narrator and character, he "leaves" himself. In this fashion, whether by his own means or by those of the god Mercury, Cervantes can say what he thought of his work and himself.

Having fulfilled these purposes, Cervantes extends the symbolic function of the poem to the métier of literature and converts *Viaje* into a mock epic of the illusions and vanities of the writer in a world where beauty and poetry have no place anymore. This is exemplified in the poet's blind zeal for glory, again uniting the particular and the universal. In some measure and without ignoring that *Don Quijote* is a work of greater substance, we could agree with Vicente Gaos that *Viaje del Parnaso* is a kind of *Don Quijote* in miniature and in verse. It makes clear that man usually judges himself to be greater than his own merits and in the process he is swept along by a chimera. His self-concept and, to a certain degree, his aspirations, surpass the real possibility of satisfying them. There is no trace of idealism in Cervantes's utilization of self-confidence, however. The ironic reference to mythology has a very practical significance. When, upon arriving in Parnassus, the character named Cervantes finds that Apollo does not recognize him, he tells the god about his own literary career, outlining its more important achievements. There is no vanity in this, just the expression of a need to succeed in order to avoid the jealousy and the lack of appreciation of his largely mediocre contemporaries.[35]

There is also another point of contact with *Don Quijote*. If *Don Quijote* mocks the romances of chivalry, *Viaje* parodies the mythological world of classicism that Renaissance authors had abused so much. If Don Quijote makes princesses of country girls and castles of windmills, *Viaje* brings the gods down from the Olympic pedestals and grants them human stature, submerging them in an atmosphere of caricature similar to that of Velázquez's paintings.[36]

The point of departure for the poem is the appendix to Cesare Caporali's *Viaggio in Parnaso*. Cervantes himself acknowledges as much in the first line of his *Viaje* as well as in the prologue to his *Novelas ejemplares* (*Exemplary Novels*). One can only point to other possible Spanish sources: Juan de la Cueva's *Viage de Sannio* (*Journey to Sannio*), 1585; a couple of *romances* of the *Coro febeo* (*Phoebean Choir*), 1587; and some older antecedents, such as *Infierno de los enamorados* (*Lovers' Hell*) or *El triunfete de Amor* (*The Triumph of Love*), by the Marquis of Santillana. In turn, Cervantes's *Viaje* was widely read in the seventeenth century. Republished in 1624, it inspired Salas Barbadillo's *Coronas del Parnaso* (*Crowns of Parnassus*), 1635, and Jerònimo de Cáncer's *Platos de las Musas de Salas* (*The Daily Fare of the Salon Muses*), 1640.

Even if this long poem has been fully accepted as an ironic expression of Cervantes's literary criticism, it has not been well received as a poem as such. Nevertheless, it is a kind of reassessment of his ideas about literature seen from the twilight of his career. *Viaje del Parnaso* is in fact the journey to that discursive continent that is literature.[37] From this point of view, *Viaje* does not imply a search for the "self" in the tradition of Virgil, but a way of discovering the uselessness of the search for perfection in some lost paradise of poetry. Parnassus, which is nowhere, has turned its back on daily life. Italy, the country where in his youth Cervantes found the greatness of the Renaissance, has by now been sterilized by Academies that clone classicism, using it not as a cultural model but as a simple repertory of prescriptive norms. Spain (or at least the Madrid where he lives) may not be a good place for a poet to be, but it is the only place Cervantes possesses. The task of the poet is to work immersed in his or her own time and country; to work not in search of fame but in order to achieve pleasure for self and others. In a Platonic tradition, Cervantes sees the poet as a repository of moral and collective responsibilities. This is why a country that does not respect poets cannot be well governed.

The utilization of the linked tercet in Cervantes's poetry has been criticized for its monotony and its failures. Yet, it seems to us that this kind of stanza, as used in *Viaje*, is not gratuitous; it was a question of putting all poets on the same level, of stacking them to show their extensive mediocrity. Thus, there was no better way of making them indistinct than by putting all judgments and clichés in the same verse and using a redundant stanza. From another point of view, Cervantes discovers in his symbolic journey that poetry has nothing to do with a Parnassus that has turned its back on the real world; the final sense of the poem will thus clearly entail an ethical reflection about what it means to write and to be, "socially," a writer. The "terceto" stanza is more appropriate to reflexive discourse than the "octava rima," which was usually employed by his more academic contemporaries when dealing with these topics.[38] To speak of Cervantes's error[39] is not to understand Cervantes's special constructive sense which, quite justly, characterized him as a "rare inventor."

Cervantes proclaims his truth and life despite the cold reception suffered at the hands of many of his peers. Yet the possibility that he would not be understood forced him to explain his own viewpoints and perspectives. Cervantes's linked narrative(s) of *El casamiento engañoso* (*The Deceitful Marriage*)/*El coloquio de los perros* (*The Dialogue of the Dogs*) and, especially, *Don Quijote* testify to his capacity for eluding the mix that was so common in the picaresque tradition: writing and explicit construction of the self. Unlike *Lazarillo de Tormes*, for example, Cervantes did not use the "true" story of his life to answer a question not answered directly. On the contrary, he wrote a kind of literary, "fictional" story to inscribe himself in the margins, as absence. For Cervantes, life is not conceived as anecdote, but as a way of living, thinking, and writing:

> To sing with such a harmonious and live voice
> that they think I am a swan and that I am dying.[40]

This is why the end of the journey shows us not a social image of an artist, but a rediscovered "human body," tired by movement and age:

> With this I left, and, full of spite,
> I looked for my old and dark inn,
> and I threw myself vanquished on the bed;
> for tiring is a day, when it is long.[41]

NOTES

1. *Historia y relación verdadera de la enfermedad, felicísimo tránsito y suntuosas exequias fúnebres de la Serenísima Reina de España Doña Isabel de Valois, nuestra Señora.*

2.   Quien goza de quietud siempre en su estado,
         y el efecto le acude a la esperanza
         y a lo que quiere nada le es trocado,
         argúyese que poca confianza
         se puede tener dél, que goce y vea
         con claros ojos bienaventuranza. ("Elegía" vv. 133–138)

No alcanzan perezosos,
honrados triunfos, ni vitoria alguna,
ni pueden ser dichosos
los que, no contrastando a la fortuna,
entregan, desvalidos,
al ocio blando todos los sentidos. (*Don Quijote I*, 43)

Quotations from *Don Quijote* follow the edition of Luis Murillo (Madrid: Castalia, 1978). English translations of quotations from Cervantes's writing are our own, unless followed by a page number, which refers to a published translation. For *Don Quijote* we use the translation of J.M. Cohen (Baltimore: Penguin Books, 1950).

3.   Desde mis tiernos años amé el arte
     dulce de la agradable poesía
     y en ella procuré siempre agradarte. (Chap. 4, vv. 31–33)

4. See, for example, Ricardo Rojas (1948), or Gerardo Diego (1948) who likewise states that "without divine calling no poet is legitimate.... Miguel who was born a poet, died a confessed poet" ("sin la divina vocación no hay poeta legítimo.... Miguel que nació poeta, poeta confesado murió").

5.   Yo, que siempre me afano y me desvelo
     por parecer que tengo de poeta
     la gracia que no quiso darme el cielo. (Chap. 1, vv. 25–27)

6.   Pasa, raro inventor, pasa adelante
     con tu sotil disinio, y presta ayuda
     a Apolo, que la tuya es importante.
     Antes que el escuadrón vulgar acuda
     de más de veinte mil sietemesinos
     poetas, que de serlo están en duda. (Chap. 1, vv. 223–228)
     ¡Cuerpo de mi con tanta poetambre! (Chap. 2, v. 396)
     Dijo: ¿Será posible que en España
     Haya nueve poetas laureados? (Chap. 8, vv. 97–98)

7. See Valbuena Prat (1943), Schevill and Bonilla (1922), or even Alborg (1966), who speak of "painful confession," "bitter realization," and so on.

8. See Blecua (1947).

9. "Con la poca estimación que de ellos los príncipes y el vulgo hace, con sólos sus entendimientos comunican sus altos y extraños conceptos, sin osar publicarlos al mundo, y tengo para mí que el Cielo debe ordenarlo de esta manera, porque no merece el mundo ni el mal considerado siglo nuestro gozar de manjares al alma tan gustosos."

10. "Privilegios, Ordenanzas y Advertencias que Apolo envía a los poetas españoles" (Adjunta al *Viaje del Parnaso*):

Es el primero, que algunos poetas sean conocidos tanto por el desaliño de sus personas como por la fama de sus versos.

Item, que si algún poeta dijere que es pobre, sea luego creído por su simple palabra, sin otro juramento o averiguación alguna.

Ordénase que todo poeta sea de blanda y de suave condición, y que no mire en puntos, aunque los traiga sueltos en sus medias.

Item, que si algún poeta llegare a casa de algún su amigo o conocido, y estuvieren comiendo, y le convidare, que aunque el jure que ya ha comido, no se le crea en ninguna manera, sino que le hagan comer por fuerza, que en tal caso no se le hará muy grande.

Item, que el más pobre poeta del mundo, como no sea de los Adanes y Matusalenes, pueda decir que es enamorado, aunque no le esté, y poner el nombre a su dama como más le viniere a cuento, ora llamándola Amarili, ora Anarda, ora Clori, ora Filis, ora Fílida, o ya Juana Téllez, o como más gustare, sin que desto se le pueda pedir ni pida razón alguna....

Item, se advierte que no ha de ser tenido por ladrón el poeta que hurtare algún verso ajeno y le encajare entre los suyos, como no sea todo el concepto y toda la copla entera, que en tal caso tan ladrón es como Caco. (Ed. Gaos, 188–190)

11.   Si a militar concierto se reduce
      cualquier pequeño ejército que sea,
      veréis que como sol claro reluce,
      y alcanza las victorias que desea;
      pero si a flojedad él se conduce,
      aunque abreviado el mundo en él se vea,
      en un momento quedará deshecho
      por más reglada mano y fuerte pecho.

12.   1. Los conocimientos de tipo intelectual, herméticos, son captados por "ingenios aptos a las cosas divinas e intelectuales y mente conservativa de las verdaderas ciencias y no corruptivas de ellas."

2. En cuanto al "provecho", es asignado a las mentes según tres grados: (a) "las mentes bajas pueden tomar de las poesías solamente la historia con el ornamento del verso y su melodía"; (b) "las otras más levantadas comen, además de esto, el sentido moral"; y (c) "otras más altas pueden comer, allende de esto, del manjar alegórico, no sólo de la filosofía natural, mas también de la astrología y la teología."

13. We are thinking, for example, of the perfection of *The Ballad of Jealousy* (*Romance de los celos*):

      Where the sun sets
      between two boulders split asunder
      lies the entrance to the abyss,
      I mean by that a cave ...
      Yace donde el sol se pone
      entre dos partidas peñas
      una entrada del abismo,
      quiero decir una cueva ...

14. See, respectively, the following poems:
      Although you think that I am happy
      I carry grief within me (*The Baths of Algiers*)

      Aunque pensáis que me alegro
      conmigo traigo el dolor (*Los baños de Argel*)

      Child, you spilled the waste water
      and did not say: "There it goes." (*The House of Jealousy*)

      Dearramaste el agua niña
      y no dijiste: "Agua va." (*La casa de los celos*)

15.   El fruto que fue sembrado
        por mi trabajo contino,
        a dulce sazón llegado,
        fue con próspero destino
        en mi poder entregado.

        Y apenas pude llegar
        a términos tan sin par,
        cuando vine a conocer
        la ocasión de tal placer
        ser para mí de pesar.

        Mostróseme a la vista
        un rico albergue de mil bienes lleno;
        triunfé de su conquista,
        y cuando más sereno
        se me mostraba el hado,
        vilo en escuridad negra cambiado.

16.   Vuela mi estrecha y débil esperanza
        con flacas alas, y aunque sube el vuelo
        a la alta cumbre del hermoso cielo,
        jamás el punto que pretende alcanza.
        Yo vengo a ser perfecta semejanza
        de aquel mancebo que de Creta al suelo
        dejó, y, contrario de su padre al celo,
        a la región del cielo se abalanza.

        Caerán mis atrevidos pensamientos,
        del amoroso incendio derretidos,
        en el mar del temor turbado y frío;
        pero no llevarán cursos violentos,
        del tiempo y de la muerte prevenidos,
        al lugar del olvido el nombre mío.

17. If, as Gerardo Diego intelligently states, Cervantes had a tin ear that was "not receptive or passive, but active and thunderous" ("no receptiva o pasiva sino activa o entonadora"), how does one account for the fact that through the years he persists in his poetic work and in the orchestration of his prose?

18. "Esta dificultad de las rimas, la cual como saben los que mejor escriben en este género de poesía, disturba muchas y hermosas sentencias; que no se pueden narrar con tanta facilidad y clareza."

19. "Debe el poeta regirse más por el sonido, que por otra ninguna vía; y para esto suelen algunos ir cantando lo que van componiendo ... Es menester que tenga para cada compostura su sonada ... Cuando estudiaba me leía mi maestro a Virgilio cantando, porque decía él, que de aquella manera se sentía mejor la suavidad del verso, y que Virgilio al tiempo que los iba componiendo, los iba también cantando."

20. The preoccupations of treatise writers on aspects of tone and time of verse rhythm in the sixteenth century [one of whose most sublime examples is Francisco Salinas (the blind musician immortalized by Fray Luis) in his *De musica libri septem* (1577)] are not documented in the seventeenth century, when the problem of rhythm is reduced to a matter of meter and rhyme, e.g., in Juan Caramuel's *Rhythmica* of 1665.

21. "Pero como la belleza corpórea se divide asimesmo en dos partes, que son en cuerpos vivos y en cuerpos muertos, también puede haber amor de belleza corporal que sea bueno. Muéstrasela una parte de la belleza corporal en cuerpos vivos de varones y de hembras, y ésta consiste en que todas las partes del cuerpo sean de por sí buenas, y que todas juntas hagan un todo perfecto y formen un cuerpo proporcionado de miembros y suavidad de colores. La otra belleza de la parte corporal no viva, consiste en pinturas, estatuas, edificios, la cual belleza puede amarse sin que el amor con que se amare se vitupere." (II, 44–45)

22. "Y según a mí me parece, este género de escritura y composición cae debajo de aquél de las fábulas que llaman milesias, que son cuentos disparatados, que atienden solamente a deleitar, y no a enseñar; al contrario de lo que hacen las fábulas apólogas, que deleitan y enseñan juntamente. Y puesto que el principal intento de semejantes libros sea el deleitar, no sé yo como pueden conseguirle, yendo llenos de tantos y tan desaforados disparates; que el deleite que en el alma se concibe ha de ser de la hermosura y concordancia que ve o contempla en las cosas que la vista o la imaginación le ponen delante; y toda cosa que tiene en sí fealdad y descompostura no nos puede causar contento alguno. Pues ¿qué hermosura puede haber, o qué proporción de partes con el todo, y del todo con las partes, en un libro o fábula donde un mozo de dieciseis años da una cuchillada a un gigante como una torre, y le divide en dos mitades, como si fuera de alfeñique, y cuando nos quieren pintar una batalla, después de haber dicho que hay de la parte de los enemigos un millón de combatientes, como sea contra ellos el señor del libro, forzosamente mal que nos pese, habemos de entender que el tal caballero alcanzó la victoria por sólo el valor de su fuerte brazo? Pues ¿qué diremos de la facilidad con que una reina o emperatriz heredera se conduce en los brazos de un andante y no conocido caballero?" (I: 564–565)

23. See Vicente Gaos (1971).

24.   Mira, Clemente, el estrellado velo
        con que esta noche fría
        compite con el día
        de luces adornando el cielo;
        y en esta semejanza,
        si tanto tu divino ingenio alcanza,
        aquel rostro figura
        donde asiste el extremo de hermosura.

25. See Karl Selig (1962).

26. "Despabilé los ojos, limpiémelos, y vi que no dormía, sino que realmente estaba despierto; con todo esto me tenté la cabeza y los pechos, por certificarme si era yo mismo el que allí estaba, o alguna fantasma vana y contrahecha; pero el tacto, el sentimiento, los discursos concertados que entre mi hacía, me certificaron que yo era allí entonces el que soy aquí ahora."

27. For these concepts as used here see Emilio Orozco Díaz (1970).

28. ELICIO: Esle tan fácil a mi corta suerte
                ver con la amarga muerte
                junta la dulce vida
                y estar su mal a do su bien se anida,
                que entre contrarios veo
                que mengua la esperanza, y no el deseo.
                            (*La Galatea, vv.* 43–48)

SAAVEDRA: En la veloz carrera apresuradas
            las horas del ligero tiempo veo
            contra mí con el cielo conjuradas
            queda atrás la esperanza, y no el deseo.
                    (*Los tratos de Argel*, I)

29. See Alonso Zamora Vicente (1947), who speaks of the "veiled voice" of Cervantes in the poem.

30. See Blecua (1948).

31. Tú que ganaste obrando
     un nombre en todo el mundo
     y un grado sin segundo.

32. His purpose was not to duplicate what he had already achieved in "Canto de Calíope" ("Calliope's Song") of *La Galatea*. As José Manuel Blecua noted, Cervantes was not merely praising contemporary poets, but was alluding to something much more profound and serious. Nor was it a matter, as Menéndez y Pelayo stated around the turn of the century in Cervantes, considerado como poeta" (Rpt. 1941) of "an elegant/ingenious and discreetly critical poem" ("un elegante/ingenioso y discreto poema crítico"). Scholars have usually compared *Viaje* with Lope de Vega's *Laurel de Apolo* (*The Laurel of Apollo*), judging Lope's version to be superior to that of Cervantes. Yet, it is clear that those two works do not have much in common and that *Viaje* should be related to the rest of Cervantes's production.

According to F. Rodríguez Marín, Cervantes conceived his *Viaje* both as escape to a nostalgic past and to celebrate, in passing, his contemporary poets.

33. ¡Oh tú—dijo—que los poetas
     canonizaste de la larga lista,
     por causas y por vías indirectas!

    ¿Dónde tenías, magancés, la vista
    aguda de tu ingenio, que así ciego
    fuiste tan mentiroso cronista?

34. Aquel que de poeta no se precia,
     ¿para qué escribe versos y los dice?
     ¿Por qué desdeña lo que más aprecia?

    Jamás me contenté ni satisfice
    de hipócritos melindres; llanamente
    quise alabanzas de lo que bien hice.

35. This autobiographical inscription has been noted by Elias L. Rivers (1970) and Jean Canavaggio (1977). See also Francisco Márquez Villanueva (1990). Jordi Gracia García (1989) points out how the *Viaje* shows the literary and moral abjection as origin of the sad situation of the poets.

36. See Rodríguez Marín (1935).

37. See a brilliant analysis of the poem in Francisco Márques Villanueva (1990), who cites an extensive bibliography on this topic.

38. Ibid.

39. See, for example, Rodríguez Marín (1935), and Schevill and Bonilla (1922).

40. Cantar con voz tan entonada y viva
      que piensen que soy cisne y que me muero.
          (Chap. 4, vv. 564–565)

41.   Fuíme con esto, y, lleno de despecho,
       busqué mi antigua y lóbrega posada,
       y arrojéme molido sobre el lecho;
       que cansa, cuando es larga, una jornada.
                         (Chap. 8, vv. 454–457)

DOMINICK FINELLO

The Galatea

During the early 1580s, after five years of captivity in Algiers and a decision to embark upon a career in writing, Cervantes produces the *Galatea*, his earliest record of substantial contact with the pastoral. Since he is an untried author, one might dismiss this novelistic experiment as blind accommodation or servility to a popular convention; but the fact that he is unknown perhaps explains his motive for writing in this particular form.[1] The *Galatea* draws attention to its author as a new face on the literary scene who, wishing to leave his mark by gaining friends, takes as his guide this genre, which is a vogue among the established writers. While commentators on the *Galatea* (of which there have been many in the recent past) differ in their judgments about Cervantes's adherence to Arcadian conventions, each agrees that the work offers original features.[2] Let us, then, examine its purpose, its response to poetics and the pastoral tradition, and its narrative and lyrical style.

Cervantes writes partly in admiration of poets like Garcilaso, Fernando de Herrera, and Luis Gálvez de Montalvo. In his dedicatory letter to the literary patron Ascanio Colonna he bows to "los que alguna virtuosa ciencia profesan, especialmente los que en la poesía se ejercitan" (those who profess whatsoever science, especially the poetic profession) (*La Galatea* 1:1–2),

From *Pastoral Themes and Forms in Cervantes's Fiction.* © 1994 by Associated University Presses, Inc.

hoping some day to perfect his poetic skill. Meanwhile, as he is involved in
the composition of the *Galatea*, the *Pastor de Fílida* comes off the presses in
1582[3]—a fortuitous occurrence for him; and when the *Galatea* arrives in
1585, Gálvez de Montalvo pays tribute to Cervantes with a sonnet for a great
soldier who, upon his return to Spain after a protracted imprisonment, joins
her muses. Here are the tercets:

> Pero después que diste al patrio suelo
> tu alma sana y tu garganta suelta
> dentre las fuerzas bárbaras confusas,
> descubre claro tu valor el cielo,
> gózase el mundo en tu felice vuelta,
> y cobra España las perdidas musas.

> [But after you gave to your country's soil
> your honest soul and your daring voice
> among the confused barbarous forces,
> heaven discovers your valor,
> the world enjoys your happy return,
> and Spain receives its lost muses.]
> (1:11)

Here and throughout, the pastoral serves as a repository for homages to
friends and patrons. In the case of Gálvez de Montalvo's *Pastor de Fílida*, his
patron, Don Enrique de Mendoza y Aragón, is one of the protagonists
(Mendino); tributes on its final pages reveal at least three poems from the
Mendoza;[4] and the panegyric to famous women at the end of part 6 (473–77)
is calculated to laud the Mendoza and the Infantado branch of that house. At
the beginning of part 3, Gálvez de Montalvo introduces the action with
words praising the cream of Spain among the shepherds in the woods:
"Paréceme que de España lo mejor se recoge en estas selvas" (It seems that
the best of Spain are found in these woods) (421).

In the *Canto de Calíope* (she, the muse of eloquence and heroic poetry)
Cervantes honors Gálvez de Montalvo:

> ¿Quién pudiera loaros, mis pastores,
> un pastor vuestro amado y conocido,
> pastor mejor de cuantos son mejores,
> que de Fílida tiene apellido?
> La habilidad, la ciencia, los primores,
> el raro ingenio y el valor subido

de Luis de Montalvo, le aseguran
gloria y honor mientras los cielos duran.

[Who could give commendation due shepherds,
Your shepherd true, beloved and recognised,
The best of all who are acknowledged best;
De Fílida his appellation is;
Ability, science, prime qualities,
Uncommon genius, courage elevated,
To Luis de Montalvo is assured,
Glory and honour while the heavens endure.]
(2:198–99)[5]

This recognition of Gálvez de Montalvo provides impetus for the completion of the *Galatea*. Luis Astrana Marín has suggested that the success of Gálvez de Montalvo's intriguing roman à clef encourages Cervantes to finish the *Galatea*.[6] Furthermore, Gálvez de Montalvo's novel offers a model for the conception of the *Galatea*, since Cervantes creates figures for his work based on those of real life.[7] As a newer writer, Cervantes not only wants to celebrate the bonds of friendship between poets of Spain but, like Gálvez de Montalvo, and even Montemayor, he mounts scenes that resemble intimate personal dramas. The *Pastor de Fílida* for its part corresponds with the love affairs of the author (Siralvo) and his above-mentioned patron. Although the *Galatea* is not drawn as systematically closely to real life as the *Pastor de Fílida*, actual friendly relationships that Cervantes wishes to record for posterity undoubtedly occupy a high position on his list of priorities (they include Siralvo and other shepherds of the *Pastor de Fílida*). In this spirit of friendship and awareness of his fellow writers—a topic that will be examined shortly— he composes the *Galatea*.

ECLOGUE AND THE ART OF POETRY

In the prologue of the *Galatea* ("Curiosos lectores" [Curious readers]), Cervantes says that the definition and function of pastoral poetry itself is another of his work's primary concerns. In this prologue, one of his least cryptic, he openly admits to a desire to write in the pastoral manner with the aim of one day mastering its lyricism:[8] "puedo alegar de mi parte la inclinación que a la poesía siempre he tenido, y la edad, que, habiendo apenas salido de los límites de la juventud, parece que da licencia a semejantes ocupaciones" (I can truly allege what predilection I have entertained for poetry, for when I was scarce emancipated from my youthful shackles, I gave way to these identical pursuits) (1:6). He declares that poetry is advantageous because it nourishes the vernacular for higher enterprises, such as "enriquecer el poeta considerando su propia lengua, y enseñorearse del artificio de la elocuencia que en ella cabe, para empresas más altas y de mayor importancia" (enriching the poet relatively to his mother tongue, and so as to rule over the artifices of eloquence therein comprised, with a view to higher aims and of more serious import) (1:6). This is a brief preparation for the *Canto de Calíope*, an homage to poetry and Spanish poets.[9] Cervantes then defends poetry against those who would discredit it: "Y así, por esta causa, los insignes y claros ingenios que en ella se aventajan, con la poca estimación que dellos los príncipes y el vulgo hacen, con solos sus entendimientos comunican sus altos y estraños conceptos, sin osar publicarlos al mundo" (Hence the famous intellects which abound in Spain, though little appreciated by some, by their energy communicate lofty and unusual conceptions, without daring to publish them to the world) (2:226–27). Later in his career, especially in part 2 of the *Quijote* and in the *Viaje del Parnaso*, Cervantes writes less flatteringly about poets.

On the whole, the *Galatea* contains a limited number of comments that speak passionately to the crucial contemporary issue of the justification of poetry,[10] while the activity of theorists grows throughout Europe and is manifested in Spain as well with the landmark publication of Fernando de Herrera's *Anotaciones* (1580).[11] Yet the well-known tradition of attacking fiction that accelerates during the Spain of the Habsburgs continues among humanists, and their criticism of the chivalry book sometimes includes the pastoral. Therefore, it is not surprising to find defense mechanisms cautiously built into the prefatory material of pastoral novels. Montemayor advises his readers that the stories in his *Diana* are "casos verdaderos" (true tales); Gil Polo sidesteps the issue by deeming his *Diana enamorada* a "recreación" (diversion), casting his project in a positive light;[12] Bartolomé López de Enciso, *Desengaño de celos* (Disillusionment of jealousy) (1586), lauds the pleasurable sounds of the shepherd's lute by dressing his delicate story of jealousy in bucolic garb; Bernardo González de Bobadilla, *Primera parte de las ninfas y pastores de Henares* (First part of the nymphs and shepherds of Henares) (1587), somewhat contrite, uses a humility formula, asking forgiveness for "este pobre librillo mío" (this poor little book of mine); and Gálvez de Montalvo also employs the "libro humilde y pequeño" (small and humble book) axiom. Cervantes for his own part echoes concerns by beginning his prologue with a mild complaint that the occupation of writing eclogues at a time when poetry is so forsaken will not be esteemed as a laudable exercise, though it will be indispensable to give some special satisfaction to those who rate this employment as little less than labor and time lost (1:5). Anyone familiar with Cervantes's prologues will agree that his later ones are less direct though more trenchant. Here he is a grieving writer on the defensive, while in later prologues he switches to the offensive, upbraiding readers and critics. Yet this posturing in 1585 is for Cervantes no mere rhetorical exercise, since besides these *disculpas* (apologies), constructive statements make their bow in the *Galatea*, especially with regard to *invención*, the ability to create imagined or fictional subjects with proper arrangement of material (*disposición*) aimed at pleasing the reader: "Las demás que en la invención y en la disposición se pudieren poner" (The remaining objections must be placed to the account of the invention and disposition of the piece) (1:8–9). This remark can be appreciated fully in the context of two subsequent remarks: his claim that he is the first to novelize in Spain,[13] and "Yo soy aquel que en la *invención* excede a muchos" (I am the one who excedes many when it comes to invention).[14]

NOVELTY AND VERISIMILITUDE

Cervantes is not especially aggressive in the *Galatea*'s Prologue. He does not insist that his work be placed in a high position among pastorals, and though he writes in a climate he considers hostile toward poetry and imaginative fiction, he does not meet the controversy over them head-on. But the lack of experimental spirit in the prologue is compensated for in the body of the work, as Cervantes seeks novelty in its stories themselves.[15] Later, in the scrutiny of the *Galatea* in part 1, chapter 6 of the *Quijote*, Cervantes confesses that he was disturbed over never having carried out the full potential of his earlier work. Attentive to formal problems of the pastoral romance, he exhibits maturation of his ideas in the *Quijote* by subjecting the *Galatea* to very high artistic standards in a kind of self-reproach. The Priest and Barber speak: "Pero ¿qué libro es ese que está junto a él?—*La Galatea*, de Miguel de Cervantes—dijo el barbero.—Muchos años ha que es grande amigo mío ese Cervantes, y se que es más versado en desdichas que en versos. Su libro tiene algo de buena invención; propone algo, y no concluye nada: es menester esperar la segunda parte que promete; quizá con la enmienda alcanzará del todo la misericordia que ahora se le niega; y entre tanto que esto se ve, tenedle recluso en vuestra posada, señor compadre" (But what book is that next to it? "The *Galatea* of Miguel de Cervantes," said the Barber. "That Cervantes has been for many years a great friend of mine, and to my knowledge he has had more experience in reverses than in verses. His book is not without imagination; it presents us with something but brings nothing to a conclusion. We must wait for the Second Part he has promised; perhaps it will show enough improvement to win the unrestricted praise that is now denied it. In the meantime, my good friend, keep it shut up in your own quarters") (1.6.75). The *Galatea*'s inclusion in Don Quijote's library has a twofold purpose. First, Cervantes says in hindsight that with all good intentions it was a youthful, incomplete statement about art, "propone algo, y no concluye nada" (it presents us with something but brings nothing to a conclusion); and second, he admits it lacks some originality, "*algo* de buena invención" (not without imagination), despite his genuine desire at the time to change the artistic configuration of the pastoral novel.

Perhaps it is the notion of traditional romance—the implied need for a definitive ending or resolution—that leads Cervantes to refuel his obsession over the *Galatea*'s unfinished state once more in his last dedicatory letter (1616), in which he says that if God gave him more time, he would finish the *Galatea*.[16] Nevertheless, this lingering preoccupation suggests at least that the pastoral does not deserve the same sort of censure as the chivalric in Cervantes's mind. One wonders, then, why he never returned to the *Galatea*, and the question must certainly be satisfied by a careful reading of the pastoral episodes of the *Quijote*, whose abrupt disintegration is more than mere coincidence.

The insecurity that surfaces with these comments about the *Galatea* twenty years after its publication has much to do with the sixteenth century's attention to truth in fiction. Cervantes, as noted already, is mindful of the difficult business of writing pastoral material (*églogas*). This, coupled with the statement at the end of his prologue that it seems awkward that simple shepherds should sit about all day inventing love philosophies, makes the pastoral a vehicle for testing degrees of truth in fiction: "pues el príncipe de la poesía latina fue calumniado en algunas de sus églogas por haberse levantado más que en las otras, y así no temeré mucho que alguno condemne haber mezclado razones de filosofía entre algunas amorosas de pastores, que pocas veces se levantan más que a tratar cosas del campo, y esto en su acostumbrada llaneza. Mas advirtiendo—como en el discurso de la obra alguna vez se hace—que muchos de los disfrazados pastores della to eran sólo en el hábito, queda llana esta objeción" (the very prince of Latin poetry was blamed for making some of his eclogues more elevated than others. Hence have no fear that I shall be criticised because some philosophical reasons are interspersed with certain amorous arguments of shepherds, who rarely rise in discourse beyond country affairs, and this, too, with a congenial simplicity. Yet noting [as in this work is found] that many of the disguised shepherds are so only in attire, this objection is cleared) (1:8). The problem stated here involves the acceptance of shepherds as symbolic figures, not as real guardians of herds. Montemayor and Gil Polo shift smoothly to and from the isolated world of shepherds; but the happy medium between the world of shepherds and the real world appears to be difficult for Cervantes to strike, at times, in the *Galatea*. Moreover, incompatibility between the hard realities of shepherd life and Arcadian idealism is also more prevalent in the *Galatea* than in the *Pastor de Fílida*, which, as we know, is the pastoral exemplar closest to Cervantes. Gálvez de Montalvo for his own part thinks that the he faces complaints about believability because his motives for mixing the rustic duties of shepherds with their poetic practices are not well understood. For this reason, he points out in a passage at the beginning of part 6 the incongruous juxtaposition of the rustic and the literary, and attempts to explain the combination of the two:

> Possible cosa será que mientras yo canto las amorosas églogas que sobre las aguas del Tajo resonaron, algún curioso me pregunte: Entre estos amores y desdenes, lágrimas y canciones, ¿cómo por montes y prados tan poco balan cabras, ladran perros, aullan lobos? ¿dónde pacen las ovejas? ¿a qué hora se ordeñan? ¿quién les unta la roña? ¿cómo se regalan las paridas? El segundo objeto podrá ser el lenguaje de mis versos. También darán mis pastores mi disculpa con que todos ellos saben que el ánimo del amado mejor se mueve con los conceptos del amador que con el viento las hojas de los árboles. La tercera duda podrá ser si es lícito donde también parecen los amores escritos en los troncos de las plantas, que también haya cartas y papeles: cosa tan desusada entre los silvestres pastores. (464)

> [Perhaps as I sing the amorous eclogues that resonated on the waters of the Tagus someone may ask me: Among these loves, disdains, tears, and songs, why do goats bleat, dogs bark, and wolves howl so little in the mountains and pastures? Where do the sheep graze? At what hour are they milked? Who coats their scabs? Who takes care of the females who have recently given birth? The second matter could be my poetic language: My shepherds will be forgiven for knowing that the soul of the lover is better moved by the lover's conceits than the leaves of the trees are moved by the wind. The third doubt may have to do with the fact that as love's messages are written on the trunks of trees, they are also written in letters and papers, a habit seldom seen among wild shepherds.]

He is not entirely happy with his attempt at creating the illusion that the world in which his shepherds roam is credible. Yet we can see that the contrast of styles in the *Pastor de Fílida* is not as stark as the author would have us believe, once we realize that the specific backdrop of this novel is actually the drama and intrigue of documented courtly love affairs in the admitted guise of pastoral. Gálvez de Montalvo therefore does not have to explain how simple shepherds are capable of poetically inspired love. But since readers may misunderstand his intention, which, of course, is not to combine the world of the authentic shepherd and that of the elegantly disguised court shepherd, he pauses to prove that he is aware of the differences between the two.

The clash of reality and fiction is more evident in the *Galatea*. For example, concrete touches of a so–called rustic picnic are not totally convincing in book 1 (1:80–88). As Teolinda's tale ends, the rest of the elegant company sit to entertain themselves among "rústicos manjares" (rustic foods) and "rebaños" (flocks), and when Cervantes introduces the "desamorado" (unloved) Lenio with his "zampoña" (rustic flute), "en cuyo pecho el amor jamás pudo hacer morada" (in whose breast love never could find an abode), and recounts that the company listens earnestly, the tangibles of the everyday shepherd do not correspond with the harmony struck by the literary shepherds (1:80). A debate about love ensues (Lenio, Elicio, and Erastro), and the first book concludes with the return of the shepherds to their huts: "Y habiéndole acompañado Elicio hasta media lengua de su cabaña, le tornó a abrazar" (and having accompanied Elicio half a league to his cabin, he turned and embraced him) (1:87). Symbolic action again appears out of place with the backdrop of the prosaic hut. In book 2, however, after Teolinda narrates the second part of her tale, Cervantes accomplishes a smoother transition, turning his attention to the arrival of other shepherds with a lyrical formula, "Y de allí a poco oyeron que al son de la zampoña el de un pequeño rabel se acordaba" (At a little distance from the pipe was a slender rebeck which kept time) (1:104). But at the beginning of book 4, as in other places, incongruities recur. Teolinda walks along the banks of the Tagus looking for Artidoro, and Galatea offers to send one of her father's shepherds to find him, an abrupt turn to everyday pragmatism: "de enviar algón pastor de los de su padre a buscar a Artidoro por todas las riberas de Tajo y por donde se imaginase que podría ser hallado" (of sending some shepherd of her father to look for Artidoro everywhere on the banks of the Tagus to see where he might be found) (2:7). The attempt to combine real places and things with the conversation between Galatea and her friends in book 1, such as the preoccupation with herding sheep, misses the desired effect. She tells Elicio that "desde ayer concertamos las dos [Florisa and Galatea] de apacentar hoy allí nuestros ganados, y como yo venía descuidada sonando mi zampoña, la mansa borrega tomó el camino de las Pizarras, como della más acostumbrado" (only yesterday we agreed so to do, and feed our flocks, and as I came along thoughtlessly tuning my pipe, the gentle ewe took the road towards the pebble stream as the most accustomed) (1:55). Characters thinking as literary shepherds and yet mindful of the tasks of laboring peasants would present a problem for Gálvez de Montalvo. These words come from Teolinda's story: "Mejor harías de tener cuenta con to honra y con to que conviene al pasto de tus ovejas, y no entremeterte en estas burlerías de amor" (Better attend to your honour, and what concerns the pasture of your flock, and not interpose yourself in those love-fooleries) (1:66). Such awkward posturing recalls the shepherdess Marcela of the *Quijote*, who claims to spend her days in the company of her flock and other shepherdesses, an activity incompatible with her upbringing.

In later works, Cervantes resolves these disparities resulting from the portrayal of rustics and shepherds. In the *Coloquio de los perros*, Berganza, a canine interlocutor of this exemplary novel, draws a clear distinction between real shepherds and literary ones, and in the *Quijote*, the reality of the workaday world is mounted as an independent medium for artistic expression.

The desire to hear and tell stories, which, as we know, is fundamental to the composition of pastoral novels as a whole, is explicit in the *Galatea*. While Cervantes shapes his work with a wide variety of stories, and thereby satisfies the artistic necessity to please ("la voluntad del autor, que fue de agradar," 1:9), he also strikes new chords in pastoral art having to do with interdependence. He features a historical plot against the grain of the poetic substance of songs, verse, feasts, and other less routine activities.[17] The simplest profile of this suspenseful plot will bear this out: The *Galatea* begins with the plaints of Elicio, whose story is tied to Erastro and Galatea. Lisandro appears and tells how he killed Carino for the love of Leonida. Enter Teolinda, in pursuit of Artidoro, and focus then shifts to a debate between Lenio and Elicio. Teolinda's tale continues, and then follows the most complicated story in the novel, a Byzantine tale narrated by Silerio, friend of Timbrio and lover of Nísida. Other shepherds, Daranio and Silveria, plan to be married, but the relationship is complicated by Mireno, who is in love with Silveria. Teolinda then encounters Leonarda, her long lost sister, who is journeying with Rosaura, a shepherdess in search of Grisaldo. A debate about the effects of Love between Tirsi and Lenio ensues, followed by the reunion of Nísida Timbrio, Silerio, and Blanca. Silerio weds Blanca, but Leonarda tricks Artidoro into betrothal. All the lovers go to the Valley of the Cypresses to pay tribute to Meliso. After the homage, Calliope sings her *canto* in praise of Spanish poets. Part 1 of the *Galatea* ends as

Galatea attempts to prevent her arranged marriage to a Portuguese shepherd while Elicio threatens force in support of her.

The artistic effect of intertwining stories suggests that Cervantes's shepherds have formed an interdependent chain binding their friendship, a vital ingredient of the pastoral and a major building block of the *Galatea*. The energy and movement of its tales are probably the result of the author's anxiety to focus sharply on sweeping a multitude of people into proximity with one another.[18] The overall effect is one of an inscrutable force joining characters who had not necessarily been acquainted; some come from the nearby village and others from parts unknown. It is Cervantes's aim to have his figures move on collectively, wandering and suffering—often in unison—while telling stories and reciting poetry to vent their emotions. As the company grows, the characters partake of each others' concerns, and it becomes obvious that friendship is a key motive of this novel.

FRIENDSHIP AND COMMUNITY

In the final analysis the *Galatea* succeeds because its design follows its characters' needs for harmony. Ultimately, all of this contributes to a strong collective spirit; friendship and community are stressed throughout the work. The desire for companionship, introduced briefly in chapter two, and the interaction within a group of intellectually intimate friends such as an academy, defines the *Galatea* as effectively as other traditional motifs and antecedents do. One may recall Cervantes's wish to be in the good graces of the writers and poets of Spain; and one may note his anxiety to involve people with one another, an objective of both his early and later writing. Together, these two facts have important thematic implications for his pastoral art, because the intended harmony of the shepherd points to a deep and broad bond among poets and writers. For these and other reasons, friendship is generally one of the most revealing common denominators for character analysis in the pastoral.[19] Thus, happy reunions consume much of the characters' time in the *Galatea*. Moreover, while such gatherings are common to almost all pastorals, they develop to a high degree in the *Galatea*, with the result that at times they become the novel's guiding force.

Montemayor and Gil Polo symbolize this unifying impulse in the person of Felicia, who possesses the magic that makes people live happily. When the shepherds come to her temple they celebrate gleeful reunions. This deus ex machina of the *Diana* and *Diana enamorada* evolves into a system of mutual advice and dependence in the *Galatea*. Cervantes presents people from different places who cling to one another for self-protection. They have few guides but find strength in numbers, and consequently the company scene becomes prevalent. This tendency toward unity, resulting in the mobilization of the characters into an aggregate, makes the evocation of collective human profiles one of the most successful techniques of Cervantes's early work. It is a key to the temporal and spatial structure of the *Galatea* because shepherds constantly gravitate toward and console one another, shifting their focus to anyone of the company who deserves special attention. A group of shepherds prepares to talk about love and its varied effects near the end of book 1:

A la sazón que Lenio cantaba lo que habéis oido, habían ya llegado con sus rebaños Elicio y Erastro, en compañía del lastimado Lisandro, y pareciéndole a Elicio que la lengua de Lenio en decir mal de amor a más de lo que era razón se estendía, quiso mostrarle a la clara su engaño, y aprovechándose del mesmo concepto de los versos que él había cantado, al tiempo que ya llegaban Galatea, Florisa y Teolinda y los demás pastores, al son de la zampoña de Erastro, comenzó a cantar.

[While Lenio was singing what we just heard, both Elicio and Erastro, with their wind instruments, came up, in company of the much-to-be-lamented Lisandro, and it seemed to Elicio that the evil which Lenio spoke of love, as far as it extended with reason, went to show clearly his deception; and while availing himself of the same ideas as are found in the verses which he had recited, Galatea, Floriso, and Teolinda arrived with the other herdsmen, to the sound of the rebeck of Erastro; Elicio began this strain.] (1:82)

Here is the scene after which Lauso recites tercets in book 4 introducing a discussion of the theory of love:

Mas no hubieron andado mucho, cuando vieron venir de lejos algunos pastores, que luego fueron conocidos, porque eran Tirsi, Damón, Elicio, Erastro, Arsindo, Francenio, Crisio, Orompo, Daranio y Marsilo, con todos los más principales pastores de la aldea, y entre ellos el desamorado Lenio, con el lastimado Silerio, los cuales salían a tener la siesta a la fuente de las Pizarras.

[They had not progressed very far when they encountered several shepherds, their acquaintances, for there were Thirsis, Damón, Elicio, Erastro, Arsindo, Francenio, Crisio, Orompo, Daranio,

Orfenio, and Marsilio, with all the foremost shepherds of the vicinity, and among them the disenamoured Lenio, with the melancholy Silerio, all of whom had sallied forth for a *siesta* at the stone fountain.] (2:30)

To survive, characters appear to huddle with each other, a picture frequently found in the *Galatea*. In book 4, Cervantes evinces the effect of an inscrutable human bond:

> Cuando Arsindo volvió a decir lo que con la pastora había pasado, halló que todos aquellos pastores habían llegado a consolar al enamorado pastor, y que las dos de las tres rebozadas pastoras, la una estaba desmayada en las faldas de la hermosa Galatea, y la otra abrazada con la bella Rosaura, que asimesmo el rostro cubierto tenía. La que con Galatea estaba era Teolinda, y la otra, su hermana Leonarda, las cuales, así como vieron al desesperado pastor que con Gelasia hallaron, un celoso y enamorado desmayo les cubrió el corazón, porque Leonarda creyó que el pastor era su querido Galercio, y Teolinda tuvo por verdad que era su enamorado Artidoro; y como las dos le vieron tan rendido y perdido por la cruel Gelasia, llególes tan al alma el sentimiento, que sin sentido alguno, la una en las faldas de Galatea, la otra en los brazos de Rosaura, desmayadas cayeron.

> [When Arsindo reverted to what had passed with the female, he found all the other swains had joined to console the love-affected shepherd, and that of two of the disguised shepherdesses, one had fainted in the folds of the lovely Galatea, and the other was embracing the attractive Rosaura, whose face was also shrouded from sight. Teolinda was with Galatea, and the other, her sister Leonarda. On sight of the despairing swain, whom they found with Gelasia, a sort of jealous and enamoured fainting fit pervaded their hearts, for Leonarda believed that the shepherd was her cherished Galercio; and Teolinda found it for a truth to be her beloved Artidoro, and so witnessing him persecuted and lost by the heartless Gelasia, they sympathetically joined their sentiments, so that the result was that one, fainting, fell into the folds of the vest of Galatea, and the other fainted in the arms of Rosaura.] (2:81)

This motif of intimacy is one for which the reader need not look far. Descriptions from book 2 express the familiar camaraderie among these shepherds. Elicio and Erastro are often together: "Estaba Elicio en compañía de su amigo Erastro, de quien pocas veces se apartaba por el entretenimiento y gusto que de su buena conversación recibía" (Elicio was in company with his tried friend, Erastro, from whom rarely he separated, as his conversation and taste were in unison with his own) (1:112). Elicio tells Tirsi: "Bien conforma tu agradable semblante, nombrado Tirsi, con lo que de tu valor y discreción en las cercanas y apartadas tierras la parlera fama pregona; y así, a mí, a quien tus escriptos han admirado e inclinado a desear conocerte y servirte, puedes de hoy más tener y tratar como verdadero amigo" (In sweet accord is thy well-favoured countenance, renowned Thirsis, with what thy valour and sobriety in near and remote lands speaking fame announces. So to me, who have admired your writings, and have desired and have been inclined to know and serve you, may you hold me to be, and treat me, as your well-tried friend) (1:114). The act of engaging each other to talk figures prominently here, as it does in Cervantes's later works. Moreover, if characters want to listen to someone's story, this could mean that it has the potential of being interesting. Silerio's tale continues in book 2 with the following introductory words of Erastro, reminiscent of Dorotea's reaction to Don Luis's appearance in the *Quijote*, part 1, chapter 43; here, friendship is celebrated, not surprisingly, in song: "Deteneos, pastores, que según pienso, hoy oiremos todos lo que ha días que yo deseo oir, que es la voz de un agradecido mozo.... [Le] he sentido tocar una harpa y entonar una voz tan suave, que me ha puesto en grandísimo deseo de escucharla ... Y aunque con hablarle he procurado hacerme su amigo, ofreciéndole a su servicio todo lo que valgo y puedo, nunca he podido acabar con él que me descubra quién es" (Stay, swains, for methinks this day we shall hear what I have longed to hear of a long season, namely, the voice of a pleasing youth.... I have heard him play a harp accompanied by a voice so soft, that my desire has been awakened to hear it.... Yet in conversation with him have I made myself his friend, offering him all I could, and all I have; never could I learn who he was) (1:121–22).

On the whole, while fostering interdependence does not originate with Cervantes, its artistic expression in the *Galatea* stands out among pastorals. Consequently, friendship and community are crucial for the novel's interpretation. This kind of interaction is developed further in the Grisóstomo–Marcela episode of the *Quijote*. The opening of the deceased shepherd's papers and the reading of his lament is a high point in the novel's first pastoral interlude, and it attracts people from far and wide to pay homage to a poet and friend. When Don Quijote learns that the words of Grisóstomo will be made public beside his tomb, nothing can prevent him from visiting the site.

ACADEMY AND COLLOQUIUM

Friendly gatherings and reunions, which loom as a forum for communication specifically among writers, have other dividends for the pastoral. Through the exchange of ideas, authors elevate their dialogue gradually to a broad philosophical plateau, and this dialogue eventually points up the pastoral artist's quest for universal harmony among men, not only among personal friends. This often occurs in literature that reproduces academic interaction, which a look at the text of the *Galatea* will disclose.

In academic settings of the Renaissance, friendship arises out of oneness of purpose among people gathered for artistic competitions and other intellectually motivated pastimes. Hence, academic literature, like some pastoral novels, relies significantly on friendship enhanced by artistic contests and rivalries. In this regard, Andrew Ettin offers the following observation of the first part of Evelyn Waugh's *Brideshead Revisited*, which carries the title "Et in Arcadia Ego," and shows, in this sense, that little has changed in the modern pastoral. It is concerned, he says, with "an artificial and playful society of almost carefree young men whose main interests are literature, entertainment, and comradeship; most of it is set in the sheltered environment of the university."[20] The *Galatea* likewise celebrates brotherhood by mounting the human drama inherent in the solemnization of intellectual discourse, poetic competition, feasts, games, and masquerades, whose purpose is to focus sharply the value of the characters not, of course, as humble shepherds but as fellow poets joining symbolically to form a community of compatible artists. This is how the dialectic core of the *Galatea* re-creates customs of the Renaissance colloquium and of the more formally structured academy, which begin to take shape in the dialogue of book 1 about the relative merits of love, described as a "graciosa pendencia" (gracious quarrel) (1:86). Here, not only do Cervantes's shepherds share similar concerns about love and its spiritual rewards, but on another level their conversation, interspersed generously with poems, celebrates poets' mutual admiration for their own skills. Cervantes thus honors courtier-poet friends by exhibiting his command of the craft dear to them. In an academic setting the shepherds and shepherdesses share each other's enthusiasm and learning. Teolinda describes the new arrivals, Tirsi and Damón, in book 2, recognizing their intellectual talents as well as their camaraderie: "tan aventajados los dos en todo género de discreción, ciencia y loables ejercicios, que no sólo en el circuito de nuestra comarca son conocidos, pero por todo el de la tierra conocidos y estimados" (supreme in general discretion, science, and commendable exercises, who not alone in our circuits are known, but far and wide enjoy estimation and respect) (1:105). In book 4 of the *Galatea*, where a pivotal discussion of love takes place, references to the cultural impulses that motivate the philosophical debate between Lenio and Tirsi set these interlocutors squarely in the academic world of disguised shepherds. Lenio speaks of Tirsi, "cuya crianza en famosas *academias* y cuyos bien sabidos estudios no pueden asegurar en mi pretensión sino segura pérdida" (whose education is celebrated in *academies*, and whose well-grounded knowledge indicates an assurance to me that I cannot be victor in the contention) (2:43). Other comments about both shepherds facilitate the transition away from the rustic world toward that of a kind of academy situated in groves and woods: "Tirsi, cuyas razones y argumentos más parecen de ingenios *entre libros y las aulas criados*, que no de aquellos que entre pajizas cabañas son crecidos" (Thirsis, whose reasons and arguments appear more ingenious among those educated *in halls and in literature* than among those whose nativity and culture are amidst village cabins) (2:71); and: "la crianza del nombrado Tirsi no ha sido entre los árboles y florestas, sino en *las reales cortes y conocidas escuelas*.... Y aunque el desamorado Lenio ... ha confesado la rusticidad de su vida ... te aseguro que los más floridos años de su edad gastó, no en el ejercicio de guardar las cabras en los montes, sino en las riberas del claro Tormes, en loables estudios y discretas conversaciones" (the education of the renowned Thirsis has not been confined to trees and woods, but in the *royal courts and recognised schools*.... And though Lenio, disenchanted of love, ... has confessed the rusticity of his life, ... I assure you that he did not melt down the marrow of his youth in goat keeping on the hills, but on the banks of the fluent Tormes, in laudable studies and judicious conversational exchanges) (2:72). Paolo Savj-López profiles the *Galatea* and its learned shepherds as academics; he calls them "sabios pastores" (learned shepherds) who discuss the subtleties of court and country life like a group of academics congregating in the gardens of the Renaissance ("como podía hacerlo una reunión de *académicos* congregados en los huertos del renacimiento").[21] J.B. Trend characterizes the society of the *Galatea* as that of young men and women who, for a period of time, retire from their routine labors and create a utopian community in which they talk about literature, music, and philosophy on a daily basis.[22] This is the business of Arcadian academies of Italy in the sixteenth and seventeenth centuries, whose members in their capacity as academics establish rules that make everyone equal and even permit women to join as "académicos de número" (regular members). Spaniards who visit Italian academies during the period employ pastoral names, precisely the custom re-created in the *Galatea*.

Book 4 confirms the fundamental idea that the academy pervades the pastoral. Characters are young, well-educated, and have studied what they talk about. Elicio terms it "buena conversación" (good conversation),[23] which supports the Renaissance genre of dialogue or colloquium: "Con hacer, señor, to que nos mandas, cumpliremos nuestro deseo, que por agora no se estendía a mas que venir a este lugar a pasar en él en buena conversación" (Now to do, my lord, what you desire, replied Elicio, we concur, but it extends no further than pursuing a conversation) (2:31). Colloquium substantially advances the limits of pastoral form by allowing it to introduce diverse topics familiar to a courtly or academic public. Cervantes, in fact, shapes this raw material into some of the most dynamic dialogues of the *Quijote*, a topic explored in part three of this study. In book 3 of the *Galatea*, his shepherds are joined by courtiers, Damón and Darinto, and these courtiers, inspired by the setting, talk about and praise country life in polite discussion during the long, hot afternoon.[24] The picture calls to mind Giorgione's masterful *Concert champêtre*, in which courtiers rapturously enjoy the life they have been dreaming about. The "gallardos pastores" (elegant shepherds) of the *Galatea* invite the richly adorned ladies and gentlemen to chat about the advantages of country life over court life as Cervantes portrays bucolic yearning in the locus *amoenus* (2:31–32). Darinto speaks, beginning with a Garcilasian formula: "Cuando me paro a considerar, agradables pastores, la ventaja que hace al cortesano y soberbio trato el pastoral y humilde vuestro, no puedo dejar de tener lástima a mí mesmo, y a vosotros una honesta envidia" (When I stop to consider, agreeable shepherds, the advantage which your pastoral and humble carriage hath over the haughty bearing of a courtier, I cannot but pity myself, and be really jealous of your deportment) (2:32–33). And he says further: "¿Qué te diría, pues, si quisiese, de la sencillez de su vida, de la llaneza de su condición y de la honestidad de sus amores?" (Who would speak, then, of the simplicity of their lives, the evenness of their state, and the integrity of their loves?) (2:33–34). The topic of bucolic honesty and simplicity on the one hand, and its antipode, the corrupting city and court on the other, finds many adherents in academic circles.

From the above analysis the following key features of the *Galatea* emerge. First, the communal pattern as an allegory of the brotherhood of poets is central to the *Galatea*; and in a broader sense this stands for the bonds between men. Second is the portrayal of a pluralistic group of people caught up in the excitement of exchange of mutual concerns. The following vignette of characters moving nervously about in the preparations for the nuptials of Daranio and Silveria at the end of book 2 is yet another of Cervantes's unique portraits of shepherds gleefully involved with one another:

> vieron venir hacia ellos hasta una docena de gallardos pastores puestos en dos hileras, y en medio venía un dispuesto pastor,

coronado con una guirnalda de madreselva y de otras diferentes flores. Traía un bastón en la una mano, y con grave paso poco a poco se movía, y los demás pastores andando con el mesmo aplauso, y tocando todos sus instrumentos, daban de sí agradable y estraña muestra.... Y a esta sazón llegó *el montón alegre de pastores*, los cuales conociendo a Elicio, y Daranio a Tirsi y a Damón, sus amigos, con señales de grande alegría se recibieron, y renovando la música y renovando el contento, tornaron a proseguir el comenzado camino, y ya que llegaban junto al aldea, llegó a sus oídos el son de la zampoña del desamorado Lenio, de que no poco gusto recibieron todos, porque ya conocían la estremada condición suya.

[they observed about a dozen lively swains in lines, and in the centre a shepherd was posted, crowned with a honeysuckle garland, and divers flowers. He bore a staff in his hand, and walked very deliberately, and the other shepherds to the same sounds, touching instruments, indicating an agreeable and unusual sympathy.... And at this season came *a crowd of jocund swains*, who, recognising Elicio, and Daranio, and Thirsis, and Damón, his friends, received all with evidence of unalloyed joy, and setting the music off again, and renewing contentment, they pursued the beaten path; and, as soon as they reached the hamlet, that which struck on their ears was the oaten pipe of the unenamoured Lenio, and this gave infinite pleasure to all, for they were aware of his forlorn state.] (1:160–61)

Cervantes strikes at the core of life—people acting in concert with one another and with the realization that each is integral in the human mosaic. Capturing humanity in scenes like this one that teem with life becomes one of the stamps of Cervantine art.

Further, although Cervantes echoes established rules for the pastoral genre in the prologue of the *Galatea*, in his earliest work he begins to realize that beyond them the writer has the greater responsibility of finding a proper activity for people in a novel. What people in a novel do and what novels are supposed to be about are questions Cervantes surely must be asking himself at this time. As a result, he comes up with a plot that is attractive to his reading public perhaps because of its suspense or because of its riddles of identity.

Finally, in the *Galatea* there are few real shepherds in rustic settings, for they have little to do with its conception. They are left for the *Quijote*, where problems about method of the pastoral are resolved as the prosaic and lyrical worlds confront one another. As for the *Galatea*, Cervantes the apprentice author attempts to celebrate his profession, and the work, then, remains a testament to his love for writing and his spiritual unity with fellow writers, a theme highly profiled in the work's lofty conception of friendship.

NOTES

1. For the most recent comments on the circumstances surrounding Cervantes's decision to publish the *Galatea*, see Avalle-Arce, "*La Galatea*: Four Hundred Years Later"; "*La Galatea*: The Novelistic Crucible"; and the introductory article to his edited volume, "*La Galatea*" *de Cervantes: Cuatrocientos años después*.

2. See Wellington, "*La Arcadia* de Sannazaro y *La Galatea* de Cervantes"; and Ricciardelli, "Originalidad de *La Galatea* en la novela pastoril española."

3. It is noteworthy that a work like Gálvez de Montalvo's, admired so much by Cervantes, has attracted only a few short commentaries in the last one hundred years. See Menéndez Pelayo, *Orígenes de la novela* 2:317–42; Rennert, *The Spanish Pastoral Romances*, 104–15; Rodríguez Marín, "La *Fílida* de Gálvez de Montalvo"; Astrana Marín, *Vida ejemplar y heroica de Miguel de Cervantes Saavedra* 3:222–32; Avalle-Arce, *La novela pastoril española*, 144–53; Solé-Leris, *The Spanish Pastoral Novel*, 118–21; and Siles Artés, *El arte de la novela pastoril*, 122–26. There are also a few shorter discussions of verse technique.

4. Luis Gálvez de Montalvo, *El pastor de Fílida*, in *Orígenes de la novela*, ed. Marcelino Menéndez Pelayo, 483–84. All subsequent references to and quotations of this work are cited (by page number) parenthetically in the text.

5. In the *Quijote*, the Priest calls the *Pastor de Fílida* a "precious jewel": "No es ése pastor sino muy discreto cortesano; guárdese como joya preciosa" (No shepherd that but a highly polished courtier; let it be preserved as a precious jewel) (1.6.74).

6. Astrana Marín, *Vida ejemplar y heroica de Miguel de Cervantes Saavedra* 3:233.

7. Stagg uses the term *bal masqué* to describe the *Galatea*, because it requires identification for a satisfactory interpretation. "A Matter of Masks," 255.

8. It is not uncommon for poets of the Renaissance to use pastoral verse for early experiments. See Congleton, *Theories of Pastoral Poetry in England*, 16.

9. And for Telesio's admiration of the art in the pages that follow it: "Y no penséis que es pequeño el gusto que he recibido en saber por tan verdadera realción cuán grande es el número de los divinos ingenios que en nuestra España hoy viven, porque siempre ha estado y está en opinión de todas las naciones estranjeras que no son muchos, sino pocos, los espíritus que en la ciencia de la poesía en ella muestran que le tienen levantado, siendo tan al revés como se parece, pues cada uno de los que la ninfa [Calíope] ha nombrado al más agudo estranjero se aventaja, y darían claras muestras dello, si en esta nuestra España se estimase en tanto la poesía como en otras provincias se estima" (And think not that it is a small matter and enjoyment that I have received the knowledge exactly how great is the number of those exalted geniuses which still breathe vital air in our Spain; for it always has been, and still is, the opinion of foreign nations that many there are not especially in the science of poetry. This being contrary to the fact, for each one called by name by the nymph would show well in comparison of any stranger, and would establish the truth that in Spain poesy is estimated at its due worth) (2:226).

10. Riley states: "For, while it is perfectly clear that Cervantes was well acquainted

with Aristotelian theory when he wrote the *Quixote*, no such conclusion can be drawn from the critical comments (which are much fewer) in the *Galatea*." *Cervantes's Theory of the Novel*, 11.

11. The pastoral genre's entrance into the debate about fact and fiction begins with Guarini's *Il pastor fido* (1590), and is led by Giason Denotes in these same decades.

12. Alberto Porqueras-Mayo believes that Cervantes used this prologue as his model for the *Galatea*. See "En torno a los prólogos de Cervantes," 76–77.

13. Cervantes, *Novelas ejemplares* 1:64 ("Prólogo").

14. Cervantes, *Viaje del Parnaso*, in *Poesías completas* 1:103. Regarding *invención* and *disposición*, see Weiger, *The Substance of Cervantes*, 117–21.

15. Weiger, *The Substance of Cervantes*, 117.

16. Cervantes, *Los trabajos de Persiles y Segismunda*, 46.

17. Avalle-Arce observes that the mythical-pastoral world in the *Galatea* is generally invaded by circumstance. See *La novela pastoril española*, 243–44.

18. Rhodes, "The Poetics of Pastoral," 152 n. 10.

19. Poggioli says friendship is a "state of grace or spiritual communion," the highest form of which is the funeral elegy, which may often serve as a centerpiece of the pastoral work. *The Oaten Flute*, 20.

20. Ettin, *Literature and the Pastoral*, 57. He also describes Virgil's bucolics as a close society of family friends. Ibid., 153. Thomas Rosenmeyer, *The Green Cabinet*, 106 and 155, emphasizes in Theocritus's idylls the interconnection between song and mutual benefit, with dialogue one of the resulting forms of expression. Poggioli, *The Oaten Flute*, 26, avers that the pastoral projects the human condition in terms or a universal brotherhood.

21. Savj-Lopez, *Cervantes*, 53.

22. Trend, "Cervantes en Arcadia," 503.

23. Avalle-Arce says regarding this *buena conversación*: "con estas palabras se introduce uno de los placeres capitales del hombre renacentista: el de la conversación, que se fija artísticamente en uno de los géneros literarios predilectos del período, el de los diálogos" (with these words one of the capital pleasures of Renaissance man is introduced: that of conversation, which becomes artistically fixed as one of the favored literary genres of the period, that of the dialogue). *La Galatea* 2:31 n. 31.

24. Werner Krauss asserts that the pastoral centers around poetic contests and other court activities. See "Localización y desplazamientos en la novela pastoril española," 368–69.

IAN WATT

Don Quixote of La Mancha

Unlike Faust, the character Don Quixote was not based on an actual historical person. There has been a little talk of real-life originals, such as Alonso Quijada, Cervantes's wife's uncle, who may have believed that the romances of chivalry were true. But there has been no agreement among scholars, and any firm identification is improbable. The hero of *El ingenioso hidalgo Don Quijote de la Mancha—The Ingenious Gentleman Don Quixote of La Mancha*—published in 1605 and 1615, almost certainly had no real-life original;[1] and yet, like all myths, that of Don Quixote has taken on a very simple form in the popular consciousness. It is mainly with how this form reflects some of the major values and conflicts of modern Western civilization that we are concerned.

THE FIRST EXPEDITION

A poor *hidalgo* (that is, a member of the lowest order of the Spanish nobility), whose surname is Quixada, Quesada, Quexana, or Quixano—the narrator claims not to know—and whose age is "bordering on fifty," lives in a village in La Mancha. In the times when he has nothing else to do, "which was mostly all the year round," we are told, he gives himself up "to reading of books of chivalry."[2] It becomes an obsession. He sells off "many an acre of

From *Myths of Modern Individualism: Faust, Don Quixote, Don Juan, Robinson Crusoe.* © 1996 Cambridge University Press.

tillage land to buy books of chivalry" and so deeply commits his imagination to the belief that all these inventions and fancies are true that "to him no history in the world was better substantiated" (p. 26). Finally, he "hit upon the strangest notion that ever madman in this world hit upon"; he decides, for both "his own greater renown" and "the service of his country," that he will "make a knight-errant of himself, roaming the world over in full armor and on horseback in quest of adventures." So he tries to "put into practice all that he had read of as being the usual practice of knights-errant."

First, he refurbishes some rusty and mildewed armor left him by his ancestors, that had "for ages been lying forgotten in a corner" (p. 27). Next, he spends four days ruminating about what high-sounding and distinctive name he should confer on his old and very emaciated horse, before deciding on Rocinante, combining *rocín*, the word for a hack, with the suitably sonorous ending of "ante," meaning "formerly" or "foremost." Next, eight whole days are passed in devising a name for himself, until he finally hits on Don Quixote: this combines Don, the proper appellative for a man in a high rank of the nobility, with a lofty-sounding variation on his own surname. But it is still not lofty enough for him, until, remembering that the prime model of knight-errantry, Amadís of Gaul, had "added the name of his kingdom and country to make it famous," Don Quixote adds "de la Mancha" (p. 28). The province of La Mancha, south of Madrid, was something of a byword for poverty and remoteness, and *quijote* is the word for thigh armor, so the name as a whole embodies a parodic intention which is suggested by some modern equivalent as Lord Greaves of the Badlands. Armor, steed, heroic name; only one more thing is necessary to complete the requirements of the chivalric hero—"Nothing more was needed now but to look for a lady to be in love with." Don Quixote fixes on a "very good-looking farm-girl" from the nearby village of Toboso (p. 29). He decides that a suitable, though somewhat remote, variant on her baptismal name of Aldonza Lorenzo would be Dulcinea: so she becomes, for him, Dulcinea del Toboso.

Spurred on by "the thought of how much the world would suffer because of his tardiness," Don Quixote sets out before dawn one July day "without anybody seeing him." He takes the way "which his horse chose," in the belief that in this "lay the essence of adventures" (p. 30). Nothing whatever happens all day, and by nightfall Don Quixote is tired and hungry. But since "everything our adventurer thought, saw, or imagined seemed to him to be fashioned and to happen on the same lines as what he had been reading" (p. 31), when he comes to an inn he takes it for a splendid castle. As readers we might well expect that the end to his adventure, and his delusion, must come now, at his first contact with the outside world. But no; the innkeeper, afraid of Don Quixote's contentiousness and his arms, finds it more prudent to humor the visitor's folly. Don Quixote is received according to the role he has assumed, and, after being fed, spends the night with his arms piled on the water-trough, his version of the ritual night's vigil of an aspirant to knighthood. Next morning he successfully assaults two muledrivers who innocently try to move his armor from the water-trough; and then the innkeeper, in a hurry to get rid of him, mimics the ceremonial of dubbing him a knight. So Don Quixote, feeling himself at last a properly qualified knight-errant, hurries forth; the innkeeper is so glad to get rid of the troublemaker that he demands no payment for the food and lodging given man and horse.

The second day brings two adventures. First, Don Quixote stops a farmer from flogging his young shepherd, Andrés, for not watching his sheep properly; he makes the farmer promise to pay the boy his wages, and rides off very pleased with himself. The farmer, as soon as his back is turned, almost flays Andrés alive; and the narrator ironically comments "Thus did the valiant Don Quixote right that wrong" (p. 41). Later, he falls in with a train of Toledo merchants; he decides he must force them to admit the peerless beauty of Dulcinea; but he falls off his horse and is brutally beaten by one of the muleteers. Left on the ground, unable to move, Don Quixote comforts himself by singing a mournful "romance" or ballad about Baldwin, one of Charlemagne's paladins, who had been wounded and left alone in the mountains. Fortunately a kindly man from his own village happens along, hoists him up on to his donkey, and discreetly takes him home.

Cervantes's main intention in the five chapters which comprise Don Quixote's first expedition is very evidently a direct burlesque of the chivalric romances. The idea was by no means new when Cervantes started to write Don Quixote in about the year 1597. A century earlier, the great Italian poets of the Renaissance had already treated the chivalric heroes in a spirit of sophisticated comedy—most notably in poetic narratives about the love and madness of the paladin Orlando by Boiardo (*Orlando innamorato*) and Ariosto (*Orlando furioso*), works Cervantes knew and admired.[3] More recently, and nearer home, there had been a short farcical dramatic treatment of the theme in the anonymous Spanish *Entremés de los romances* [*Interlude of the Ballads*] (1592).[4] In this work a peasant called Bartolo, who has heard too many popular ballads about knightly exploits, goes mad and imagines himself to be a romance hero. He puts on some ridiculous old armor and sets forth in quest of adventures. Trying to rescue what he imagines to be a persecuted maiden he stumbles into what is actually a lovers' quarrel; the angry gallant wounds him, and he is taken back home declaiming appropriately mournful ballads.

Like the English and Scottish Border ballads, the Spanish *romances* dealt with heroic and tragic events of love and war, and were often based, like the song Don Quixote sings, on parts of the traditional Carolingian cycle of stories dealing with Charlemagne and his twelve famous knights, the paladins.[5] The satiric targets of the *Entremés* are obviously the same as those of *Don Quixote*. Moreover, there is a further parallel in that neither work operates through the usual methods of parody or burlesque, but through an essentially realistic dramatic treatment of a comic psychological idea: to show the ridiculous results that ensue when a devotee of romance totally confounds his fictional world with the real one, and tries to maintain his imagined ideal against the cruel batterings of quotidian reality.

How can so simple an idea be made capable of convincing narrative development? In the *Entremés* the contradiction between Bartolo's idea and reality is so brutal and unqualified that it can hardly go on for any longer than one confrontation. Cervantes realized this; his Don Quixote is not always the loser—a fact vividly illustrated by Vladimir Nabokov in an elaborate listing of Quixote's "Victories and Defeats," which shows that in the total of Don Quixote's encounters there are twenty victories, perfectly balanced by twenty defeats.[6]

Cervantes certainly brings a great many mediating psychological factors into play so that the contradiction between the real and the ideal is not total: some people, like the innkeeper, go along with Quixote's fantasies because they do not want any trouble, and are afraid of his sword and lance. On other occasions, Quixote unconsciously summons his own psychological defense mechanisms into play. Usually any defeat can be rationalized in terms that protect and even fortify his original delusion: for instance, when he has been beaten by the muleteer it seems to Quixote that "this was a real knight-errant's mishap"; his failure is due entirely "to the fault of his horse" (p. 44). Later, he attributes his defeats to various magical enchanters whom he believes to be his enemies. There is, then, a continuing dialectic between Quixote's mind and the realities he encounters, a dialectic which is capable of infinite variety and complexity, and which gives Don Quixote a place of unique importance in the history of the novel.

What transforms *Don Quixote* into a myth is a development of this idea. As Cervantes went along, he discovered that Don Quixote's obsessional mania is, after all, not a wholly private one; everyone Quixote comes into contact with already knows something about the chivalric romances, and they usually prove to have complex and often contradictory attitudes towards them. It is true that in the Prologue Cervantes's friend advises him to keep his "aim fixed on the destruction of that ill-founded edifice of the books of chivalry [*invectiva contra los libros de caballerías, SM*, p. 185] hated by so many yet praised by many more" (p. 13); and at the end of the story Cervantes claims that his "desire has been no other than to cause mankind to abhor the false and foolish tales of the books of chivalry [*las fingidas y disparatadas historias de los libros de caballerías*, SM, p. 593]." But, of course, many others praised knight-errantry as an admirable ideal; and the widespread support for the chivalric romances, and their embodiment—however problematic—in *Don Quixote*, no doubt lay in their being a fictional expression of many of the most essential values in both the classical and the Christian heritage of Western civilization.

THE ROMANCES OF CHIVALRY

The term *chivalry*, like the analogous words for a knight or gentleman in French, Italian, and Spanish, *chevalier*, *cavaliere*, and *caballero*, of course starts with the idea of "riders of horses." Man's taming of the horse gave the human possessor a power, height, and mobility that became both the actual and the symbolic basis of a military and social elite. In the dark ages of Europe the feudal horsemen, the original knights, pillaged the countryside and preyed on the weak; to counter this threat the Christian church attempted to civilize knighthood. The results were most spectacular during the period of the Crusades, from 1096 to 1291. The Crusades themselves, with participants vowing on the cross to follow the ethic of the gospels, were a way of bringing the warrior caste under some control by the church; and there soon arose the great military orders, such as the Knights Hospitallers (Order of the Hospital of St. John of Jerusalem, founded c. 1099), the Knights Templars (Order of the Poor Knights of Christ and the Temple of Solomon, founded c. 1119), and the Teutonic Knights (German Order of the Hospital of St. Mary, founded 1190). Originally inspired by the monastic ideal of life, and devoted to tending the sick and protecting pilgrims, the knightly orders soon became powerful and exclusive fraternities with great financial and territorial possessions; they exemplify, at least in theory, the general pattern by which the military class as a whole, which held the exclusive right to bear arms, was converted both to the social ideals of honor, abnegation, and courtesy, and to the Christian virtues of charity and succoring the weak. Knighthood, with its elaborate chivalric code, reached its fullest development in the twelfth century; and with it there arose an associated literature, the whole tradition of romance, which constitutes the first body of original writing in the vernaculars of medieval Europe.

Our word "romance" derives from the Old French *romanz*, originally meaning the "roman" language of popular speech, as opposed to classical Latin in which nearly all written literature had previously been composed. The word *romanz* soon came to mean the very varied stories for which the written vernacular was mainly used, and especially the vast international cycles of tales concerning Charlemagne, and King Arthur, and their knights. These cycles of romances share several features with *Don Quixote*; most generally, they contain very much the same, not necessarily conscious, conflict between the Christian ideals of the culture and its secular values. This division is well expressed in two of the main groups of Arthurian legends. On the one hand there is the evangelizing Christian theme, which dominates the legends of the quest for the Holy Grail. After the crucifixion, Joseph of Arimathea is supposed to have kept Christ's blood in the Grail; and the knights of the Round Table vow to seek it. The quest can only be accomplished by a knight who, true to his knightly vows, is pure in spirit and cleansed from sin; Galahad and two exemplary companions achieve a vision of Christ, and receive the Grail from him. But on the other hand there are many knights of the Round Table who are concerned with secular, more specifically with adulterous, love. Lancelot, for instance, is the lover of Queen Guinevere, Arthur's wife; and Galahad himself is the fruit of Lancelot's amours with the princess Elaine, whom he had believed to be Guinevere as the result of an enchantment.

The two narrative elements combined here, the idealized religious and the quotidian erotic, became standard features of the romances. The use of supernatural enchantment—that is, of non-Christian magic—in both elements is significant: it accounts for much of the church's hostility to romances; it constitutes the most obviously ridiculous aspect of traditional chivalric narrative in *Don Quixote*; and it also underlies our current usage of the term "romance" for an unrealistic and far-fetched kind of story. Meanwhile, it was the erotic which occasioned the church's most explicit, though never very concerted or effective, opposition to the new literary genre and its sexual ideology. Love in the romances means religious adoration; and it is this tradition that requires Don Quixote not to stir until he has his Lady Dulcinea to whom, as is the proper service of a knight, he can dedicate all his glorious actions.

It is also the treatment of love in the Arthurian and Carolingian romances that gives us our daily-life meaning of the term "romance," as a love affair, or a story about one. In general the medieval romances, like the poems of the troubadours, were produced with a special audience in view, that of the queen or great noble lady at her feudal court. There had arisen in southern France, and rather earlier than the romances, the now famous, though still controversial, code of courtly love.[7] This was essentially an application of the feudal service that the knight owed his lord; but it took the form of the male's complementary poetic, or possibly sexual, adoration of his lady love. The French romances, and particularly those of the greatest and most influential of the writers of the late twelfth century, Chrétien de Troyes, did much to spread the cult of courtly love, whether in the form of tragic faithfulness unto death, as in the Tristan stories, or in a lighter vein of skeptical sophistication, as in *Lancelot*. Both *Tristan* and *Lancelot* deal with adulterous love, but present that love as lifelong, faithful, and, at least in theory, chaste.

The concept of courtly love was not confined to France, but was taken up in different ways in Italy, most famously by Petrarch and Dante, and in Germany, by the Minnesingers. In the course of time its literary expression tended to become more idealized, and the element of adultery was subordinated either to a wholly platonic love, or to the developing ideal of a romantic monogamous marriage. But whatever the differences of literary treatment, courtly love gave chivalry and its literature the theme of an idealized love for an unattainable lady; this, of course, is the model for Don Quixote's adoration of his unattainable and indeed nonexistent Dulcinea.

By the fourteenth century many of the active military functions of knighthood had begun to decay. The Crusades were over; and new military techniques, weapons, and organization were making the heavily-armored horseman a relic of the past. Foot soldiers using the pike, the longbow, and the crossbow proved their effectiveness against mounted knights during the Hundred Years War; and the use of gunpowder, most spectacularly at the Turkish capture of Constantinople in 1453, ended the power of the castle, the home of feudal knighthood, as well as of the military dominance of cavalry. Don Quixote bewails the "diabolic invention" of gunpowder (p. 303); it had destroyed forever the chivalric phase of warfare, as Cervantes knew. In Cervantes's own time the great Spanish conquests of Charles V both in the Old World and in the New had been won, not by noblemen, but by professional and enlisted soldiers who wielded a new and relatively light firearm, the arquebus, a matchlock gun.

Having lost its monopoly of military power, chivalry for the most part became a ceremonial and social institution connected with royal and princely courts. In the fourteenth and fifteenth centuries the old warrior code was gradually adapted to the purposes of leisure and social display in the elaboration of highly complicated rules of honor, dueling, and jousting at tournaments. New, and largely honorific, orders of knighthood were created, such as the English Order of the Garter in 1344, and the Burgundian Order of the Golden Fleece in 1429; at the same time the increasingly centralized power of kings diminished the military and political autonomy of the knightly class. Royalty took control of such matters as precedence and armorial bearings—in England by the foundation of the College of Arms, a royal corporation, in 1433; and kings became the heads of the old chivalric orders: since 1489, for instance, the kings of Spain have been Grand Masters of the ancient crusading Order of Calatrava.

One of Cervantes's major themes in *Don Quixote* is whether chivalry and its ideal values can ever be an operative force in the real world. Historically it seems clear that medieval knighthood's ideals of honor and courtesy had some occasional effects even on the actual conduct of war as late as the sixteenth century, and gave a distinctive character to the lives of a good many people. The point of honor against taking unfair advantage led the Castilian Don Henri de Trastamara to give up the advantages of terrain, and thus lose the battle of Navarrete to the Black Prince in 1367; the ideal of saving lives through individual trial by combat actually operated in the famous duel of Bayard and Sotomajor in 1503, and was twice proposed by Emperor Charles V to the King of France, in 1526 and 1536.[8]

One obvious escape from the decline in the functions of organized knighthood was offered by the ideal of knight-errantry. This is the extreme example of chivalry, to use Johan Huizinga's description of it as "a sublime form of secular life" that was essentially "an aesthetic ideal assuming the appearance of an ethical ideal."[9] The idea of a freelance—the medieval reference of the term is telling—and footloose style of life for the individual knight was in part literary, and remained so. The chivalric romances as they developed in the early sixteenth century had knights-errant as their heroes. These heroes, unlike those of epics or *chansons de geste*,[10] inhabit a world largely free of national, political, or geographical constraints; they fight, not for their liege lord, but for the purpose each knight-errant has individually chosen, most typically the winning of his lady, and the overcoming of the various obstacles which that involves: enemies, rivals, giants, and enchantments. The pattern of action in the chivalric romance is not collective but individual; and its climax is not the battle but the adventure— the danger or opportunity that comes along the road by chance.

Apparently the first occurrence of the term "knight-errant" in English is in the greatest English poem of Arthurian chivalry, the fourteenth-century *Sir Gawain and the Green Knight*. There were, however, actual knights-errant, or *chevaliers errans*, long before,[11] such as William Marshall in the days of Richard I of England ("the Lion-Hearted"), or even as early as the tenth century;[12] and they were common later.[13] Spain, for example, had real knights-errant during the fifteenth century and many writings about them, historical or fictionalized, have survived.[14] Of course, by the very nature of its separateness from economic and social institutions, knight-errantry in real life can only have been embodied in a relatively occasional and fragmentary way. Still, the idea of an individual quest for glory clearly survived in the countries of western Europe. The most famous of all the later real-life knights-errant was Pierre du Terrail Bayart (c. 1473–1524), the celebrated *chevalier sans peur et sans reproche*.[15] He was a soldier of incredible courage who was also famous for his devoutness, generosity, and gentleness to the weak. The continuity between medieval chivalry and the humanism of the Renaissance is neatly illustrated by the fact that François I of France, the great patron of art and letters, chose to be dubbed a knight by the Chevalier Bayart.[16]

The most complete literary example of the fusion of the old chivalric and the new humanistic ideals was the romance most dear to Don Quixote, *Amadís de Gaula*. The figure of Amadís dates back to a fourteenth-century or earlier Spanish or Portuguese original; but the *Amadís* in its earliest extant version, by the Spaniard Garcia Ordóñez (possibly Rodriguez) de Montalvo, was published in 1508. The hero, Amadís, is the son of the King of Wales; he falls in love with Oriana, a British princess, and after a long series of incredible sufferings and triumphs finally wins her hand. The romance contains most of the standard Arthurian characters and situations, including wicked enchanters, and the tutelary fairy, Urganda; but, despite the vast number of characters and adventures, the narrative is carefully organized, and the most refined spirit of courtesy, verbal elegance, and idealized love pervades, not only in the paragon Amadís, but in the language, atmosphere, and sentiments of the whole work.

Amadís was tremendously popular, not only in Spain but throughout western Europe, and especially in France. It had innumerable continuations and descendants, of which *Palmerin of England* is the only book of chivalry that, along with *Amadís*, is spared from the flames when the priest and the barber carry out their ruthless destruction of Don Quixote's library (pp. 48–54). The popularity of *Amadís* and its successors stimulated general interest in the chivalric romances, and many of them filtered down to a larger public through abbreviated chapbook versions, plays, and ballads.

The books of chivalry were not merely popular; they were also a powerful cultural force. In its own time *Amadís* was certainly not regarded merely as a work of entertainment. It numbered François I of France and the devout Charles V of Spain, as well as eminent scholars and moralists such as Montaigne, Juan de Valdés, Luis Vives, and Fray Luis de Granada, among its admirers; it was widely regarded both as a manual of courtly deportment, and as a work that could inspire its readers to glorious achievements. There are a good many testimonies as to its actual effects on human behavior. For instance, when the Conquistadores under Cortés first saw Tenochtitlán, the Aztec capital, they likened it to the enchanted city in *Amadís*;[17] and the name! "California," which they wrote on the map of the New World, was derived from a utopian island in *Esplandián*, the first continuation of *Amadís*.[18] Even more convincing evidence comes from the two greatest religious figures of sixteenth-century Spain. Both Ignatius de Loyola and

Santa Teresa recorded the appeal that *Amadís* made to their youthful imaginations: it was reading chivalric romances that spurred them to rise above the pettiness of the self and the mundane world. At the same time, we should recall that *Don Quixote* was by no means the first attack on the romance of chivalry—Riquer lists thirty-five written in sixteenth-century Spain;[19] nor should we forget that the chivalric romances remained very popular long after the publication of *Don Quixote*.

THE SECOND EXPEDITION

On almost every page of *Don Quixote* there are allusions, usually unexplained, which show that Cervantes assumed that his readers were familiar with the main characters and situations of many of the chivalric romances. There is no doubt that in its own time the work was regarded as primarily a comic, and in some sense a satirical, attack on chivalric romances; but that in itself is not enough to create a myth. How could *Don Quixote* have attained mythical proportions in later generations, for whom chivalric romance had ceased to be topical or even familiar?

One reason, certainly, is that although the setting in time and place is that of Spain in Cervantes's own time, the novel retains much of the freedom from the particularities of real life that characterizes the world of romances (and also the worlds of modern adventure fiction or Western movies). Don Quixote traverses the arid Spanish tableland where the people and places that he encounters are wholly devoted to the ordinary purposes of daily life, and where the heat and dust are real. In another sense, however, time and place are less real than is usual in the modern novel; as in the chivalric romances, cause and effect have none of the intractable and imperative quality of real life. Anything can happen in *Don Quixote*, and in more or less any order; the whims of the hero—and the caprices of his horse—seem to be the main determinants of the course of the action.

The narrative also shares with that of the chivalric romances the greatest possible simplicity of situation with the greatest possible capacity for variation and expansion. It is this that makes *Don Quixote* in some ways like other mythical tales such as those of Faust, Don Juan, and Robinson Crusoe: the protagonist sets out on a course of action with a very simple idea in mind, whose realization can involve an infinite number of adventures. Moreover, Cervantes also takes up the interest in individual psychology that had distinguished the chivalric romances from the earlier *chansons de geste*, and that had been further developed in the articulate self-consciousness which had formed one of the more innovative aspects of the *Amadís* hero. As a result, Cervantes's infinite expansion of the narrative action is complemented by an equal degree of expansion in psychological internalization of the action. As in romance, we start with a noble hero who goes out to face a world that is apparently neatly divided into good and evil. But very soon the question of what is good or bad, or real or unreal, in that world, and in Don Quixote's perception of it, makes everything seem problematic. The contradictions and mysteries and riddles that are resolved in romance remain largely unresolved in *Don Quixote*; and they remain unresolved because they deal in a new way with problems that have always puzzled mankind, and that continue to puzzle the thought—and the fiction—of the modern world.

Several of the basic mythic elements of *Don Quixote*, of course, are absent in the first expedition. Quixote's own motives at this point are somewhat grosser than later: for instance, he particularly admires Reinaldos of Montalbán in *Orlando innamorato* for "sallying forth from his castle and robbing everyone he met"; and he particularly itches to "have a bout of kicking" Ganelon, the villain in the Charlemagne cycle (p. 27). Cervantes's early effects are very broad: after Don Quixote is beaten by the muleteer, he actually imagines that he is one of the heroes of the ballads—Baldwin or Abindarráez (pp. 44–45); and this parodic exaggeration tends to reduce his psychology to mere lunacy. In the second expedition, however, which occupies the remaining forty-seven chapters of the first part of *Don Quixote*, a much subtler and more complicated psychological pattern emerges.

The transition between the first and second expeditions is introduced by a lengthy discussion of the books in Don Quixote's library; his niece, his housekeeper, the village barber, and the curate resolve to destroy the books that they blame for Quixote's madness, and most are burned. Quixote is undeterred. He sees, however, that in his earlier venture he had failed to provide himself with one essential appanage of a knight, a trusty squire. So he now enlists a neighboring peasant, Sancho Panza, promising him that, as Amadís had done for his squire, so he, Don Quixote, will bestow some island won by his sword on his squire as recompense for his services. Sancho Panza is not, of course, a squire of the traditional kind, such as the nobly-born apprentice to knighthood in Chaucer's Prologue to *The Canterbury Tales*, of Gandalín in *Amadís*. Instead—and this is essential to the story and its meaning—Sancho is a comic bumpkin who begins his career as squire with the idea that he can profit by it. But Quixote is in a hurry, and takes him because he happens to be at hand. After raising what money he can, patching his helmet, and borrowing a shield from a friend, Don Quixote finally rides out with Sancho Panza one evening, secretly—presumably for fear of being prevented or brought back.

The first part of the story, which, like the original *Amadís*, came out in four separate volumes, is increasingly occupied by interpolated stories and complicated subplots concerning various characters Quixote meets on his way. Much of this incidental matter is still interesting, and is arranged in a way that has an indirect but cumulative bearing on the themes and incidents of the main narrative, while some of the interpolations are fine examples of complicated baroque plotting.[20] But the stories and subplots are not really part of the myth; after all, very few people remember Cardenio and Don Fernando, Leonela and Anselmo, Dorotea and Doña Clara, or even the captive's tale of his life and adventures. The myth centers on the long series of Don Quixote's personal encounters; and it is one of these which finally brings his second expedition to a close. First the Holy Brotherhood, a kind of mobile police, present a writ for his arrest as a result of one of his greatest apparent triumphs, when he forced the release of some galley slaves. Then the curate and barber from the village, having finally caught up with him, persuade him that his destiny—through the pronouncement of a great magician—commands that he go home as a prisoner in a cage. So poor Don Quixote is taken home in a cart; and as he arrives at midday on a Sunday, his return this time is both public and humiliating.

Don Quixote's adventures in his second expedition usually follow a pattern of action that in itself is very simple: a visual stimulus; a misinterpretation of the stimulus by Quixote in terms of his chivalric compulsions; a realistic correction by Sancho Panza, overridden by his master's complacent imaginative expertise; a challenge; a battle and its result; and a conclusion, in the form of a highly entertaining discussion between Quixote and Sancho, that the reader gets into the habit of eagerly awaiting.

Both the pattern of the action, and the conversations the action provokes, are usually related to the chivalric theme on the one hand, and the more general perspectives concerning human life on the other. The best-known episode, as far as the myth is concerned, largely follows this standard pattern of narrative and theme. Don Quixote sees the windmills on the plain of Montiel; he is sure that they are "thirty or more monstrous giants"; by slaying them all he hopes to enrich both Sancho and himself from the spoils; moreover "it is God's good service" for him to "sweep so evil a breed from off the face of the earth." Sancho patiently explains that the windmills are windmills, but Quixote replies contemptuously: "It is easy to see ... that you are not used to this business of adventures." He shouts his defiance at the windmills, commends himself and his cause to Dulcinea, and charges the nearest windmill at full gallop. He succeeds in thrusting his lance into the sail, but, alas! "the wind whirled it around with such force that it shivered the lance to pieces," dragging horse and rider with it, and sending the knight rolling, badly injured, across the plain. Sancho ventures an "I told you so," but Quixote silences him with an instant rationalization: that same sage

Frestón who carried off my study and books, has turned these giants into mills in order to rob me of the glory of vanquishing them" (pp. 59–60). We have entered a world of self-perpetuating delusion that no reality can destroy; and on the whole we are very glad to do so, for it means that our hero will be miraculously immune from the greatest of all humiliations, knowing that he has made a fool of himself.

The jousting with the windmills is unique in one respect, because it involves inanimate objects which are so huge and unmistakable that the encounter provides a starkly representative pictorial image for the myth; its emblematic quality is shown in the adoption of the common phrase, "tilting at windmills." The phrase presumably denotes an enterprise whose total impracticality derives from the ridiculous disparity between an imagined individual purpose and the powerful imperviousness of its object. In popular usage the phrase also has a specifically idealistic connotation: the individual is not seeking any personal advantage; he is inspired by a noble but illusory idea of helping humanity.

The disparity between individual desires on the one hand, and reality on the other, is not, of course, peculiar to Don Quixote; the confusion of romantic wishes with historical truth is a universal tendency. In essence, Don Quixote unconsciously responds to the same imaginative pressures as the romances themselves: he personifies the attempt to redress the actual course of history since the golden days of a heroic past. Miguel de Unamuno defiantly articulates this aspect of Quixote's quest: "Quixotism is simply the most desperate phase in the struggle between the Middle Ages and the Renaissance."[21]

That transition, of course, includes science as one of its modern elements. In his book on Quixote, Ortega y Gasset wrote:

> When the vision of the world which myth supplies is deprived of its command over human souls by its hostile sister, science, the epic loses its religious gravity and dashes forth in search of adventures. The *libro de caballerías* ... were the last great sprouting from the old epic trunk ... The book of chivalry retains the epic characteristics, except the belief in the reality of what is told.[22]

The belief in that reality is a necessity for Don Quixote, and it makes him see the general course of history as one of decline. He holds this view with conviction and consistency, as we see in his famous discourse to the goatherds on the golden age: in that blessed age all was held in common, concord and friendship reigned, justice was not perverted by favor and self-interest, and maiden modesty could roam freely without fear. It is that ideal of civilization which has made Quixote turn to his present vocation. "In this hateful age of ours," he continues (calling it "the iron age"), as "wickedness increased, the order of knights-errant was instituted, to defend maidens, to protect widows, and to succor the orphans and the needy" (pp. 74–75). In this context knight-errantry, indeed, serves a vital religious function. The monk's profession, Don Quixote later argues, may well be as austere as the knight's, "but I am very much inclined to doubt whether the world is equally in need of it." Churchmen may "pray heaven for the world's welfare," but they do it "in peace and quiet": knights-errant, on the other hand, not only have to endure severe privation and danger, but in their deeds they perform what the monks only pray for; knights-errant, in fact, are "God's ministers on earth and the arms that implement his justice" (p. 85).

Both the narrator, who remarks that the discourse on the golden age "might very well have been omitted" (p. 75), and the people to whom Quixote addresses himself, see his views as patent nonsense; Don Vivaldo, for instance, pretends to take them seriously only to give "the occasion for him to utter further absurdities" (p. 85). Later Cervantes has his hero suggest, in all seriousness, that the best way for the King of Spain to defend himself against a threatened Turkish invasion would be "to command, by public proclamation, the knights-errant scattered all over Spain to assemble on a fixed day in the capital. Even if no more than half a dozen come, there may be one among them who alone will suffice to destroy the entire might of the Turk" (p. 427). Absurd, indeed: and yet, though Quixote's military and political sense is wanting, his idea has an irrefutable imaginative logic. In the present degenerate state of the world we need all the admirable values of the past: those of pastoral and the golden age, those of the Christian knights of romance and the Greek and Roman heroes who were often equated with them in medieval and Renaissance thought; and we therefore need people— knights-errant—who will attempt to make those values live again in a world that lacks all their virtues.

THE THIRD EXPEDITION

The first part of *Don Quixote* was an instant and enormous success: there were four authorized and three pirated editions in its first year alone;[23] further editions followed, including two in Brussels and one in Milan; very soon there were translations into French and English. In 1613 Cervantes announced that he was bringing out a sequel, a possibility which had been hinted at in the last chapter of Part I. In 1614, however, he was anticipated: a spurious continuation written by a still unidentified author using the pseudonym Alonso Fernández de Avellaneda was published in Tarragona.[24]

Cervantes's own continuation came out at the end of 1615. Since 1617 both parts have normally been published together, and are justly considered to form a single work.

Part II of the story concerns the third and last expedition of Don Quixote. This expedition is considerably longer than both the earlier forays combined; and yet it is more unified, for it contains fewer stories and episodes not directly concerned with the main protagonists. It begins with Don Quixote determining that he must get Dulcinea's blessing on his new adventure. Sancho Panza cannot find her in Toboso, and so he persuades Don Quixote that one of three village girls he meets by chance is really Dulcinea in the form given her by a wicked enchanter. This claim is maintained by a later trick in which someone impersonating the great Arthurian wizard Merlin announces that Dulcinea can only be restored to her own shape when Sancho shall "On his own sturdy buttocks bared to heaven / Three thousand and three hundred lashes lay" (p. 623).

The main adventure that Quixote has in mind for his third sortie is to win renown at a ceremonial tournament to be held at Saragossa. In fact he never reaches the tournament. Instead the narrative describes the encounters which occur to Quixote and Sancho on the way. Don Quixote begins with a real success: he defeats the Knight of the Mirrors in single combat. The Knight, however, is actually one Sansón Carrasco, a student who, in collusion with the barber and the chaplain from Quixote's native village, had hoped to get Quixote home by defeating him in battle and requiring his return as a penance; Quixote's unexpected victory frustrates the plan. The central portion of the expedition is spent with a duke and duchess who, bizarrely, have read Part I of *Don Quixote*; they entertain themselves by contriving diversions at the expense of Quixote and Sancho, culminating in an arrangement for Sancho to become temporary governor, if not of the promised island, at least of a town in the duke's dominions. At the conclusion of this episode, Sancho and Quixote journey to Barcelona where, through the initiative of a bandit chief, Roque Guinart, who is also a devotee of the first part of *Don Quixote*, they make a triumphal entry. But the end is in sight. Don Quixote is challenged to combat by the Knight of the White Moon, who is actually Sansón Carrasco making a return appearance. This time Sansón's trick is successful: Don Quixote is defeated; he agrees to go back home and promises to give up knight-errantry for at least a year.

The greater part of the third expedition is kept going through the deliberate pretenses of characters who actually know Don Quixote's earlier story. To that extent it obviously has less narrative excitement for the reader than the earlier expeditions; but if the game-playing element is much more obtrusive, it also gives Part II many rich intellectual and literary qualities of a new depth and complexity. Most obviously, Don Quixote and Sancho Panza have already become mythical figures, to themselves and to others; and we now see these legendary persons acting in the real world. The relationship between fiction and history has been given a new twist. The romances had turned quasi-historical persons into fictitious characters; Cervantes has turned his fictional characters into authentic historical celebrities.

DON QUIXOTE AND SANCHO PANZA

Any attempt to evaluate Cervantes's achievement in *Don Quixote* must begin with the apparent contradictions in the hero's character.

As soon as Don Quixote sets out on his first expedition many people call him mad, and no one seriously disagrees—least of all the narrator, who continually and ostentatiously obtrudes a total contempt for the evident lunacy of Quixote in taking romances seriously. It is hardly credible, however, that Don Quixote should have become so universally popular a figure if he were indeed mad in the modern sense. In Cervantes's time madness, or lunacy, was not regarded as creating an absolute separation of kind between one person and another;[25] according to the prevailing theory of humors, any exceptional mental or imaginative power was regarded as the result of an excess of one physical component in the body, which was likely to produce corresponding excesses in thought and behavior. This is quite consistent with most of what we observe in Quixote. He is a beloved figure in his village, where he is known as Alonso Quixano the Good (p. 829). He often astonishes his hearers by his learning and eloquence—indeed, some of his speeches, notably those on the golden age, and on arms and letters, have since become classics of the Spanish schoolroom. Broadly speaking, Quixote is mad only in the colloquial sense of "crazy"; his behavior is markedly obsessional, but only on a defined and limited range of matters. More specifically, one might say that Quixote manifests a single extreme but highly localized interpretative mania; and that mania is entirely concerned with romances and knight-errantry. As the narrator tells us, "he only talked nonsense when he touched on chivalry, and in discussing all other subjects he showed that he had a clear and unbiased understanding" (p. 657).

There are difficulties in going much further than this in any attempt to analyze Quixote's sanity, or the lack of it. The dry and often critical objectivity of the narrator does not take us deeply or authoritatively into his hero's mind; Quixote is obviously thoughtful and reflective, but we can only surmise the nature of his introspections from his words and actions. Both of these, however, suggest that he is in fact very self-conscious on the question of madness. For instance, to show his desperation at how Dulcinea has spurned him, he goes mad as a penance. He speaks of this with a nice combination of logic and obsession, as a conscious literary imitation: No thanks, he says, are due to a "knight-errant for going mad when he has cause"; in the present case he acts thus "to let my lady know, if I do this without any excuse, what I would do if I had one" (p. 179). This sophisticated awareness of the problem of madness is soon given a further complication when Quixote says that if Dulcinea is not overcome by the tribute of his madness, "I shall become mad in earnest. Being so, I shall suffer no more." Freud would no doubt have agreed with this view of the therapeutic function of neuroses and psychoses.

Don Quixote seems to negotiate a very fine balance between truth and his darling fictions. In the second part of *Don Quixote* there is a discussion of how truthfully his actions were reported in the first part. Initially what Quixote says seems to show an unequivocal allegiance to literal truth: "History is to some extent a sacred thing, for it should be true, and where the truth is, there God is" (p. 442). But when Sansón Carrasco reports that some readers wish that the narrator had left out some of the beatings Quixote received, the knight's comment shows a fine mastery of defensive skepticism: "There is no need [to] record events which do not change or affect the truth of a history, if they tend to bring the hero of it into contempt. Aeneas was not in truth and earnest so pious as Virgil represents him, nor Ulysses so wise as Homer describes him" (pp. 439–40). There are other occasions when Don Quixote rejects a blind devotion to the romance pattern: for instance, he decides that on grounds of common-sense realism he will "improve" on the customary practice of the romances by rewarding his squire with a governorship as soon as possible, and not so late that Sancho will be too old to enjoy it (p. 58). Quixote also has moments of real doubt: when the duchess wonders whether Dulcinea may not be a creation of his imagination, he answers: "God knows whether there is any Dulcinea or not in the world, or whether she is imaginary or not imaginary. These are things the proof of which must not be pushed to extreme lengths" (pp. 606–7).

There are many other ways in which Cervantes qualifies his picture of Don Quixote as an insanely literal imitator of the chivalric model. For one thing, Quixote retains many ordinary human characteristics that are quite independent of that model: he is not always sanguine, impatient, and enthusiastic, but can also be sober, skeptical, and matter-of-fact. On several occasions Don Quixote also falls short of the chivalric ideal of exemplary courage and selflessness. At the inn, when Sancho is tossed in a blanket, Quixote is too "bruised and battered" even to dismount and try to defend his squire (p. 116). Later, when the villagers knock Sancho unconscious because they think he is mocking them with his realistic imitation of asses braying, Quixote flees in terror from their crossbows and muskets, and "every minute he took a deep breath to see whether he still could" (p. 581).

Don Quixote is even further from the chivalric ideal in the matter of selfless altruism. He has some of the self-centeredness of a solitary old man, and this often makes him capricious and domineering. This is especially—and unpleasantly—obtrusive for the reader in his repeated insistence that Sancho should give himself the number of lashes supposed necessary before Dulcinea can be disenchanted; on the other hand he is too kind and sympathetic to be able to stand by when Sancho (who is actually merely lashing the trees) produces a particularly convincing cry of pain (pp. 815–16).

Other, and more general, egotistic motives may be surmised from Don Quixote's turning knight-errant: that in fact it advances his own psychological and social interests; that it is a projection of a more gratifying image of the self than that forced upon him by the constricting dullness of village life; and that it assumes a rise in the social scale from the by no means exclusive gentility implied by the term *hidalgo*[26] to the much more prestigious rank of *caballero*. Thus Sancho Panza reports to him about the local reaction to the first part of the novel: "The *hidalgos* say that, not content with being a gentleman, you have assumed the 'Don,' and made a knight of yourself when all you own is a few vines and a couple of acres of land and the shirt on your back" (p. 436).

But, on the whole, Don Quixote has no more faults and weaknesses than are needed to make him seem real and human. We notice that he wins over not only his readers but also almost every character he comes into contact with in the novel. Those characters who mock him—and Quixote's character is nowhere more psychologically convincing than in his fear of mockery—in the end make the ordinary mental and social norms by which they live seem dull, cautious, and selfish. When the duke plays his last farcical trick on Quixote, the narrator comes much closer than elsewhere to siding with Quixote's madness, commenting "that personally he considers the concocters of the joke as crazy as the victims of it, and that the duke and duchess came very close to looking like fools themselves when they took such pains to make fun of a pair of fools" (p. 810).

The duke and duchess are only two among the innumerable characters in the novel who pay inadvertent tribute to one remarkable quality of Don Quixote's folly: it is highly contagious. Reality is, after all, what our personal vision perceives; and though we are schooled in hiding that vision from public scorn or obloquy, we cannot but admire those who do not. This makes us sympathize with the casuistry that Don Quixote often needs to protect his personal vision from the rebuffs of reality. Thus when he is making his helmet he spends a week improvising a visor out of cardboard; it is immediately demolished by his first testing sword thrust; he makes a stronger one; but then, "not caring to try any more experiments with it, he accepted and commissioned it as a helmet of the most perfect construction" (p. 28).

This is a familiar kind of foolish protective strategy; most of us would prefer to risk disaster at a later date rather than expose as useless something on which we have invested our best efforts. Much of the comedy of *Don Quixote* comes from observing the various devious strategies whereby the hero tries to protect his delusions from the realities that would expose them. We identify with Don Quixote, hope that he will triumph over reality, and are both relieved and envious when he succeeds, time and time again, in making everybody else play his own game merely by his obstinate refusal to play any other. At the same time, we find the narrator's mockery of Quixote gratifying, because it helps us acknowledge the feeble caution of our own irresolute attempts to live the life of our dreams.

Another aspect of the enduring universality of the myth arises from the fact that Cervantes creates not one but two convincingly rounded characters; he presents the relationship of Don Quixote and Sancho Panza in a way that is both psychologically authentic and also an enactment of many of the book's larger themes.

If we should ever see a stick and a ball advancing together side by side down a road, we would immediately recognize them as Don Quixote and Sancho Panza. Their visual appearances evoke so many oppositions that they seem to encompass everything: Quixote, ramrod stiff, like a dilapidated Gothic spire trying to reach the heavens; and Sancho, short and squat, looking down on his big belly and wondering what will come its way next. Their mounts complete the comic double dyad: Rocinante, the skeletal horse, and Dapple, the globular ass, two beasts who are, like their masters, ridiculously mismatched and yet inseparable.

That Don Quixote and Sancho Panza, unlike Faust or Don Juan, should have become visual myths, is no doubt partly due to the way they are characterized by Cervantes. Their physical features are etched with a pitiless clarity of outline that matches the harsh light of the Castilian landscape; and Cervantes seems to have anticipated what the future would bring, for he makes many references to the pictorial rendering of his work. At the beginning of Part I, the narrator explains that the source of his story is an old Arabic manuscript that he found in Toledo, and that on the first notebook "an artist had depicted the battle between Don Quixote and the Biscayan to the very life" (p. 67); there follows a fairly detailed description, not only of the fight, but also of the knight, the squire, and Rocinante. In the second part of the novel, Sancho remarks prophetically: "I'll bet ... that before long there won't be a tavern, roadside inn, hostelry, or barbershop where there isn't a picture of our deeds" (p. 817).

Their visual images embody many of the contrasts between the ideas for which they stand. These contrasts begin in basic physical differences—thin and fat, tall and short—but they extend into some of the most general and symbolic dualities. Psychologically Quixote and Sancho stand for the polarities of spirit and flesh, brain and belly, heaven and earth, dream and reality, past and present, literature and life; in the social domain there is the dichotomy of the knight and the peasant, the proclaimed hero and the professed coward, the introvert and the extrovert, the solitary and the gregarious, the bachelor and the husband. George Orwell has written very well of their connection, arguing that between the two of them Don Quixote and Sancho Panza represent many of the dualities that compose humanity as a whole:

> Two principles, noble folly and base wisdom, exist side by side in nearly every human being. If you look into" your own mind, which are you, Don Quixote or Sancho Panza? Almost certainly you are both. There is one part of you that wishes to be a hero or a saint, but another part of you is a little fat man who sees very clearly the advantages of staying alive with a whole skin. He is your unofficial self, the voice of the belly protesting against the soul ... it is simply a lie to say that he is not part of you, just as it is a lie to say that Don Quixote is not part of you either.[27]

Orwell surely expresses here one of the main psychological reasons for the appeal of the myth, and for our sense of its wisdom. However, the emphasis of his formulation involves two kinds of simplification: it takes no account of the extent to which the characters of Quixote and Sancho are not polar opposites, but themselves both share some elements of that complex mixture that Orwell finds in "nearly every human being"; and it neglects the way in which that human complexity develops and changes in the course of their association.

Sancho Panza is no doubt earthy and animal; panza is the Spanish word for "paunch," and Sancho's saddlebags are as conspicuous in our visual memory as Don Quixote's armor. Sancho is—to use the Spanish term—a gracioso: not a buffoon or clown, but a droll fellow worthy of being taken seriously.[28] He is not, of course, a Dionysian figure:[29] in the Sierra Morena, Quixote, wanting to demonstrate the proper madness of a chivalric lover, says to his squire, "I should like you, I say, to see me stripped to the skin and performing a dozen or two insanities" (p. 186). Sancho seems genuinely shocked at this: "For the love of God, master ... don't let me see your worship stripped. It will upset me, and I won't be able to keep from tears" (p. 187). The closest Sancho gets to indecency occurs in an amusing interchange when Quixote is being taken home at the end of the second expedition. Sancho, with infinite precaution, asks how his master manages his bodily functions when he is shut up in a cage: "This is what in my heart and soul I was longing to know" (p. 381).

Sancho Panza, then, is earthy but very decent. He is also said to be a coward. In general there is, no doubt, a consistent contrast between Don Quixote's reckless pursuit of danger, with consequent suffering bravely borne, and his squire's pitifully comic fear of danger, with his unabashed refusal to maintain a stiff upper lip when he gets hurt. Still, Sancho freely chooses to continue a life of danger and hardship with Quixote; he sometimes fights well; and although he often finds his circumstances incomprehensible, perhaps mad, he goes on risking his skin to the end. He is illiterate, but he has a fine sense of the oral tradition—a tradition which, especially in the form of popular proverbs, proves rich enough to enable him easily to hold his own in any discussion with his master, for all Quixote's knowledge of history and literature. Sancho is also extremely intelligent, not only in practical and prudential things, but in his quick understanding of logical and analogical matters, as we see with his resourceful use of rhetorical skills to maintain his own point of view in argument. When Sancho becomes the governor of Barataria, he forgets his original idea of making it a profitable source of wealth and comfort for himself, indeed, he hardly seems to need Quixote's lectures, so spontaneous is his disinterested sense of equity and justice. One must, then, so far qualify the various polarities in which Sancho is allotted the physical, the material, and the selfish side of things by adding that, as against these tendencies of his temperament and his situation, there is behind Cervantes's conception of his character a settled belief in natural law and right reason as powers available to guide all human beings, whatever their station. Sancho is clearly entitled to say "I don't understand those philosophies," and yet be rightly confident that "I have as much soul as another" (p. 389).

Don Quixote is a different matter. Though he falls short of his ideal on occasion, as we have seen, we must surely view the physical and mental rigidity of his posture as the necessary defenses of his foolish idealism in its battle against the destructive powers of reality. Nevertheless he is very aware of the material realities, as we can see in the very practical and understanding way in which he handles Sancho's departures from the chivalric standard in such matters as money, food, and drink, his constant complaining about ill-usage, and his groaning when in pain. We must therefore assume a richly human and realistic substratum in Quixote's consciousness; it is this substratum that, despite the domination of the doctrines of knight-errantry, enables him to relish Sancho, and even his humor—a quality which Quixote himself completely lacks. It is this side of Quixote's character which provides a bridge to the world of his squire, and enables him to pay Sancho a very handsome tribute:

> Sancho Panza is one of the most amusing squires that ever served knight-errant. Sometimes there is a simplicity about him so shrewd that it is an amusement to try and make out whether he is simple or sharp; he has mischievous tricks that show him to be a rogue, and blundering ways that prove him to be a fool. He doubts everything and believes everything; when I think he is about to fall headlong from sheer stupidity, he comes out with something shrewd that raises him up to the skies. Finally, I would not exchange him for another squire, though I were given a city to boot. (p. 609)

The many dualities that Don Quixote and Sancho Panza represent are not, then, absolute and monolithic. In fact, the book's general intellectual perspective is fairly close to that of Erasmus's *In Praise of Folly* or Rabelais's *Gargantua and Pantagruel*; the wisdom of Sancho's folly is the perfect complement to the folly of Quixote's wisdom. The more we look and listen the clearer it becomes that, contrary to the various simplifications of their relationship that are implicit in the popular view as expressed by Orwell, Cervantes actually represents Quixote and Sancho with such invincible and humorous concreteness that they cannot be reduced to any set of social, moral, or psychological opposites.

One of the most explicit and compelling expressions of this view is that of the critic Salvador de Madariaga: he argues that the characteristics of the two men cannot be "converted into two series of antagonistic values," whereby from "Don Quixote is drawn the series 'valour-faith-idealism-utopia-liberalism-progress', while the Sancho series is made to develop in the opposite direction as 'cowardice-skepticism-realism-practical-sense-reaction.'"[30] For one thing, their characters are too densely human to exhibit any unmixed elements. Quixote's "faith," for instance, is by no means absolute and assured, as we observe from his frequent rationalizations, and the many occasions on which he shrinks from putting his beliefs to the test. As for Sancho's cowardice, he can actually be belligerent and hot-headed, when the occasion demands it, as with the goatherd (pp. 174–75), or the Squire of the Grove (pp. 495–97).

1134567891011121314151617181920

Don Quixote and Sancho Panza, then, are not opposites; more than that, they adopt each other's traits in the course of their association. The sad veracity of the whole third expedition, especially, can be seen as a dialectical process whereby Sancho's faith in his chivalric role slowly rises, while Quixote's assurance in it declines; this decline is accompanied by the knight's adoption of the realistic and skeptical attitudes that his squire has progressively abandoned through the influence of his master's earlier credulity. By the end, one can say with Madariaga that Sancho has been largely "quixotized," while Quixote has been sufficiently "sanchified" to be ready to abandon the dream by which he had come to live. When the duchess argues that "If Don Quixote is mad, crazy, and cracked, and Sancho Panza his squire knows it, and notwithstanding, serves and follows him, and believes his empty promises, there can be no doubt he must be even madder and sillier than his master" (p. 612), she is unanswerable, but not finally correct, at least as far as Sancho is concerned. For, as the book proceeds, Sancho's thinking is more and more dominated by his role as squire; it becomes a second nature in which he finds more satisfaction than he had ever before experienced as a peasant farmer. But the change in Don Quixote is more ambiguous; it owes less to Sancho and more to the way in which his own increasing doubts about himself are reinforced by his failures.

Don Quixote's differences from the world at large remain unchanged and unmediated; there must be no neat dialectical resolution of his quarrel with reality. In his relationship with Sancho, however, it seems likely that by exaggerating the already great differences between the two men at the moral and intellectual level, Cervantes has reinforced their kinship at the emotional and human level. The mere sharing of a life of adventure far away from the normal stabilities and confinements of ordinary existence gives their relationship an unexampled intimacy; and this helps to isolate Sancho Panza and Don Quixote into a representative image of a human pair. Of course, there is no question of the heroic equality of a Roland and Oliver; they remain master and squire; they keep many of their other original differences of character; and they continue their comic role in mocking or abusing each other on occasion almost to the end—for instance when Quixote abuses Sancho for his impudence in venturing to defend his master's sanity in public (p. 748), or when Sancho rudely wonders how Altisidora can possibly be in love with Don Quixote when "in truth often I stop to look at your worship from the sole of your foot to the topmost hair of your head, and I see more to frighten a person than to make one fall in love" (p. 745).

Still, their mutual loyalty and devotion are boundless. Don Quixote records it in his will: "If, as when I was mad I had a share in giving him the government of an island, now that I am in my senses, I could give him that of a kingdom, it should be his, for the simplicity of his character and the fidelity of his conduct deserves it" (p. 828). Sancho is characteristically more emotional and unrestrained. There are many occasions when he expresses his affection and loyalty, as when he says to the duchess: "If I were wise I would have left my master long ago. But ... I can't help it; I must follow him. We're from the same village, I've eaten his bread, I'm fond of him, I'm grateful, he gave me his ass-colts, and above all I'm faithful. So it's quite impossible for anything to separate us, except the pick and shovel" (p. 612).

If Sancho Panza and Don Quixote, with all their differences, seem, as the priest says, to be "cast in the same mold" (p. 434), so equally do their mounts. Cervantes delights in reminding us of the friendly constancy of the two animals, and in one elaborate passage recounts "how eagerly the two beasts would scratch one another when they were together and how, when they were tired or full, Rocinante would lay his neck across Dapple's, stretching half a yard or more on the other side. The pair would stand thus, gazing thoughtfully on the ground, for three days" (pp. 484–85). The narrator even claims that in the original version the author of the story "devoted some special chapters" to the two beasts, and recorded that their friendship was "so unequaled and so strong that it is handed down by tradition from father to son." Moreover, "the author left it on record that he likened their friendship to that of Nisus and Euryalus, and Pylades and Orestes. If that is so it may be perceived, to the admiration of mankind, how firm the friendship must have been between these two peaceful animals, shaming men, who preserve friendships with one another so badly."

PUZZLES OF INTERPRETATION

After his defeat by the Knight of the White Moon, Don Quixote feels beaten, and beaten by his own fault—by his unwillingness to recognize unpleasant realities: "Each of us is the maker of his own Fortune," he tells Sancho, and adds, "my presumption has therefore made me pay dearly; for I ought to have realized that Rocinante's feeble strength could not resist the power and size of the Knight of the White Moon's horse" (p. 792). On the way back home Quixote talks with Sancho about how they will employ the coming year. Quixote must, according to his promise, abandon knight-errantry; but he is unwilling to give up their companionship. Perhaps they will live as shepherds, according to the models of the pastoral romance: "I under the name of the shepherd Quixotiz and you as the shepherd Pancino, we will roam the woods and groves and meadows singing songs here, lamenting in elegies there, drinking the crystal waters of the springs or limpid brooks or flowing rivers" (p. 797). But the old buoyancy has gone from his fantasies, especially after he and Sancho meet their most ignominious encounter yet, when they are overrun by a drove of pigs (pp. 801–2). Then, as they enter the village, two incidents strike Quixote as bad omens; hearing a boy's chance remark about a stolen cage of crickets— "you'll never see it again as long as you live"—Quixote thinks it refers to Dulcinea; watching a hunted hare take temporary shelter under Dapple, Quixote is convinced that "I am never to see Dulcinea again" (p. 822). Once home, Don Quixote takes to his bed with a fever brought on, we are told, either "from the melancholy his defeat produced, or by heaven's will that so ordered it" (p. 825).

After a six-hour sleep, he awakens and cries out: "Blessed be Almighty God, who has shown me such goodness" (p. 826). The blessing, he explains, is that "My reason is now free and clear, rid of the dark shadows of ignorance that my deplorable constant study of those detestable books of chivalry cast over it." Don Quixote is worried that he "should be remembered as a madman; for though I have been one, I would not like to perpetuate that fact with my death." He goes on to confess to the priest, draw up his will, receive all the sacraments; this done, we see him "dying in his bed so calmly and so like a Christian" (p. 829).

Sancho is heartbroken. He has previously tried every device, including reporting that Dulcinea is no longer enchanted, in an attempt to rally his master's chivalric spirit. Then he urges that "the most foolish thing a man can do in this life is to let himself die without rhyme or reason, without anybody killing him or any hands but melancholy's doing him in" (p. 828). To this Don Quixote returns, in Sancho's own proverbial style, the saddest of life's permanent truths: "'In last year's nests there are no birds this year.' I was mad, now I am in my senses."

The unqualified severity of this deathbed disavowal, carrying with it, as it does, Don Quixote's own emphatic support to the narrator's repeated anathematizing of the chivalric romances as models of action, has disappointed many modern readers. In earlier times there was no particular difficulty about the ending, since *Don Quixote* was usually taken at its face value as a comic exposure of the folly of the books of chivalry. The difficulty arises when we interpret Don Quixote and his values in a primarily serious, sympathetic, and symbolic way, and therefore wish to find an excuse for disregarding the overt and repeated disavowals of the chivalric romances by the narrator.

In pursuing any challenge to the narrator it is relevant to point out various discrepancies in the authority of the text itself. At the moment of crisis in his fight with the Biscayan, early in Part I, Don Quixote is left with his sword held aloft over his enemy while the narrator announces: "At this

suspenseful point the delightful history came to a stop and remained
curtailed with no indication from the author where the missing part could be
found" (p. 65). There follows, first, the comment of the narrator that "I
could not bring myself to believe that such a gallant tale had been left
maimed and mutilated." Then the narrator goes on to tell us how he
happened to come across some papers that were being sold for wrapping in
the marketplace of Toledo; one parchment book turned out to be *The History
of Don Quixote of La Mancha*, written by "Cide Hamete Benengeli, an Arab
historian." The narrator describes how he commissioned a Moor to translate
the text faithfully into Castilian, for "fifty pounds of raisins and two bushels
of wheat" (p. 67); it is this translation, according to the narrator, which
provides the basis of the text for all the rest of the narrative.

    If we waive the unlikely coincidence of the narrator having chanced to
find the continuation of the manuscript just at the place where the first
source had stopped, several other puzzles remain: especially, the key question
of Cide Hamete's own veracity. The narrator remarks that lying is very
common among Arabs, and that Cide Hamete, "where he could and should
have licensed his pen to praise so worthy a knight, he seems to me
deliberately to have written nothing" (p. 68). The narrator, in fact, claims
that the Arab was motivated by racial malice towards a Spaniard. Later, when
Cide Hamete writes, "I swear as a Catholic Christian" (p. 576), the narrator
comments on the dubious nature of any such authentication, coming, as it
does, from a Moor. We may add that there is a logical impossibility in the
time scheme of the novel as a whole, since a chance document by a
presumably dead author turns out to have anticipated history, and supplied a
continuation of the story in which all the world has read the first part
published ten years before. These doubts are raised even while the narrator
pretends to be authenticating the literal truth of his history. There are many
other complex narrative devices or apparent inconsistencies which seem to
show that Cervantes was amusing himself with an elaborately gratuitous
hide-and-seek game between the reliable (that is, the real and authentic) and
the unreliable (that is, the unreal and imagined) portions of the history.

    In a larger critical view this seemingly conscious play of multiple
literary perspectives[31] raises complicated semiotic and philosophical
problems;[32] but although we will consider one aspect of this later, we can, for
the moment, conclude that while Cervantes's inmost intentions, if any, are
lost to us in the infinite regress of his multiplying ironies, we should not take
any overt comment made either by the narrator in his own voice or by "Cide
Hamete Benengeli" as being necessarily of an unqualified reliability.

    It may be that the underlying reason for the ironic contradictions in the
way Cervantes presents his narrative is related, not so much to the possibility

that the Inquisition forced Cervantes into very devious modes of expressing his bitter criticism of the life of his time,[33] as to the lack of any antecedents for what, in essence, Cervantes was trying to do in this work. There is, first of all, Don Quixote's "need to escape from the harsh oppression of immediate circumstances";[34] consequently, his "efforts and energy were concentrated and drained in the creation of his new *being*"; and this brings about an unprecedented conflict: "The quixotic character and a world that is not quixotic are going to confront one another."[35] These are modern problems, at least as far as literary consciousness is concerned; and they involve not only the end of such standard fixed oppositions as good and evil, truth and illusion, knowledge and folly, but also a new kind of complexity in the relation between the actual writer, Cervantes, and his narrative. It is difficult to formulate such ideas without excessive abstraction;[36] but they can perhaps be illustrated in one of the subtlest episodes in the second part, Don Quixote's visit to the cave of Montesinos.

According to the Carolingian ballads, Durandarte, one of Charlemagne's paladins, fled after Roland's defeat at Roncevalles. Before he died he asked his friend Montesinos, who had followed the trail of his blood, to cut out his heart and take it to his love, Belerma; when Montesinos did this, she, not surprisingly, fainted, and then, more unexpectedly, shed tears of blood. The cave of Montesinos is famous because of its connection with the story, and Don Quixote decides to explore it. He is lowered down on a rope, in circumstances of comic fear, but half an hour later he is pulled up again as if in a deep sleep. After eating, he recounts his vision, which is mysterious, poetic, ridiculous, and infinitely problematic. He found himself, he says, "in the midst of the most beautiful, delightful meadow that nature could produce or the most lively human imagination conceive" (p. 550). The first problem raised is about the reality of this pastoral paradise, and, therefore, of his own identity. Did he really see it?

> I opened my eyes, I rubbed them, and found I was not asleep but thoroughly awake. Nevertheless, I felt my head and breast to satisfy myself whether I myself was there, or some empty delusive phantom. But touch, feeling, and the collected thoughts that passed through my mind all convinced me that I was the same then and there as I am at this moment.

Here, surely, we have Don Quixote revealing the extent to which in his inner being he wonders whether he can believe either in the identity of his self, or in the reality of how it sees the world. The narrator reports Cide Hamete's comment that he cannot believe that the cave of Montesinos episode really happened, and yet it is "impossible for me to believe that Don Quixote could lie" (p. 558). Much of what Quixote reports is certainly convincing, down to the most trivial unheroic details: enchanted beings, he reports, neither eat nor defecate, "though it is thought that their nails, beards, and hair grow" (p. 555). This last is confirmed by the appearance of Montesinos, who acts as Quixote's guide, and who has a white beard down to his waist; but Quixote's testimony is rendered suspect, if only by his answer to Sancho's characteristic question, "Do the enchanted sleep?" "Certainly not," Quixote replies, "At least, during the three days I was with them not one of them closed an eye, nor did I either." But Sancho knows that his master was actually only down in the cave for "little better than an hour" at most (p. 554), and both on Quixote's arrival there (p. 550) and on his return (p. 549) we are told he was in a deep sleep. These are direct and obvious contradictions.

Beyond such epistemological perplexities, the episode turns both inwards and outwards on many general themes. Outwardly, Don Quixote gets into an amusing but characteristic altercation with Montesinos, who has dared to prefer the beauty of Belerma to that of Dulcinea; whereas, Quixote reports, in reality Belerma has bad teeth, a sickly complexion, and dark rings around her eyes—disadvantages not caused, we are assured, by the menstrual cycle, which she has not experienced for "many months and even years," but from "the grief her own heart suffers for the heart she ceaselessly holds in her hand," her lover's withered relic (p. 504). The macabre sadness of this description has its own evocative power; but we can surely see it as part of Don Quixote's wish to translate the fictional Belerma into the same disappointing reality as his own imaginary Dulcinea, originally seen as a village girl.

Dulcinea, too, reappears in his vision in the cave; she is with her maidens, gamboling in the field like she-goats, along with Guinevere and other ladies of past times. Quixote is disappointed that she will not answer him when he calls; instead she runs off too fast for him to catch up. Then two curious things happen. First, one of the maidens comes back to ask on behalf of her mistress for six reals, giving as deposit a new cotton skirt. This sounds like a disguised version of a commoner kind of transaction between poor girls and old men, and one wonders what may be vaguely present in Don Quixote's mind about the true nature of his Dulcinea. In any case, he gives the maiden what he has—only four reals. And then there comes the second surprise: "instead of making me a curtsy she cut a caper, springing two full yards into the air" (p. 557). We are reminded that when Quixote tried to help Aldonza, the village girl from Toboso, to remount after she had fallen off her ass, "the lady, getting up from the ground saved him the trouble ... going back a few paces, she took a short run, and putting both hands on the croup of the ass, she vaulted into the saddle more lightly than a falcon" (p. 476). What Quixote sees in the cave of Montesinos seems to be a delicately fanciful and yet severely comic echo of this equestrian feat; and the gloomy direction of his unconscious thought—which again casts a rather demeaning light on Dulcinea—may well be strengthened by the vastly more experienced Montesinos's argument that there is nothing surprising about the request for money, since "need is to be met with everywhere. It penetrates all quarters and reaches everyone, and does not spare even the enchanted" (p. 557).

The climax of this disillusioning dream occurs when Don Quixote comes upon Durandarte, "of actual flesh and bone" (p. 551). His right hand "lay on the side of his heart," and he lies stretched out on a marble sepulcher under the enchantment of Merlin. Montesinos gives a few apologetic details of how much care he took when he cut the heart out, but Durandarte still occasionally complains and sighs, and cries out one of the stanzas of the ballad that made him famous. Montesinos is much affected, but he finally tells Durandarte to "open your eyes and you will see" Don Quixote, "of whom the sage Merlin has prophesied such great things ... With his intervention and aid it may come about that we shall be disenchanted, for great deeds are reserved for great men" (p. 553). Here the report of Quixote's vision of his self is flattering, but not very convincing; and then comes the paladin's laconic reply: "And if that may not be, said the wretched Durandarte in a low and feeble voice, if that may not be, then, O cousin, I say 'patience and shuffle the cards.'"

It is a stunning reversal of tone and topic. The homely colloquialism makes one wonder. Are the rats gnawing at the foundations of the castle of romance?

Although in his dream Don Quixote still feels himself to be a great man, the heroic peer of Roland is as grotesquely sad and disillusioned a figure as his beloved Belerma. Durandarte can find a strong voice in which to intone the ballad of his fame, but even he is really whistling in the dark; as far as the future is concerned, he is resigned to a diet of minimal expectations with only card games to pass the time. Together, the dislocating discrepancies of this episode form a distillation of the clash between the past and the present, the grandiose and the petty, the touching and the ridiculous: the contradictions embodied in Don Quixote's own experience, and the endless counterpoint of myth.

"The Knight of the Mournful Countenance" was originally the title of a character in one of the *Amadís* romances; but it is appropriated for Quixote by Sancho Panza because "hunger and the loss of your teeth have given you such an ugly face" (p. 130). We may think of Quixote as mournful because, on his long *via dolorosa*, he never encounters the Dulcinea of his dreams, but the Spanish phrase *triste figura* has less dignified and more derisory connotations: it may mean that to those who are not initiates he has a miserable-looking face. There is the same mixture in what he tells us of his visit to the cave. We do not know if the Montesinos episode is a vision or a reality. We do not see Quixote in the cave directly, but only through his later account of it. Is it a continued and contradictory presentation by the narrator? Is the disjunction between the inner subjective and outer objective worlds intended by Cide Hamete? Or the narrator? Or Cervantes? In general, as E.C. Riley has suggested, the message "of *Don Quixote* surely is what most readers have always taken it to be: that personal visions must be accommodated to the eternal facts of living."[37] Of course, this begs the question of priorities. But, as Riley also points out, despite Don Quixote's sadness and defeats, "he is admirable ... in that he never quite gives up."[38] The extreme of this position is that of W.H. Auden, who sees Quixote as "A Christian Saint."[39] But is Don Quixote a saint because he "suffers himself intentionally," or because he finally becomes sane?

Quixote himself informs us, after the first part of the novel has been published, that "my history ... will require a commentary to make it intelligible" (p. 461); Cervantes has neglected to supply a reliable one. He is the least confessional of writers, much too proud to give us any notion of his own personal experiences of humiliation and defeat. We may possibly think that we are given an avowal of personal identification between Cervantes and his hero at the end of the last book, as he hangs up his quill pen for ever: "For me alone was Don Quixote born, and I for him; it was his to act, mine to write; we two together make but one" (p. 830). But, ironically, the voice is that of Cide Hamete; the final words, "*solos los dos somos para en uno,*" represent his claim to secret and exclusive kinship with Quixote, while Cervantes withholds his endorsement. On the basis of this evasion Leo Spitzer has ingeniously inverted the usual terms of the problem. "It is not so much," he writes, "that Cervantes' nature is split in two (critic and narrator) because this is required by the nature of Don Quijote, but rather that Don Quijote is a split character because his creator was a critic-poet who felt with almost equal strength the need of illusionary beauty and that of pellucid clarity."[40]

Cide Hamete ends the novel with an already familiar claim: that his desire has been "to cause mankind to abhor the false and foolish tales of the books of chivalry" (p. 830). This final reassertion is contrary both to his alleged spiritual kinship with his hero, and to the reader's general feeling that some of the more positive chivalric virtues in the myth of *Don Quixote*—and indeed in the romances themselves—cannot have been wholly alien to Cervantes. Indeed it has even been argued that *Don Quixote* is the "definitive and perfect" book of chivalry, although Ramón Menéndez-Pidal prefers to give this tribute to Cervantes's last work, *The Wanderings of Persiles and Sigismunda*.[41] Cervantes surely shared Don Quixote's nostalgia for the golden age and the heroic past, the triumph of good over evil, the exciting life over quotidian boredom, inspirational dream over everyday reality, madness over prudence. How these contradictions and ambiguities could be expressed was no easy matter to resolve; and Cervantes apparently found nothing better to offer than the foolish but shared enterprise of Don Quixote, Sancho Panza, and their ungainly but lovable quadrupeds in a real modern world. The complexity of the narrative suggests that it was, perhaps, no more than a dream, or a game; but it answered the need to express how the association of values of a long-gone world with the rewards of human fellowship in a common purpose could endure even amid the insoluble contradictions and brutalities of their contemporary world. As the myth still does in ours.

NOTES

1. *El ingenioso hidalgo Don Quijote de la Mancha*, ed. Justo Garcia Soriano and Justo Garcia Morales (Madrid: Aguilar, 1973), p. 32; cited hereafter in the text as *SM*. See also William Byron, *Cervantes: A Biography* (New York, 1978), p. 305.

2. *Don Quixote*, by Miguel de Cervantes, trans. John Ormsby, revised Joseph R. Jones and Kenneth Douglas, Norton Critical Edition (New York and London, 1981), p. 25. The Ormsby translation, though old (1885), is accurate and of considerable literary quality. Quotations and references are to this edition, and are cited hereafter, by page numbers, in the text. I have also consulted the translation by Samuel Putnam, 2 vols. (New York, 1949).

3. There had been a closer anticipation of the *Quixote* theme even earlier; the Italian short-story writer Franco Sacchetti (c. 1330–1400) had pictured a seventy-year-old Florentine gentleman so crazed by the ideal of chivalry that he sets out to a local tournament on a lean nag, hoping to gain great honor but only making himself ridiculous. See especially Ramón Menéndez-Pidal, trans. George I. Dale, "The genesis of *Don Quixote*," in *Cervantes across the Centuries*, ed. Angel Flores and M. J. Benardete (New York, 1747), pp. 32–55.

4. The *Entremés* is contained in the Norton edition of *Don Quixote*.

5. The term "paladin" originally meant an officer of the palace; it was Charlemagne's "paladins" who gave the term its modern meaning of heroic champion.

6. *Lecturer on Don Quixote*, ed. Fredson Bowers (London, 1983), p. 110. Nabokov charmingly ascribes this balance to "the harmonizing intuition of the artist."

7. On the history and ideology of courtly love, see the now classic works by Denis de Rougement and C.S. Lewis. Lewis, *The Allegory of Love* (London, 1936), formulates the convenient summary that courtly love has four elements: humility, courtesy, adultery, and the religion of love. De Rougement, *L'amour et l'occident* (Paris, 1939), has been translated in England as *Passion in Society* (London, 1950) and in the USA as *Love in the Western World* (New York, 1956). For a less favorable view, see Alexander J. Denomy, *The Heresy of Courtly Love* (New York, 1947), and for a more recent scholarly summary see Roger Boase, *The Origin and Meaning of Courtly Love: A Critical Study of European Scholarship* (Manchester, 1977).

8. Johan Huizinga, *The Waning of the Middle Ages* (1924; New York, 1954), pp. 100, 97.

9. Huizinga, *Waning of the Middle Ages*, p. 69.

10. That is, the group of medieval "adventure poems" mainly concerning Charlemagne and his circle.

11. See Maurice Keen, *Chivalry* (New Haven, 1984), pp. 20–22. Keen's is an excellent survey with fine illustrations.

12. See the classic study by George Duby, trans. Cynthia Postan, *The Chivalrous Society* (Berkeley, 1977), pp. 156–57.

13. Examples include Nuno Alvares Pereira in the fourteenth and George Von Ehingen in the fifteenth century. See, respectively, Edgar Prestage, ed., *Chivalry: A Series of Studies to Illustrate its Historical Significance and Civilizing Influence* (New York, 1928), pp. 153–54, and *El Viaje de Jorge de Ehingen*, in *Libros de Antano* 8, pp. 37–38.

14. See Martin de Riquer, "Cervantes and the romances of chivalry," and its bibliography, in *Suma cervantina*, ed. J.B. Avalle-Arce and E. C. Riley (London, 1973), pp. 273–92; reprinted in the Norton edition of *Don Quixote*, pp. 895–913.

15. Keen, *Chivalry*, p. 78.

16. Keen, *Chivalry*, p. 238.

17. Cited in R.O. Jones, *The Golden Age: Prose and Poetry*, in *A Literary History of Spain* (London, 1971), p. 54.

18. Erwin G. Gudde, *California Place Names* (Berkeley, 1962), "California."

19. Riquer, "Cervantes and the romances of chivalry," Norton edition, pp. 901–5. For a close analysis of Cervantes's imitation of this tradition, see Howard Mancing, *The Chivalric World of Don Quijote: Style, Structure, and Narrative Technique* (Columbia, MO, 1982).

20. See especially the illuminating article of Joaquin Casalduero, "La composición del Quijote," *Rivista de Filologica Hispanics* 2 (1940), trans. Esther Sylvia as "The composition of *Don Quixote*," in Flores and Benardete, *Cervantes across the Centuries*, pp. 56–93.

21. Trans. J.E. Crawford Flitch, *The Tragic Sense of Life* (1912; New York, 1954), p. 322.

22. Ortega y Gasset (1914), trans. Evelyn Rugg and Diego Marín, *Meditations on Quixote* (New York, 1963), p. 130.

23. William Byron, *Cervantes: A Biography* (New York, 1978), p. 444.

24. This work is amusingly discussed by Don Quixote and Sancho Panza in the fifty-ninth chapter of Cervantes's sequel, while the narrator pursues Avellaneda with obsessive and rather rancorous mockery throughout.

25. See R.O. Jones, *The Golden Age*, pp. 177–78, and E.C. Riley, *Don Quixote* (London, 1986), pp. 48–57, 62–63.

26. According to Antonio Domingues Ortiz, about a tenth of the families in Castile towards the end of the sixteenth century were noble. See *The Golden Age of Spain 1516–1659* (New York, 1971), p. 114.

27. George Orwell, "The art of Donald McGill," in *A Collection of Essays* (New York, 1954), p. 120.

28. See Samuel Putnam's note 16 to chapter 59 in the Norton edition.

29. See Arthur Efron, *"Don Quixote" and the Dulcineated World* (Austin, TX, 1971).

30. *Don Quixote: An Introductory Essay in Psychology* (Oxford, 1935), pp. 82–83.

31. See Leo Spitzer, "On the significance of *Don Quijote*," and E.C. Riley, "Literature and life in *Don Quixote*," both reprinted in *Cervantes: A Collection of Critical Essays*, ed. Lowry Nelson, Jr. (Englewood Cliffs, N.J., 1969).

32. See Alban K. Forcione, *Cervantes and the Mystery of Lawlessness* (Princeton, 1984), pp. 187–94, and notes.

33. See Américo Castro, *Hacia Cervantes* (Madrid, 1957), pp. 271, 159–66.

34. Américo Castro, *Cervantes y los casticismos españoles* (Madrid, 1966), p. 57.

35. Castro, *Cervantes y los casticismos españoles*, p. 62.

36. For example, Michel Foucault, in *The Order of Things* (London, 1970), writes that, on linguistic grounds, "Don Quixote is the first modern work of literature because in it language breaks off its old kinship with things and enters into that lovely sovereignty from which it will reappear, in its separated state, only as literature" (pp. 48–49).

37. Riley, *Don Quixote*, p. 172.

38. Riley, *Don Quixote*, p. 147

39. "The ironic hero: some reflections on Don Quixote," in *Cervantes*, ed. Nelson, pp. 75, 77.

40. "On the significance of *Don Quijote*," in *Cervantes*, ed. Nelson, p. 95.

41. "The genesis of Don Quixote," in *Cervantes across the Centuries*, ed. Flores and Benardete, p. 55.

HENRY W. SULLIVAN

The Two Projects of the Quixote
and the Grotesque as Mode

*D*on Quixote, Part II is a literary production written a decade after, and in a different voice, from Part I. Despite the almost universal tendency to refer to Cervantes's masterpiece in the singular, as "the *Quixote*," thereby erasing the independence of the two parts, the fact remains that the *Quixote* is composed of two different novels that deserve to be read for their differences. Very frequently, studies that appear to address the *Quixote* as a whole prove, on closer scrutiny, to be dealing with Part I almost exclusively, and with Part II partially or almost by the way. As noted previously, there is a very extensive literature on the key incident in Part II—the episode of the Cave of Montesinos—but, surprisingly, there exists to date no dedicated and comprehensive interpretation of *Don Quixote*, Part II.

Part II cannot, of course, be examined entirely in isolation, especially given the continuing function of Part I as the founding authority of Part II. But Part II addresses different concerns than its predecessor, and the two basic projects of each book are different. The major purpose of this chapter is to bring these differences to the fore, both in terms of thematics and novelistic mode. I shall argue that Part I implicitly sets forth this pair of questions: (1) What is the most perfect career? and (2) What is the most perfect marriage? Part II sets forth a different pair of questions: (1) What is the most perfect death? and (2) What is the most perfect path to salvation?

From *Grotesque Purgatory: A Study of Cervantes's Don Quixote, Part II.* © 1996 by The Pennsylvania State University.

225

Part I, in other words, is concerned with work and love, while Part II is concerned with death and immortality. As regards novelistic mode, I contend that, for reasons arising from this difference of thematic, Part I is comic, while Part II is grotesque.

These may seem like surprising contentions, and the formula "the most perfect" may seem especially odd. Surely perfection admits of no degrees; either something is perfect or it is not. In Neoplatonic currents of thought in the sixteenth and seventeenth centuries, however, this was not a meaningless question. The sixteenth century, in particular, was full of idealistic striving towards perfection (courtly, Neoplatonic, humanist, mystic, Catholic, Protestant) and replete with idealizing theories of perfect love (Sullivan 1985). Calderón actually posed the question in a kernel refrain that furnishes the title of one of his cape-and-sword comedies: *¿Cuál es la mayor perfección, hermosura o discreción?* This phrase uses the comparative, rather than the superlative, form of the adjective in Spanish to mean: "Which is the greater perfection, beauty or discretion?" But even to pose such a question establishes that for the epoch of Cervantes and Calderón there could be shades of perfection; that one might rank perfection in greater or lesser degree. The concept also survives in the opening lines of the American Constitution: "We the people of the United States, in order to form a *more perfect Union* ..." (Preamble 1787; my emphasis). It is in this traditional Renaissance sense that I am suggesting issues of career, marriage, death, and salvation may be submitted to comparative scrutiny within ascending orders of perfection.

THE PROJECT OF *DON QUIXOTE*, PART I, AND THE MIDLIFE CRISIS

The critic who has written most eloquently and searchingly on Don Quixote's unexpected and drastic switch of careers in midlife is Carroll B. Johnson. He compares Don Quixote to real-life figures such as Paul Gauguin, who left a secure job as stockbroker in Paris in 1891 to go to Tahiti and paint naked women. Johnson's principal thesis is that the attractive young niece in his household (Johnson dubs her Sobrina), who has now flowered into nubile womanhood, precipitates a sexual crisis in her fifty-year-old uncle by reason of the threat of incest with her. Thereupon, Alonso Quijano loses his wits, reinvents himself as Don Quixote, and in this new career flees the presence of the girl who has unhinged him (Johnson 1983).

It is not my purpose, for the reasons set out in my preamble above, to dwell overlong here on a discussion of Part I, except to stress its differences from the sequel. But the theme of the most perfect career is already predicated in the decision of the now deranged hidalgo: the mission of a knight-errant is a more perfect undertaking than the sequestered routine of a mildly well-to-do country squire. It is developed in Don Quixote's ringing speeches on the choice between the career of arms or letters. The theme is played out again in the Captive's Tale, where the Viedma brothers choose three different distinguished careers: the eldest son follows the profession of arms; the second son chooses a life of profitable commerce in the New World; while the youngest opts for a career of letters that raises him to the position of a high court judge in Mexico. The several interviews with the galley-slaves prior to their liberation are a kind of comic inversion of this: What are the less perfect career choices or mistakes that led to a life of corrective hard labor?

Formal Implications for the Structure of Part I

The main business of Part I is Don Quixote's attempt to make good on the program or project behind his career decision: reviving the values of the Golden Age of chivalry. But this fundamental datum or *fons et origo* of the novel has many implications for the subsidiary thematics and form of Part I. The Knight is celibate and has had no sexual experience; it is the threat of sexuality and incest with his niece, according to Johnson, that unhinges his reason. As he tells the Duke and his entourage in self-defense in Part II, chapter 32: "I am in love, only because knight errants are obliged to be so; and, being so, I am not one of those depraved lovers, but of the continent and platonic sort" (675). Don Quixote can love the fictitious Dulcinea del Toboso in his imagination, therefore, but he cannot have a love life in the novel.

The consequences of this strategic novelistic decision around the career question—chivalresque mission and celibacy of the hero—are crucial to the question of the perfect marriage. For how could Cervantes (or most other novelists, for that matter) conceive of a work of fiction that contained a "continent and platonic sort" of hero and no love interest? Given the author's fundamental characterization of the Knight, the novel's love imbroglios clearly had to come from elsewhere. It is for this reason that Cervantes places his romantic intrigue in the plethora of much-maligned episodes, digressions, and interpolated tales that make up the tangled skein of Part I's subsidiary plots. The course of these many love stories is not straightforward or happy, moreover, despite their final resolution. On scrutinizing the stories carefully, it becomes clear that the impediments that stand in the path of true love are more than just the stock-in-trade of fiction. Each of the relationships that should or could lead to marriage is barred by an obstacle of specifically theological nature, according to the canons and decrees of the Council of Trent.

For reasons of space and critical focus on Part II, I refer the reader to
the checklist of theological impediments to matrimony between the various
couples in *Don Quixote*, Part I, set out in Appendix A. There are eight main
couples with plans to marry who people the interpolated stories, and whose
unions are either pronounced valid (4), nonvalid (3) or, in the single case of
the Tale of Foolish Curiosity, valid, but doomed by procuration of adultery.
The list indicates once more, as in his *Rufián dichoso*, Cervantes's firm
theological grasp of the Tridentine decrees, as well as their potential for
imaginative literature. The love stories emerge as a series of subplots that
complement the main story of the celibate knight-errant, while themselves
being thematically united in their internal problematic. Taken together and
singly, they ask: What are the obstacles or taints that hinder the
consummation of a perfect Christian matrimony? Or, more simply,
according to the lights of the Counter Reformation: What is the most
perfect marriage?

So the main plot concerns work and career, and the subsidiary plots
concern love and marriage. These are characteristically the preoccupations
of a younger man, finding himself in work and love, donning his manhood,
and gradually beginning to learn by his mistakes. By the 1590s, the decade
generally suggested as the terminus a quo for the conception of the first
Quixote, Cervantes was in his mid-forties and with many a career
disappointment behind him (student, soldier, Christian slave, playwright,
novelist, royal commissary, tax farmer). His marriage to Catalina de Salazar
y Palacios was a distant affair and probably a failure. And in early middle age,
it is only too common for career and marriage to be submitted to a searing
scrutiny. That is the sense of the midlife crisis: a choice between carrying on
in the same work and altering the character of the matrimony; or else,
retaining the matrimony intact and launching into a new career; or, at worst,
casting all to the winds. Don Quixote's solution is a kind of compromise
between these last two options.

THE PROJECT OF *DON QUIXOTE*, PART II

It should be clear from the foregoing that Part II is not a sequel to the first
novel in the sense of simply providing more of the same. As E.C. Riley
observes: "To achieve any fruitful new development Cervantes had to
introduce some significant new factor or exploit some elements present in
the first part. He did both" (Riley 1986, 93). Part II has a number of the same
protagonists in common, and some of the same premises. But the characters
of the two principals begin to change. Riley notes correctly that Don
Quixote no longer misreads physical appearances in spontaneous fashion;

rather, he misinterprets the reality behind the appearance because other people mislead him. The incidents in Part II consequently have a contrived and theatrical quality. Sancho grows from a mere fount of proverb lore and folk wisdom into a Solomon or sage in judgment. Part II has an important new protagonist in the shape of Sampson Carrasco, who supplants Sancho—now inebriated with the drug of fame—as a foil. The formal structure is far more artistically integrated; and Cervantes uses the existence of Part I as the informational means by which new characters know all about Don Quixote and Sancho in advance and fabricate situations for them to react to (Riley 1986, 93–94). Later, Cervantes uses the extraneous existence of Avellaneda's spurious Quixote to achieve even stranger complications of distancing and reduplication.

Most important of all, the basic project of Part II is different. Its author is writing from a different vantage point in life. This is the novel of a master in the sunset of his days. Its double question, as we have said, interrogates death and immortality: What is the most perfect death, and what is the most perfect path to salvation? Here, we may say, lifework has become redefined, in the expression of J.-B. Pontalis, as "death work" (Pontalis 1978, 92; Ragland-Sullivan 1986, 72; 322). The meaning of how life's energies should be spent is submitted to questioning, not from its beginning or midpoint, but from its end, or a retroactive point beyond death. This could be understood as Lacan's paradoxical statement that the death instinct is merely a concept, but the only place where man can approach the register of life (Lacan 1978, 113).

A key passage for this reading of Part II is the significantly placed chapter 8. There is a symmetry at work here. In Part I, the second sally had been preceded by seven chapters of preliminaries, and the pair had set off at the end of this seventh chapter. The same is true of Part II. At the end of chapter 7, Sampson Carrasco accompanies them partway out of the village on the road to El Toboso, and the expedition proper begins with chapter 8. But chapter 8 is remarkable for its new manifesto and the forensic and dialectical skills displayed by Sancho. Their conversation about Dulcinea and the desire of winning fame takes an unexpected turn when Sancho begins to argue down his master. In a kind of cross-questioning, Sancho insists that the value of a life quest for fame is best sized up retroactively from the standpoint of death. And the theme of Purgatory is now introduced, since, when Sancho inquires of the whereabouts of the heroes of old, he is told by his master that the heathens are in Hell, but the Christians, "if they were good Christians, are either in Purgatory or in Heaven" (*DQ* II: 8, 518).

The gist of Sancho's case is that the fame of a saint or holy man, capable of raising the dead in his own lifetime and adored by the faithful after his own death through the relics he has left, is superior to the fame of heathen emperors and knights errant. Judged from the standpoint of how a life is to be viewed in retrospect (that is, by the degree of perfection of its obituary and posthumous memory), Sancho tells his master that "it's better to be a humble little friar, of any order you like, than a valiant and errant knight" (*DQ* II: 8, 519; Pope 1984, 170). Sancho's stunning conclusion to the argument, for which his master can find few rejoinders, is that "we should set about turning saints. Then we shall get the good name we're aiming at rather sooner" (*DQ* II: 8, 519).

Sancho's project for sainthood finds its response in Don Quixote's remarks on salvation at the close of the chapter. He tells Sancho that not everyone can be a friar and that "many are the ways by which God bears His chosen to heaven. Chivalry is a religion, and there are sainted knights in glory" (*DQ* II: 8, 520). My critical contention is that, by a strange and roundabout route, precisely this is the eventual outcome of the third and final sally. The chivalric project of Part I now becomes a salvific project in Part II. It is not that the pair knowingly seek out the means to attain sainthood. Nor is it the deliberate intention of anyone else to subject them to a religious purification. But the outcome—sanctification through Purgatory in this life—is, I submit, eventually the same.

Formal Implications for the Structure of Part II

There are, it seems to me, three principal consequences for the formal structure of Part II that arise from this new alignment of its thematic: (1) transformation is the underlying process of the novel, a transformation wrought by Providence; (2) the focus of the action must, therefore, bear steadily on both protagonists in this process of transformation; and (3) all incidents and digressions must be built up around the protagonists or out of them. To take up the first of these points, transformation, or purgatorial sanctification, is achieved by Cervantes's idiosyncratic manipulation of a narrative perspective in what one can only call, with John Jay Allen, an "operation of Providence" (Allen 1980, 184). Allen was the first critic to see that all of Cervantes's fictional world is governed by a single beneficent Providence that both rewards and punishes; a world in which man is autonomous certainly, but not abandoned by God (Allen 1980, 194).

The manipulation of perspectives to this end is best exemplified in *Don Quixote*, Part II, by the events at the ducal palace that fill the center of the novel (chapters 30–57). The harrowing incidents stage-managed on their country estate, and inflicted on the pair for the grandees' own sport by the Duke, Duchess, and their retinue, may be classified as jests from the point of view of the onlookers (*burlas*), but they are felt as true suffering from the point of view of Don Quixote and Sancho (*veras*). The discrepancy between these two points of view (*burlas/veras*) is further complicated by the status of the protagonists, and their tormentors, at varying times, as the "deceiver deceived" (*el engañador engañado*).

But Cervantes's narrative perspectives allow the reader to embrace all these points of view and to sense a greater will, or Providence, presiding over the events presented, which transforms the pair through suffering. If it seems difficult to imagine a writer assuming the position of divine intelligence in this way, one can only respond that such a posture did not trouble Cervantes's contemporaries. Spanish playwrights regularly dramatized the will of God in hagiographical or other religious plays; while verse epics in twelve or twenty-four cantos, detailing God's influence on the lives of His saints, was a thriving, if not especially fortunate genre. Cervantes assumes for himself an even more providential role as author in the *Persiles* (Allen 1980, 187, 193–94).

Our second formal consequence arising from the novel's theme of sainthood as project concerns the necessary focus of the action on the two protagonists in the process of their transformation. Don Quixote and Sancho are rarely out of the spotlight in Part II. During the telling of stories in Part I, the two had often been reduced to the status of passive listeners, virtually disappearing from view, while other characters took up center-stage (during the Tale of Foolish Curiosity, for example, or the Captive's Tale, or the narrated tribulations of Cardenio, Lucinda, Dorothea, and Ferdinand). But, in Part II, even when an adventure centered on someone else arises (such as Camacho's wedding, dealing with the loves of Basilio and Quiteria), Knight and Squire become directly involved in the adventure's development and outcome. But their centrality comes through most of all in the torments contrived and inflicted on them in a series of incidents that focus pertinently on the temperament of the two protagonists.

Their sufferings at the ducal estate, we may say, are person-specific; measured out with a certain semicriminal intelligence. Don Quixote's celibate resolve is tortured in the flesh and in the spirit by the blandishments of Altisidora, and by the perhaps innocent attentions of Doña Rodríguez. When the duenna enters his bedroom at night, he believes she is a soul in Purgatory wandering abroad, though she explicitly denies this (chapter 48). But, while a woman's aggressive sexual attention would be exciting to some men, to the chaste and faithful Knight it is a source of horror. He is tortured more literally by Altisidora and the Duke in the incident of the alarming cats and bells, and even has "pussy" thrust figuratively in his face, when his nose gets badly scratched by the claws of the panicked felines.

The bon vivant and roly-poly Sancho is tormented in the flesh during his governorship of Barataria through being deprived of food and drink by the bogus diet of Doctor Pedro Recio de Agüero, and also by being starved of sleep. He is crushed and bruised in the pseudo-attack on the island; and later punished with slaps (*mamonas*), pinches, and pinpricks on his arms and loins in the bogus resurrection of Altisidora (chapter 69). The 3,300 lashes that Sancho is supposed to inflict on himself for the disenchantment of Dulcinea are also a violent penitential sentence, but with a purportedly talismanic efficaciousness. It would probably be true to say, furthermore, that these torments are not simply interchangeable. The ascetic Don Quixote, long used to physical injury, vigils, hunger, and denial of the body, would not have been unduly afflicted by the physical toils imposed on Sancho. Sancho, by the same token, would not have been repulsed by the attention of women; he would have been perplexed perhaps, but charmed that ladies of a higher social rank forced themselves on him.

So both are systematically compelled to suffer in ways tailor-made to fit the nature of each's vulnerability. Indeed, the whole sojourn on the Duke's estate is a kind of theater of sadism that encloses the two protagonists, while not making them privy to the true nature of their roles. Their situation is almost comparable to a kind of "persecuted innocence," which lends a refined psychological dimension of cruelty to the whole. The comparison with a bullfight (where all participants except the bull know what is going to happen) might be appropriate, except that Don Quixote and Sancho—unlike animals—possess human discourse and self-awareness, but are the dupes of aristocratic prestige and carefully constructed lies. Such a comparison is not exactly appropriate for another reason: Don Quixote and Sancho are not entirely innocent either.

The third formal consequence of setting up a new, death-and-salvation thematic in Part II lies in Cervantes's general disposition of the main plot and subsidiary incident. In the "review of reviews" section of Part II, chapters 3–4 (where current opinions of Part I are related), complaints had been lodged by readers against Cervantes's use of interpolated stories, because they were out of place and had nothing to do with Don Quixote. This criticism undoubtedly irked Cervantes; first, because he knew it was true and, second, because he could not bear to harp forever without variety on a single storyline. In Part II, he adopted a new strategy and explained it in very straightforward fashion through the mouth of his alter ego, Cide Hamete Benengeli.

In the opening paragraph of chapter 44, Benengeli bewails his lot "for having undertaken so dry and cramped a story; since he seemed always to be restricted to Don Quixote and Sancho, not daring to launch out into digressions and episodes that would have yielded both pleasure and profit" (*DQ* II: 44, 745). Being confined to a single subject and to so scanty a list of characters, says Benengeli, was an unbearable hardship, which he had tried to alleviate in Part I by the introduction of short tales, in a sense, separate from the story. The new solution that the pseudo-author has found is the following: "he decided not to insert any tales, either detached or connected, in this Second Part, but to include some similar episodes *arising out of the actual happenings themselves*; and even these should be sparing and no longer than their bare narration required" (*DQ* II: 44, 746; my emphasis).

In order to continue this new, and highly disciplined, technique of narration in practice, Cervantes resolved on a bold stroke. In chapter 44, as good as his word, he literally split his plot in two, dispatching Sancho Panza to Barataria to take up his governorship, and retaining Don Quixote in the ducal castle to endure new afflictions in his loneliness. The next dozen chapters are then symmetrically divided; the even chapters (44, 46, 48, 50, 52, 54, and 56) dealing primarily with Don Quixote, and the odd chapters (45, 47, 49, 51, 53, and 55) dealing almost exclusively with Sancho. It is also observable here that the author derives more variety and incident from the Sancho sequence than from the *Quixote* sequence. They are reunited in chapter 55, when Don Quixote, out exercising Rocinante, comes upon Sancho trapped and lamenting in the underground pit.

There is a precedent for the separation of Knight and Squire in Part I, of course, when Sancho was sent off to deliver his master's letter to Dulcinea, leaving Don Quixote to his antics in the Sierra Morena (chapters 26–29). But this new creation of what is virtually a double novel, each strand centering on the specificity of its protagonist, is much more ambitious. And Cervantes's method for involving himself in a proliferation of incident without straying from his main story requires him also to consolidate the narrative in other ways. Here, he essays what seems almost like an embryo of the epistolary novel. There are letters from the Duke to Sancho (chapter 47), from the Duchess to Teresa Panza (chapter 50), from Don Quixote to Sancho (chapter 51), from Sancho to Don Quixote (chapter 51), from Teresa to the Duchess (chapter 52), and from Teresa to Sancho (chapter 52), all of which keep the principals abreast of events and advance the action.

It is hard to agree with Riley's view of these six letters: "There are signs here, if not of a crisis in the composition of the work, at least of a disturbance, or a hiccup, in the inventive flow" (Riley 1986, 96). The epistles are an ingenious solution, necessitated by both thematics and aesthetics. Still less can one concur with Riley that the sequel coheres better than the work of 1605, "despite the continuing absence of a central intrigue or plot" (Riley 1986, 96). As I show in this section, the central intrigue of

Part II concerns Sancho's blithely announced project for sainthood; the
providential purification emanating from this project; and the Knight's
purgatorial progress toward a model Christian death, salvation, and
immortality. The formal techniques explored and realized by Cervantes in
these pages conform suitably and necessarily with the implications of this
new thematic.

THE GROTESQUE AS MODE

What has been said so far might well seem prima facie plausible to the reader
of this study, but rather out of tune with the overall impression he or she has
carried away from *Don Quixote*, Part II, over the years. Surely the claims for
the new and different thematic of Part II make of it too solemn and long-
faced an interpretation to be credible? Professor Peter Russell, after all,
iconoclastically proclaimed the *Quixote* to be a "funny book" and blamed
Sismondi and the romantics for seeing it as a sad one (Russell 1969). The
same position was reaffirmed and developed at length by Anthony Close in
his much-read *Romantic Approach to "Don Quixote"* (Close 1978; reviewed,
Sullivan 1980). But, in a 1992 letter to me, John Jay Allen remarks that the
more serious line of interpretation "has been somewhat overshadowed in
recent years by what I would characterize as an overemphasis on the comic
aspects of Part II, a reaction in turn against contrary (and unconvincing)
emphases deriving ultimately from nineteenth-century Romanticism." In
another 1992 letter to me, Professor Diana de Armas Wilson speaks of the
"astonishing darkness of this text." How is it possible, then, to reconcile
Russell's "funny book" with the dark solemnity of transformation in *Don
Quixote*, Part II?

In Chapter 3, I shall demonstrate the theological viability of
"Purgatory in this life" during the Counter Reformation. But fun and
solemnity, I believe, can be reconciled by an understanding of the grotesque
as mode. The vale of woe through which the two pass is a "grotesque
Purgatory"; that is to say, its dimensions of distortion and fantastic ugliness
are the vehicle by which laughter may be provoked, while the underlying
seriousness of the narrative may also be maintained. I refer deliberately to
the grotesque as a mode; not as a genre or an artform. Comedy can assume
a grotesque mode (Ionesco, Pinter); and so can tragedy (Hamlet's ravings in
Shakespeare's play); so normally can a lampoon (political cartoonists).
Painting and drawing can be grotesque (Goya's etchings known as *Los
disparates* [Absurdities]); and so can music (the rickety timpani theme from
the scherzo of Beethoven's Ninth Symphony; some of the enfant terrible
works of Prokofiev). Carl Friedrich Flögel, indeed, proclaimed Calderón's

autos sacramentales to be "grotesque-comic" as long ago as 1788. But in what precisely does the grotesque consist?

The Renaissance Rediscovery of Ancient Roman Grotesque

The grotesque differs from apparently related categories, such as the burlesque, pastiche, parody, satire, persiflage, and sarcasm, in a number of important ways. It will be convenient here to touch on (1) its standard definition, (2) its external history, (3) its etymology, (4) its relation to the body, and (5) its relation to the unconscious. To take these points in numerical order, we may note that some standard dictionary definitions of the term are the following: "1. Distorted, incongruous, or fantastically ugly in appearance or style; bizarre; outlandish. 2. Characterized by fantastic combinations of human and animal figures with conventional design forms, as ornamental work" (*Funk and Wagnalls*); "1. b. A work of art in this style. Chiefly pl[ural], figures or designs in grotesque; in popular language, figures or designs characterized by comic distortion or exaggeration; 2. A clown, buffoon, or merry-andrew" (*OED*); "... human and animal forms often combined with each other and interwoven with representations of foliage, flowers, fruit, wreaths, or other similar figures into a bizarre hybrid ... aesthetically satisfying but that may use distortion or exaggeration of the natural or the expected to the point of comic absurdity, ridiculous ugliness, or ludicrous caricature" (*Webster's*).

These definitions point well enough to the linkage between a form of design, fantastic distortion, and the ridiculous. But what of the term's external history? How did this semantic progression come about? Grotesques were rediscovered in modern times during the Renaissance in Italy, in the course of excavations of the Domus Aurea, or vast palace ordered built by Nero after the conflagration that destroyed Rome in A.D. 64. It had a subterranean labyrinth of passageways and rooms dubbed "grottoes" by the Italians, decorated with elaborate statuary and murals. The murals exhibited a central representation, framed by an ornamental fringe; and it was this fringe, in particular, that consisted of anatomical impossibilities, extraordinary excrescences, human heads and torsos, all convoluted with indeterminate vegetation (Robertson 1991, 17–18).

Although ancient authorities obviously did not apply the term "grotesque" to such decoration, the nonrealistic and supposedly degenerate qualities of such design had already been condemned by both Horace and Vitruvius in the classical era (Robertson 1991, 21–24). But the artists of the late fifteenth century in Italy began to imitate the grotesques' fantasy and dynamism, and the vogue achieved its greatest expansion, in both painting and sculpture, during the sixteenth century, above all the 1560s and 1570s, the period when the youthful Cervantes was soldiering on the Italian peninsula. The term *crotescque* is recorded in French by Gay as early as 1532 (*Larousse*), and in an English wardrobe inventory with the same spelling in 1561 (*OED*).

After these brief remarks on the definition of grotesque and its external history, a word on its etymology is called for. As stated above, the word grotesque is derived from grotto, that is, a masculine reflex of the Italian *la grotta*, meaning an artificial, cavelike structure. The Italian word also has a cognate in *la gruta*, one of several Spanish terms for a cave (*cueva; caverna*), although most Spanish authorities claim that *grotesco* has always been an exotic borrowing in Castilian (*Enciclopedia Universal Ilustrada* 1925, 26: 1386b–1387a). Finally, Italian *grotta* is derived from the Latin *crypta* and, ultimately, from the ancient Greek *krypte*, meaning a chamber or vault, especially one beneath a temple, used as a place of burial. The related Greek adjective *kryptós* retains its meaning of "hidden" or "cryptic" in modern English.

The interest of these etymological connections is that they suggest a constellation of meaning between cryptic and enigmatic; crypt or underground vault; and, perhaps, the grotesque as an artistic or literary mode. But, before exploring this constellation of meaning, it is necessary to stress that the difference between a cave and a crypt or vault lies in the distinction between the natural and the artificial. A cave is hollowed out by geological movements or by erosion, while a crypt is fashioned by the hand of man for ritual or artistic purposes. A crypt, in other words, is an artifact of human intelligence and imagination; a product of fantasy. Or, in Lacanian terms, a cave is an effect of the Real; a crypt is an effect of the Imaginary (see Appendix D).

The same Lacanian distinction applies in the difference between the organism and the body. The organism—the living matter that composes humans as born in nature—belongs to the Real. The body, however, is an Imaginary construct. This perhaps surprising claim is based on Lacan's view that early infant perception (during the mirror stage, especially) construes the body in parts, or as discrete part-objects, rather than as a totality. There is, according to this view, no necessary link in the child's perception between the mother's arm, her face, or her breast, etc. The advent of language confirms this separation of body parts through naming. The signifier of language, Lacan would have it, "cuts" the body into different and arbitrary sections, unjustified by the Real continuity of the organism. In this way, a limb is divided for signifying purposes into fingers, hand, wrist, lower arm, elbow, upper arm, and so on. Some body parts are attributed greater and lesser value. Thus, the head is deemed to be more "noble" than the buttocks; facial hair is regularly exposed, but pubic hair is normally concealed. Someone suffering from *anorexia nervosa* may really weigh 100 pounds, but experience her "overweight" body in the mirror as weighing 200 pounds. The body is said, then, to be a construct produced by the Imaginary order of perception.

The relation of the grotesque to the body, it seems to me, can be understood in these terms. What the ancient Roman grotesques portrayed was the human body fragmented—which is a normal effect of signification and the Imaginary order according to Lacan—but fragmented in an unfamiliar and incongruous manner. So, for example, a human face is depicted at the center of a flower; a torso is depicted separate from a complete body; half-statues rise from roots and stalks, and human heads sit atop the neck and shoulders of a horse. It is as if the Imaginary had done its work, and then some: introducing limbs and part-objects from animals and plants, and splicing them with dismembered fragments of human bodies, in disturbing and "grotesque" fashion.

Now the dismemberment of the body, or the falling apart of its Imaginary unity, is an anxiety- or terror-provoking experience. Horror films trade on the fact unmercifully. The fragmentation of the body, in hallucination, is also an attested symptom of delirium tremens or the descent into psychosis. What the grotesque achieves in art is an aesthetic transformation of this unpleasant experience in a halfway acceptable form. But, because the root of the grotesque is a subjective experience of terror at bodily bounds being dissolved, I believe we are justified in calling the grotesque *sensu stricto* a mode, not a genre or artform, and it can turn up in a wide variety of genres and artforms (lyric poetry, drama, novel, music, plastic arts, cinema, etc.).

Having explored the relation of the grotesque to the body, we may now ask, What is its relation to the unconscious? It should be remarked in the first place that Imaginary perception is largely unconscious. We do not stop to think about our linguistic cutting up of the body, attribution of special value to body parts, or derivation of the countless metaphors we live by from bodily features or attitudes, and the like (Lakoff and Johnson 1980). So the construction or dismemberment of the body takes place in a locus more difficult of access than the conscious mind. It takes place, so to speak, in an underground vault or crypt of consciousness that Freud termed the unconscious (*das Unbewußtsein*). This, it seems to me, is the heart of the matter and the reason why the term *grotesque* is so felicitous.

The unconscious, like the crypt, is in significant measure an artificial construct of the Imaginary. The unconscious also has a logic of its own:

cryptic, enigmatic, paradoxical, but a determining logic all the same. The strangeness or "uncanniness" (*Unheimlichkeit*) of dreams is a good example of this. I am suggesting, therefore, that the presence of the grotesque signifies an encounter with the strange world of putting together and taking apart that is the unconscious mind, functioning according to a logic of its own. The Cave of Montesinos episode in *Don Quixote*, Part II, can be viewed as a descent into a grotto or "crypt of consciousness," rather than as a literal descent into a cave. To quote E.C. Riley: "The marvellous events and beings of Montesinos Cave were truly alive and real. But not in the Cave. They were alive and real within Don Quixote. Don Quixote was not in the marvellous world of the Cave; he was asleep, alone, down a hole in the ground. The Cave of Montesinos was inside him" (Riley 1982, 119).

DON QUIXOTE, PART II, AS A NOVEL IN THE GROTESQUE MODE

This theoretical digression on the grotesque was undertaken to answer the question of how fun and solemnity could be reconciled in Cervantes's novel of 1615. I term the travails of the two protagonists a "grotesque Purgatory." Many critics before me have also applied the term *grotesque* to *Don Quixote*, Part II. Though Menéndez-Pidal (1964) disagreed with him, Paolo Savi-López stated as long ago as 1917 that Part I of Cervantes's masterpiece was "comic," whereas Part II was "grotesque" because the hero becomes a caricature of himself (Savi-López 1917). Francisco Ayala claimed that, in Part II, the grotesque becomes quintessentalized and touches frequently on the magical (Ayala 1947). Percas de Ponseti said that the end of the Montesinos episode, portraying Dulcinea's distress, was "grotesque" (Percas de Ponseti 1968, 379); and Renée Sieburth noted that "the lovely ballad relating the tragic lives of Montesinos, Durandarte, and Belerma has been changed into a nightmarish, *grotesque* story" (Sieburth 1981, 6; my emphasis). What is the justice of these and similar judgments in the critical literature? Does the Cave of Montesinos episode, or the novel as a whole, fit the definitions and meanings of the grotesque that I have put forward?

When we examine the specifically grotesque elements in the Montesinos story, we note that they are (1) the excision of Durandarte's "two-pound" heart and its being sprinkled with salt, even though he is still alive; (2) the fact that it is pointed out, in discussing her sallow appearance, that Belerma is no longer menstruating; and that she also wears a huge turban; (3) the fact that "Dulcinea," in her distress, offers Don Quixote the *faldellín* or underskirt she wears as collateral for a loan; and (4) the fact that her lady-in-waiting takes the proffered four reals and jumps six feet in the air before running off. It may be further remarked that the overall outer framework of the spelunking episode has a grotesque and incongruous air.

Now all the key narrative elements noted above have at their center the body (the heart, the uterus or womb, the legs) or extensions of the body (headgear, underwear). These Imaginary elements would not, of themselves, be incongruous or grotesque, were it not for the Symbolic framework against which they are set (see Appendix D). A poet might very well praise a woman's body parts from the head down (it was a Renaissance topos); and poets might refer to the heart or womb in figurative ways in celebration of an individual, a dynasty, etc. (they frequently did so). The point is that, in the Montesinos episode, these mentions of body parts and bodily extensions are literally denoted in a formal and heroic context that would normally proscribe them; they intrude the Imaginary body improperly into a Symbolic framework.

To change the Symbolic framework for purposes of illustration, we may remember the classic gag where a comedian loses his pants and reveal his legs and underwear in a public performance; it would be inconceivable for a politician to do so in the middle of a formal speech. When the president of the United States vomits into the lap of the Japanese prime minister during a state visit, this is comic for those who can see the humor; a tragic diplomatic disaster from the official point of view, and by any standards grotesque. Both of these last examples depend on the sudden projection of bodily part-objects into public, Symbolic-order contexts that cannot accommodate them.

When we consider the Purgatory through which Don Quixote and Sancho arguably pass in Part II, it is striking how much of their suffering is related to the body and clothing, and to the soul as an indirect outcome. Indeed, they are not aware of direct spiritual torment, or they would revolt in some fashion. The mocking of Don Quixote's celibacy is a taunt to his private parts; Altisidora pretends the parting pair have stolen her garters; Don Quixote's face is scratched by cats; his hose is full of holes; he is trampled by bulls, by a herd of swine, lampooned with a sign on his back in Barcelona, thrown from his horse on the beach, deluded with fake, speaking heads, "speaking" monkeys, carved wooden bodies of puppets, the firework-filled body of a wooden horse, and so on. Sancho is starved, kept thirsty, kept awake, trampled, slapped, pinched, pricked with pins, cajoled to flagellate himself, and thrown around like a ball and battered by the oarsmen of a galley.

The difference between these torments and the knockabout humor of Part I lies in their contrived, pseudoformal framework. In Part I, Don Quixote's injuries arose from attacks he undertook of his own free will, however ill-advised, and punishment was meted out to him by rightly outraged persons. The same is true of the scrapes into which Sancho is unwillingly dragged. But virtually everything that befalls Knight and Squire in Part II is offered up by jokers as if it were a true public ceremony or honorific event. In other words, a Symbolic-order context is created for these cruel japes and jests, however bogusly, while those in the know look on with tongue-in-cheek. When the physical intrusions occur, it is into this falsely public and official setting, thus producing what we have defined as the essence of the grotesque: body parts detached and thrown in incongruous fashion into the coherence and formality of the Symbolic order.

In this chapter I have distinguished the different nature of the thematics and humor of Parts I and II; while Part II continues to be a "funny book," it also develops a solemn theological thesis: This difference in the quality of the humor, grotesque rather than simply comic, depends in turn on the fundamentally different preoccupations of the aging author: a man now debating issues of death and immortality, rather than those of career and marriage. Part II is, therefore, a different and independent novel: a work of literature to be considered in its own right.

The years between 1605 and 1615 had been highly significant. The temptation of posterity to blend these diptych masterworks into a single novel, one conceived as such, is well-nigh irresistible, but it must be resisted. It is true that publishers almost always reprint Parts I and II together as one volume; while critics and readers alike refer in shorthand and in the singular to "the *Quixote*." But Cervantes's 126 chapters do not form an epic novel of single conception, similar to Hugo's *Les Misérables* or Tolstoy's *War and Peace*. Part I is comic and funny. And Part II continues to be a "funny book," but of a different kind. It is the grotesque of the body subjected to pain, contextualized within a mock ceremonial order, that raises the uncertain smile. And, as Nietzsche observed, it is "a bitter tale" (Drake and Finello 1987, 27).

Select Bibliography

Allen, John Jay. 1980. "The Providential World of Cervantes' Fiction." *Thought* 55.217: 184–95.

Ayala, Francisco. 1947. "La invención del *Quijote como* problema técnico-literario." *Realidad: Revista de Ideas* 2.5: 183–200.

Close, Anthony J. 1978. *The Romantic Approach to "Don Quixote."* Cambridge: Cambridge University Press.

Drake, Dana B., and Dominick L. Finello. 1987. *An Analytical and Bibliographical Guide to Criticism in Don Quijote (1790–1893)*. Newark, Del.: Juan de la Cuesta.

Johnson, Carroll B. 1983. *Madness and Lust: A Psychoanalytical Approach to Don Quixote*. Berkeley and Los Angeles: University of California Press.

Lacan, Jacques. 1978. *The Four Fundamental Concepts of Psychoanalysis.* Trans. Alan Sheridan. New York: Norton.

Lakoff, George, and Mark Johnson. 1980. *Metaphors We Live By.* Chicago. University of Chicago Press.

Percas de Ponseti, Helena. 1968. "La cueva de Montesinos." *Revista Hispánica Moderna* 34: 376–99.

Pontalis, J.-B. 1978. "On Death-Work.". *Psychoanalysis, Creativity and Literature: A French-American Inquiry.* Ed. Alan Roland. New York: Columbia University Press. 80–95.

Ragland-Sullivan, Ellie. 1986. *Jacques Lacan and the Philosophy of Psychoanalysis.* Urbana: University of Illinois Press.

Riley, Edward C. 1982. "Metamorphosis, Myth and Dream in the Cave of Montesinos." *Essays on Narrative Fiction in the Iberian Peninsula in Honour of Frank Pierce.* Ed. R. Brian Tate. Oxford: Dolphin. 105–19.

Robertson, Kim Alton. 1991. "The Grotesque Interface: Deformity, Debasement, and Dissolution." Ph.D. diss., University of Texas at Austin.

Russell, Peter E. 1969. "'Don Quixote' as a Funny Book." *Modern Language Review* 64: 312–26.

Savi-López, Paolo. 1917. *Cervantes* [1913]. Trans. from the Italian by Antonio G. Solalinde. Madrid: Calleja.

Sieburth, Renée. 1981. "Metamorphosis: The Key to an Interpretation of Don Quixote's Adventure in the Cave of Montesinos." *Revista de Estudios Hispánicos* (United States) 15: 3–16.

Sullivan, Henry W. 1980. Review of Anthony Close, *The Romantic Approach to "Don Quixote."* Cambridge: Cambridge University Press, 1978. *Canadian Review of Comparative Literature* 7.1: 114–18.

———. 1985. "Love, Matrimony and Desire in the Theatre of Tirso de Molina." *Bulletin of the Comediantes* 37.1: 83–99.

MANUEL DURÁN

Picaresque Elements in Cervantes's Works

As I write this essay I am aware that I do so five hundred years after Columbus's first voyage toward the New World. It was virtually impossible to resist an analogy between the invention of the picaresque, a new kind of novel destined to explore social and psychological spaces hitherto unknown, and the travels of exploration and conquest starting in 1492.

In both cases the initial discovery was followed by a period of uncertainty and doubt. Columbus looked in vain for Oriental landmarks and landscapes as described by Marco Polo that he could not possibly find because they were not there. What had he really discovered, and how could his discovery become useful to all? The problem was not solved right away. Similarly, after the initial discovery of new literary lands with *Lazarillo de Tormes* in 1554, a period of confusion follows. Neither the readers, however enthusiastic, nor the critics, and even less the possible imitators of the intriguing, amusing, and disquieting novel knew exactly what to do with it. Hence the long hiatus between the first picaresque novel and its sequel, the full-blown, overlong, fully self-conscious second picaresque novel, *Guzmán de Alfarache*, published in 1598. Forty-four years of silence and infertility (at least in the field of the picaresque novel, since *Lazarillo* did not have a progeny until almost the end of the century) constitute a negative record by any standard, especially given the infectious and enduring vitality the new literary trend was about to acquire.

From *The Picaresque: Tradition and Displacement.* © 1996 by the Regents of the University of Minnesota.

An explosion of new knowledge, of new facts and new possibilities, is bound to create anguish, chaos, vertigo. After a while an attempt is made to put the pieces together in a rational way and understand what has happened. Exploration is followed by description of the new lands, the drawing of maps, conquest and settlement.

The settlement of the immense lands in the realm of literature opened up by the discovery of the picaresque mode in the novel has lasted until the very present and will probably continue for a long time to come. Opening at random novels by Camilo José Cela, by Günter Grass, by selected American authors (Fanny, by Erica Jong, comes to mind) will show us that picaresque attitudes are still very much with us.

Conquest and settlement assume a victory, announcing the creation of an empire. Fortunately for the writer and his or her readers the expansion of literary empires does not entail bloodshed, victims, or slaves. It does frequently upset the system of values that most people had taken for granted, therefore accelerating social change in the short run, political change in the long run. Our modern world owes much to those who, like the creators of the picaresque novel, and like Cervantes, introduced a new sensitivity and changed forever in subtle or obvious ways our way of seeing man and society—a new vision is also a new way of judging and creates often an urge to change things in order to correct the crooked, distorted view that the new sensitivity has surpassed.

After the initial period of confusion and chaos that the increase in information entails seems to abate, another need comes to the fore. It is imperative to consolidate and beautify the land that had been previously discovered and partially explored. Out of the ruins of Tenochtitlán, Mexico City, with its baroque cathedral and its Main Square, is about to emerge.

While this great activity of consolidation and reconstruction goes forward in the Spanish Empire that Columbus and Cortés helped to create, another effort aimed at transforming and beautifying existing structures takes place in an invisible empire, one that we could perhaps call by its eighteenth-century name, the "Republic of Letters." Cervantes is about to rework and rearrange, rethink and transcend, the materials that have been handed to him, and of course to any thoughtful reader and author, by the picaresque Revolution.

It was indeed a revolution: it broke down old taboos related to idealization that had been a part of Western culture since the ancient Greeks, since Phidias and Plato—even before that, since the first systematic idealizations of the human body by Egyptian carvers and relief sculptors. Anything ugly, humble, despised, debased, misshapen, could now be treated seriously and become a source of knowledge and wisdom. Everyday life in its triviality and imperfection was worthy of attention and could become a springboard to wisdom. Thus an omelette made with rotten eggs, eggs in which the chickens are already visible, a shocking, nauseating experience for young Guzmán at the very beginning of his adventures, becomes an image, a paradigm, a summing up of a rotten society in which no one scruples to cheat, to deceive, to rob, to poison, for the sake of a few coins or a feeling of self-esteem, vanity, pride, arrogance. Small, humble, debased objects and people are all around us: we must see them, really see and understand them, if we want to understand the world and our role in it, since the ugly, debased, humble objects and people make up perhaps nine-tenths of what exists and condition the rest.

Cervantes, however, would not agree. Not, at least, wholeheartedly, not without reservations. Perhaps Cervantes remembered that it was not the first time a gloomy vision of the world around us had been offered in a literary work. There was a text considerably older than the *Lazarillo*, a text much admired by Cervantes, who calls it "divine," if only human failings and errors had been more carefully disguised in it. This text is, of course, *La Celestina*, and more specifically its end, the final speech by Pleberio.

A case can be made that the whole of picaresque literature came out of Pleberio's speech. Life, Pleberio claims, is a trap, a bait we swallow without realizing we have also swallowed the hook. Life is a vale of tears. Every moment of hope has to be paid for by many moments of despair. Pleberio's daughter has just committed suicide, and neither Pleberio nor his wife realized until it was too late that Melibea had a secret life her parents knew nothing about. Life is indeed a dark passage, full of ugliness and suffering. Can there be a clearer blueprint for the picaresque novels that are to follow?

Obviously, we may object that *La Celestina* is not a true novel, and moreover that Pleberio's despair has a metaphysical, philosophical, existential quality that bears little resemblance to the urgent problems poverty and low birth introduce in the picaresque novels. Yet many of the gloomy musings of Guzmán parallel Pleberio's statements.

Is it perhaps due to the fact that both Rojas and Alemán are *conversos* who have abandoned the traditional security of their original religion and yet are not quite at ease within the framework of their brand-new Christianity? If this is so, if only *conversos* possess the magic touch that allows them to write true picaresque literature, how are we to explain Quevedo's success, whose *Buscón* exhibits all of the classic characteristics of the genre, and moreover offers wit and cold bitterness beyond all expectation? (We know, of course, that Quevedo is not only a true "Old Christian," but also the most rabid anti-Semite, possibly, that the Spanish Golden Age produced.)

La Celestina, it is true, was not a novel—yet it offered a reader such as Cervantes a literary model that in many respects could be more useful than the example of the picaresque novels. The situations outlined in *La Celestina* are psychologically richer, more varied, than the monotonous misadventures and setbacks that can be found in most picaresque novels. Basically a picaresque text offers us one single viewpoint; it shows us the world through the eyes of its hero, whose personality, problems, and predicament change slowly or not at all. The opposite is true in *La Celestina*. Dialogue is at its very core, and through dialogue we can witness the deep changes that take place in each main character. Duplicity is, for Celestina, the name of the game, and she shows us many facets of her complex personality, many colors, as a chameleon would, before being overtaken by death. Calixto, seen at first as a young lover intoxicated by the lofty feelings and conceits of *cancionero* poetry, will later become a young man totally dominated by his sexual urge, who will almost rape Melibea, tearing off her clothes and justifying his actions with the coarse comparison that one has to pluck a bird in order to eat it. Both Pármeno and Sempronio change in the course of the play. Briefly, the message is one of dynamic interaction and deep change in the behavior and personality of the characters, a secondary message being that of misunderstanding. Neither Calixto nor Melibea nor even clever Celestina fully hears what the other characters say; they hear only or mostly what they want to hear.

Obviously *La Celestina* offers also many instances of what we might call *ur*-picaresque characters and situations. The banquet at Celestina's house is not only a possible parody of Plato's *Symposium* but also a clear vision of the world as seen from below, by characters such as Areusa who are full of resentment at the advantages that a young lady, Melibea, has been granted by society or destiny.

Briefly, Cervantes could find in *La Celestina* a text so rich and complex that practically all the elements needed for a novel as sophisticated and innovative as *Don Quixote* can be found in it: idealization, parody, misunderstandings, slow changes of mind, evolution of characters, interaction among characters, dialogue, a sad yet illuminating ending, and, of course, a profusion of "lowly" details, characters, and situations. These are building blocks that the picaresque novels would later appropriate and standardize. The only drawback, yet a considerable one, was that *La Celestina* was not a true novel.

Let us now try to identify ourselves with Cervantes as he must have felt in 1598. *Guzmán de Alfarache* had just appeared, Cervantes had read it and enjoyed it, and he was also aware of the instant success of that novel. It had become almost from the very beginning what we would call today a "best-seller," just what Cervantes needed to write, what he must have prayed for, the only possible solution to his anguishing economic situation. Cervantes was in need of a clear literary success. It would have been easy for him, given his talent, to write a novel very much like the *Guzmán*, not necessarily a sequel to it, simply a good picaresque novel patterned after it.

No writer works in a vacuum. Literary tradition always stands behind the writer, providing him or her with models and building blocks, with materials to be recycled and used once more. This is still true today but was especially true during the Middle Ages and the Renaissance: imitation was not only not frowned upon, it was encouraged. Literature was seen as a continuum, and the good writer could insert himself into it only by acknowledging the existence of literary traditions and attaching his own works to the wave of time that continued and preserved such literary traditions. It is only after the Romantic experience that writers search deliberately for the new, the original, the pristine word, the dream never before dreamed, the character absent from every previous novel, and plunge "au fond de l'Inconnu pour trouver du nouveau," according to the Baudelairian prescription. Cervantes was not averse to come to terms with literary tradition, but he also had found certain artistic principles that he was not about to forsake. The use of picaresque materials, situations, and characters could give his works a most necessary fashionable look, yet such materials had to be handled in such a way that they could be integrated into a more complex literary structure. Perhaps an example taken from the discipline of art history will show more clearly what, according to my interpretation, Cervantes had in mind when, after reading *Guzmán de Alfarache*, he was getting ready to start *Don Quixote*.

All along the sixteenth century tension grows between two approaches to the plastic arts, and especially painting. On the one hand, the Italian style, with its refined, idealized figures set in a framework dominated by symmetry, true perspective, and allusions to classical antiquity. Leonardo, Raphael, Michelangelo, and Titian are among the high priests of this style, which becomes more and more fashionable and slowly invades the rest of Europe. On the other hand, in Northern Europe, especially in Germany and Flanders, a realism still rooted in the Gothic world gives birth to robust, down-to-earth pictures of everyday life, often without any attempt at idealization. A good example of this style can be found in the paintings of Pieter Bruegel. In sixteenth-century Flanders the legacy of the Middle Ages was strong. The primary aim of art was still to preach Christian morality or instill pious feelings. Man was seen as clumsy and small, his habitual follies ruthlessly exposed. Everything in his paintings is to be judged and enjoyed both as a symbol and as an accurate portrayal of real life. Bruegel's canvases stir with life, everyday life devoid of glamour, with man working at worldly enterprise—but doomed to final failure. There is scarcely a hint of personal feeling in any of his paintings and never any appeal for the viewer's sympathy.

Bruegel's cripples, his beggars, his blindmen tumbling into a ditch are just there, part of the world as it is. This, Bruegel seems to say, is the world. This is man. Take him or leave him if you can. There is a feeling of malaise and pessimism in many of his canvases that relates them to the Spanish picaresque novels. A close friend of Bruegel's, the scientist and mapmaker Abraham Ortelius, makes his pessimistic views clear enough in letters kept secret at the time: "We live in a very disordered time, which we have little hope of seeing soon improved. The patient [Flanders, or probably all of Western Europe] will soon be entirely prostrate, being threatened with so many and various illnesses, as the Catholic evil, the *Gueux* fever [that is, the rebellious Protestant Dutch] and the Huguenot dysentery."[1] Or, to put it in other words, a pox on both your houses. Pieter Bruegel probably agreed with him. It is quite probable that Bruegel took no sides at all, and that, like the philosopher Erasmus, he disapproved of all violence committed in the name of Christianity, by Calvinists and Catholics alike.[2] Erasmus, whose influence upon Spanish thought and letters was thoroughly researched by Marcel Bataillon many years ago, seems to have influenced Bruegel, the anonymous author of *Lazarillo de Tormes*, and also Cervantes.

Grotesque elements, as well as the acceptance of ugliness as part of everyday life, came to characterize many Flemish and German painters, although their attitude in turn was sternly criticized by Italian artists:

> Flemish use of perspective, it was pointed out, was determined more by rule of thumb than anything else and fell far short of Italian geometric exactitude. Flemish handling of the human figure too, far from being noble and stately, was sometimes downright grotesque. Flemish Virgins, notably those by the Master of Flémalle and Memling, were often dumpy-looking and pale as a poached fish. Hugh van der Goes's Eve, naked in the Garden of Eden, was plainly pot-bellied and stringy. Such things were entirely against Italian Renaissance principles. It was not long before the greatest artist and most powerful personality of the South, Michaelangelo himself, was denigrating the Flemish fondness for chatty detail and for painting everyday things as they are. "Their paintings," he observed in conversations collected by the Portuguese artist Francesco da Hollanda, "are of stuffs, bricks, mortar, the grass of the fields, the shadows of trees ... and little figures here and there. And all this, though it may appear good in some eyes, is in truth done without ... symmetry or proportion."[3]

The struggle between Platonic idealization and realistic caricature took place in the mind of Cervantes not once but throughout his career as a writer. We must not forget his Italian experiences, his love for Renaissance Italian literature, and the fact that his first novel, *La Galatea*, published in 1585, is a pastoral novel, with all the idealization and rhetoric that the pastoral genre entails. Four days before his death, while writing the preface to his *Persiles*, he still remembers fondly his first novel and hopes to write an addition or second part to it if God allows him a few months of life. We can find pastoral subjects and descriptions in several of his works, especially in *Don Quixote*, where pastoral themes in a literary framework appear in the episode of Marcela and Grisóstomo, and a rustic pastoral scene is described in the chapters dealing with Camacho's wedding. A great Spanish critic, Américo Castro, has pointed out that "the pastoral subjects are ideologically and aesthetically essential to Cervantes" (190).

Yet the same Cervantes who praises the nobility and harmony of pastoral life is capable of approaching this same world with mocking irony. In *El coloquio de los perros* one of the dogs, Berganza, who has lived among shepherds, comes to the conclusion that pastoral novels lie, for shepherds in real life do not sing beautiful songs accompanied by bagpipes, violins, and other musical instruments, but rather scream or grunt, and pass the time killing the fleas that infest them and mending their muddy rustic sandals.

Cervantes's mind is, we have to assume, extremely complex. The opposition between lofty ideals and everyday life with all its imperfections and even its ugliness is a problem that cannot be totally solved by Cervantes and will become a part of his worldview during all his career. There are problems that cannot be made to disappear, yet they stimulate the creative mind, helping us to create a new, more subtle, more complex image of the world around us. Cervantes did believe in an ideal reality, one that could be as real as everyday reality. In it one could find a myriad of perfect values, all worthy of his admiration and his attention, even if they were reflected only in part, only imperfectly, in the everyday world in which we all must live. But this ideal world was to be found only in the mind of the artist, the philosopher, the lover, all exceptional beings, and to enter this ideal world was both an exhilarating experience and a discouraging limitation, since it meant giving up on the world of everyday events, the world that for most of Cervantes's contemporaries was the only real world.

Cervantes could not be entirely satisfied by being inside the world of idealization and high moral values, yet being outside it was felt by him as a loss, almost a fall into a private hell. Hence the need to ironize and criticize both worlds. We have seen how the pastoral is mocked in *El coloquio de los perros*. Yet, we may conclude, perhaps a dog is not the best judge of the world of shepherds and shepherdesses: perhaps there is more to the pastoral world than meets the eye of a dog.

All along his literary career, from his first novel to his last, Cervantes will experiment with two opposing forces, the idealizing attitude with roots in the Italian Renaissance and courtly love, and the world of caricature, want, cruelty, and petty crime with medieval roots. We must emphasize, of course, the continued presence of the second force, the picaresque elements, in the author's life, in his total experience, from boyhood to old age.

Yet there was for him, Cervantes the avid reader, another world. Cervantes was an admiring reader of Garcilaso, and no doubt had also read Petrarch, Sannazaro, Ariosto, in their original Italian text, as well as Jorge de Montemayor and Gaspar Gil Polo, the creators of the Spanish pastoral novel, in Spanish, together with hundreds of texts permeated with courtly love, Platonic idealization, fantasy, a quest for beauty and truth. Cervantes had written love poetry and a pastoral novel. On the other hand, he had known thieves and pimps while in jail, or perhaps out of jail while in Seville, and his descriptions of the Seville underworld in *Rinconete y Cortadillo* ring true.

Two worlds in opposition that somehow seem to coexist in Cervantes's mind and experience: one might be tempted to compare them to matter and antimatter, which are supposed to destroy each other on contact.

Cervantes will avoid such a dangerous contact by conducting a series of experiments in which idealization and the picaresque are brought close to each other in limited quantities and different proportions.

His main experiment, one that turned out to be totally successful, consists in placing idealization and the picaresque face to face, making them confront each other, but in a privileged space where whatever happens cannot affect us directly since we are far removed from such a space, protected from it by an invisible barrier. This privileged secluded space is of course the mind, and the vital experiences, of a madman. We can examine the clashing principles inside the mind and the adventures of Don Quixote without being involved in the painful surprises and constant readjustments this clash entails: after all, we are mere spectators of a unique event, one that cannot be repeated in our own mind and our own experience. Similarly, another great Spaniard, Velásquez, will allow idealized, exquisite beauty and misshapen, grotesque ugliness to confront each other in his most famous painting, *Las Meninas*, where the young Spanish princess is shown very close to a dwarf: this happens also in a privileged space, the royal court of the Spanish Hapsburgs, a place where the whim of kings and princes overrules all principles of aesthetics and harmony.

There is another characteristic of picaresque novels that must have intrigued Cervantes: the fact that they are "open works," without a clear conclusion, lacking a definite end. Their characters remain restless, ready to depart for a new adventure like Quevedo's Pablos, who announces a voyage to the New World in the last page of the novel, and lets us know that the results of his American adventures were not happy, as it was to be feared, since he had changed his surroundings without getting rid of his roguish behavior.

Neither *Lazarillo* nor *Guzmán* ends in ways that could be considered satisfactory to a reader or a writer examining them under the guidance of Aristotle's *Poetics*. For Aristotle a literary work reaches perfection only if the fable turns around one single action, whole and complete, having a beginning, a middle, and an end. Picaresque novels, with their truncated endings, would be shapeless and monstrous when judged by an Aristotelian. Was Cervantes an Aristotelian in his own writings, as we have been told so many times during the past thirty years? The problem is much more complex than it appears at first.

Among the galley slaves that Don Quixote frees in Chapter 22 of Part I is a famous rogue, Ginés de Pasamonte, also known as Ginesillo de Parapilla. He has written the story of his life, and a fine book it is: "It is so good ... that Lazarillo de Tormes will have to look out, and so will everything in that style that has ever been written or ever will be." Don Quixote then asks Ginés if his book is finished. "How can it be finished," replies Ginés, "if my life isn't?"

It is fitting that the picaresque novel being written by Ginés de Pasamonte should remain unfinished, just as unfinished as the other canonic picaresque novels of the Golden Age, and should be described by its author as such, in a manner that recalls Umberto Eco's definition of an "opera aperta." Yet what can we say about the end of *Don Quixote, Part I*?

It is obvious today, and was equally obvious to Cervantes's contemporary readers, that the end of Part I remains open. We do not know exactly what happened to Don Quixote and Sancho. Don Quixote's death has been reported, yet in an uncertain way. His epitaph has been written, but this fact in itself proves nothing. Moreover, Cervantes himself invites other writers to continue Don Quixote's adventures in his quotation of Ariosto: "For's altri canterà ... con miglior plettro. Perhaps somebody else will sing Don Quixote's song, or ballad, with a better voice than Cervantes himself. (Obviously Cervantes regretted this quotation more than once, as soon as Avellaneda's novel appeared: Cervantes had openly invited someone else, anyone else, to continue his novel, and Avellaneda had accepted the challenge.)

Considering the results of Part I having been left open at the end it is not surprising, and on the contrary it is totally predictable, that Cervantes would take great pains to close Part II of his novel as tightly as possible, with Don Quixote's last will and testament, his death, and the admonition to any future novelist that Don Quixote was created by Cervantes and no one else should attempt to write anything on this subject.

Our first conclusion must be that Cervantes learns from the picaresque novels the art of leaving his novels open-ended. Not only *Don Quixote, Part I*, also *Rinconete y Cortadillo*, another work by Cervantes in which the picaresque elements are paramount, remains open at the end, against the best Aristotelian advice. Which does not mean, of course, that Cervantes approves the picaresque attitude, philosophy, and character creation (or should we say character deformation). On the contrary. He makes use of fragments, materials taken from the picaresque quarry, without building a picaresque house for his own characters. Since he does not reject picaresque materials, for he finds them useful and much in demand among his contemporary readers, and yet he considers them ultimately unacceptable, debasing, even abhorrent, he is forced to neutralize them the best way he can. One of the devices he uses is to take away the sting of the "pícaro" by turning him into an artificial character, a masked figure worthy of a carnival ball. This is what happens in the short novel (or long short story, or "novella") *La Ilustre fregona*.

The tale is relatively simple: two young men belonging to noble families leave home, pretending to go to Flanders to fight in the war, and actually disguise themselves as "Pícaros." They are eager to live the adventurous life of the "Pícaros," but Cervantes underlines that they are the sons of noble and rich gentlemen, and under their rags they hide bags of gold doubloons. These young men, Carriazo and Avendaño, are playing the picaresque game, just as much as Don Quixote plays the game of chivalry, but they only resemble Don Quixote in his moments of lucidity in Part II and are in any case much less complex than the "Ingenioso Hidalgo" of Cervantes's great novel. Their role is often that of "voyeurs," taking part in picaresque life without being totally submerged in it, always aware of the possibility of getting out of the picaresque atmosphere, a privilege that is not given to any true "Pícaro" by the authors of true picaresque novels. Yet they are reluctant to leave the Toledo inn they have reached because one of them, Avendaño, has fallen in love with a beautiful girl, Constanza, who works at the inn polishing silver. The young men accept to work at the inn, one of them taking care of horses, the other one of water supplies, and as love develops, Avendaño serenades Constanza and writes love poems for her (which will be discovered by the innkeeper among a list of supplies for the inn's horses) while a rich tapestry of picaresque life unfolds before the eyes of Cervantes's readers.

We examine the ceaseless activity of many rogues, guided by the attraction of money or sex, plotting swindles or rehearsing erotic dances, yet it is all a spectacle, a game, a show that our young heroes enjoy from the outside without being actually full partners of the picaresque game. The end is predictably both happy and contrived, since Constanza turns out to be the daughter of a noble lady, our young men's parents finally reach the inn looking for them, and Constanza and Avendaño get married in the final pages and fade into the sunset of wedded bliss.

Angel Valbuena Prat classifies *La Ilustre fregona* as "realistic-idealistic," in an oxymoronic definition that means that realistic observations about everyday life are mingled with a Platonic conception of love. *La Gitanilla* is, according to Valbuena Prat, another example of this mixture. I agree that the mixture exists, and I suspect such a mixture points to the core of Cervantes's approach to the art of fiction, as a generous effort to embrace and transcend opposites and contradictions. Cervantes does not deny the existence of picaresque situations and characters, yet does his best to redeem or go beyond them through wit, irony, or love, and if it is not possible to turn the picaresque into something made of nobler ingredients Cervantes will always create a door or a window through which his characters can escape the picaresque prison if they really wish to do so, for Cervantes truly believes in freedom, and through this belief, which he infuses into each one of the characters he creates, he subverts or destroys the very foundation of the picaresque world.

I would now hazard a guess, or perhaps a hypothesis, not susceptible of complete proof, yet a plausible hypothesis. It is this: of all the characters created by him, Cervantes must have felt closer to someone like the young heroes of *La Ilustre fregona*. He must have, in any case, envied them, he must have wished his life had been like theirs. Cervantes, the son of a "shabby-genteel" family, had been too close to the picaresque atmosphere from the very beginning of his life. Poverty, debts, hasty displacements in order to avoid debtors, were very much a part of his childhood memories. Later on, once more poverty, debts, together with long months spent in jail, wanderings in southern Spain staying at country or city inns that attracted thieves and pimps: Cervantes's adventurous existence brought him in and out of the picaresque milieu, too close for comfort and at the same time looking at it from his own protected, fortress-like inner self, a mixture of ironic detachment and amused curiosity. Perhaps, when we are trying to define the relationship between Cervantes and the picaresque characters offered in abundance by his society and his contemporary novelists, the key word is "curiosity," which implies both interest and detachment, sympathy and superiority.

As a novelist, Cervantes is an active member of what Marshall McLuhan has called "the Gutenberg Galaxy." A consequence can be easily deduced from the very bulk of many Renaissance novels (*Guzmán de Alfarache* and *Don Quixote* come easily to mind), as opposed to the much more slender appearance of a book of poetry, and that is the role that technology, in the specific shape of Gutenberg's printing press, played in the development of the novel in modern times. A lengthy novel seems to demand the presence of a printer who with his printing press will make the novel available to a large public; copying a long novel by hand is exceedingly tedious and will result in a small number of expensive copies. The novel was from the beginning a democratic genre and was written for the masses of readers, young and old, but especially young, that the schools of the Late Middle Ages and early Renaissance were beginning to mass-produce.

Another distinctive feature of the modern European novel, born at the crossroads between medieval and Renaissance times, is that it was born not only democratic but also Christian. In his brilliant book of critical essays on realism in Western literatures, *Mimesis*, published first in German in 1946 and translated into English in 1953, Erich Auerbach shows how Christianity's strong belief that the souls of all sorts and conditions of men are potentially of equal value produced a narrative tradition very different from the classical literary theory of the separation of styles, according to which serious treatment was restricted to "noble" subject matter, while everyday reality and humble people were considered appropriate only for comic or satiric treatment. We find servant women treated with the utmost interest and respect in great Western novels, from Joanot Martorell's *Tirant lo Blanc* to Benito Pérez Galdós's *Misericordia*, in which the servant Benina often takes center stage and at the end forgives her mistress with words that remind us of the New Testament. Tolstoy, Balzac, and Proust will write some of their best pages about characters that we might consider socially unimportant.

A small masterpiece close to the picaresque genre is the novelette *Rinconete y Cortadillo*. It allows us a close-up of the underworld of Seville in the late sixteenth century, as seen through the eyes of two runaways who hope to find an easy life in it. What they find is initially astonishing: a picaresque organization that is run like a successful corporation, with a first-rate chairman of the board whose name is Monipodio and who supervises everybody's transgressions. Policemen are bribed, even saints and heavenly patrons are duly appeased. Members help each other. The inescapable conclusion is that on the whole the underworld is better run, more harmonious, even more productive, than the "normal" society around it.

We feel almost from the first page the honesty and accuracy of

Cervantes's portrait of the Seville mafia. He had been there, both inside and outside the jails of Seville, and his firsthand contact is obvious in the way he handles the rogue's language and describes the situations in which they develop their tricks.

Yet there are noteworthy differences between Cervantes's text and the most typical picaresque novels. Perhaps the most outstanding difference is that Cervantes's novelette is not written in the first person, as Juan Luis Alborg underlines: the very existence of a dialogue between the two main characters separates Cervantes's novelette from the picaresque literary norm.[4]

What Rinconete and Cortadillo achieve is exactly the opposite of what Lázaro or Guzmán do: the young heroes of Cervantes's novelette observe, judge, compare; finally one of them abandons the picaresque life, which he has found wanting, and goes home, while his friend, who has taken a liking to his new existence, remains in Seville and will become with time a full-fledged pícaro. Decisions such as the ones taken by these boys imply a high degree of inner freedom, which is always lacking in the true picaresque hero. This has been remarked by Joaquín Casalduero, for whom the essential fact is that the two lads depicted by Cervantes have not lost control over their own destinies.[5] Both critics agree thus with Menéndez y Pelayo, who in "Cultura literaria de Miguel de Cervantes y elaboración del Quijote" points out the independence of Cervantes's art vis-à-vis the picaresque viewpoints: Cervantes is a "genre painter," inspired by real-life models, not by a fixed ideology such as the picaresque literature assumes.[6]

The psychological traits that allow Cervantes to turn mud into gold in his narrative are above all a stubborn optimism, a faith in himself and also in mankind in general, a great deal of tolerance, bordering on cynicism, and above all a spirit of forgiveness that excuses vice when it is a by-product of the general corruption of society. Perhaps Monipodio and his gangsters are not only picturesque but mirror, as would a distorting convex mirror, the corruption of the so-called normal society.

Another neutralizing agent that destroys or eliminates the acids of the picaresque is humor, especially when combined with irony and farce, which are the main ingredients of *El casamiento engañoso*. Lieutenant Campuzano is not only a rogue who marries doña Estefanía de Caicedo because he falls in love with the contents of her hope chest, which he estimates is at least two thousand five hundred gold ducats, but also a "miles gloriosus" that Plautus would have applauded, a braggart such as the one Cervantes paints in one of his satirical sonnets. The whole plot of this "novella" would have pleased Boccaccio. After the wedding doña Estefanía disappears, taking with her Campuzano's meager earthly goods. The deceiver has been deceived, and on

top of this misadventure he is now infected with a sexually transmitted
disease that he is trying to get rid of through a sweating cure at the hospital.

Closer to the traditional picaresque fiction is the second part of this
"novella," *El coloquio de los perros*, since one of the dogs, Berganza, narrates his
adventures in the first-person singular, and the other dog, Cipión, plays the
role of enlightened and judicious listener. Much like Lázaro or Guzmán,
Berganza has served many masters and traveled a great deal. He is now in a
position to reveal the cheating and lying that permeate Spanish society. Most
probably Cervantes wrote this "novella" soon after settling in Valladolid,
when his memories of the Seville jail and its inmates were still fresh in his
mind. Satire and social criticism are perhaps more biting in this text than in
any other by Cervantes. Yet the effect is one of unreality. Time and time
again we are reminded that it is two dogs that are speaking, and the fact that
Campuzano is feverish and has taken strong medicine may indicate to the
reader that probably he has imagined the dogs' dialogue. This in turn means
that the criticism of Spanish society is not backed up by the direct experience
of the narrator, if we assume Campuzano imagines the tale, or, if the dogs
really speak, how much do dogs understand about the human world, how
well can they judge it? The sting remains, yet the problem of who speaks and
who has lived through the fascinating adventures told in the dialogue softens
some of the sharp edges of Cervantes's satire.

For if the dogs speak we are dealing with a miracle, and like any miracle
it is quite inexplicable. The very tale that unfolds supposedly picaresque
situations "falls under the category of those things they call miracles," as
Cervantes puts it. We are now beginning to suspect that Cervantes's tale,
instead of being a picaresque text, is on the contrary a satire of all picaresque
literature. As Carlos Blanco Aguinaga points out, "It is not difficult to see the
jest implied in the fact that the attempts at moralizing are put in the mouth
of a dog who, because he can miraculously speak, thinks that he is more
intelligent than he is and that he has the right to judge" (144).

Berganza thinks he knows so much that he can judge everything and
everybody (just as Guzmán de Alfarache had been doing all through the
pages of the novel that bears his name), but Cipión corrects him and tries to
instill in him some humility: "Just look at your paws," he says to him, "and
you'll stop playing the dandy, Berganza. What I mean is that you should
realize that you are an animal lacking in reason, and if for the moment you
show some reason, we have already settled between the two of us that it is a
supernatural and unprecedented thing." Cipión's final advice to Berganza is
also an appeal to moderation and humility, reminding him that our
knowledge is relative and our place in this world a modest one: "You see,
Berganza, no one should intrude where he is not invited, nor should he ever

undertake anything not within his competence." "It would seem, then, that the Colloquy is hardly a burlesque of the pastoral novel; it is rather a parody of the picaresque novel as a dogmatic and self-complacent form. In its formal and thematic 'realism' the picaresque is as ideal, absolute and fixed as the chivalric novel is in its: the naturalistic novel and the idealistic novel thus stand in contrast to the objective realism of Cervantes whose spirit does not allow, either in theme or form, any fixity. At the ultimate bottom of the box of several bottoms that is the *Deceitful Marriage* and *Colloquy of the Dogs* (in the Prologue Cervantes himself calls his novels 'a game of billiards') we encounter, among other things, a frontal critique of the way of writing novels [the picaresque way] which Cervantes *seems* to have followed" (Blanco Aguinaga 144–45).

There is no doubt that Cervantes acknowledged the existence, the power, the influence of picaresque novels. He read them and understood their message, and his admiration for a text that may have inspired them, *La Celestina*, he stated clearly.

The picaresque novels had sharpened the vision of Cervantes's contemporaries by describing characters and situations that had remained previously beyond the pale of Literature. Once more we should acknowledge that the Renaissance was a culture, whether in Italy, in France, in Spain, or elsewhere, given to extreme idealizations, class distinctions, and basic all-encompassing snobbery—and inasmuch as the picaresque novels introduce a new subject, the life of the humble, the poor, the oppressed, even if they are painted as debased criminals, these novels are bound to enlarge our sensitivity and our awareness of a complex world in which even the picaroons have a role to play. They are a counterweight to the excessive idealizations of the pastoral genre and courtly love.

It is possible, therefore, to state in conclusion that the picaresque texts that Cervantes read were both necessary to his creative endeavors and also insufficient. Much of what he found in them must have excited his sensitivity and his imagination, yet many of the situations, literary techniques, and characters in the picaresque novels must have seemed to him deficient, incomplete, one-sided. Two important recent books dealing with Spanish picaresque fiction are helpful in delineating Cervantes's debt to the picaresque mode and also point out the many ways in which Cervantes's art transcends the picaresque tradition.

Peter N. Dunn's *Spanish Picaresque Fiction: A New Literary History* attempts to soften, even blur, the contrast between Cervantes's art and the picaresque tradition, underlining instead the complexity of the picaresque texts, the divergent strains in picaresque writing, and ultimately the important influence they exerted upon Cervantes: "without *Lazarillo* and

Guzmán he could not have written *Rinconete y Cortadillo* or the *Coloquio de los perros* or *La ilustre fregona*" (219). Dunn is harshly critical of Carlos Blanco Aguinaga's 1957 article in which he identifies the picaresque completely with Alemán, since, according to Dunn, *Guzmán* "is not the determinist tract that it is often represented to be; the protagonist's message to his readers is 'If I could break free from my inheritance and my circumstance, so can you'" (208–9). Yet, in spite of his efforts to find picaresque elements in Cervantes's works, he is compelled to admit the basic divergence between Cervantes's art and the picaresque as seen in Alemán: "It is likely that Cervantes found *Guzmán* objectionable for its preaching and for its direct haranguing of the reader, two procedures that he never employed without irony, or without the mediation of a different voice" (218). Dunn goes on to point out that one of the triumphs of Cervantes's art is the play of many voices, a polyphony to which the voice of the narrator is subtly responsive, varying its own tone and distance. "With his vocation for theater, Cervantes was not inclined to allow a single voice either to define the imagined world or to hold uncontested sway over it" (219). It is therefore not surprising that Cervantes did not follow *Lazarillo* and *Guzmán* in adopting the first-person narration throughout, "for to have done so would have deprived him of the opportunity for multiple perspectives and narratorial comment" (219). The influence of the picaresque is ultimately felt with anxiety by Cervantes, yet wittily sublimated: Dunn quotes with approval Joaquin Casalduero's phrase, "Cervantes skirts the picaresque without wanting to plunge right in" (219).

Finally, in *Celestina's Brood: Continuities of the Baroque in Spanish and Latin American Literature*, Roberto González Echevarría devotes a long chapter (pages 45–65) to the relationship between Cervantes and the picaresque. His point of departure is Harry Sieber's interpretation of *Lazarillo*. Sieber, in *Language and Society in La Vida de Lazarillo de Tormes*, sees in young Lázaro a lad trying (and succeeding) to survive by means of adjusting to social pressures and changes by mastering the codes of language and society. The greatest value in Sieber's book, González Echevarría points out, is the way in which he underlines the major preoccupation in the picaresque: the emergence of writing and its relation to authority. Lázaro subverts and preserves authority at the same time. He learns enough from the blindman to blind him, but his own authority at the end is based on his own willed blindness to his wife's infidelity (González Echevarría 53). González Echevarría goes on to state: "though Cervantes never wrote a picaresque following Alemán's model, he did leave a complex critique of how this new literature was changing the rules of the game" (53–54). In *El casamiento engañoso* and *El coloquio de los perros* Cervantes "reveals how the picaresque has an inner connectedness provided by the way in which the turning points of a picaresque *vida* allude, through appeal to a metaphoric field drawn for sexuality, to the origin and disposition of writing" (57). By uncovering the metaphoric stratum in the picaresque text, Cervantes lays bare a contradiction at the core of this new form of writing: it pretends to be a legal document, related to truth and authority, yet its inner connections remit us to literature, not to the outside world of power and authority. Thus Cervantes has reached a sort of "metapicaresque." Whether his attitude may be described as parody or metapicaresque, both González Echevarría's conclusions and those of other critics seem to validate Casalduero's basic idea: Cervantes surveys the picaresque, goes around it, inspects it, but never fully plunges into its core, its system of values, its technical and ethical approach to literature, and to the description of man's relationship to society and the cosmos.

Looking back to the beginning of this essay, to the role of the discovery and conquest of the Americas by Columbus, Cortés, Pizarro, and so many others, a process that can be described also as an "encounter of cultures" in which both sides fight each other but also learn from each other, groping toward a synthesis that has eluded us yet tantalizes us and appeals to us from the future, we can place the picaresque novels on the side of the fight and the conquest of a new space, a new awareness. Conquests do not take place without bloodshed and destruction. The picaresque novels created a new space for literature, yet the realism they defined was only part of what realism could be. Ideology was a hidden luggage that picaresque writers carried into literature. Sometimes the target of their ideology was the establishment, the status quo, the very fabric of society with its centers of power and oppression. A strong attraction for utopias of all kinds is a characteristic trait of Renaissance thought. The picaresque novel may have produced the shadow image of the many positive Utopias created in Renaissance times, a negative Utopia that in its humble way attempted to validate the positive Renaissance utopias that never came to life. If the world as the picaresque authors describe is so bad, so corrupted, it is perhaps because it is the mirror image, inverted and distorted, of a much better world, the opposite world of Platonic ideas and Christian principles. It offers us a clear-cut choice, a smooth flat image, a "yes-or-no" approach to our view of the world.

Cervantes, on the other hand, gives us an ambiguous multifaceted presentation of lives coming into being, influencing each other, coming to terms with each other, coexisting, evolving before our eyes. Realism is not absolute truth versus false illusion, but rather uncertain, free, unforeseeable life unfolding in time, without a single point of view presented in advance, accepting doubt and uncertainty, giving ugliness, physical and moral ugliness, its place besides idealized Platonic beauty and integrating both in an overview that could be called a synthesis but is too fluid and changing to admit of a single definition. Cervantes is thus not Columbus, discovering uncharted land, which is precisely what the writers of picaresque novels had already achieved, but Cortés, subduing the new lands, bringing them closer to the old metropolis, and transforming them in an enduring way. His conquest and transformation of the picaresque lands will be acknowledged later by Fielding, Stendhal, Flaubert, Galdós, and many other great novelists. The empire created by him in the lands of the novel has turned out to be more durable even than the empire conquered by Cortés: it has lasted almost four centuries and it remains even today prosperous and expanding.

NOTES

1. Quoted by Timothy Forte, *The World of Bruegel* (New York: Time-Life Books, 1968) 99.

2. Forte 99.

3. Forte 17.

4. "Por su ambiente y protagonistas bien se ve que *Rinconete y Cortadillo* pertenecen al mundo de la novela picaresca. En líneas generales, así es. Pero Cervantes, que tantos préstamos tomó de todos los moldes literarios de su tiempo, los rompía cada vez al henchirlos con su propia fuerza y medida. De la narración picaresca habitual se diferencia el *Rinconete* en aspectos formales, o de técnica más bien diríamos: estos pícaros cernantinos no cuentan su propia vida, según norma creada por el *Lazarillo* y seguida por todos los demás" (Alborg 91).

5. "Parece que nos encontramos en el mundo de la picaresca, pero observamos que Rincón y Cortado no son pacientes, sino agentes de la acción. En la picaresca se nos presenta siempre al hombre en su choque con la vida, adquiriendo una experiencia a costa de su dolor. Indefenso, en su salida al mundo, en su nacer, la vida le despierta y abre los ojos para que, echando una mirada a su alrededor, contemple la bajeza y villanía humana" (Casalduero 103–4).

6. "La novela picaresca es independiente de él [Cervantes], se desarrolló antes que él, camina por otros rumbos: Cervantes no la imita nunca, ni siquiera en *Rinconete y Cortadillo*, que es un cuadro de género tomado directamente del nat ural, no una idealización de la astucia famélica como *Lazarillo de Tormes*, ni una profunda psicología de la vida extrasocial como *Guzmán de Alfarache*. Corre por las páginas de *Rinconete* una intensa alegría, un regocijo luminoso, una especia de indulgencia estética que depura todo lo que hay de feo y de criminal en el modelo" (Menéndez y Pelayo I: 398–399).

WORKS CITED

Alborg, Juan Luis. *Cervantes*. Madrid: Gredos, 1966.

Blanco Aguinaga, Carlos. "Cervantes and the Picaresque Mode." *Cervantes: A Collection of Critical Essays*. Ed. Lowry Nelson Jr. Englewood Cliffs, N.J.: Prentice-Hall, 1969.

Casalduero, Joaquín. *Sentido y forma de las Novelas Ejemplares*. Buenos Aires: Imprenta y Casa Editora Coni, 1943.

Castro, Américo. *El pensamiento de Cervantes*. Madrid, 1925.

Dunn, Peter N. *Spanish Picaresque Fiction: A New Literary History*. Ithaca and New York: Cornell Univ. Press, 1993.

González Echevarría, Roberto. *Celestina's Brood: Continuities of the Baroque in Spanish and Latin American Literature*. Durham and London: Duke Univ. Press, 1993.

Menéndez y Pelayo, Marcelino. "Cultura literaria de Miguel de Cervantes y elaboración del Quijote." In *Obras completas*. Santander: Edición Nacional. 1941.

Sieber, Harry. *Language and Society in La Vida de Lazarillo de Tormes*. Baltimore: Johns Hopkins Univ. Press, 1978.

ROBERTO GONZÁLEZ ECHEVARRÍA

Introduction to Don Quixote

Miguel de Cervantes Saavedra's masterpiece has endured because it focuses on literature's foremost appeal: to become another, to leave a typically embattled self for another closer to one's desires and aspirations. This is why *Don Quixote* has often been read as a children's book and continues to be read by or to children. Experience and life's blows teach us our limits and erode the hope of living up to our dreams, but our hope never vanishes. It is the soul's pith, the flickering light of being, the spiritual counterpart to our DNA's master code. When the hero regains his sanity at the end of Part II, he dies. As the last chances of living an imaginary life disappear, so must life itself. Don Quixote's serene passing reflects this understanding; he knows that the dream of life is over, and as a Neoplatonist and Christian, his only hope now is to find the true life after death.

Stories endure because they either express an archetype or create a new one. The epic and other oral narratives, including tragedy, retell known stories: think of Ulysses, Oedipus, Roland, the Cid. *Don Quixote* creates an archetype that is, appropriately, the archetype of type—the founding story of printed literature.[1] It is the tale of the reader, who indulges his imaginative needs not in a collective setting such as the theatre or the public square, but alone with his private yearnings, listening to his inner voices and those to which he gives life in his soul's stage as he scans the pages. Because of print

From *The Ingenious Hidalgo: Don Quixote de la Mancha*. Translated by John Rutherford. © Roberto González Echevarría, 2001. All rights reserved.

the reader is more educated; his memory is not only his or his people's, but that of many other individuals and cultures. Unlike those listening to singers or actors performing, the reader can go back and replay a scene, relish again what he liked, giving his own tempo to the unfolding of the story, taking time to let the pleasure of his imaginings sink in slowly or flipping the pages quickly to come to the end of an adventure and learn his hero's fate. This is what we, the readers of *Don Quixote*, imagine that the hero himself did as he read his cherished romances of chivalry. It is what we ourselves do as we savour our favorite passages, rereading isolated episodes, suspending the malleable time of fiction to postpone or really just forget our own inevitable demise.

Alone with ourselves and a book we can be children again. You cannot get up in the theatre and challenge an actor, and you would be smothered by the crowd if you interrupted the minstrel's performance. But in our own private space, huddled under the cloak of our fantasies with the book, we can counsel our hero, sigh for a damsel, shout insults at the wrongdoers, and enter the fiction in soul, if not in body. This last thing is, of course, what Don Quixote attempted to do: to bring his reader's imaginings to the bruising world of tangible reality and to the withering present. The book's archetype would not be complete if the hero remained in the ideal world of literature. Human desire is all too human; it longs for actualization in bodies and things, in the here and now of the sensory and the sensual. These are, of course, not as pliable as our fantasies and the world of books, and therein lies *Don Quixote*'s power—and the frontier between children's stories and those for adults.

There was nothing even remotely like *Don Quixote* before 1605, when the novel appeared. There were chivalric, pastoral, and Byzantine romances; epics in the style of Ludovico Ariosto's; stories like Giovanni Boccaccio's or, closer in time, Malteo Bandello's; and of course, picaresque novels since the publication in 1554 of *La vida de Lazarillo de Tormes* and in 1599 the defining *Primera parte de la vida del pícaro Guzmán de Alfarache*. Shakespeare and Molière worked within established theatrical conventions dating back to the Greeks, as did Cervantes when he wrote plays. But *Don Quixote*, which drew from all the prose genres that preceded it (and some poetic ones, too), had no beaten paths to follow.[2] In fact, such is the book's novelty that this novelty is incorporated as an issue into its own fabric. Don Quixote is too old to be a picaresque anti-hero, an epic champion, a pastoral lover, or a knight, and as a petty nobleman of the lowest rank he would make an unlikely courtier. So much for the available literary roles. Protagonists his age, even in Cervantes's other works, were usually husbands cuckolded by their younger wives or sages beyond desire or adventure left, to voice useless warnings to the young. As much else in *Don Quixote*, the parts do not fit, provoking laughter, to be sure, but also wonder that leads to profound reflection. This is why Georg Lukács calls the novelistic genre, whose founding was *Don Quixote*, "the epic of a world that has been abandoned by God," and adds that "the objectivity of the novel is the mature man's knowledge that meaning can never quite penetrate reality, but that without meaning, reality would disintegrate into the nothingness of inessentiality."[3] It is as difficult to overstate *Don Quixote*'s originality as it is to relive the surprise of its first readers when it reached their hands.

Postromantic habits of thought have led some to make Cervantes into a rebel or an outcast, if not the member of a religious minority chafing under oppression. How could the author of such an original book, so deviously ironic, not be working against established authority? The paucity of documentary evidence about Cervantes's life has allowed for no small amount of speculation along these lines, fueled by commonplaces about the Spain of the Counter-Reformation, redolent with hooded inquisitors, and by the racial and religious strife of our own era. It is just as hard to disprove as to prove anything about Cervantes, given how little is known, but what we do know, together with a sensible reading of his works, makes it reasonably clear that the author of *Don Quixote* was a loyal Spanish Catholic, and a patriotic one at that. Spaniards did not have to stop being Spanish or Catholic to be audacious and modern. Younger than Cervantes, Diego Velázquez, a genius in his art, was a court painter, and his contemporary, Pedro Calderón de la Barca, a major playwright also at the court, wrote more than a hundred *autos sacramentales* celebrating the eucharist. Like them, Cervantes probed pitilessly into the human condition, speculated about the nature of his own art, and produced masterpieces in sharp dialogue with the greatest works of the Western tradition. One of the outstanding features of Cervantes's Spain was the plethora of artistic and literary luminaries, sometimes within a few blocks of one another in Madrid: El Greco, Lope de Vega, Francisco Zurbarán, Tirso de Molina, Luis de Góngora, Francisco de Quevedo, and many others. This is why it is called the Golden Age in conventional literary histories. We will never know what produces a talent like Cervantes's, but commonplaces about rebelliousness in the contemporary sense should be the first to be discarded.

Cervantes's life, though far from easy, was relatively ordinary for someone of his class and background. His commonality, in fact, is relevant to the genesis of *Don Quixote*, to his career as a writer, and to literary history. It was new for someone who lacked social rank and a thorough humanistic education to dare to become an author. With Mateo Alemán and Lope de Vega, Cervantes belongs to the first generation of writers who attempt to make a living from their craft, creating new literary genres that deviate from Renaissance theory and practice.[4] Lope de Vega, writing prolifically and mostly for the theatre, succeeded. Cervantes did not, and he had to depend (futilely and sometimes pathetically) on the support of aristocratic patrons. This precarious professional status, which undermined his authority as a writer, is why Cervantes so often incorporated himself in his fiction and the humblest cause for the notorious self-reflexivity of his work. With what authority, other than the weight of my own mundane experience, do I dare to write this book? How can I, a lowly being, dare to pretend to be the source of these inventions? Are they mine, and if so in what way? Cervantes realized that he was his own most alluring mystery, and that his story as writer was the most interesting of all. *Don Quixote* is the tale of the reader because it is also that of the writer.

Even if Cervantes led a fairly ordinary life, it was rich in experiences, and it is projected not only onto obviously autobiographical stories, such as the captive's in Part I, but onto nearly all the lives told in *Don Quixote*. It also informs the overall structure of the book, which tells Don Quixote's life by adhering not to Renaissance poetic formulas about well-wrought plots but rather to the picaresque *vida*. A life told by someone like Cervantes, who had lived almost his own entire life, is a shape understandable to all, not just to those steeped in the classics and their commentators. Cervantes being Cervantes, however, tells the life of Don Quixote as the character he wills himself to be, with little or no information about his "real" life, meaning his family background and how he arrived at the decision to become a knight-errant. But all the stories in *Don Quixote* are subsumed into that of the hero's life as the novel unfolds toward its natural and expected conclusion in his death. Cervantes's transmutation of his own experiences into the stuff of literature has its specular image in the hero's efforts to elevate his life into fiction. Cervantes and Don Quixote find each other in the book.

Throughout his life Cervantes met with repeated failures and misfortunes; when literary recognition at last came, it brought few worldly or—spiritual rewards—it was as ironic a turn of events as those in his fictions. Born in Alcalá de Henares, a university town a few miles east of Madrid, probably on September 29, 1547, Miguel was the fourth of Rodrigo de Cervantes's and Leonor de Cortinas's seven children. Had his family been wealthy or enjoyed exalted aristocratic status, his not being a firstborn male would have added to Cervantes's woes later on. But Rodrigo, though he belonged to the gentry like Don Quixote (an *hidalgo*), was a man of modest means who was once even incarcerated for nonpayment of debts. In 1564, when Miguel was seventeen, Rodrigo stated in a document that he was a "surgeon," a profession that was then barely above that of barber and that neither required much education nor produced much income. Nothing definite is known about Miguel's early education, but it has been inferred that he studied with the Jesuits in Córdoba and Seville and with the humanist Juan López de Hoyos in Madrid. He was then in his late teens and early twenties, had published some poems, and had had his first scrape with the law for wounding a man in a duel. As a result of this incident he left in 1570 for Rome, where he joined the retinue of Cardinal Julio Acquaviva, having duly given proof, as was required in Spain, that he was of "clean blood" (having no Jewish or Arabic ancestors) and an *hidalgo*. Italy, where he enlisted in the Spanish forces deployed there under John of Austria, was a decisive intellectual experience for Cervantes; but nothing was as traumatic as his military exploits, which literally marked him for life. At the naval battle of Lepanto, fought against the Turkish fleet in 1571, Miguel went on deck for hand-to-hand combat and fought bravely though he was ill with a fever. A harquebus shot to his left arm maimed him for life and led, in the Spanish-speaking world, to the rhyming epithet by which he is known to schoolchildren: "el manco de Lepanto," the one-handed man from Lepanto. He was proud of his wound, a badge of courage and loyalty that he boasted about as late as the prologue to Part II of *Don Quixote*, which appeared in 1615, a year before his death. From then on, Cervantes also frequently petitioned rewards from the Crown for his distinguished military record.

In spite of his injury, Cervantes continued his military service, but when he was finally furloughed in 1575 and had begun his trek home, he suffered a greater misfortune: he and others were seized by Barbary pirates and taken hostage to Algiers. Hostage-taking was rampant in the contested Mediterranean. The letters attesting to his military exploits, which Cervantes planned to use in his pleas before the court, led his captors to believe that they had stumbled upon a greater prize than they had expected. After three failed escape attempts, he was finally ransomed in 1580 and made his way back to Spain. He was twenty-eight when he was captured, thirty-three when he regained his freedom. Cervantes had wasted his late twenties and early thirties as a slave in Algiers, an experience that would enrich his fiction, but at a great price.

As if trying to make up for lost time, Cervantes wrote several plays upon his return to Spain, among them *La destrucción de Numancia* (his best) and *Los tratos de Argel*, both staged in Madrid in 1581. He also wrote and published in 1584 a pastoral novel, *La Galatea*, which met with relative success and shows hints of what was to follow in the mixture of styles and the intrusion of erotic violence in the ideal world of the shepherds. Or, as Richard L. Predmore eloquently put it, "he began to see how myths could be deflated with injections of real life and real life ennobled in mythical robes;

he began to explore the possibility of catching the complexity of human life in a net of ambivalence."[5] But Cervantes was already thirty-seven years old; his work for the theatre—the only profitable literary activity—was only modestly successful, and he had to earn a living to support his new wife Catalina de Palacios Salazar Vozmediano. It was not his only responsibility. As a result of a liaison with, another woman, Ana Franca de Rojas, Cervantes also had an illegitimate daughter, Isabel de Saavedra. And so he obtained a position as commissioner and tax collector in Andalusia, around Seville, as the Crown was stockpiling wealth and supplies for what would be the disastrous Armada of 1588. Cervantes suffered terrible ordeals in this job, then as now an unpopular one. Disputes over the handling of his accounts landed him in Seville's jail, and he was once excommunicated by the general vicar of that city. Throughout his forties Cervantes was imprisoned several times, resulting in more experiences that enriched his work, but again at a steep price. He claimed in the prologue to Part I of *Don Quixote* that it was in Seville's jail that he first had the idea for *Don Quixote*.

In the waning years of the sixteenth century Cervantes was in Valladolid, though he also spent time at Esquivias, where his wife owned vineyards, and he shuttled back and forth to Seville because of his job. He was by then writing *Don Quixote*, which went to press in 1604 and appeared early the next year. Cervantes was about to turn fifty-eight when the book was published, always an advanced age to begin making your mark as writer, but particularly then, when it was rare to live to be sixty. He had only ten years of life left, but they were as productive and successful as anyone could hope for. *Don Quixote* went through several printings and was soon translated into English and French. Publishers were suddenly interested in printing not only Cervantes's fiction, but also, his theater. In 1613 the *Novelas ejemplares*, a splendid collection of twelve short novels, was published, as was *Viaje del Parnaso* in 1614, a long poem in which Cervantes surveys the literary scene of his time. That same year, an apocryphal second part of *Don Quixote* appeared, signed by someone calling himself Alonso Fernández de Avellaneda. Cervantes, who was halfway through writing his own second part, was spurred to finish. It appeared in 1615, as did a volume of his plays. He was ill and rushing to complete what he thought would be his masterpiece: the Byzantine romance *Los trabajos de Persiles y Sigismunda*. He did finish it, but he did not live to see it published, dying in Madrid on April 22, 1616.[6] The *Persiles* was published posthumously the next year. In its moving prologue, Cervantes bid farewell to his friends and mused with humour about his late-found fame with the same composed tone of Don Quixote's parting words on his deathbed.

Cervantes's irony, elegant self-mockery, and disclaimers of authorship are certainly at the core of his mind and work. In *Don Quixote* the author pretends to be merely the translator of a manuscript written by Arabic historian Cide Hamete Benengeli. He dramatizes this by stopping the action in Chapter 8 of Part I, protesting that he has run out of text and then telling an elaborate story about how he found the remaining chapters and secured the services of a translator. Thus the rest of the novel would be the work of this translator, who is intrusive enough to append impudent comments about the characters or the plausibility of their speech. There are also remarks by the author about the translator's comments, as well as on the incongruity of the high-flown rhetoric of certain passages. Many segments are parodies of recognizable literary genres, such as the chivalric romances and the pastoral, as well as the rhetoric of the courtly love tradition, full of paradoxes and trite figures. And so there are layers upon layers of discourse, commenting on one another, blurring the source, intention, and ultimately the legitimacy and truth of the final product. Further ironic distancing is provided by the blatantly literary nature of the "found manuscript" device, which makes the whole thing appear to be a sham from the start, and by allusions to Cervantes's other works, such as *La Galatea* in the episode of the scrutiny of the knight's library. If the Cervantes mentioned by the priest is the same as the one on the cover of the book we read, is he a fictional character in *Don Quixote* or its author? Is the whole of reality a book whose characters we are and the author of which is too grandiose for us to fathom? If we are on the same level of reality as this author-character, the inescapable conclusion is that we, too, inhabit a fictional realm. But if Don Quixote's inability to distinguish literary fiction from reality is what makes him a madman, where does that leave us?

We are aware, of course, that all this charade is in jest, but knowing it is also part of the game. Yet we do continue to play it, and there is the rub and the road that leads to the deepest and darkest recesses of this series of interlocking ironies: does Don Quixote really believe in his fictions, as when he emerges from Montesinos's cave in Part II and tells a tall tale that he insists others should believe, or does he act in the knowledge that it is all bogus? The mirror play leads to a disquieting questioning of the self's coherence, of the mind's very existence as a thinking, feeling, and willful entity to which we can attribute our actions and beliefs. Joaquín Casalduero maintains, in a disturbing insight, that at the Duque's house, when Don Quixote is finally treated like the knight-errant he wants to be, the hero has a distanced, ironic perception of himself as a parody of his desires: "Don Quixote, a spiritual man, sees his own image as a knight-errant, which he had heretofore always contemplated in the purity of his own actions: it is an image of his external self. The honors, social status, the fame that society can grant a man of the spirit are nothing but a burlesque image, a distortion of his inner life."[7] It is at this level that irony's humour becomes serious indeed, and Cervantes's disclaimers as author acquire a deeper meaning, one that affects the very nature of *Don Quixote*.

In Cervantes's delightful prologue to Part I he calls himself stepfather to the book, yet he tells the reader how he is hard at work writing the very prologue that he is reading because he truly does not know how to legitimize his relationship to t(his) creation. A helpful friend then appears (Cervantes always favours dialogue, as the splitting of his authorial self here attests), and tells him to make up what today we would call "an index of names" or bibliography, to lend authority to the book. By suggesting that the tradition from which *Don Quixote* presumably emerges can be fabricated, Cervantes is subtly underscoring the book's and his own originality. The literature produced by the new writers will be new, therein its value in every sense, including monetary.

Consideration of *Don Quixote*'s composition is not limited to the prologue and to the passages mentioned about the origins of Cide Hamete's manuscript and the commentaries by the translator and the author or transcriber: it is embedded in the games of chance, improvisation, and error that are so much a part of the book. It is a play that takes us outside the fiction. One topic of *Don Quixote* criticism since the publication of Part I in 1605 has centered on Cervantes's various gaffes or oversights. Though there are others, the most blatant is the appearance of Sancho on his donkey when it had been stolen from him in an earlier episode. Cervantes makes light of this in the prologue to Part II, though he did make hurried emendations of the book between printings of Part I. But the errors feed right into the issue of authorship, authorial intention, irony, and the structure of the novel. In short, they undermine the authority of the author and highlight his ironic stance before the final product. Is this mine, the issue of my imagination, or is it partly the product of chance? How much of its creation obeyed my intentions? Should I not humbly accept the role of chance in the composition of the book and admit with humility my crass errors, where my limited powers could not totally master the universe of fiction that I tried to invent?

So effective was Cervantes's ironic stance that it allowed him to deal brilliantly with the biggest threat to face him as author: the publication of Avellaneda's spurious *Don Quixote*, purporting to be a continuation of the original. It now seems as if Cervantes would have had to invent Avellaneda had he not existed (it is not known who this author really was, for it is fairly certain that he used a pseudonym). Cervantes was writing Chapter 59 of Part II when the rival book appeared in 1614. Avellaneda had misread Cervantes's masterpiece, as did most of his contemporaries, reducing it to its comic elements. He also insulted Cervantes, mocking him for, among other things, his physical handicap, and boasted that his book would ruin the sales of the real Part II if and when it appeared. But Avellaneda had only played into Cervantes's hand. His response was, as Stephen Gilman put it, "to encompass [Avellaneda] in a web of irony."[8] He absorbed the fake book and pirate author into the fiction of his own, even having his novelistic characters attest to the counterfeit nature of their doubles. Avellaneda became another one of Cervantes's characters, one of the fictions that play at undermining Cervantes's authority, while at the same time strengthening it.

Cervantes's own doubts about his agency as author tend to lend credence to a theory about the genesis of *Don Quixote* proposed in 1920 by the noted Spanish scholar and philologist Ramón Menéndez Pidal.[9] Characteristically, as the greatest expert of Spanish popular balladry, Menéndez Pidal maintained that the source of the book was an *entremés*, a comic one-act play, in which a man goes insane trying to reenact the exploits of great epic and chivalric heroes sung about in the *romances*, or Spanish ballads. This *Entremés de los romances* would have given Cervantes the idea for a short novella, like those he published in 1613 as *Novelas ejemplares*, about a gentleman who suffered the same fate as Don Quixote trying to imitate the actions of knights in the romances of chivalry. Be that as it may, the most significant part of the theory is that *Don Quixote* was going to be a novella that would end with the hero's first return home, when he is picked up by his neighbour Pero Alonso while babbling lines from a ballad about Baldwin and the Marquis of Mantua, characters in the Charlemagne cycle. If that were so, the rest of *Don Quixote* grows out of this narrative kernel, being made up as it goes without model or plan. The fortuity of the narrative structure, which depends on chance encounters at roads and inns, would mirror this fortuitous beginning, sharing with it a delicate balance between chance and invention. It is the blueprint for errancy and error, as well as for the questioning of authorial design.

The most significant addition to Don Quixote as the plot proceeded beyond the first sally was Sancho Panza, whose presence allowed Cervantes to indulge his penchant for dialogue and multiple perspectives. Sancho gives a voice to the world of slovenly inns, innkeepers, prostitutes, muleteers, criminals—a whole panoply of people living in the present as they had for centuries—that Cervantes had adapted from picaresque fiction and observed first-hand in his travels as a tax-collector and in the jail. In terms of the development of the novel as genre, Sancho is as important as Don Quixote because he develops as the plot progresses and circumstances place him in new situations. A topic in Cervantes criticism has been that Don Quixote becomes Sanchified and Sancho Quixotized as their lives intertwine. Cervantes removed from picaresque fiction the inherent penchant for evil of characters drawn from the lower classes, and Sancho is the prime example, but only one of many. Maritornes, the grotesque prostitute at Juan Palomeque's inn, is kind and tender to Sancho and Don Quixote, and Ginés de Pasamonte is a clever rascal but not malevolent by nature. Sancho governs his bogus Island of Barataria with common sense, honesty, and compassion. Through him Cervantes shows that any man can rise to the occasion on the strength of his God-given wit and goodness.

But Sancho's most important role is as foil to the knight's deranged plans; warning him of his wild misperceptions. "What giants?" asks Sancho when Don Quixote points to the windmills and rejoices in the anticipation of adventure. Of course, Sancho becomes enmeshed in Don Quixote's fictions not only because he is gullible but also because of the need to lie to get out of difficult situations. He winds up defending the existence of Dulcinea in Part II to cover earlier prevarications and falls for the Duque's contrivances. All of this is hilariously funny, particularly in the original because Cervantes had an uncanny ear for the variations of Spanish according to social class and region. The point is, however, that Sancho is not in possession of the truth because of his simple nature and common sense. Neither he nor Don Quixote is ultimately right, as the episode of Mambrino's helmet shows: the reader knows that it is a barber's basin, but from outside the fiction and aided by the narrator. In the fiction, as no doubt in the reader's own world, the truth is a matter of negotiation and compromise. Sancho is as befuddled as Don Quixote because he, too, is human and he also has a penchant for error and self-delusion in the midst of a changing reality. Together Sancho and Don Quixote sketch the shape of the emerging modern self.

If the Renaissance, or early modern period as it is now called, meant renewed faith in the human capacity to make, organize, and control—from politics to urban design, from painting and sculpture to architecture—*Don Quixote* signals that the resulting new science and philosophy have also led to radical doubts about the self. Sancho's island is the distorted version of utopias such as Thomas More's and well-run kingdoms like the ones envisaged by Niccolò Machiavelli. The wooden horse Clavileño may not have soared to real heights, yet his flight mocks the limitations of ancient conceptions of the cosmos, with solid spheres and fixed stars. The boundlessness of the universe discovered and contemplated brought about a crisis whose names are Galileo Galilei and René Descartes. The emerging modern self experiences a frightening freedom when, armed with its limited if autonomous powers, it faces the immensity of the universe. It is Don

Quixote setting out alone on his first sally, at dawn, heading aimlessly toward the broad Castilian plain. It is the starry night sky seen by the characters through the ramshackle roof of Palomeque's flimsy inn, which offers no shelter and provides no limit. Descartes's relentless questioning left him only with a self that exists because it thinks and poses questions. Literature allowing more margin than philosophy to speculate, Cervantes ventured further, questioning the nature and cogency of that self. This is the issue raised by Don Quixote's madness. What is a sane self? Cervantes begins where Descartes leaves off. His response to this quandary was a comical hero too old to be enmeshed in his family romance (there is nothing about his parents) and an author too jaded to have confidence in the effectiveness of his own will and intentions to create.

The elusiveness of Cervantes's irony has led some to think that he was a follower of Erasmus and to view *In Praise of Folly* as an important influence on *Don Quixote*. Whether Cervantes had read the Rotterdam humanist or been a follower of his many disciples in the Peninsula is difficult to prove or disprove.[10] But it is clear that Cervantes's irony goes further than Erasmus's. *In Praise of Folly* is an elegant exercise in doublespeak: everything Folly says in her monologue is played off against the sane way a Christian should approach faith and doctrine. There is no stable truth against which to measure Cervantes's irony, which whorls in a spiral of infinite evasiveness. This, of course, is more daring than Erasmus's presumably sacrilegious ideas (such as reading the Bible directly in Hebrew and Greek). In *El pensamiento de Cervantes*, Américo Castro went as far as to call the author of *Don Quixote* "a skillful hypocrite."[11] Castro masterfully argued in that book that Spanish humanists had kept up with philosophical and scientific developments elsewhere in Europe, particularly in Italy, and had devised a method to absorb their findings without provoking the Church. It was a system of double truth: the universe was guided by its own laws, free of God and religious doctrine, which however enveloped it all, including potential discrepancies and contradictions. One's individual opinions were left out, as if the whole thing could not affect personal faith. It was a gesture similar to the formula by which laws sent to the New World irrelevant to local conditions were received: "se acata, pero no se cumple" (obeyed, but not enacted).

It is worthy of notice that of the two literary archetypes created during Spain's Golden Age, Don Quixote and Don Juan, it is the second that has been most often taken up by later writers, not to mention by composers. Don Quixote's musical legacy cannot compare to Don Juan's. Perhaps this is so because eros will always be more appealing than the reflective humour of Cervantes's masterpiece and the desire of the protagonist to be other than himself. But the disparity is obvious only if one takes the mad gentleman to be the sole archetype in the novel. From within literature, however, the most important character in Cervantes's novel is the narrator, the implicit author whose ironic games concerning his product are the foundation of the modern novel. This was understood immediately by writers such as Alain-René Lesage, Laurence Sterne, and Henry Fielding, who picked up Cervantes's legacy explicitly, and by every novelist who has put pen to paper since then. A host of modern Latin American writers—Jorge Luis Borges, Alejo Carpentier, Gabriel García Márquez, Carlos Fuentes—have understood that Cervantes, more than Don Quixote, is the origin of narrative fiction and have turned him into a character or a problem in their works.[12] Don Quixote, of course, has heirs of his own in Stendhal's Julien Sorel, Gustave Flaubert's Emma Bovary, Herman Melville's Captain Ahab, and James Joyce's Leopold Bloom. In a memorable book, René Girard argued that desire mediated by literature harkened back to *Don Quixote* and was the essence of the novel as genre.[13]

Leo Spitzer and Erich Auerbach coincided in locating what is "Cervantine" in the difficulty of pinning Cervantes down on any given topic, in his play of perspectives. Auerbach states that "the theme of the mad country gentleman who undertakes to revive knight-errantry gave Cervantes an opportunity to present the world as play in that spirit of multiple, perspective, non-judging, and even non-questioning neutrality which is a brave form of wisdom."[14] Spitzer's brilliant analysis of linguistic perspectivism in *Don Quixote* (beginning with the uncertainty about the mad gentleman's last name: Quesada, Quejana, Quijada) concludes that "in our novel, things are represented, not for what they are in themselves but only as things spoken about or thought about; and this involves breaking the narrative presentation into two points of view ... the only unquestionable truth on which the reader may depend is the will of the artist who chose to break up a multivalent reality into different perspectives. In other words, perspectivism suggests an Archimedean principle outside the plot—and the Archimedes must be Cervantes himself."[15] But, of course, we have already seen how elusive Cervantes the author is. While agreeing with Spitzer's definition of Cervantine perspectivism, Ciriaco Morón Arroyo comments that the author of *Don Quixote* was no relativist when it came to morals and adds the following: "Perhaps we ought to point out here that perspectivism is inherent to Christian thought. Perspectivism as a form of modesty that recognizes the limits of all judgement and human knowledge is, indeed, Christian humility and intelligence in its strictest sense: the capacity to perceive the limit of our own creations: *eironeia*."[16]

To my mind the "Cervantine" is found in the ease, the elegance and apparent effortlessness, with which the intertwined and complicated stories, happening in different levels of the fiction, resolve themselves, with multiple suggestions about a variety of profound themes, none of which is mentioned directly or in abstract terms. A case in point is the episode in which Don Quixote attacks the wineskins, while dreaming that he is in pitched battle with Pandafilando de la Fosca Vista, the giant made up by Dorotea when she concocts the story about being Princess Micomicona. This story is a translation into chivalric fiction of what happened to her with her suitor Don Fernando, whose name cleverly rhymes with that of the giant. Like the giant, Don Fernando is a voracious lover of all; the Greek *pan* and *philos* give the clue here. Fernando and the giant are "Panphilanderers with a Menacing Gaze"—the gaze being the mark of lasciviousness and will to possess. As Javier Herrero, whose superb analysis of this scene I am following here, observes, the fact is that Don Quixote has by his actions slain the giant and brought to a happy conclusion Dorotea's ordeal.[17] This is all very funny, no doubt, except to the innkeeper whose wine has been spilled, but at the same time it is worthy of profound reflection. Here is a madman solving a real conflict while engaged in a dream battle with a giant who is the product of a lie. Don Quixote has become the instrument of a weird kind of Providence. An equally masterful, if even more complicated, design is the Pageant in the Forest in Part II, when Sancho's lies about Dulcinea result in a baroque performance in which the imaginary lady (a "metacharacter" invented by the other characters) materializes as a beautiful page who is playing her role. This transvestite Dulcinea opens a Pandora's box of suggestions and suggestiveness worthy of the most modern and daring of writers. As in Pandafilando's story, one senses here the presence of an ironic and elegant creator unwilling to show his hand any more than he has to, aware of the significance of it all yet feeling that it would be unworthy of him to point it out. The reader, this reader, gratefully understands, and humbly marvels at the unsurpassed mastery.

NOTES

1. See Ian P. Watt, *Myths of Modern Individuality: Faust Don Quixote, Don Juan, Robinson Crusoe* (New York: Cambridge University Press, 1996).

2. The genres mentioned are incorporated into the fiction of *Don Quixote* as characters afflicted by the same malady as the hero attempt to play out in real life roles drawn from books. Hence Marcela and Grisóstomo the pastoral, Cardenio the courtly lover, Ginés de Pasamonte the rogue and picaresque author, and so forth. In some cases, such as Grisóstomo's, the result turns out to be tragic.

3. *The Theory of the Novel: A Historico-Philosophical Essay on the Forms of Great Epic Literature* [1920], tr. Anna Bostock (Cambridge, Mass: MIT Press, 1971), p. 88.

4. See Otis H. Green, "Originality: The New Literary Genres," in his *Spain and the Western Tradition*, vol. 4 (Madison: University of Wisconsin Press, 1968), pp. 210–85.

5. *Cervantes* (New York: Dodd, Mead, 1973), p. 107.

6. The reader will note the proximity with the date of Shakespeare's death (April 23, 1616), but England had not adopted the Gregorian calendar, so the death of the two writers is separated by several more days.

7. *Sentido y forma del Quijote (1605–1615)* (Madrid: Ediciones ínsula, 1949), pp. 294–95.

8. "The Apocryphal *Quixote*," in *Cervantes Across the Centuries*, ed. Angel Flores and M. J. Bernardete (New York: The Dryden Press, 1947) p. 247.

9. There is an English version of this paper in *Cervantes Across the Centuries*, ed. Flores and Bernardete, pp. 32–55.

10. Spanish Erasmianism was studied by Marcel Bataillon in his monumental *Erasme et l'Espagne* (1937). The Spanish translation published in 1950 and 1960 by the Fondo de Cultura Económica in Mexico as *Erasmo y España* is an expanded version of the original.

11. Américo Castro, *El pensamiento de Cervantes*, Anejos de la Revista de Filología Española—Anejo VI (Madrid: Imprenta de la Librería y Casa Editorial Hernando, 1925), p. 249.

12. See my "Cervantes y la narrativa hispanoamericana moderna: Borges y Carpentier," *Unión* (Havana), 10, no. 37 (1999): 4–13.

13. *Deceit, Desire, and the Novel: Self and Other in Literary Structure* [1961], tr. Yvonne Freccero (Baltimore: Johns Hopkins University Press, 1965).

14. *Mimesis: The Representation of Reality in Western Literature* (Princeton, N.J.: Princeton University Press, 1953), p. 357.

15. "Linguistic Perspectivism in the *Don Quijote* [1948]," in *Cervantes*, ed. Harold Bloom (New York: Chelsea House, 1987), p. 22.

16. "La historia del cautivo y el sentido del *Quijote*," *Iberoromania* (Tübingen), 18 (1983): 103.

17. Javier Herrero, "Sierra Morena as Labyrinth: From Wildness to Christian Knighthood," *Modern Language Studies* 17, no. 1 (1981): 55–67.

DAVID QUINT

Cervantes's Method and Meaning

INTERLACE

Cervantes indicates to his reader how to read *Don Quijote*, as a whole and not as the sum of it parts, in the story of Leandra in Chapter 51, the last of the interpolated tales in Part One of *Don Quijote*. It is a kind of laboratory case set inside the novel to demonstrate one of the book's salient literary techniques, for it picks up echoes and details of *all* the other interpolated tales that precede it.

The charlatan soldier Vicente de la Roca, who runs off with Leandra, her jewels, and her father's money, is a debased version of the Captive, Captain Viedma, who recounts his escape from Algiers with his beloved Moor Zoraida, (Chapters 39–41). When the beautiful Leandra is compared to a miracle-working image ["imagen de milagros" (502; 506)] we are reminded of Zoraida, who brought about the Captive's "miraculous delivery" ["milagrosa libertad" (429; 431)], and who is closely associated with the Virgin Mary, whose name she takes as her own and whose images ["imágenes" (430; 432)] she recognizes when she first enters a church in Spain.[1] The phrase also anticipates Don Quijote's last exploit in the First Part, his attack on the disciplinants who are carrying an image of the Virgin Mary in the following Chapter 52. In its pastoral setting, and in the behavior of those lovers of Leandra who accuse her of disdain without ever having

From *Cervantes's Novel of Modern Times: A New Reading of Don Quijote*. © 2003 by Princeton University Press.

spoken to her, the episode obviously repeats the first of the interpolated stories, the episode of Grisóstomo and Marcela (Chapters 12–14). The songs that Vicente sings to Leandra evoke the story of Luis and Clara (Chapters 42–43). Leandra, the rich farmer's daughter who is seduced and abandoned, resembles Dorotea, dishonored and abandoned by Fernando (Chapter 28). The narrator of the tale, Eugenio, has a rival, Anselmo, whose name recalls the Anselmo of the "Curioso impertinente" (Chapters 33–35). When Eugenio, who has decided to blame the fickleness of women for his loss of Leandra, brawls with Don Quijote and Sancho in the next chapter, we should be reminded of Cardenio, who, similarly inveighing against the supposed falseness of Luscinda, fights with the hidalgo and his squire in the Sierra Morena (Chapter 24). Finally, when the braggart Vicente is said to claim that his right arm is his father, his deeds his lineage, and that as a soldier he owes nothing, even to the king (504; 507), he becomes a parodic mirror of Don Quijote himself, who in Chapter 4 had made the proverbial declaration that every man is the son of his own works (76; 57) and at the end of Chapter 45 had asserted to the police force of the Holy Brotherhood that he and other knights-errant were exempt from all jurisdiction (462; 465).[2]

As it recapitulates the episodes of Part One of Cervantes's novel, the story of Leandra suggests how these episodes interpolated into the adventures of Don Quijote and Sancho Panza are themselves interconnected. The stories of characters whom Don Quijote meets on his way (Marcela and Grisóstomo, Cardenio, Dorotea, Eugenio), the stories of the characters who arrive at the inn (the Captive, Don Luis, and Clara), the story of the "Curioso impertinente" that is labeled precisely as an interpolated tale, drawn out of a trunk and read at the inn, and, not least of all, the miniature chivalric romance that Don Quijote tells to Sancho in Chapter 21, itself another inset tale—these are all thematically linked not only to the deeds of knight and squire, but to one another. They take up the larger part of the narrative space of the first installment of the novel, and for long stretches can seem to crowd Don Quijote out of his own story.[3] The first readers of the novel appear to have objected particularly to the "Curioso impertinente"; Sansón Carrasco tells us in Chapter 3 of Part Two that they complained that the story "is out of place and has nothing to do with the history of his worship, Don Quijote" ["por no ser de aquel lugar, ni tiene que ver con la historia de su merced del señor don Quijote" (549; 562)]. Still later in Chapter 44, Cervantes seems to be answering his critics when the narrator Cide Hamete links the "Curioso impertinente" with the Captive's Tale as digressions and episodes that seem detachable from the rest of the book ["como separadas de la historia" (833; 848)].[4]

Cervantes is being ironic. These first critics were not strong readers.

And it is still one of the weaknesses of the tradition of criticism on *Don Quijote* that it has generally treated the novel's episodes individually rather than as integral parts whose mirroring relationship creates its larger whole.[5] In doing so, such criticism may have emphasized the picaresque elements of *Don Quijote* over its inheritance from the chivalric romances the novel sets out to destroy and replace.[6] To accomplish this satirical demolition, Cervantes treats the picaresque and the chivalric romance as inversions of one another, transforming the quest of his mad knight-errant into a series of picaresque wanderings. He signals the overlay and reciprocity of the modern and the medieval genres early on in Chapter 3 of the novel, when the first innkeeper whom Don Quijote meets poses as a retired knight and describes his own earlier picaresque career as thief and criminal as a series of chivalric adventures (69; 49).[7] Cervantes thus gives his novel the formal appearance of a picaresque narrative, a collection of disparate episodes, one thing after another. Claudio Guillén writes that the picaresque "novel is loosely episodic, strung together like a freight train and *apparently* with no other common link than the hero."[8] In *Lazarillo de Tormes*, the ur-picaresque novel that Cervantes evokes in Chapter 22, the hero, as his name implies, appears to die and be reborn from one episode to the next as if to denote the discrete quality of each and the discontinuity of his human experience. (So, to a certain extent, does Don Quijote dust himself off after each defeat, assess the damage to his body, and ride off to his next adventure.) Guillén is careful to suggest, however, that despite appearances, even the picaresque narrative finds ways to link its parts together.

For the purpose of making such connections, *Don Quijote* turns back to the model of chivalric romance itself. Cervantes's method of playing one episode of the novel off against another derives from and is inspired by the technique of narrative *interlace* ("entrelacement") that organizes the great chivalric romances of the Middle Ages such as the prose *Lancelot*.[9] The romance follows the careers of some eight or ten questing knights, telling a segment of one knight's story before turning to a segment of another's, and thus keeps multiple plots going at once. The plots parallel one another and may share common motifs, and the reader begins to realize that the romance coheres and generates meaning not so much from the endings of the knights' stories, which are hardly in sight, as from the juxtaposition of the stories and their reflection upon one another.[10] Narrative strands that initially seem to be discrete can turn out to be symbolically related. To take an example from the *Lancelot*: when one knight fights a giant in his story line, and another knight kills a villainous baron oppressing a damsel in his, we are invited to see the baron as a kind of giant.[11]

So, in a rather clear-cut Cervantine adaptation of this technique in

Chapter 29 of *Don Quijote*, Dorotea, cast by the Curate and Barber in the role of Princess Micomicona, tries to kiss the hands of Don Quijote after he has promised to champion her against the giant who persecutes her (295; 295). A few pages earlier Dorotea has in her own person tried to kiss the feet of Cardenio, who has promised to defend her honor against her seducer Don Fernando (290; 291). The reader sees the parallel between Dorotea's real-life situation and the chivalric scenario invented for the benefit of Don Quijote—Don Fernando is like a wicked giant, she is a genuine damsel-in-distress. Cervantes gives this narrative juxtaposition his typical psychological twist when Dorotea improvises upon and embroiders this scenario in Chapter 30: she seems quite conscious of the parallel and to be indulging in autobiography beneath the fiction that she is an exotic princess.[12] We may be led to a secondary reflection that if one inverts the parallel, the fantastic stories of chivalry may contain disguised versions of lived human experience in the first place.[13]

Interlace is the principle of narrative organization in Ludovico Ariosto's *Orlando furioso* (1516), the literary work that most deeply influenced Cervantes in *Don Quijote*.[14] Not only does Ariosto juxtapose, contrast, and compare the adventures of the myriad knights and ladies who zigzag across the map of his romance; he also introduces interpolated tales, often in the form of Bocaccian novellas, into its sprawling narrative. The "Curioso impertinente" is a rewriting of the two novellas in Canto 43 (9–46; 72–143) of the *Furioso* that recount husbands testing the fidelity of their wives, and Cervantes signals his debt by giving his overly curious husband Anselmo the same name as the jealous husband in Ariosto's second tale. It is important to emphasize that Ariosto builds these tales into the larger interlace structure of his poem: thus these stories of Mantuan and Ferrarese husbands and wives comment on the climactic marriage of the heroes Ruggiero and Bradamante, who will found the Este dynasty that produced Ariosto's patrons, the Cardinal of Ferrara and the Duchess of Mantua. In a more pointed example, the notorious, salacious novella that Ariosto advises his lady readers to skip in Canto 28 describes sexual intercourse with the conventional metaphor of horseback riding; in the next canto the mad Orlando rides the horse of his beloved Angelica to death in what is clearly a symbolic substitution for rape; in between, the woman-hating Rodomonte, for whom the novella was told, journeys by boat to save wear and tear on his own horse: the juxtaposition tells us something about men who treat women like horses, horses like women, horses better than women.[15]

Cervantes masters his own version of interlace in Part One of *Don Quijote*. While he does not present a series of concurrent stories and jump from one to another—though he *will* do something of this sort in Part Two when he alternates chapters between Don Quijote's experience in the castle of the Duke and Duchess and Sancho's tenure of his "governorship" (44–53)[16]—he makes full use, as I have already suggested, of the interpolated stories of other characters and of the interpolated tale itself. He establishes connections among them and between them and the main plot of Don Quijote's madness with an artistry that can be dizzying. Thus he requires his reader not only to understand a given episode of *Don Quijote* on its own terms, but to juxtapose it with other episodes that may at first appear unrelated to it. A motif central to one story will turn up displaced in a peripheral position in another, as seemingly out of place ("no ser de aquel lugar") as the entire interpolated tale of the "Curioso impertinente." But in this scheme, nothing, in fact, may be out of place in the novel; the apparently extraneous detail, no less than an entire digressive episode, can be found to fit into a larger web of meaning. The reader or critic does not need to share a romantic notion of the organic unity of the literary work of art or a classical aesthetic of the work's architectonic unity.[17] The practical experience of reading literature itself produces the axiom that precisely those elements of the text that on the face of it do not seem to fit—the digression, the subplot, the story-within-the-story—will almost always reward close attention and offer commentary, often through contrast and irony, upon a principal or central story. In Part One of *Don Quijote* the madness and career plans of Don Quijote reveal their full implications in the stories of the other characters that jostle for narrative space in the novel alongside his own. *Their* stories, reciprocally, are deepened by parallels among themselves—and to Don Quijote's motives, ideas, and behavior: an obvious, continuous irony of the novel suggests, sometimes gently, sometimes savagely, that these other characters are not much saner than the mad hidalgo.

ARMS AND LETTERS

The analyses that follow in this book seek to apply a method of reading *Don Quijote* by tracing and examining Cervantes's technique of interlacing his novel's episodes and of distributing its thematic motifs. They also propose an interpretation of the novel that emerges from this method. To suggest how one gets from the first to the second, I want to look now at two secondary instances of Cervantine interlace; they will give some idea of the technique in question. The first of my examples arches across nearly the entirety of Part One of the novel. It concerns the debate between arms and letters—that is, which is the nobler profession, that of the soldier or that of the man of learning?—a time-honored topos in Renaissance writing at least since the discussions of Castiglione's *Book of the Courtier* (1.42–46).[18]

Don Quijote, who is always ready to spout long passages from his reading, and who thereby repeatedly gains from those around him the opinion that he is a man of good sense when he is not pursuing his chivalric mania, gives an elaborate version of the debate of arms and letters in Chapters 37 and 38. The would-be knight naturally enough awards primacy to arms, whether or not he reflects the opinion of Cervantes, who could claim experience both as man of letters and as soldier. The author of *Don Quijote* had been wounded and lost the use of his left hand at the battle of Lepanto in 1571, as he tells us in the Prologue to Part Two, "the greatest occasion that present, past, or future ages have ever seen or can ever hope to see" ["la más alta ocasión que vieron los siglos pasados, los presentes, ni esperan ver los venideros" (526; 535)]. Cervantes weaves his character's version of this by now commonplace debate into a whole sequence of episodes in the novel, and we are invited to watch how its terms develop and change: the logic of this development will turn out to be *historical*, suggesting a movement from an earlier feudal social formation to the modern, money-driven society of Cervantes's age. This historical logic governs both the shape and the meaning of the first part of *Don Quijote*; it becomes a main subject of the larger novel.

The theme emerges as a joke that the Curate and Barber of Don Quijote's village make at Sancho Panza's expense when they greet him as he returns from the Sierra Morena on his mission to El Toboso and Dulcinea in Chapter 26. When Sancho tells them that he is to be rewarded with an island and governorship once his master rises through his prowess to become emperor or king, they play along and tell Sancho that it is very possible for Don Quijote "to become in time an emperor, as he had suggested, or at least archbishop, or something equally important" ["a ser emperador, como él decia, o, por lo menos, arzobispo, o otra dignidad equivalente" (260; 257)]. The offhand quip about the archbishop greatly worries the married Sancho, for he would be ineligible for the ecclesiastical benefices that Don Quijote in his capacity as archbishop-errant—one of the "arzobispos andantes," as Sancho calls them—would be able to bestow on him instead of the promised island. The Barber reassures him that Don Quijote will more easily become emperor than archbishop since he is "more of a soldier than a scholar" ["más valiente que estudiante"]. The contrast between Don Quijote's career options is thus cast explicitly in terms of the stereotyped opposition of arms and letters. Cervantes introduces this opposition in its most socially conservative form as one between martial aristocracy and church, in the feudal distinction between those who fight and those who pray.

These are the same backward-looking terms with which Don Quijote himself had already defined his mission as knight-errant much earlier in the novel in Chapter 13. When his traveling companion Vivaldo comments that the rules of knight-errantry appear to be stricter than those of the Carthusians, Don Quijote replies that "holy men, in all peace of tranquillity, pray to Heaven for the welfare of the world, but we soldiers and knights carry out what they ask for ... not under shelter but under the open sky, exposed as target to the intolerable beams of the sun in summer and to the piercing frost of winter" ["los religiosos, con toda paz y sosiego, piden al cielo el bien de la tierra; pero los soldados y caballeros ponemos en ejecución lo que ellos piden ... no debajo de cubierta, sino al cielo abierto, puesto por blanco de los insufribles rayos del sol en el verano y de los erizados yelos del invierno" (131–32; 118)]. Don Quijote thus claims for the soldier-knight a sacred calling—he is one of God's ministers on earth—even as he is careful not to pretend that the state of the knight-errant is as good as that of the monk: the two represent distinct but related careers. In the same passage Don Quijote lets himself think about just how high the chivalric career can aspire: some knights, he says, "rose to be emperors by the valor of their arms" ["algunos subieron a ser emperadores por el valor de su brazo" (132; 119)]. He returns here to his daydreams in the very first chapter of the novel, where he fancied himself "already crowned Emperor of Trebizond by the valor of his arm" ["ya coronado por el valor de su brazo, por los menos, del imperio de Trapisonda" (59; 38)]. When the Curate and Barber make their joke about Archbishop-as-opposed-to-Emperor Quijote, they thus pick up, without knowing it, the hidalgo's own opposition of religious and chivalric vocations. Even the joke itself has its precedent in the novel: back in Chapter 7, the delirious Don Quijote, recovering from his first sally, had addressed the same Curate as "arzobispo Turpín" (93; 76), evoking a character of the chivalric romances who had really been an archbishop-errant.

The same opposition of the religious versus the military life reappears in a very different context in Chapter 33 inside the interpolated tale of the "Curioso impertinente," in a prime example of Cervantes's technique of displacing the thematic motifs of his novel from one episode to another. In the tale, Lotario is responding to his best friend, Anselmo, who has asked him to test the chastity of Anselmo's wife, Camila, by pretending to court her. In urging Anselmo to consider what he may gain from this project, Lotario includes an odd and roundabout argument. There are, he says, three goals for human endeavors (none of which Anselmo can accomplish by his testing of his wife):

> Man undertakes arduous enterprises for the sake of God, for the
> world's sake, or for both. The fast are undertaken by the saints,
> who strive to live as angels in human form; the second are

accomplished by men who sail the boundless ocean and endure
the vagaries of climates as they rove through far-off lands in quest
of what are called the goods of fortune; the third, which are those
that are undertaken for the sake of God and man, are the
achievements of staunch soldiers, who no sooner see a breach in
the enemy's rampart made by a single cannonball than, shedding
all fear of the perils that threaten them from all sides and soaring
on the wings of the desire to conquer for their faith, for their
country, and for their king, they hurl themselves forward into the
jaws of death, which awaits them in a thousand guises ... but the
project you would now attempt will earn you neither heavenly
glory, nor goods of fortune, nor fame among men. (332)

Las cosas dificultosas se intentan por Dios, o por el mundo, o por
entrambos a dos: las que se acometen por Dios son las que
acometieron los santos, acometiendo a vivir vida de ángeles en
cuerpos humanos; las que se acometen por respeto del mundo son
las de aquellos que pasan tanta infinidad de agua, tanta diversidad
de climas, tanta estrañeza de gentes, por adquirir estos que llaman
bienes de fortuna. Y las que se intentan por Dios y por el mundo
juntamente son aquellas de los valerosos soldados, que apenas
veen en el contrario muro abierto tanto espacio cuanto es el que
pudo hacer una redonda bala de artillería, cuando, puesto aparte
todo temor, sin hacer discurso ni advertir al manifiesto peligro
que les amenaza, llevados en vuelo de las alas del deseo de volver
por su fe, por su nación y por su rey, se arrojan intrépidamente
por la mitad de mil contrapuestas muertes que los esperan ... Pero
la que tú dices quieres intentar y poner por obra, ni te ha de
alcanzar gloria de Dios, bienes de la fortuna, ni fama con los
hombres. (333–34)

Here, too, the man of religion and the man of war are opposed, even as they
are shown to share some common goals. We should note that the soldier
["soldado"] in question is a modern one, apparently an infantryman and no
longer Don Quijote's knight ["caballero"]. Like the saint, this soldier pursues
the glory of God as he fights for his faith, though he also seeks for worldly
glory. In the second formulation of the opposition, however, it is the latter—
fame among men—that seems to characterize the soldier and to place him
squarely in a secular realm. That realm is defined further by the new, third
term that the passage has meanwhile introduced: the merchant whose,
ventures now take him to a literally New World, undreamt of in earlier

times, a world that Cervantes's Spain had taken a leading role in discovering and colonizing. If there is a suggestion that the merchant's hardships rise to a quasi-heroism—it is he who suffers the changeable weather that Don Quijote had earlier ascribed to the soldier-knight—Lotario's speech decidedly places the motive of commerce, the mere gain of worldly wealth, beneath the goals of religion and military honor that seek in complementary and divergent ways to transcend the world. Heroism belongs most vividly to the soldier, and the speech expands into a brief set piece to celebrate military courage in the face of death.

Lotario's speech has no place in its own context except to amplify his admonishment to Anselmo not to pursue his "impertinent" curiosity about the fidelity of his wife. Its larger function is to point forward in the novel, as a kind of connecting bridge, to Don Quijote's long set speech defending arms over letters in Chapters 37–38 and to the ensuing interpolated tale of the Captive, Captain Viedma, newly come from Algiers with Zoraida. Don Quijote's speech on arms and letters is, like so much of his discourse in the novel, a piece of book-learning; the topic was a favorite for rhetorical debate, and, as such, designed as much to demonstrate rhetorical and literary skill as to decide the issue. Lotario's vivid little scene of land battle before a breach in the enemy ramparts has its counterpart in Don Quijote's much expanded description of a sea battle in Chapter 38. Here, too, soldiers charge into near certain death into a tight space, on two planks of a battering ram, to reach the enemy ship: "inspired by the honor that spurs him on, he allows himself to be the mark for all their fire and endeavors to force his way by that narrow path into the enemy vessel" ["llevado de la honra que le incita, se pone a ser blanco de tanta arcabucería, y procura pasar por tan estrecho paso al bajel contrario" (391; 393)]. The passage evokes Cervantes's experience at Lepanto, and it is directly linked to Captain Viedma's ensuing narrative in Chapter 39, where he recounts how he was captured during Lepanto after he had jumped onto an Ottoman galley and found himself cut off from his own ship (396; 399)—turning Don Quijote's rhetorical example into true life-history.

If Don Quijote treats arms in a way consistent with the earlier appearances of the arms-versus-letters motifs we have traced in the novel, the same cannot be said for his discussion of letters. For the beginning of Don Quijote's speech in Chapter 37 now explicitly separates the vocation of letters from a religious calling:

> The aim and goal of letters—I am not now speaking of divine letters, whose sole aim is to guide and elevate the soul of man to Heaven, for with that sublime end none can be compared—I speak of human letters, whose end is to regulate distributive

justice, to give every man his due, to make good laws, and to
enforce them strictly: an end most certainly generous, exalted,
and worthy of high praise, but not so glorious as the aim of arms,
which is peace, the greatest blessing that man can enjoy in this
life. For the first good news that the world ever received was
brought by the angels on the night that was our day when they
sang in the skies: "Glory be to God on High and peace and on
earth to men of goodwill"; ... This peace is the true end of war,
and by war and arms I mean the same thing. (387–88)

Es el fin y paradero de las letras ..., y no hablo ahora de las
divinas, que tienen por blanco llevar y encaminar las almas al
cielo; que a un fin tan sin fin como éste ninguno otro se le puede
igualar: hablo de las letras humanas, que es su fin poner en su
punto la justicia distributiva y dar a cada uno lo que es suyo, y
entender y hacer que las buenas leyes se guarden. Fin, por cierto,
generoso y alto y digno de grande alabanza; pero no de tanta
como merece aquel a que las armas atienden, las cuales tienen por
objeto y fin la paz, que es el mayor bien que los hombres pueden
desear en esta vida. Y así, las primeras buenas nuevas que tuvo el
mundo y tuvieron los hombres fueron las que dieron los ángeles
la noche que fue nuestro día, cuando cantaron en los aires:
"Gloria sea en las alturas, y paz en la tierra a los hombres de
buena voluntad"; ... Esta paz es el verdadero fin de la guerra; que
lo mesmo es decir armas que guerra. (389–90)

Don Quijote links the soldier, once again in the novel, to a higher, sacred
calling. Here is an early formulation of the paradoxical idea espoused by
military establishments that peace is their business. Arms may still bear some
link to religion and to *divine* letters. But the thrust of Don Quijote's speech
is to redefine—and in the process somewhat devalue—letters as purely
human letters, and more specifically, to connect them to the career of the
jurist and the magistrate.

Such was the usual construction given to the profession of letters by the
end of the sixteenth century. "Letrado" perhaps primarily designated a
lawyer, and the opposition of arms and letters evoked a social divide between
a traditional martial aristocracy and a new legal elite that filled government
positions in the early-modern state: what in France would be called the
"noblesse de la robe," in Italy the "nobiltà della toga."[19] Like the church, this
legal profession allowed some degree of social mobility: when Don Quijote
takes up the subject again in Part Two of the novel (Chapter 24), he concedes

that "more great families have been founded by letters than by arms" ["han fundado más mayorazgos las letras que las armas" (701; 718)]. He suggests as much here by describing the poverty of the student, even though he acknowledges that not all students are poor (388; 390). Through letters, the poor boy can make good.[20] And, Don Quijote concludes in Chapter 38, he is more likely to do so than the soldier who is most likely to meet his death, however honorable and glorious it may be, in battle (390; 391–92).

This redefinition of letters as a secular career leading to fortune and social position prepares the way for the Captive's Tale that immediately follows (Chapters 39–41) and the further story of Captain Viedma's brother and his family (42–45) that follows in turn. Just as Don Quijote's long set speech on the Golden Age in Chapter 11 precedes the pastoral episode of Grisóstomo and Marcela (12–14), so here his discourse on arms and letters precedes the Captive's story—which the Curate will later compare to an old wives' tale—of the three brothers of the Viedma family who set out to make their fortunes in the world. To be sure, they come of blue blood from León, and their father, a former soldier, lives the aristocratic life of liberality—that is, he lives beyond his means and is impoverishing himself. So the sons, who imitate their father's generosity by giving him back part of their inheritance, must find their own ways in the world.

The sons are instructed by their father to choose among the three vocations summed up in the Spanish proverb: "Iglesia o mar o casa real":

If you want to be powerful and wealthy, follow the Church, or go to sea and become a merchant, or take service with kings in their palaces ... one of you should pursue letters, another commerce, and the third should serve the king in his wars because it is difficult to obtain a place in his household, and although war does not bring much wealth it gradually brings great fame and renown. (394)

Quien quisiere valer y ser rico, siga, o la Iglesia, o navegue, ejercitando el arte de la mercancía, o entre a servir a los reyes en sus casas ... uno de vosotros siguiese las letras, el otro la mercancía, y el otro serviese al rey en la guerra, pues es dificultoso entrar a servirle en su casa; que ya que la guerra no dé muchas riquezas, suele dar mucho valor y mucha fama. (396)

These three careers repeat the three callings described earlier by Lotario—ecclesiastic, merchant, and soldier—and we can see how that passage inscribed within the "fictional" tale of the "Curioso impertinente" now becomes actualized in the "real" world of the novel. The difference here is that all three—including the churchman's—are now described as worldly careers whose aim is wealth and power. The soldier's career may be distinguished on a higher level than the other two, but the fame and renown he seeks are worldly nonetheless—and Lotario's soldier, we also remember, was motivated by human fame as well as by heavenly glory.

The story of the Viedma brothers, moreover, conforms to Don Quijote's discourse on arms and letters by shifting the category of letters away from an ecclesiastical profession already conceived in primarily secular terms to the profession of law. One of the brothers (Cervantes is inconsistent as to whether it is the youngest or middle one) "said that he wanted to follow the Church or finish his studies in Salamanca" ["dijo que quería seguir la Iglesia, o irse a acabar sus comenzados estudios a Salamanca" (394; 397)]. The sentence is remarkably subtle and seems to enact the shift in which I am interested. Studies at Salamanca could lead to a career in the Church— Sansón Carrasco, bachelor of Salamanca, appears headed for one in Part Two. But the "or" suggests an alternative career in letters, and, in fact, when we meet this brother, who arrives at the inn shortly after the Captive has finished his tale, we find that he has studied the law and become a judge; he is on his way to Mexico, where he will sit as the king's "oidor" on the supreme court (42). The opposition between arms and letters is played out in the Viedma family in the careers of the gallant Captain, who returns penniless to Spain from his captivity in Algiers, and his brother the judge who pursued "letters, in which God and my own exertions have raised me to the position in which you see me" ["las letras, en las cuales Dios y mi diligencia me han puesto en el grado que me veis" (435; 437)]. The judge speaks of his worldly rise with the satisfaction of the self-made man.

What early in the novel thus begins, at least in the nostalgic imagination of Don Quijote, as a choice between two holy vocations— fighting knights and praying clerics—has, through the progressive unfolding of the motif of arms and letters, been reconfigured into a more modern choice among thoroughly secular careers. The noble father of the Viedma brothers, too, looks backward with his proverbial wisdom, but the Church is no longer the only—perhaps not even the primary—destination for the "letrado." The full extent of this secularization is suggested by the third, absent brother, the merchant.[21] He is absent from the scene of the novel, and he finds no place in Don Quijote's opposition of arms and letters as the two possible careers that a man of honor can follow. Yet this brother, and the worldly means—money—that he has at his disposal, are in fact crucial to judge Viedma's story. In the next sentence, the judge tells us:

My younger brother is in Peru, so wealthy, that with what he has sent to my father and to me he has fully repaid the portion he took with him and has even given my father enough to satisfy his natural prodigality. Thanks to him, I have been able to follow my studies with more becoming fashion and authority, and so to reach my present position. (435)

Mi menor hermano está en el Pirú, tan rico, que con lo que ha enviado a mi padre y a mí ha satisfecho bien la parte que él se llevó, y aun dado a las manos de mi padre con que poder hartar su liberalidad natural; y yo, ansimesmo, he podido con más decencia y autoridad tratarme en mis estudios, y llegar al puesto en que me veo. (437)

Having chosen the career whose aim—as Lotario earlier defined it—is the "goods of fortune," this brother has amassed a fortune in the colonial trade, money that, in fact, finances and makes possible both his father's generous way of life as an old-fashioned aristocratic man of arms *and*, perhaps more significantly, the judge's own career as man of letters. The judge did not live the life of the impoverished student described earlier by Don Quijote; his brother's money helped give him "authority" and it may have helped him to buy a lower court office (royal judgeships themselves were not for sale). Nor, he now acknowledges, is he entirely self-made: the repetition within two sentences, "me han puesto en el grado que me veis ... y llegar al puesto en que me veo," leaves the reader to decide just how much of judge Viedma's prominence in the legal profession is due to his own "diligencia," how much to the money that flowed in from the New World and allowed him to cut a dignified figure.

In the absent *perulero* brother the novel *Don Quijote* acknowledges, without quite being able to represent on its fictional stage, a modern mercantile capitalism that has brought about a new social fluidity. The moneyed economy has opened new avenues for social advancement, including Spain's colonial system that links together the two Viedma brothers, the soon-to-be Mexican judge as well as the Peruvian merchant. In the third brother, the gallant Captain who goes East rather than West to fight the traditional religious enemy of Islam, Cervantes, the survivor of Lepanto, may still try to invest soldiery with higher, more disinterested values; if the soldier is not fighting as a crusader, he does at least pursue valor and fame. But, as I shall argue in Chapter Three, the money that ransoms the Captive and that he and his fellow Christians try to carry off from Zoraida's father in Algiers marks the novelist's simultaneous awareness of the extent to which worldly motives now infiltrate all professions.[22]

The debate between arms and letters that runs through Part One of *Don Quijote*, taken up by apparently disparate episodes that are thus unexpectedly linked together, contains an implicit narrative of modernity. It eventually introduces commerce as a third term that cannot be fitted into the traditional opposition of martial versus clerical careers; yet the monetary forces and secular spirit of an emergent capitalism come to dominate and transform the nature of those careers and of the larger social order. The selfless knight and churchman, the imaginative projections of a receding feudal order cited by Don Quijote toward the opening of the novel, now have their modern, mercenary counterparts in the soldier and judge. Part Two of *Don Quijote* will take up this opposition of arms and letters in the opposition of Don Quijote himself to Sancho Panza, when the latter takes up his position as governor and judge and, as an illiterate "letrado," briefly accomplishes the most dramatic social ascent chronicled by the novel.[23]

LUSCINDA AT THE WINDOW

My second example of how Cervantes links the motifs of Part One of *Don Quijote* is much more briefly told. It occurs in the space of two pages in the middle of Cardenio's story of his erotic woes in Chapter 27, and concerns two moments by the barred window of the house of his beloved Luscinda. The first records Cardenio's last conversation with Luscinda; she is troubled and her eyes fill with tears. Cardenio contrasts the moment with his recollection of earlier happier meetings by the window, always conducted, he notes, with propriety:

> the greatest freedom I permitted myself was to take, almost by force, one of her lovely white hands and to press it to my lips as best I could, despite the narrowness of the bars that separated us. (268)

> y a lo que más se estendía mi desenvoltura era a tomarle, casi por fuerza, una de sus bellas y blancas manos, y llegarla a mi boca, según daba lugar la estrecheza de una baja reja que nos dividía. (266)

The second passage comes a paragraph later, when Cardenio tells us how a letter from Luscinda was delivered to him: the bearer had passed by her window and been asked, as a Christian ["si sois cristiano"] to take the letter to the absent Cardenio. Luscinda added a further incentive:

'And in case you want money to do it, take what you find wrapped in this handkerchief.' 'With these words,' the messenger went on, 'she threw out of the window a handkerchief in which were wrapped a hundred reals, this gold ring that I am wearing, and the letter that I have given you ...' (269)

"y para que no os falte comodidad de poderlo hacer, tomad lo que va en este pañuelo."—Y diciendo esto, me arrojó por la ventana un pañuelo, donde venían atados cien reales y esta sortija de oro que aquí traigo, con esa carta que os he dado ..." (267)

The memory of kissing Luscinda's hands through the railing, the handkerchief filled with coins she throws down from her window to the messenger: neither of these details is strictly necessary to Cardenio's story. But the first links the story backward in the novel to the model chivalric romance that Don Quijote tells to Sancho in Chapter 21, where a princess newly enamored by the knight-errant who has come to stay at her father's castle meets him for a nocturnal tryst; she will "give her white hands through the railing to the knight, who will kiss them a thousand times and bathe them with his tears" ["dará sus blancas manos por la reja al caballero, el cual se las besará mil veces, y se las bañará en lágrimas" (205; 198)]. The second looks forward to Chapter 40 and to the moment in the Captive's Tale when Zoraida lowers from *her* window a cloth ["lienzo"] filled with coins to Captain Viedma and his fellow companions in their captivity in Algiers; she, too, is searching for a Christian (405; 408).

The effects of this juxtaposition of episodes in the novel are complicated. First of all, it places the genre of the story of Cardenio, Luscinda, and Cardenio's rival, Don Fernando—an erotic novella— somewhere between the stereotypes of chivalric romance that fill Don Quijote's imagination and the "true history" of the Captive's Tale and, perhaps more specifically, to the reality principle that lends the tale its verisimilitude: the presence of money. Thus here, too, *Don Quijote* seems to be telling, on the level of literary history, a story of modernity, the transition of fiction itself from the fantasy world of chivalry, the literature of an outmoded feudal past, to the depiction of lived experience in a modern materialistic world, the new realm of the novel that Cervantes is inventing. Cardenio's kissing Luscinda's white hand is a gesture of old-fashioned romance and suggests something of the unreal, excessively literary quality of his love for her. It links him and the penitence he imposes upon himself to Don Quijote the lover of Dulcinea, the lady who is almost exclusively the creature of Don Quijote's literature-fed imagination. On the other hand,

Cardenio is tied by money to the real world: the hundred reals that Luscinda
wraps in her handkerchief ["pañuelo"] recall the very first appearance of
Cardenio himself in the novel in Chapter 23, not in person, but in the form
of his traveling bag that contains four shirts of Holland linen and a hundred
"escudos" wrapped in a little cloth or handkerchief ["pañizuelo" (222; 216)],
money—it may or may not be the same money—that Sancho happily
appropriates. Here, too, Cervantine interlace is at work, for the first
innkeeper whom Don Quijote meets in Chapter 3 advises him to carry
money and clean shirts (70; 49), and the knight is careful to do so (96; 79) as
he prepares in Chapter 7 for his second sally. Even when Cardenio goes mad
for love, he is similarly prudent enough to pack the necessities. Cardenio's
money, moreover, acquires a life of its own in the novel, for in Chapter 3 of
the Part Two Sansón Carrasco states that many readers of Part One want to
know what Sancho did with it: "for it is one of the substantial points that is
missing in the work" ["que es uno de los puntos sustanciales que faltan en la
obra" (551; 564). Money, Cervantes punningly asserts, is a matter of
substance in his novelistic world.

THE TWO LOVES OF DON QUIJOTE

These two examples of Cervantes's technique of interlacing together the
thematic motifs and episodes of his novel are themselves related by the
similar stories they tell about the arrival of a modern world reshaped and
increasingly dominated by money. *Don Quijote* is a novel whose central
character chooses to reject the modern world, to turn back the clock and to
live in a idealized and fabulous realm of feudal chivalry derived from the
romances he consumes. Don Quijote has a weaker sense of the anachronism
he is committing than has the second innkeeper in Chapter 32, who believes
just as firmly as the mad hidalgo in the literal truth of the chivalric romances,
but who acknowledges that knight-errantry is no longer the custom ["ahora
no se usa to que se usaba en aquel tiempo" (324; 325)]. At times Don Quijote
speaks of "reviving" ["resucitar" (186; 188)] chivalry and a lost golden age
(Part One, Chapter 20); at the beginning of Part Two, on the other hand, he
appears to believe that there are other knights-errant than he still wandering
across Spain (Chapter 1). Through its hero who wants to live in the past,
even or especially because it is an imaginary past, Cervantes's novel depicts
the factual reality of the modern present.

Don Quijote's nostalgic, anarchic impulses—manifested above all in his
refusal to pay money for his stays at inns and his claimed exemption from the
king's laws that is symbolically enacted in his freeing of the galley slaves in
Chapter 22—are what make visible the imprisoning bars of this reality, and

Don Quijote himself is literally imprisoned in his cage and escorted home by the king's troopers at the end of Part One. (As we shall see in Chapter Three, it is a triumph of the novel and of its method of interlace to suggest that the inn itself is a kind of prison from which only money—i.e., paying one's bills—can allow one to escape.) What Don Quijote rides up against is not only the material solidity of windmills but the social arrangements of a moneyed economy and the nation-state.[24]

My examples suggest, furthermore, a progressive narrative unfolding in Part One that brings the novel from a nostalgic evocation of earlier social conditions and values (the knight and the monk as sacred vocations; the hand of the idealized lady) to the conditions and values of modernity that supersede them (the soldier, the judge, and the merchant as secular careers of worldly success; the hand of the lady that contains a packet of money). This progress is written large in Part One by the sequence that moves from its two main clusters of interlaced narratives, each organized around a separate chivalric-erotic fantasy of Don Quijote himself. These clusters will, respectively, be the focus of my next two chapters.

The first, which I want to label the "Dulcinea" cluster, comprises the remarkably closely interlaced stories of Cardenio, Luscinda, and Don Fernando and of the "Curioso impertinente," as well as the earlier pastoral story of Marcela and Grisóstomo; these stories of women variously idealized and victimized by the egotistic male imagination and the cult of male honor all comment on Don Quijote's apparently selfless worship of Dulcinea, his ideal lady who may or not exist. The second, the "Princess Micomicona" cluster, includes the Captive's Tale, the story of Don Luis and Clara, and the story of Leandra, and it comments on Don Quijote's project, which he outlines to Sancho in Chapter 21, of marrying the daughter of a king and ascending to the throne himself: his project of making himself emperor. This scheme seems about to be realized when Dorotea, disguised as the Princess Micomicona, promises to marry Don Quijote after he has defeated the giant who is oppressing her kingdom.

The fantasies involving Dulcinea and "Princess Micomicona" are both, to be sure, fantasies of self-aggrandizement and omnipotence—the peerlessness of Dulcinea makes her chosen knight (or the knight who chooses *her*) without peer, while the princess raises him to royalty—but the latter has an evident social correlative where the former does not. In the first "Dulcinea" narrative cluster, the lady is the object of intersubjective rivalry among men all conceived more or less as social equals—for Don Quijote, Dulcinea is the token by which he surpasses other, similar knights-errant—and these stories may thus look historically backward to what Jacob Burckhardt called the "medieval caste sense of honor" that preceded the more fluid and confused arrangements of rank and class that characterize the modern society of Burckhardt's Renaissance.[25] In the second "Micomicona" cluster, the lady is both the trophy and, in part, the cause of an advancement in worldly fortune, and these stories belong to a world of social ambition and mobility—and to the marriage-and-money plot of the novel, the new genre of this new, modern world.[26]

TABLE 1.1
DULCINEA VS. "PRINCESS MICOMICONA"

Chapter		
12	D	(Marcela)
13	D	(Don Quijote describes Dulcinea; Marcela)
14	D	(Marcela)
16	M	(Don Quijote, Maritornes, and the Inn-Castle)
21	M	(Don Quijote's fantasy of the chivalric career)
23–24	D	(Cardenio's story)
25–26	D	(Don Quijote describes Dulcinea; Don Quijote's penance)
27	D	(Cardenio's story)
28	M	(Dorotea's story)
29–30	M	(Dorotea as Princess Micomicona)
33–34	D	("Curioso impertinente")
35	M	(Don Quijote and the wineskins)
35–36	D	("Curioso impertinente"; reunion of the lovers)
37–41	M	(Captive's Tale)
42	M	(The judge)
43–44	M	(Luis and Clara)
47, 50	M	(Canon of Toledo and Don Quijote on social mobility)
51	M	(Leandra and Vicente de la Rosa)
51	D	(Eugenio and Anselmo as shepherd-suitors of Leandra)

It is possible to map these two clusters of stories—those organized around Don Quijote's ideal love for Dulcinea, those organized around his fantasy of a rise to power and riches and its supposed embodiment in "Princess Micomicona"—across the narrative of Part One and to see how they intertwine. The first cluster is marked D, the second M in Table 1.1.

If the two clusters of stories alternate in the first two-thirds of the narrative of Part One, this diagram suggests that from the Captive's Tale on, the second cluster of stories succeeds and very largely replaces the first. The novel and its stories, that is, come increasingly to recognize the importance of money and class mobility. They do so in ironic counterpoint to Don Quijote's own progress in the novel: his mobility as a knight-errant virtually ceases as the action stops at the inn and he is imprisoned in his cage in Chapter 46, five chapters after the Captive tells of his own liberation from captivity in Algiers. The larger narrative plan of Part One thus seems to follow a historical trajectory, traced in its stories of erotic intrigue, that moves from the idealized feudal past of Don Quijote's chivalric fantasies to the mentality and social arrangements of Cervantes's present-day Spain. Tales about lovers driven by old-fashioned notions of jealousy and honor are succeeded by others that bring us closer to the way that we live and love now, stories of modern desire.

It is not surprising that when Don Quijote is asked to choose between his two fantasies—as he is in Chapter 30, when Sancho urges him to marry Princess Micomicona immediately then and there (and keep Dulcinea as a mistress on the side), and still earlier in Chapter 16, when he imagines that the serving girl Maritornes is the princess of his dreams coming to a nocturnal assignation with him—he professes his unswerving devotion to Dulcinea. The ideal lady Dulcinea is not only a censoring device to keep real women at a distance for a character who we may begin to suspect has never had any sexual experience at all. The very disinterestedness of Don Quijote's love for Dulcinea and his simultaneous spurning of the wealth and power offered by the "princess"—his rejection of the poor-boy-makes-good, social-success story thinly veiled in chivalric garb—represent his spurning of the conditions of modernity. Don Quijote will not, finally, be in it for the money.

If Cervantes uses Don Quijote to criticize the mercenary motives and materialistic values of the modern world into which he is cast, he nonetheless skewers his hero's efforts to transcend that world: Don Quijote's attempt to return to the supposed ethos of an earlier time and to dedicate himself to his ideal lady. Cervantes does so not so much by bringing the knight into contact with the demands of a real, material existence; for, as we have just seen, Don Quijote can still choose in such a case to cling stubbornly to his ideals, choosing Dulcinea over Micomicona. Rather, Cervantes discredits Don Quijote's apparently selfless idealization of Dulcinea on its own terms by revealing just how selfish it actually is, how much this idolatrous cult of the lady feeds Don Quijote's male ego. Through the parallels among their interpolated stories, Cervantes criticizes Don Quijote as lover of Dulcinea by associating him with the monstrously self-centered lovers Cardenio, Grisóstomo, and the Anselmo of the "Curioso impertinente"—all madmen in their own way. Perhaps the most remarkable feature of this association is the way in which it conversely links these stories of male jealousy to the *premodern* mentality of Don Quijote's project. The code of male honor itself, so dear to the Spanish cultural and literary imagination, is viewed as a holdover from an aristocratic feudal past that is gradually being replaced in that imagination by the modern allure of wealth and the worldly career.

Part One of Cervantes's novel does not have much good to say for this new ethos that it represents in terms of marrying for money instead of for love. It may share, that is, many of its hero's apprehensions that the modern, moneyed world is bereft of heroism and human values. But, unlike Don Quijote, it has little use for the feudal values of the world that preceded it. Ten years later, as we shall see in Part Two of the novel, Cervantes and Don Quijote together begin to make peace with and discover positive worth in the conditions of modern society. Part One of *Don Quijote* is interested in depicting; as the very sequence of its episodes suggests—the succession of the "Dulcinea" by the "Princess Micomicona" cluster—how the atavistic values of an earlier social order come into conflict with and gradually yield to a modern social ethos, and how this shift is registered in a refocusing of human desire itself. It charts the emergence of modern times.

NOTES

1. All citations from *Don Quijote* are taken first from the English translation of Walter Starkie, *Don Quixote of La Mancha* (1957; reprint, New York: New American Library, 1979), then from the Spanish text of Martin de Riquer, *Don Quijote de la Mancha*, 2 vols. (Barcelona: Editorial Juventud, 1971). I have occasionally altered Starkie's translation. The citations from the Spanish text appear in brackets. Page numbers in parentheses refer first to the English, then to the Spanish text. All other translations, unless specified, are my own.

2. Edwin Williamson notes some of these parallels in "Romance and Realism in the Interpolated Stories of the *Quixote*," *Cervantes* 2 (1982): 43–67. See also John Weiger, "The Curious Pertinence of Eugenio's Tale in *Don Quijote*," *Modern Language Notes* 96 (1981): 260–85. In a further interlaced parallel, which will be discussed in Chapter Three, Leandra's suitor, Vicente de la Rosa, is aligned with Diego Garcia de Paredes (504; 507), the braggart-soldier whose "modest" account of his own life and superhuman exploits is drawn out of the trunk at the inn in Chapter 32, along with the history of his commander, Gonzalo Hernández de Córdoba, the Great Captain, whose title and true history align *him* with Captain Viedma.

3. The role that the tales have in the architecture of Part One is discussed by Raymond Immerwahr, "Structural Symmetry in the Episodic Narrative of *Don Quijote*," *Comparative Literature* 10 (1958): 121–35.

4. Criticism has often agreed that the interpolated tales must fit into the larger narrative of Part One of the *Quijote*, but most analyses nonetheless treat the tales as self-contained. For a thoughtful discussion, see Williamson, "Romance and Realism." Vicente Gaos usefully questions the sincerity of the apparent "retraction" on the part of the Cervantine narrator in Chapter 44 of Part Two, who seems to regret having included the

tales in Part One and who forswears such interpolations in the second installment of the novel; see the chapter "El *Quijote* y las novelas interpoladas," in Gaos, *Cervantes: Novelista, dramaturgo, poeta* (Barcelona: Planeta, 1979), pp. 47–57. Ana L. Baquero Escudero compares the stories of Marcela, of the Captive and Zoraida, and of Leandra in "Tres historias intercaladas y tres puntos de vista distintos en el primer *Quijote*," *Actas del Segundo Coloquio International de la Asociación de Cervantistas: Alcalá de Henares, del 6 al 9 de noviembre de 1989* (Barcelona: Anthropos, 1991), pp. 417–23.

5. This critical disposition informs the most recent monument of Cervantes scholarship, the now indispensable commentary assembled by Francisco Rico to the edition prepared for the Centro para la Edición de los Clásicos Españoles, *Don Quijote de la Mancha* (Barcelona: Instituto Cervantes, Critica, 1998). The commentary is organized into separate treatments of individual chapters of *Don Quijote*.

6. For another account of how *Don Quijote* emerges as a different kind of novel from the picaresque novel even as it adapts many features of picaresque fiction, see Walter Reed, *An Exemplary History of the Novel: The Quixotic versus the Picaresque* (Chicago and London: University of Chicago Press, 1981), esp. pp. 71–92; for Reed, it is the revelation of the "insufficiencies of literature" that distinguishes Cervantes's contribution to the novel.

7. Edward C. Riley, "Romance, Picaresque, and *Don Quixote I*," in *Studies in Honor of Bruce W. Wardropper*, ed. Diane Fox, Harry Sieber, and Robert Ter Horst (Newark, Delaware: Juan de la Cuesta, 1989), pp. 237–48.

8. Claudio Guillén, *Literature as System: Essays toward the Theory of Literary History* (Princeton: Princeton University Press, 1971), p. 84.

9. See Edwin Williamson, *The Half-Way House of Fiction* (Oxford: Clarendon Press, 1984), p. 163: "This interweaving of plot and episode suggests that in search of variety Cervantes was experimenting with a species of *entrelacement* so typical of medieval and Renaissance romances." This study will attempt to flesh out Williamson's critical observation.

10. For remarks on the technique of interlace in medieval romance with particular application to the *Amadís de Gaula* and *Don Quijote*, see Williamson, *The Half-Way House of Fiction*, pp. 34–50, 163–65. See also Ferdinand Lot, *Étude sur le "Lancelot en Prose"* (Paris: Champion, 1918); Eugene Vinaver, *The Rise of Romance* (Oxford: Clarendon Press, 1971).

11. See for example the quests of Yvain and Bors in the prose *Lancelot* in *Lancelot-Grail: The Old French Arthurian Vulgate and Post-Vulgate in Translation*, ed. Norris J. Lacey (New York and London: Garland, 1995), 3:171–82; for another, more ironic juxtaposition, compare the quests of Hector, who kills a tyrant who dishonors women, and of Yvain, who kills a knight who has stolen a sparrowhawk from a damsel, at 3:103–8.

12. It is worth pointing out a further interlaced parallel in this episode. Dorotea is supposed to play the damsel-in-distress Princess Micomicona in order to cure Don Quijote, or at least to help the Curate and Barber bring him home (291; 292). The appearance on the scene of the distressed real-life Dorotea *does*, in fact, cure the other madman of the episode, Cardenio, who champions her cause.

13. On Dorotea and her story, see Francisco Márquez Villanueva, *Personajes y temas del "Quijote"* (Madrid: Taurus, 1975); Joaquin Casalduero, *Sentido y forma del "Quijote"* (Madrid: Ediciones Ínsula, 1949), pp. 142–43; Ruth El Saffar, *Distance and Control in "Don Quixote": A Study in Narrative Technique* (Chapel Hill: University of North Carolina Press, 1975), pp. 66–68.

14. For a related discussion of the debt that Cervantes owes to Ariosto's formal techniques, see Thomas Hart, *Cervantes and Ariosto: Renewing Fiction* (Princeton: Princeton University Press, 1989), pp. 16–38. I have published an earlier version of the

present argument in "Narrative Interlace and Narrative Genres in *Don Quijote* and the *Orlando Furioso*," *Modern Language Quarterly* 58, no. 3 (1997); 241–68. See also Margot Kruse, "Ariosto und Cervantes," *Romanistisches Jahrbuch* 12 (1961): 248–64; Maxime Chevalier, *L'Arioste en Espagne* (Bordeaux: Féret and Fils, 1966), pp. 461–63.

15. Marco Praloran discusses the innovations of this technique, particularly the suspension of the outcomes of individual episodes, in the narrative practice of Ariosto's predecessor, Matteo Maria Boiardo, in "Il modello formale dell'entrelacement nell'*Orlando innamorato*," in *Tipografie e romanzi in Val Padana tra Quattro e Cinquecento*, ed. Riccardo Bruscagli and Amedeo Quondam (Modena: Panini, 1992), pp. 117–27; in his further extension of his narratological analysis to the *Furioso*, Praloran's focus is less on interlace itself than on the temporal loops in the poem: see "Temporalitá e tecniche narrative nel *Furioso*," *Studi italiani* 6, no. 1 (1994): 5–54. Valuable analyses of Ariosto's interlace at work are offered by Elissa Weaver, "Lettura dell'intreccio dell'*Orlando furioso*: Il caso delle tre pazzie d'amore," *Strumenti critici* 11 (1977): 384–406; Robert Durling, *The Figure of the Poet in Renaissance Epic* (Cambridge: Harvard University Press, 1965), pp. 140–76; and Albert Russell Ascoli, *Ariosto's Bitter Harmony: Crisis and Evasion in the Italian Renaissance* (Princeton: Princeton University Press, 1987). On the suspensions of the narrative of the *Furioso*, see Daniel Javitch, "*Cantus Interruptus* in the *Orlando Furioso*," *Modern Language Notes* 95 (1980): 66–80.

16. Chevalier, *L'Arioste en Espagne*, p. 463. L.A. Murillo labels these chapters as "interlace" in *A Critical Introduction to "Don Quixote"* (New York: Peter Lang, 1988), pp. 215–20; see Williamson, *The Half-Way House of Fiction*, p. 179.

17. E.C. Riley discusses the issues of variety and unity, episode and whole in Cervantes's own literary culture in *Cervantes's Theory of the Novel* (1962; reprint, Newark, Delaware: Juan de la Cuesta, 1992), pp. 116–31; see also Riley's earlier essay, "Episodio, novela, y aventura en *Don Quijote*," *Anales Cervantinos* 5 (1955–56): 209–30.

18. A critical treatment of this theme is found in Michel Moner, *Cervantès: Deux thèmes majeures (L'amour, les Armes et les Lettres)* (Université de Toulouse-Mirail: France-Iberie Recherche, 1986), pp. 71–136; for Part One of *Don Quijote*, pp. 71–85. The social reality is treated in Javier Salazar Rincón, *El mundo social del "Quijote"* (Madrid: Gredos, 1986), pp. 120–37. For a discussion of Don Quijote's discourse on arms and letters in Chapter 38, see Elsa Leonor di Santo, "Análisis de los discursos sobre la edad dorada y las armas y las letras," in *Cervantes: su obra y su mundo: Actas del I Congreso Internacional sobre Cervantes*; ed. M. Criado de Val (Madrid: EDI-6, 1981), pp. 799–808. See also the comments in Américo Castro, *El pensamiento de Cervantes* (1925; reprint, Barcelona: Noguer, 1972), pp. 215–19.

19. See Jean-Marc Pelorson, *Les "letrados" juristes castillans sous Philipe III* (Le Puy-en-Velay: University de Poitiers, "L'Eveil de L'Haute Loire," 1980).

20. On student life in Golden Age Spain, see Richard L. Kagan, *Students and Society in Early Modern Spain* (Baltimore: Johns Hopkins University Press, 1974).

21. For remarks along the same lines about this third brother, see Caroll B. Johnson, *Cervantes and the Material World* (Urbana and Chicago: University of Illinois Press, 2000), p. 82; see also Salazar Rincón, *El mundo social*, pp. 123–24.

22. This point is also noted by Moner, *Cervantès: Deux thèmes majeures*, p. 80.

23. The episode is analyzed by Jean-Marc Pelorson in "Le discours des armes et lettres et l'épisode de Barataria," *Les Langues Néo-Latines* 212 (1975): 41–58.

24. Timothy Hampton has emphasized the importance of the nation-state and its institutions in his analysis of *Don Quijote* in *Writing from History* (Ithaca and London:

Cornell University Press, 1990), pp. 237–96. See also Luis Rosales, *Cervantes y la libertad* (1960; reprint, Madrid, Cultura Hispánica, 1985).

25. Burckhardt, Jacob, *The Civilization of the Renaissance in Italy*, trans. S.G.C. Middlemore (1860; English trans. Hammondsworth: Penguin, 1990), p. 104.

26. I am suggesting that *Don Quijote* already anticipates developments in the novel one century later. The classic account that aligns the growth of the English novel with the emergence of a middle-class and its economic individualism is Ian Watt, *The Rise of the Novel* (Berkeley and Los Angeles: University of California Press, 1957). On marriage and social mobility in this genre, see pages 138–48, 220–28. See also Michael McKeon, *The Origins of the English Novel, 1600–1740* (Baltimore and London: Johns Hopkins University Press, 1987), pp. 286–87.

Chronology

1547	Miguel de Cervantes Saavedra is born in Alcalá de Henares to Rodrigo de Cervantes and Leonor de Cortinas, his wife. Baptized on October 9.
1568	Writes poems commemorating the death of Isabel de Valois, third wife of Philip II.
1569	Travels to Rome, in the service of Cardinal Giulio Acquaviva; enlists in military.
1571	Wounded in battle of Lepanto, where Turks are defeated. Loses the use of his left hand.
1575	With his brother Rodrigo, captured by Turks, brought to Algiers, enslaved, and held for ransom.
1576–79	Makes four attempts to escape captivity.
1576	Rodrigo, ransomed by his family, released; arranges brother's rescue, which fails.
1580	Ransomed by Trinitarian monks; returns to Spain.
1581	Attempts career as dramatist in Madrid.
1584	Daughter Isabel de Saavedra born to Ana Franca de Rojas; marries Catalina de Salazar y Palacios.
1585	Publishes first book, a pastoral romance, *La Galatea*.
1587	Becomes a commissary requisitioning provisions for the Armada.

1597	Employed as tax collector in Andalusia and jailed for irregularities in his accounts.
1605	Publishes *Don Quixote*, part 1.
1609	Joins lay confraternity of Slaves of the Most Holy Sacrament in Madrid.
1613	*Exemplary Novels* (twelve stories) published. Becomes an acolyte in the Franciscan Order of the Roman Catholic priesthood.
1614	*Voyage to Parnassus*, a mock-heroic allegory in verse, published. Continuation of *Don Quixote* published by someone otherwise unknown and possibly using a pseudonym.
1615	Publishes *Don Quixote*, part 2, and *Eight Plays and Interludes, New and Never Performed*.
1616	Dies in Madrid on April 22 or 23.
1617	Posthumous publication of *The Trials of Persiles and Sigismunda*, a romance.

Contributors

HAROLD BLOOM is Sterling Professor of the Humanities at Yale University. He is the author of over 20 books, including *Shelley's Mythmaking* (1959), *The Visionary Company* (1961), *Blake's Apocalypse* (1963), *Yeats* (1970), *A Map of Misreading* (1975), *Kabbalah and Criticism* (1975), *Agon: Toward a Theory of Revisionism* (1982), *The American Religion* (1992), *The Western Canon* (1994), and *Omens of Millennium: The Gnosis of Angels, Dreams, and Resurrection* (1996). *The Anxiety of Influence* (1973) sets forth Professor Bloom's provocative theory of the literary relationships between the great writers and their predecessors. His most recent books include *Shakespeare: The Invention of the Human* (1998), a 1998 National Book Award finalist, *How to Read and Why* (2000), *Genius: A Mosaic of One Hundred Exemplary Creative Minds* (2002), and *Hamlet: Poem Unlimited* (2003). In 1999, Professor Bloom received the prestigious American Academy of Arts and Letters Gold Medal for Criticism, and in 2002 he received the Catalonia International Prize.

HOWARD MANCING is Professor of Spanish at Purdue University. He is the author of *The Cervantes Encyclopedia*, co-editor of *The Golden Age Comedia*: *Text, Theory and Performance*, and has written numerous articles on Cervantes.

ALBAN K. FORCIONE is a professor at Columbia University. His works include *Cervantes and the Mystery of Lawlessness*, *Cervantes' Christian Romance*, and *Cervantes and the Humanist Vision*.

E.C. RILEY has been Professor of Hispanic Studies at the University of Edinburgh. He has written widely on Cervantes, including *Cervantes's Theory of the Novel* and a work on *Don Quixote*. He has also edited and translated works of Cervantes.

TERRENCE DOODY is Professor of English at Rice University. He has authored *Confession and Community in the Novel* and *Among Other Things: A Description of the Novel*.

CORY A. REED is a professor in the Department of Spanish and Portuguese at the University of Texas in Austin. She has written a book on Cervantes' *Entremes Nuevo*.

DIANA DE ARMAS WILSON is Professor Emerita of English and Renaissance Studies at the University of Denver. She has published *Cervantes, the Novel, and the New World*, and a Norton Critical Edition of *Don Quijote*. She has also co-edited *Quixotic Desire: Psychoanalytic Perspectives on Cervantes*.

NICHOLAS SPADACCINI is a professor at the University of Minnesota. He has written on the Spanish Golden Age drama, edited several Spanish classics, and co-edited many volumes on literary theory and criticism.

JENARO TALENS has been a professor at the University of Valencia, Spain and a regular visiting professor at the University of Minnesota. He has published numerous books of poetry, translated a number of European classics into Spanish, and written many books on literary criticism and theory.

DOMINICK FINELLO teaches at Rider University. He is the author of *Cervantes: Essays on Social and Literary Polemics* and *Pastoral Themes and Forms in Cervantes's Fiction*.

IAN WATT has taught at Stanford University. He is the author of several titles, among them *The Rise of the Novel* and others focusing on Conrad and Jane Austen.

HENRY W. SULLIVAN teaches at Tulane University. He is an author of a study of *Don Quixote* and has edited and written many texts focusing on Spanish literature.

MANUEL DURÁN is Professor Emeritus of Spanish at Yale University. He is the author or editor of more than forty books of criticism and anthologies, among them Twayne's *Cervantes* and *La ambigüedad en el Quijote* (*The Ambiguity in Don Quixote*).

ROBERTO GONZÁLEZ ECHEVARRÍA is Chairman of the Department of Spanish and Portuguese at Yale University. His books include *Alejo Carpentier*, *The Pilgrim at Home*, *The Oxford Book of Latin American Short Stories* (editor), and *The Cambridge History of Latin American Literature* (co-editor).

DAVID QUINT teaches at Yale University, where he is chair of the Department of Comparative Literature. He has written *Epic and Empire: Politics and Generic Form from Virgil to Milton* and is the author, co-editor, or translator of several other titles.

Bibliography

Boruchoff, David A. "On the Place of Madness, Deviance, and Eccentricity in *Don Quixote*." *Hispanic Review* 70, no. 1 (Winter 2002): 1–23.

Bowers, Fredson, ed. *Vladimir Nabokov: Lectures on Don Quixote*. NY: Harcourt Brace Jovanovich, 1983.

Carney, Carmen Vega. "Righting Wrongs: *Don Quixote* and the Rhetoric of Justice." *Indiana Journal of Hispanic Literatures* 5 (Fall 1994): 19–36.

Cascardi, Anthony J., ed. *The Cambridge Companion to Cervantes*. Cambridge, UK; NY: Cambridge University Press, 2002.

Close, Anthony. *Cervantes and the Comic Mind of His Age*. Oxford; NY: Oxford University Press, 2000.

———. "A Poet's Vanity: Thoughts on the Friendly Ethos of Cervantine Satire." *Cervantes* 13, no. 1 (Spring 1993): 31–63.

Colahan, Clark, Celia Weller, and Michael McGaha. A Symposium on *Los trabajos de Persiles y Sigismunda*. *Cervantes* 10, no. 1 (Spring 1990).

Cruz, Anne J. and Carroll B. Johnson. *Cervantes and His Postmodern Constituencies*. NY: Garland, 1999.

de Armas, Frederick A. "A Banquet of the Senses: The Mythological Structure of *Persiles y Sigismunda*, III." *Bulletin of Hispanic Studies* 70, no. 4 (October 1993): 403–414.

———. *Cervantes, Raphael and the Classics*. Cambridge: Cambridge University Press, 1998.

de Armas Wilson, Diana. *Cervantes, the Novel, and the New World*. Oxford; NY: Oxford University Press, 2000.

———. "Speaking in Tongues: Cervantes's Translator Transila." In *"Never-Ending Adventure": Studies in Medieval and Early Modern Spanish Literature in Honor of Peter N. Dunn*, edited by Edward H. Friedman and Harlan Sturm, 235–246. Newark, DE: Cuesta, 2002.

Dunn, Peter N. "Shaping Experience: Narrative Strategies in Cervantes." *Modern Language Notes* 109, no. 2 (March 1994): 186–203.

Egginton, William. "Cervantes, Romantic Irony and the Making of Reality." *Modern Language Notes* 117, no. 5 (December 2002): 1048–1068.

El Saffar, Ruth, ed. *Critical Essays on Cervantes*. Boston: G.K. Hall, 1986.

El Saffar, Ruth, Diana de Armas Wilson, and Max Hernández. *Quixotic Desire: Psychoanalytic Perspectives on Cervantes*. Ithaca, NY: Cornell University Press, 1993.

Fajardo, Salvador J. "Instructions for Use: The Prologue to *Don Quixote* I." *Journal of Interdisciplinary Literary Studies* 6, no. 1 (1994): 1–17.

———. "Narrative and Agency: The Ricote Episode (*Don Quijote* II)." *Bulletin of Hispanic Studies* 78, no. 3 (July 2001): 311–322.

Farardo-Acosta, Fidel. "The Making of a New Genre: Structure, Theme, and Image in Dante's *Commedia* and Cervantes's *Don Quixote*." *Hispanic Journal* 20, no. 1 (Spring 1999): 57–65.

Farness, Jay. "Clown and Jester in *Don Quixote*." *Indiana Journal of Hispanic Literatures* 5 (Fall 1994): 57–80.

Flores, R.M. "*Don Quixote* as a Genre of Genres." *Romance Quarterly* 40, no. 4 (Fall 1993): 211–225.

Friedman, Edward H. "Executing the Will: The End of the Road in *Don Quixote*." *Indiana Journal of Hispanic Literatures* 5 (Fall 1994): 105–125.

———. "The Muses of the Knight: *Don Quixote* and Revisionist Fiction." In *"Never-Ending Adventure": Studies in Medieval and Early Modern Spanish Literature in Honor of Peter N. Dunn*, edited by Edward H. Friedman and Harlan Sturm, 175–92. Newark, DE: Cuesta, 2002.

Fuchs, Barbara. *Passing for Spain: Cervantes and the Fictions of Identity*. Urbana: University of Illinois Press, 2003.

Gorfkle, Laura J. *Discovering the Comic in* Don Quixote. Chapel Hill: Department of Romance Languages, University of North Carolina, 1993.

Hammond, Brean S. "Mid-Century English Quixotism and the Defence of the Novel." *Eighteenth-Century Fiction* 10, no. 3 (April 1998): 247–268.

Hart, Thomas R. *Cervantes's Exemplary Fictions: A Study of the* Novelas ejemplares. Lexington: University Press of Kentucky, 1994.

Hernández-Pecoraro, Rosilie. "Don Quixote's Dorotea: Portrait of a Female Subject." *Hispanófila* 135 (May 2002): 19–39.

Holdsworth, Carole A. "Dulcinea and Pynchon's *V*." *Cervantes* 19, no. 1 (Spring 1999): 27–39.

Hutchinson, Steven. *Cervantine Journeys*. Madison: University of Wisconsin Press, 1992.

Jehenson, Yvonne. "Don Quijote and Sancho: The Wise and the Foolish." *Indiana Journal of Hispanic Literatures* 5 (Fall 1994): 181–193.

Kallendorf, Hilaire. "The Diabolical Adventures of Don Quixote, or Self-Exorcism and the Rise of the Novel." *Renaissance Quarterly* 55, no. 1 (Spring 2002): 192–223.

Kartchner, Eric J. "Dramatic Diegesis: Truth and Fiction in Cervantes's *El Gallardo Español*." *Yearbook of Comparative and General Literature* 47 (1999): 25–35.

La Rubia Prado, Francisco, ed. *Cervantes for the 21st Century*. Newark, DE: Cuesta, 2000.

Maravall, José Antonio and Robert W. Felkel. *Utopia and Counterutopia in the "Quixote."* Detroit: Wayne State University Press, 1991.

Martinez-Bonati, Felix. *Don Quixote and the Poetics of the Novel*. Ithaca, NY; London: Cornell University Press, 1992.

Mascia, Mark. "Cervantes and the Reinvention of the Picaresque Narrative in the *Novelas ejemplares*." *Atenea* 21, nos. 1–2 (2001): 33–47.

McGaha, Michael. "Nature and Grace in Don Quixote, Part 2." In *"Never-Ending Adventure": Studies in Medieval and Early Modern Spanish Literature in Honor of Peter N. Dunn*, edited by Edward H. Friedman and Harlan Sturm, 193-213. Newark, DE: Cuesta, 2002.

Motooka, Wendy. *The Age of Reasons: Quixotism, Sentimentalism and Political Economy in Eighteenth-Century Britain*. London: Routledge, 1998.

Murillo, L.A. *A Critical Introduction to* Don Quixote. NY: Peter Lang, 1990.

O'Connor, Doreen M. "Character as Caricature: Don Quixote and the Distorted Image." *Indiana Journal of Hispanic Literatures* 5 (Fall 1994): 225–236.

O'Neill, Mary Anne. "Cervantes's Prose Epic." *Cervantes* 12, no. 1 (Spring 1992): 59–72.

Parr, James A. *On Cervantes: Essays for L.A. Murillo*. Newark, DE: Cuesta, 1991.

Paulson, Ronald. *Don Quixote in England: The Aesthetics of Laughter*. Baltimore: Johns Hopkins University Press, 1998.

Power, Mary. "Myth and the Absent Heroine: Dulcinea del Toboso and Molly Bloom." *Indiana Journal of Hispanic Literatures* 5 (Fall 1994): 251–261.

Presberg, Charles D. *Adventures in Paradox: Don Quixote and the Western Tradition*. University Park, PA: Pennsylvania State University Press, 2001.

———. "'This Is Not a Prologue': Paradoxes of Historical and Poetic Discourse in the Prologue of *Don Quixote*, Part I." *Modern Language Notes* 110, no. 2 (March 1995): 215–239.

Rabin, Lisa. "The Reluctant Companion of Empire: Petrarch and Dulcinea in *Don Quixote de la Mancha*." *Cervantes* 14, no. 2 (Fall 1994): 81–91.

Reed, Walter. "*Don Quixote*: The Birth, Rise and Death of the Novel." *Indiana Journal of Hispanic Literatures* 5 (Fall 1994): 263–278.

Rhodes, Elizabeth. "Sixteenth-Century Pastoral Books, Narrative Structure, and *La Galatea* of Cervantes." *Bulletin of Hispanic Studies* 66, no. 4 (October 1989): 351–360.

Rupp, Stephen. "True and False Pastoral in *Don Quijote*." *Renaissance and Reformation* 16, no. 3 (Summer 1992): 5–16.

Russell, P.E. *Cervantes*. Oxford; NY: Oxford University Press, 1985.

Ter Horst, Robert. "Cervantes and the Paternity of the English Novel." In *Cultural Authority in Golden Age Spain*, edited by Marina S. Brownlee and Hans Ulrich Gumbrecht, 165–177. Baltimore: Johns Hopkins University Press, 1995.

———. "The Spanish Etymology of the English Novel." *Indiana Journal of Hispanic Literatures* 5 (Fall 1994): 291–307.

Weiger, John C. *The Substance of Cervantes*. Cambridge; NY: Cambridge University Press, 1985.

Williamson, Edwin. *The Half-way House of Fiction:* Don Quixote *and Arthurian Romance*. Oxford: Clarendon Press, 1984.

Yamada, Yumiko. *Ben Jonson and Cervantes: Tilting against Chivalric Romances*. Tokyo: Maruzen, 2000.

Acknowledgments

"Knighthood Compromised," by Howard Mancing. From *The Chivalric World of* Don Quijote*: Style, Structure, and Narrative Technique.* © 1982 by the Curators of the University of Missouri. Reprinted by permission.

"Madness and Mystery: The Exemplarity of Cervantes's *Novelas ejemplares*," by Alban K. Forcione. From *Cervantes and the Humanist Vision: A Study of Four Exemplary Novels.* © 1982 by Princeton University Press. Reprinted by permission of Princeton University Press.

"Ideals and Illusions," by E.C. Riley. From *Don Quixote.* © 1986 by E.C. Riley. Reprinted by permission.

"*Don Quixote, Ulysses*, and the Idea of Realism," by Terrence Doody. From *Why the Novel Matters: A Postmodern Perplex*, edited by Mark Spilka and Caroline McCracken-Flesher. © 1990 by Indiana University Press. Reprinted by permission.

"Cervantes and the Novelization of Drama: Tradition and Innovation in the *Entremeses*," by Cory A. Reed. From *Cervantes* 11, no. 1 (Spring 1991), pp. 61–86. © 1991 by the Cervantes Society of America. Reprinted by permission.

"Plot and Agency," by Diana de Armas Wilson. From *Allegories of Love: Cervantes's Persiles and Sigismunda*. © 1991 by Princeton University Press. Reprinted by permission of Princeton University Press.

"Poetry as Autobiography," by Nicholas Spadaccini and Jenaro Talens. From *Through the Shattering Glass: Cervantes and the Self-Made World*. © 1993 by the Regents of the University of Minnesota. Reprinted by permission.

"The *Galatea*," by Dominick Finello. From *Pastoral Themes and Forms in Cervantes's Fiction*. © 1994 by Associated University Presses, Inc. Reprinted by permission.

"Don Quixote of La Mancha," by Ian Watt. From *Myths of Modern Individualism: Faust, Don Quixote, Don Juan, Robinson Crusoe*. © 1996 by Cambridge University Press. Reprinted with the permission of Cambridge University Press.

"The Two Projects of the *Quixote* and the Grotesque as Mode," by Henry W. Sullivan. From *Grotesque Purgatory: A Study of Cervantes's* Don Quixote, *Part II*. © 1996 by The Pennsylvania State University. Reprinted by permission.

"Picaresque Elements in Cervantes's Works," by Manuel Durán. From *The Picaresque: Tradition and Displacement*, edited by Giancarlo Maiorino. © 1996 by the Regents of the University of Minnesota. Reprinted by permission.

"Introduction to *Don Quixote*," by Roberto González Echevarría. From *The Ingenious Hidalgo: Don Quixote de la Mancha*. Translated by John Rutherford. © 2001 by Roberto González Echevarría. All rights reserved. Reprinted by permission.

"Cervantes's Method and Meaning," by David Quint. From *Cervantes's Novel of Modern Times: A New Reading of* Don Quijote. © 2003 by Princeton University Press. Reprinted by permission of Princeton University Press.

Index